THE LIBRARY OF DR JOHN WEBSTER:
THE MAKING OF A SEVENTEENTH-CENTURY RADICAL

Medical History, Supplement No. 6

THE LIBRARY OF DR JOHN WEBSTER:
THE MAKING OF A
SEVENTEENTH-CENTURY RADICAL

by

PETER ELMER

(*Medical History*, Supplement No. 6)

LONDON
WELLCOME INSTITUTE FOR THE HISTORY OF MEDICINE
1986

ISBN   0 85484 054 0 ✓
ISSN   0025 7273 6

Supplements to *Medical History* may be obtained at the Wellcome Institute for the History of Medicine, 183 Euston Road, London NW1 2BP; or by post from Professional and Scientific Publications, BMA House, Tavistock Square, London WC1H 9JR.

CONTENTS

PREFACE

This work, as my introduction indicates, grew from my interest in John Webster's role in the so-called "witchcraft debate" of the seventeenth century. I had also become intrigued by Webster whilst completing my doctorate at Swansea University (1976–80) on the subject of religious motives in medical reform in England during the Puritan Revolution. It seemed logical therefore that, having tracked down a copy of the catalogue of Webster's library in late 1985, I should attempt the daunting task of preparing an annotated transcription of the original manuscript. Initially encouraged by Mr David Harley of Oxford, who shared my interest in Webster and the catalogue, I thus proceeded on the long and laborious job of trying to make sense of the 1501 entries, many of them authorless, which together constituted the vast library of John Webster, radical divine and alchemist.

Of course, much has been written about Webster and the radical milieu in which he lived and wrote. I have profited, as have all who work in this field, by the seminal research of Christopher Hill, Keith Thomas, and Charles Webster, as well as a host of other scholars too numerous to mention. I should, however, like to pay a special debt of thanks to Dr Stuart Clark, whose scholarly encouragement and friendly advice over the last decade has been a never-ending source of inspiration.

Of those who have offered particular help and advice with the reconstruction of the library catalogue, I would especially like to thank Dr Vivian Nutton of the Wellcome Institute for the History of Medicine in London. I am also grateful to Dr Michael Hunter for numerous illuminating discussions, as well as his invaluable help in bringing to my notice the Webster-Lister correspondence in the Bodleian Library, Oxford.

I have used the facilities of numerous libraries and archives in the completion of this work, and would like to thank the librarians and staff of the following centres for their unfailing assistance and guidance: the British Library, the Bodleian Library, Dr Williams' Library, the Library of the Society of Friends, Nottingham University Library, and Lancashire County Record Office, Preston. In particular, I am indebted to Mr Michael Powell, the librarian of Chetham's Library, Manchester, for his invaluable help and assistance with the catalogue, and would like to express a special note of thanks to the governors of Chetham's Library for allowing me to reproduce Chetham MS.A.6.47.

Finally, I should like to thank Mr Roderick Boroughs for his help in deciphering many of the Greek and Latin items in the catalogue, and Vicky for her astonishing patience of the last eighteen months.

THE LIFE AND CAREER OF JOHN WEBSTER

John Webster was born in 1611, the son of Edward Webster of Thornton-on-the-Hill in the parish of Coxwold, Yorkshire.[1] According to Anthony Wood, the young Webster spent some time at Cambridge, though his name does not appear in the extant records of the University. In 1634, he was ordained as a minister of the Church of England and was appointed curate to the remote northern parish of Kildwick in his native Yorkshire. Within a year of his appointment, however, Webster seems to have fallen foul of the clerical authorities, and in 1637, he was finally deprived of his living, a victim, in all probability, of the anti-puritan purge of Richard Neile, Archbishop of York.[2]

Webster was no puritan in the orthodox sense of the word. Unlike many of his radical contemporaries, he did not undergo a long and tortuous route through the various sects of mid-seventeenth-century England, nor did he seem to support the cause of mainstream puritan reform in the period before 1642. His first experience of non-conformity was, in fact, with a group of radical sectaries, the Grindletonians, who preached *inter alia* perfectionist doctrines and attacked the established church and its learned ministry. Webster had encountered this group in the mid-1630s when, according to his own subsequent account, he first became aware of "the sad experience of mine own dead, sinful, lost and damnable condition". In the circumstances, it is hardly surprising that his occupancy of the living of Kildwick was so short-lived and that he was forced, as a result of his dismissal in 1637, to seek elsewhere for employment.[3]

During the 1640s, two callings in particular caught the imagination of Webster's unsettled mind: medicine and teaching. He was probably practising medicine on a part-time basis throughout the 1640s, and his skills were certainly employed in 1648, when he enlisted as a surgeon in the parliamentary regiment of Colonel Shuttleworth. Prior to this appointment, Webster had taken up residence in the Lancashire town of Clitheroe, where from 1643 to 1648 he was employed as a schoolmaster in the local grammar school. Neither of these pursuits, however, proved capable of restraining Webster's deep religious yearnings, for in 1647, he was intruded into the living of

---

[1] The article by Bertha Potter in the *Dictionary of national biography* (hereinafter *DNB*), London, Oxford University Press, 22 vols., 1921–22, vol. 22, pp. 1036–1037, gives the year of Webster's birth as 1610. For this correction and much other valuable information concerning the life of Webster, I am indebted to two hitherto neglected articles by William Self Weeks in the *Transactions of the Lancashire and Cheshire Antiquarian Society* (hereinafter *TLCAS*), 1921, **39**: 55–107; and 1932, **47**: 30–59.

[2] Anthony Wood, *Athenae Oxonienses*, edited by P. Bliss, Oxford, F.C. & J. Rivington, 4 vols., 1813–20, vol. 4, col. 250; Ronald A. Marchant, *Puritans and the church courts in the diocese of York, 1560—1642*, London, Longmans, 1960, pp. 127–128, 290.

[3] John Webster, *The saints guide*, London, Giles Calvert, 1653, sig. A3v. For Grindletonian beliefs, including the rejection of clerical ordination, see Christopher Hill, *The world turned upside down*, London, Temple Smith, 1972, pp. 65–68.

Mitton, just four miles from Clitheroe, which he held for the next two years. Clearly, the change in the political and religious mood of the country after 1647 assisted Webster's apparent *rapprochement* with the church. On the other hand, there is no evidence to suggest that he received or accepted a stipend for the cure of Mitton. Not only was he reported at this time to preach *gratis* to the people of Grindleton, but for much of the period in question he must have been absent from Mitton because of his involvement in the second civil war. Whatever the case, in 1649, he finally decided to sever all ties with the established church and returned to Clitheroe where, with one notable exception, he lived until his death in 1682.[4]

That exception was Webster's appearance in London in 1653, when he briefly achieved a certain notoriety for his radical views on the church and universities. Webster was almost certainly attracted to the capital in this year because of his conviction, shared by many others in 1653, that the long-awaited millennium was about to break forth in Cromwell's England. The meeting of the Barebones Parliament in July 1653 promised radical reform in all areas of English life and many, including Webster, undoubtedly envisaged its convocation as the prelude to the imminent return of Christ to his earthly legacy. The radicals, however, were deeply divided on the crucial issue of the nature of this future kingdom of Christ, and Webster himself rejected the popular view that Christ would return in person to reign over the saints. On the contrary, throughout his published works and sermons dating from this period, Webster strongly intimated that the prophetical vision of St John was not intended to presage real events. It was rather to be understood as a powerful allegory of the age-old spiritual struggle between good and evil which, very soon, would be concluded in the heart and soul of every Christian.[5]

Shorn of its literal meaning, the biblical account in Revelation nonetheless lost none of its urgent, cataclysmic significance for Webster, who now believed that the long-expected day of universal spiritual renewal was close at hand. Moreover, in the light of Webster's subsequent denial of traditional demonological beliefs (see below, pp. 7–14), his eschatological notions in this period are highly illuminating. In sermon after sermon, Webster insisted that the concept of evil possessed no physical shape or form, nor was it circumscribed within any fixed locality. The Devil and hell were thus intended as synonyms for the depraved condition of the human soul, which ever since the fall of Adam had been covered by a "vail of darkness". In the struggle to overcome this "vail", Webster stressed that coveted human attributes such as power, physical strength, and learning were of no use. Though they seemed to offer man security

---

[4] For Webster's association with Clitheroe Grammar School in the 1640s, and his subsequent spell as a governor (1660–62), see especially C.W. Stokes, *Queen Mary's grammar school: Part I. The sixteenth and seventeenth centuries*, Publications of the Chetham Society, new series, no. 92, Manchester, 1934, pp. 97–128, 140–141. As Weeks demonstrates, there is little evidence to support the view of Charles Webster and others that Webster retired "to a living in his native Yorkshire after 1653"; C. Webster, *The great instauration: science, medicine and reform, 1626—60*, London, Duckworth, 1975, pp. 83, 188–189, 193; W.S. Weeks, 'John Webster, author of *The displaying of supposed witchcraft*', *TLCAS*, 1921, **39**: 77–84 and *passim*. Webster himself wrote in 1653 that he was "no Dean nor Master . . . neither have I tyths appropriate, nor impropriate, augmentation, nor State pay", *Academiarum examen, or the examination of academies*, London, G. Calvert, 1654, sig.A5r (preface to the reader dated 21 October 1653).

[5] For the strength of millenarian opinion at this time, see Bernard S. Capp, *The fifth monarchy men: a study in seventeenth-century English millenarianism*, London, Faber & Faber, 1972, pp. 50–75.

against eternal damnation, and so helped to put off "the Evil day from him", they were in reality "a Covenant with Death and Hell". Only when man turned to Christ, argued Webster, was he able to determine the full extent of his misery and the depraved condition of his soul, for then, "he sees that there is in him Antichrist indeed, the beast with seven Heads and ten Horns, and himself bearing the Mark and Image of the Beast".[6]

The outcome of this personal, spiritual millennium was the destruction of all established human values, which were irrevocably turned upside down so that man's wisdom was now accounted folly, "his Righteousness, Sin; . . . his Heaven, Hell". To the regenerate saint nothing was sinful, but to those still labouring under the ordinances of the Old Testament, the "veil was unrent" and continued to obscure man's understanding, not only of himself but also of the creation. In a passage of remarkable clarity, Webster thus enunciated the full implications of his simple, uncomplicated antinomianism when he wrote that, "in the Day that the Soul turns to the Lord, . . . then is the Caul of the Heart rent, then is Hell laid open in him, and the bottomless Gulf seen in himself: *And that Hell men so much talk of, he sees to be really in himself, and that himself is the very Image of the Devil*".[7]

Webster's antinomianism was a short step to the view that it was possible to live in a perfect state of grace in *this* world rather than wait, as most clergymen taught, for the uncertain reward of an after-life. A man in such a condition was not only released from the bondage of human edicts in religion, but he was also instantaneously restored to the state of perfect innocence once enjoyed by Adam in Eden, one aspect of which was the latter's comprehensive and intuitive knowledge of the creation. Whether or not Webster submitted entirely to such doctrines in the 1650s is unclear (though one should not forget his early acquaintance with this kind of thinking in the mid-1630s, above p. 1). What is certain, however, is that he did envisage vast intellectual gains for mankind in the event of a millenial revolution of the human spirit. This much is clear from his well-known views on education and the reform of higher learning in Cromwellian England, and is especially evident in the case of his advocacy of the search for the "universal language of nature", which many saw as the key to the secrets of the creation. In 1654, under the influence of the Silesian mystic, Jacob Boehme, Webster thus described this language of nature as the "Paradisical language of the outflown word which Adam understood while he was unfaln in Eden" and which was "infused into him in his Creation and so innate . . . and not inventive or acquisitive". Lost at the Fall, the only hope of its recovery was that in this present "age of the spirit" it might once again be revealed to man through the merciful gift of divine inspiration and so heal the breach between man and the rest of nature.[8]

---

[6] John Webster, *The vail of the covering, spread over all nations*, 2nd ed., London, J. Sowle, 1713, pp. 6–8, 25. The original sermon was delivered at All Hallows, Lombard Street on 23 June 1653, and was subsequently published in *The judgement set, and the bookes opened*, London, R. Hartford & N. Brooks, 1654.

[7] Webster, *The vail of the covering*, pp. 27, 38–39 (my italics). In another sermon preached at this time in London, Webster expounded at great length upon the idea that "there is no greater Deceiver to be found then is within Man: No cunninger Devil, no greater ANTICHRIST, nor no worse WITCH then what Man hath in his own heart". He went on to say that "however man is carried out to look for all these things without him, yet be sure these Sorcerers, these Wizzards, these Necromancers . . . Devils, Antichrists, all are in thine own bosome. Here is the true Necromancy and Witchcraft, the true Antichrist," *The judgement set*, pp. 159–161; cf. below pp. 11–12.

[8] John Webster, op. cit., note 4 above, pp. 25–32.

Clearly, Webster's religious, educational, and scientific beliefs were closely inter-related, his attack on the universities in 1654 (but written in 1653) being in large part a product of his radical theological stance. By the early 1650s, Webster would seem to have rejected the authority of all sects, churches, and religious organizations. In his writings, he consistently put forward the view that any attempt to intellectualize or institutionalize man's relationship with God was a perversion of divine will. It is impossible to say when exactly Webster arrived at this conclusion, though much that he wrote during this period tends to indicate a long history of disillusionment with, and dissent from, established religion ("the chains and fetters of cold and dead formality"). What is certain is that by 1653 at the latest he was a vociferous opponent of state-supported religion, be it episcopal, presbyterian, or independent, and an equally committed advocate of comprehensive religious toleration. A member of no specific sect, he would seem, therefore, to have shared the semi-mystical seeker opinions of his colleague, William Erbery, with whom he preached in an infamous debate at All Hallows Church in Lombard Street in October 1653.[9]

Alongside Erbery and others, Webster argued that all men must be free to interpret the scriptures and seek God's grace according to the light of their own consciences. Any attempt by the secular or ecclesiastical authorities to use coercion in such matters was considered "antichristian" by Webster, based as it was on the false premise that divine wisdom was acquired through human assistance (e.g., learning and preaching) rather than infused by the free gift of God's grace. The true way to salvation was thus to be found in the pursuit of faith alone and without recourse to human reason—a view to which many mainstream puritans paid lip-service in the period before 1640, despite the obvious heretical pitfalls of such a position. As John Morgan has shown, however, any apparent ambiguity in puritan circles concerning the role of reason in religious experience was firmly resolved by subordinating reason to faith and allowing only a limited role for the former in the acquisition of grace. For Webster, on the other hand, no such fine scholarly distinctions between "infused" and "acquired" learning was allowable in matters relating to salvation, for: "if man gave his assent unto, or believed the things of Christ, either because, and as they are taught of and by men, or because they appear probable and consentaneous to his reason, then would his faith be statuminated upon the rotten basis of humane authority".[10]

Indeed, Webster reminded the scholastic theologians of the universities that such a dichotomy or division between the two kinds of learning ("infused" and "acquired") had first been taught in the academies by their own predecessors. His aim in all this was

---

[9] Ibid., sig.A2r. The debate with Erbery and two anonymous defenders of the state church was first reported in *Mercurius Politicus*, no. 175, 13–20 October 1653, pp. 2795–2796. Webster replied in *The picture of Mercurius Politicus*, London, T. Webster & R. Hammond, 1653. Webster's friendship with William Erbery, whom he referred to as "chemist of truth and gospel", tends to strengthen the view that Webster at this time was immersed in perfectionist doctrines of a most radical hue. In 1658, he defended Erbery from the charge of Ranterism, insisting that Erbery's doctrine concerning the "restitution of all things, the liberty of the Creation, and Saints oneness in Christ with God" had been misinterpreted by "some weaker spirits". Needless to say, it was also alleged of Erbery that he denied the existence of eternal damnation, heaven and hell, and the Devil; see William Erbery, *The testimony of William Erbery*, London, G. Calvert, 1658, pp. 259, 260; Hill, op. cit., note 3 above, pp. 154–159.

[10] John Morgan, *Godly learning: Puritan attitudes towards reason, learning, and education 1560—1640*, Cambridge University Press, 1986; John Webster, op. cit., note 4 above, pp. 12–13, 17.

to refute once and for all the idea that grace and redemption might somehow be attained through the mere efforts of men. As Webster and his radical associates never tired of explaining, no amount of learning or biblical study could ensure possession of the gift of divine grace. On the contrary, such efforts were more likely to obscure rather than enlighten the minds of the sinful. Theology as taught in the schools was therefore obsolete in Webster's eyes, and the fact that such wisdom was considered essential to the training of the Anglican clergy merely increased the likelihood for Webster that the Anglican church was no true church of Christ.[11]

If one turns to examine Webster's detailed plan of reform for higher learning in England, it would seem logical to expect, given Webster's pronounced fideism, that the guiding principle of reform would be a secular curriculum devoid of religious content. That this was not the case is due almost entirely to the fact that Webster, in common with other radicals, was wholly oppposed to the retention of a system of learning dependant upon non-Christian sources. *Academiarum examen* (1654) should therefore be seen as an attempt by Webster to construct a reformed Christian epistemology in which the liberal arts, philosophy, science, and medicine were all represented albeit in purified form. Moreover, in this scheme Webster fully appreciated the possibility that all learning could, and should, be adapted to complement the pursuit of a holy, Christian existence. Neither was it necessary or even desirable for wisdom "acquired" in this manner to be divorced completely from spiritual or religious concerns. On the contrary, as Webster intimated in a sermon preached in June 1653, the divine creation was a constant witness to the eternal truths of Christianity: "there is not any one thing in the World but it holds forth Jesus Christ : all the whol creation is a representation of Jesus Christ: all tipes, all metaphors are resemblances of him".[12]

The application of such knowledge to overtly religious ends was always permissible in Webster's eyes as long as (a) it did not contradict the basic tenets of the Christian faith, and (b) it was not taught in such a way as to imply that herein lay the key to the mysteries of salvation.[13] Moreover, within the realm of "acquired" learning itself, it seems that Webster may have envisaged a qualitative distinction between experimental and rational modes of enquiry with far greater emphasis placed upon the virtues of the former. Consequently, pride of place in the new curriculum was reserved for men such as Paracelsus and van Helmont, Jacob Boehme and Robert Fludd, whose theosophical speculations were always more likely, for Webster, to repair the intellectual damage caused by the fall. All of these men had to some extent denigrated the faculty of human reason in scientific endeavour whilst promoting the benefits to mankind of experiential or experimental wisdom. More importantly, they all suggested the existence of an intimate relationship between experimenter and Creator whereby knowledge was perceived in part as the product or gift of divine providence. Whether or not Webster subscribed fully to the view that all knowledge was the product of divine inspiration is open to question (cf. for example his interest in the re-discovery of the Behmenist

[11] Ibid., pp. 3–18.

[12] Webster, op. cit., note 6 above, p. 10.

[13] Cf. the view of the Paracelsian translator and religious radical, Henry Pinnell, that "every part of the Creation doth its part to publish the great mysteries of mans Salvation", *Philosophy reformed and improved in four profound tractates,* London, Lodowick Lloyd, 1657, sig.A6v.

language of nature, above, p. 3). What is beyond doubt is the relative significance that he personally attached to those schools of thought which imbibed gnostic beliefs.[14]

Given such a preference, it is not surprising that Webster, throughout his life, consistently rejected an over-reliance upon human reason. In *Academiarum examen,* he poured scorn on those "unexperienced Authors" who slavishly followed the "ancients" in all aspects of learning, and he failed to understand how anyone could hope to "fathome the Universe by our shallow imaginations, or comprize the mysteries of mother nature in the narrow compass of our weak brains". Twenty years later, in the very different atmosphere of restoration England, Webster continued to decry speculative learning, and he remained especially contemptuous of "the Dark-lanthorn of Mans blind, frail and weak reason", which he believed was still the object of excessive veneration. Among those who continued to "idolize humane abilities and carnal reason" were the churchmen and philosophers who "not only applied those so much magnified Engines to the discovery of created things, wherein they have affected so little, [but] have also . . . invaded Heaven, and taken upon them to discover and determine of Celestials".[15]

Iconoclasm of this kind, dating as it does from Webster's later years, would seem to suggest that Webster never fully abandoned the radical principles upon which his personal faith was built, despite the fact that he conformed after 1660. One reason for his apparent quietism is almost certainly to be found in the profound sense of disillusionment that Webster experienced following the collapse of millenarian hopes in the mid-1650s. The failure of the millennium to materialize, as Webster explained in 1658, was a sign to the "saints" that "the restitution of all things is put afarr off". Webster now realized that he was no longer living in the promised age of "deliverance", but rather in the "time of bondage" so that "the Saints running from Mountain to Hill, is rather an exchange of one bondage for another then any reall redemption from the Ancient Yoke". Consequently, Webster reasoned that the "saints" had a duty to recognize the altered circumstances of the time and to adopt a "carriage" or attitude commensurate with their new position. Accordingly, he cautioned submission to the powers-that-be and, citing his ex-colleague Erbery as an example, he counselled that "it was the Wisdom, as well as the obedience of the Saints, to make their Captivity as comfortable as they could; [for] to shake off the yoke before the season came, was to rebel against the Lord".[16]

That Webster was referring here to his own situation, rather than that of his dead friend Erbery (d.1654), is borne out by the details of his life following his return to Clitheroe in the mid-1650s. By 1657, he had acquired sufficient property, much of it sequestered land, to qualify for the office of in-bailiff or resident magistrate to the town

---

[14] Webster quoted van Helmont to the effect that "the Lord had created the Physician, not the Schools", op. cit., note 4 above, p. 76.

[15] Ibid., p. 68; Webster, *The displaying of supposed witchcraft,* London, J.M., 1677, pp. 138, 201. By the 1670s, however, Webster's view of the traditional function of the universities had apparently softened, since he now condemned those who had "grown so rigid and peremptory, that they will condemn all things that have not past the test of Experiment . . . and so would totally demolish that part of Academick and Formal Learning that teacheth men Method and the way of Logical procedure". Ibid., p. 20.

[16] Erbery, op. cit., note 9 above, sigs. a1v-a2r (preface by J[ohn] W[ebster]).

of Clitheroe, and he held the post on three subsequent occasions (1658, 1665, 1675). He was also at this time well settled in a busy medical practice, which allowed him the luxury of an apprentice as well as an excuse to indulge his life-long passion for alchemical research. Clearly, Webster had become resigned to the fact that the revolutionary millenial moment or "season of deliverance" had passed, and that it was now his duty to adapt in the best way possible to the religious and political realities of life in interregnum England. Complete submission to the powers-that-be, regardless of what form they might take, was now the order of the day, a view which Webster seemed to find easy to translate to this period of rapidly shifting religious and political loyalties.[17]

Even the restoration of Charles II in 1660 posed few problems for Webster, whose record under the new regime was one of exemplary loyalty. In the elections to the Cavalier Parliament in 1661, Webster voted for the royalist candidate Ambrose Pudsay, and four years later, he was once again magistrate for Clitheroe, an office which he could only have held by conforming to the restored church. Such actions may, of course, have been prompted by considerations that had little relation to political idealism, particularly since Webster had acquired large amounts of royalist land in the 1650s. On the other hand, there is no reason to suppose that Webster was anything but sincere in his new-found regard for the monarchy, which as he intimated in 1658, was probably just as acceptable to the defeated "saints" as any other form of political authority.[18]

Convinced of the futility of further attacks upon the religious and political authorities, Webster thus abandoned the radical cause and began to pour his considerable energies into less controversial pursuits. In particular, more and more of his time was devoted to the study of "Experimental Philosophy" and "mysticall Chymistrye". Interest in these areas of enquiry not only formed the basis of his last two published works but also, in all likelihood, provided some form of spiritual consolation and solace for the ex-radical. In 1671, appeared *Metallographia, or, an history of metals,* a work recently described as "arguably the most effective work in its area produced by an English writer before 1700". Based on wide reading and a firm understanding of Paracelsian and Helmontian sources, it also reflects Webster's own practical involvement in alchemical research. Finally in 1677, at the age of sixty-six, Webster published *The displaying of supposed witchcraft,* a work highly critical of traditional demonological beliefs, which, in some quarters, must surely have revived memories of Webster's earlier reputation as a controversialist.[19]

Why Webster should have felt compelled to write on such a thorny subject as witchcraft in the 1670s is a matter for conjecture. There can be little doubt that the

---

[17] Weeks, op. cit., note 4 above, pp. 67–76, 90–97. Webster's last known involvement in religious controversy concerned a dispute with the local Independent minister, Thomas Jolly, between 1654 and 1656; see Henry Fishwick (editor), *The note book of the Rev. Thomas Jolly . . . Extracts from the church book of Altham and Wymondhouses,* Publications of the Chetham Society, new series, no. 33, Manchester, 1895, pp. 126, 128.

[18] W.S. Weeks, 'Further information about Dr. John Webster', *TLCAS,* 1932, **48:** 30–59, esp. pp. 37–46.

[19] Charles Webster, *From Paracelsus to Newton: magic and the making of modern science,* Cambridge University Press, 1982, p. 71. At his death, John Webster owned "Chimicall glasses" to the value of £4, as well as a "furnace house". See Appendix 1.

work itself was the product of a life-long interest in such matters, and that much of the material for the book was collected over many decades.[20] But why risk public censure and further controversy after twenty years of self-imposed restraint? One possible explanation lies in Webster's enthusiastic reception of the Royal Society, which he described in 1671 as "one of the happy fruits of his Majesties blessed and miraculous Restoration". In the same year, a Durham schoolmaster, Peter Nelson, in the course of a regular correspondence with the secretary of the Royal Society, Henry Oldenburg, referred to Webster as "a man very fit for your Correspondence". Nelson claimed to have made Webster's acquaintance "about 7 or 8 yeares agoe" [i.e., in 1663 or 1664], was aware of his radical past, but was nonetheless convinced of his potential use to the fledgling Society. It is just possible, therefore, that when Nelson wrote three years earlier to Oldenburg, in 1668, requesting to "see something from the Royall Society about Spirits and Witches" that he already had Webster in mind for the job.[21]

Though one cannot be certain of Nelson's precise role, if any, in the origins of *The displaying*, his view of witchcraft as "none of the most obvious things in Nature", which hitherto had been "discours't of with ye least of clearness and satisfaction", was surely one which Webster would have endorsed.[22] Whatever the case, a draft copy of the completed work was presented to the Royal Society as early as February 1674, and it was subsequently published in 1677 with the *imprimatur* of the Society's vice-president, Sir Jonas Moore. Despite the fact that Webster had no official ties with the Society, he did possess one vital ally and supporter in the shape of the Yorkshire naturalist and Fellow, Martin Lister. In January 1674, Webster had written to Lister requesting his assistance in "the licenseing of my booke", which had evidently met with strong disapproval in certain quarters. A month later, Webster sent Lister a draft copy of the frontispiece to *The displaying* along with an outline or "register" of chapters, and in an accompanying letter he explained the nature of his current problems with regard to publication.[23]

According to Webster, the "Ecclesiasticks" were refusing to license the work on the grounds that "I have attributed too much to naturall causes" as well as "maintaineing falne Angells to be corporeal". Under the circumstances, Webster felt obliged to send a copy to the Royal Society in the hope that it might be licensed there, and was now writing to Lister in the hope that he might "write to some of your friends there to further it". In the event that this strategy should prove unsuccessful, Webster went on to say that he was prepared, if necessary, to "habit it in Latine" and "get it printed beyond seas"—a sure indication if any were needed that the ageing physician had lost none of his contempt for intellectual authoritarianism.[24]

---

[20] Webster first encountered witchcraft in the mid-1630s when, as rector of Kildwick, he helped to expose the fraudulent practices of the local witch-finder, Edmund Robinson. A copy of the examination of Robinson is attached to the rear of Webster's *Displaying*.

[21] Webster, *Metallographia: or, an history of metals*, London, Walter Kettilby, 1671, sig. A2v; A.R. and M.B. Hall (editors), *The correspondence of Henry Oldenburg*, Madison and Milwaukee, University of Wisconsin Press, 1965–77, 11 vols., vol. 5, p. 24, vol. 7, pp. 534–535. Nelson also wrote to Oldenburg on the subject of fabulous prodigies and natural marvels (ibid., vol. 7, p. 535; vol. 9, p. 615), local iatrochemists (ibid., vol. 7, p. 326), and his own moderate and tolerant religious proposals (ibid., vol. 9, p. 616).

[22] Ibid., vol. 7, p. 24.

[23] Thomas Birch (editor), *The history of the Royal Society of London*, London, A. Millar, 1756–57, 4 vols., vol. 3, p. 192; Bodleian Library, Oxford, Lister MS. 34, ff. 145, 147–148.

[24] Ibid., f. 148.

Opinions vary as to the overall significance of Webster's contribution to the witchcraft debate in seventeenth-century England, and the work itself still awaits comprehensive analysis.[25] It was clearly intended as a reply to the familiar arguments of the demonologists, which had recently been resurrected by two well-respected Anglican clergymen, Meric Casaubon (1599–1671) and Joseph Glanvill (1636–80). Not surprisingly, the religious background of these two men, compared with Webster's own, has prompted speculation as to the underlying purpose of *The displaying* and its place in the general context of post-restoration religious polemic.[26] Casaubon, in particular, was an obvious target for Webster's pen.[27] Glanvill's appearance, however, in the witchcraft debate on the side of the traditionalists was presumably more problematic for Webster, given Glanvill's well-publicized religious moderation as well as his enthusiastic support for the "new science" and the Royal Society. One solution to this problem, proposed by Thomas Jobe, has focused on an attempt to maximize the intellectual gap between the two protagonists by portraying Glanvill and Webster as the typical representatives of two competing religio-scientific paradigms:

> The witchcraft debates took the form of a struggle between two kinds of science—Paracelsian-Helmontian science versus a mechanical corpuscularianism—but behind that struggle lay the clash of the theologies to which these sciences were linked—radical protestant versus orthodox Anglican theology. The Glanvill-Webster exchanges thus should be viewed as a continuation into the Restoration of the debate between radical Protestants and latitudinarian Anglican theologians that began in the 1650s.[28]

Although such an analysis is superficially appealing, and may well reflect the situation before 1660, as an explanation for the underlying motives in the post-restoration debate on witchcraft it undoubtedly over-simplifies what is a highly complex situation. Not all Paracelsians or Helmontians, for example, shared Webster's scepticism on such issues, nor was there unanimity among the members of the Royal Society as to belief in the reality of witches and demons.[29] It is equally improbable to suppose that hermetic science appealed exclusively to radical protestants, or that mechanical corpuscularianism was the special preserve of latitudinarian Anglicans. As to Webster's radical protestantism, there is little evidence in *The displaying* to suggest that he was *consciously* pursuing a theological controversy that had its roots in the interregnum. Indeed, in composing this work, Webster may well have employed many

[25] G.L. Kittredge, for example, was completely unable to see how Webster might "be regarded as a tower of sceptical strength in the great witchcraft controversy"; Kittredge, *Witchcraft in old and new England*, New York, Russell & Russell, 1958, pp. 348–349; cf. similar view of R.T. Davies, *Four centuries of witch-beliefs*, London, Methuen, 1947, p. 185 and n. At the opposite extreme, K. Theodore Hoppen has described Webster's work as "perhaps the most noteworthy contemporary critique of belief in witchcraft"; Hoppen, 'The nature of the early Royal Society', *Br.J.Hist.Sci.*, 1976, **9**: 15.

[26] Most notably by Thomas Harmon Jobe, 'The devil in restoration science: the Glanvill-Webster witchcraft debate', *Isis*, 1981, **72**: 343–356.

[27] An opponent of religious "enthusiasm" in the 1650s, Casaubon remained stubbornly opposed to all forms of religious or intellectual innovation, which he equated with the works of the devil. Webster, in fact, owned a copy of Casaubon's *A true and faithful relation of . . . Dr. John Dee . . . and some spirits*, London, T. Garthwait, 1659 [item 40].

[28] Jobe, op. cit., note 26 above, p. 344.

[29] This is a complex issue to which I hope to return in the near future. Needless to say, I cannot agree with Garfield Tourney's conclusion that continuing belief in witchcraft in the second half of the seventeenth century was largely the product of the "superstitious state of restoration medicine"; Tourney, 'The physician and witchcraft in restoration England', *Med.Hist.*, 1972, **16**: 153–154.

of the arguments and beliefs that had earlier characterized his commitment to radical religion (see below pp. 11–12). It is not possible to deduce from this, however, that *The displaying* was intended by Webster as yet another thinly disguised broadside against the religious establishment. On the contrary, as I have already tried to show (above pp. 6–7), all surviving evidence points to the inescapable conclusion that Webster had made his peace with the religious authorities some time in the late 1650s, and thereafter accepted with patient resignation the return of the Anglican church.[30]

If the idea of an underlying clash of theologies is largely immaterial to our understanding of *The displaying,* what of Jobe's inference that Webster and Glanvill were somehow engaged in a long-standing dispute between two irreconcilable paradigms of science? Again, the evidence is unconvincing, since it seriously ignores the extent to which Webster's scientific outlook, as expounded in *The displaying* and confirmed by the contents of his library, was based on a thorough-going eclecticism. This is evident, for example, in his praise for the achievements of Harvey and Bacon, Galileo and Descartes, as well as his genuine admiration for the scientific endeavours of the gentlemen of the Royal Society. It is equally apparent in his tendency to utilize *any* evidence, including that drawn from the "mechanical-corpuscularian school", which might lend added credence to his own views on witchcraft.[31]

When Webster wrote *The displaying* in the early 1670s, there is no reason to suppose that he was deliberately seeking to revive memories of his earlier allegiance to religious radicalism, or that he was attempting to discredit non-occult schools of scientific thought. On the other hand, because his approach to witchcraft was so obviously shaped by his earlier attachment to unorthodox religious and scientific ideas, it would be foolish to ignore their part in the final draft of *The displaying.*[32] This is particularly evident in the case of Webster's passionate concern for iatrochemistry and "mystical philosophy", which, if no longer considered entirely faultless, still remained a vital ingredient of his overall intellectual outlook. Of Paracelsus, for example, Webster wrote in *The displaying* that he was unfairly attacked by his detractors, not only for his reasonable dismissal of Galenism, "but also for striving to purge and purifie the ancient, natural, laudable and lawful Magick from the filth and dregs of Imposture . . . and Superstitions". At the same time, the Englishman, Robert Fludd, was held to be "one of the most Christian Philosophers that ever writ", whilst pride of place in this pantheon of scientific Gods was reserved for John Baptist van Helmont, "a person of profound judgment, great experience, general learning, high reputation, and now generally followed as the Chief-Standard-bearer for Philosophy, Physick and Chemistry".[33]

[30] For example, as in-bailiff for Clitheroe in 1665, Webster must have conformed to the restored Anglican church because of the provisions of the Corporation Act of 1661.

[31] Webster, op. cit., note 15 above, pp. 3–9, 14–16, 88, 268. Two leading English representatives of the "mechanical-corpuscularian school" were cited by Webster in *The displaying:* Robert Boyle (p. 251) and Thomas Willis (pp. 313, 315, 316–317).

[32] It may be significant that Webster's interest in religious radicalism and occult science coincided roughly with his first encounter with witchcraft, i.e., between 1634 and 1635. For Webster's induction into "mystical Philosophy" and chemistry through the teachings of Johannes Huniades, see Webster, op. cit., note 21 above, p. 161. This means that Webster must have spent some time in London around 1635, since Huniades was resident in the Whitechapel district of the city. For Huniades, see F. Sherwood Taylor and C.H. Josten, 'Johannes Banfi Hunyades 1576–1650', *Ambix,* 1953, 1956, **5**: 44–52, 115.

[33] Webster, op. cit., note 15 above, pp. 9, 259; cf. Webster, op. cit., note 21 above, pp. 34–35.

In eulogizing the achievements and thought of such men, Webster was inevitably drawn into the defence of some of their methods, which were themselves cited by the demonologists as evidence of the reality of witchcraft (e.g., the weapon-salve). Webster's reply to such insinuations was based firmly upon the Helmontian assertion that nature itself was completely devoid of "contrariety" or malign intentions and so could not be held responsible for the evil ends to which men might use it. The creation was brought into being by God for the benefit of all mankind, "his Creatures . . . all made to show forth his power and Godhead". It was therefore inconceivable that it might possess any trait or attribute that was innately harmful to man. More often than not, Webster concluded, it was man's ignorance of natural causation that lay at the root of continuing belief in witchcraft. Yet the problem remains: to what extent did Webster allow a real role for the Devil in the world of man and nature?[34]

It has been suggested that Webster was not altogether consistent on this and a number of related points, and that he left significant loopholes in what was otherwise a thoroughly sceptical account of the Devil's ability to interfere in the natural world.[35] As we shall see, there is certainly an element of truth in such an analysis of *The displaying*. It is, however, possible to argue that many of these apparent discrepancies can be explained to some extent as due to an understandable reluctance on Webster's part to accept in full the subversive implications of his earlier adherence to what one might term the "mystical-radical" tradition. Nowhere is this more apparent than in Webster's discussion of the properties and nature of spirits, demons and devils, and their capacity to inflict harm upon men and women. In various passages throughout *The displaying,* Webster conceded that God did occasionally allow the Devil access to this world, though his liberty to act in such extraordinary circumstances was severely circumscribed. In particular, it was considered inconceivable that any physical contact between men and devils was permitted or possible, *despite the fact* that Webster positively affirmed the corporeal quality of demons and fallen angels. Because the Devil was restricted to "the acts of his wicked and depraved will", collusion was possible between men and the Devil in the form of a mental pact. In reality, however, this did not amount to a great deal, for,

> if they object and say, that here we confess a League with the Devil and the Witch, . . . we answer, it is a gross mistake, in not observing the distinction we make between a mental and a spiritual League, such as the Devil and Judas made: *and such as all wicked men make with him; and under this League we acknowledge all Witches to be; but a visible and corporeal League we positively deny.*[36]

In consistently stressing this point—that the only contact between men and the Devil was "mental" or "spiritual"—it is difficult to avoid the conclusion that Webster was drawing upon those ideas which he had held in the 1650s, and which stated, *inter alia,* that the Devil was little more than the figurative embodiment of the idea of evil (cf. above pp. 2–3; and n7). Elsewhere in *The displaying* it is possible to detect further vestiges of Webster's radical past, as, for example, in his defence of "Allegorical, Metaphorical, Mystical and Parabolical Expositions", as well as his deprecation of "too much extolling and idolizing of Humane and Carnal reason".

---

[34] Webster, op. cit., note 15 above, pp. 17–18.

[35] See, for example, Charles Webster, op. cit., note 19 above, pp. 97–98.

[36] Webster, op. cit., note 15 above, pp. 18, 71 (my italics); cf. ibid., pp. 31, 48, 67, 70, 73–75, 77 and *passim*.

Finally, the common belief amongst interregnum radicals in an impersonal, symbolic Devil is not altogether absent from Webster's last work, as illustrated by the following allusion to Ephesians, 6, 11–18:

> Therefore we are to give heed unto the counsel of the Holy Ghost, to resist the Devil in his spiritual assaults with the spiritual weapons that God bestows upon us, and not to give heed to . . . the false Doctrine of Witchmongers, that make us watch for the Devil where he is not, and in the mean time not to resist him where he is, and that is . . . effectively in a spiritual manner, for he worketh in the children of disobedience, *and therefore a Devil within us is more to be feared, than a Devil without us.*[37]

On this basis, it was possible to dismiss most instances of supposed diabolism or witchcraft in the Bible as clear examples of mental transactions between man and the Devil. Of this nature were the temptation of Eve by the serpent (Genesis, 3, 1–6) and the account of the Witch of Endor (1 Samuel, 28, 7–25). Similarly, in the New Testament, Christ's enticement by the Devil and his transportation through the air (Matthew, 4, 1–11) were not to be interpreted as real events, but rather as manifestations of Satan's spiritual wickedness and his symbolic role as universal tempter of mankind.[38] On the one hand then, because "spirits" were essentially corporeal, Webster was loath to dismiss absolutely the hypothetical notion of demonic interference in human affairs. On the other hand, however, he stood by the belief that it was highly unlikely in this present age that God should suffer the Devil to roam the earth freely, since "miracles being long ceased, it must needs follow, that Devils do nothing, but only draw the minds of Men and Women into sin and wickedness".[39]

Moreover, if devils did exist in the sub-lunary world, a supposition that Webster never consistently owned,[40] their ability to perform real and extraordinary feats was drastically curtailed. Not only were they consigned by God to the "Caliginious air or Atmosphere" and so unable without divine permission to punish or harm men, but as impure and material beings, their knowledge of the creation was necessarily imperfect and far less than that claimed by the demonologists. It was therefore a constant theme of *The displaying* that it was both "vain and needless" to invoke the aid of demons and devils "seeing they have no advantage over us, but operate only by applying active things to passive, like as men do". Even if God did allow the Devil or his agents a special dispensation to intervene in the natural world (as the "School-men, and Divines most generally hold") the outcome remained natural:

---

[37] Ibid., pp. 138–139, 99 (my italics). Cf. the view of the Paracelsian and occult philosopher, Robert Turner, that "neither they [i.e., the demonologists] nor any man or woman in the world yet saw his Cloven-foot; but he keeps his schoole in their own bosomes. And therefore St. Paul teaches them how to make their defence against him. That ever there was any such thing as Bill or Bond by any one sealed to him; or any Contract or Covenant by any witch made with him; is impossible to be true"; Turner, *Astrologicall opticks*, London, J. Allen & R. Moon, 1655, unpaginated 'To the Reader'. Similar sentiments were expressed by Reginald Scot in *The discoverie of witchcraft*, London, W. Brome, 1584, pp. 508, 510.

[38] Webster, op. cit., note 15 above, pp. 142–150, 29–30, 290, 178–179. Other examples can be found at ibid., pp. 83–97 (lycanthropy and the impossibility of diabolical transfiguration); p. 116 (on the biblical text: "rebellion is as the sin of witchcraft", 1 Samuel, 15, 23); p. 240 (diabolic possession).

[39] Ibid., p. 278; see also pp. 225, 239, 290.

[40] See, for example, Webster's comment that although there was abundant evidence in the Bible for the ministry of "good angels . . . I do not find any one place . . . where plainly and positively any apparition of evil spirits is recorded, or that by any rational and necessary consequence such a visible appearance can be deduced or proved"; ibid., pp. 288–289.

"and so killing any person, it is only wicked and diabolical, in regard of the end, which is murther, but what Witchcraft is there in the means and operation?"[41]

The fact that Webster was somewhat inconsistent in his discussion of the nature of devils and demons was probably a reflection of his own personal faith in the devil-free nature of the age. The era of miracles and similar extraordinary phenomena having long since passed, Webster now confidently affirmed that God was to be found everywhere "by his Power, Essence and Presence, and therefore cannot literally be said to be comprehended in any locality, but after a Metaphorical sense and expression". Furthermore, because God ruled "all things according to the power . . . of his own positive and actual will", nature was largely untouched by the hand of the Devil and his minions, who were accordingly "delivered into chains of darkness" to await the Day of Judgement.[42]

With the Devil thus reduced to the role of an impotent onlooker, Webster set out to emphasize the human element in witchcraft and to stress the evil disposition of the witch, which he perceived as the crucial factor in the making of such "Rebels and Traitors against God and Christ". Reversing the demonological commonplace that it was the Devil and not the deluded witch who was responsible for hurting men and beasts, Webster therefore argued that Satan played no part in the performance of *maleficia,* which were the exclusive product of the witch's corrupted wisdom. In the process, he also felt obliged to defend all knowledge, including magic, from the imputation of diabolism on the grounds that the only meaningful distinction between "types" of knowledge consisted in "the end and use" to which they were put.[43]

If the overall message of *The displaying* differed little from that first enunciated by Reginald Scot in the sixteenth century, it should not disguise either the originality or significance of Webster's contribution to the witchcraft debate. Dependent to a large extent upon the unorthodox insights of Paracelsus, van Helmont, and other hermetic philosophers, Webster not only refused to acknowledge the traditional superiority of Satan in the sublunary world but, to the horror of his opponents, he rejected the spiritual being of man's arch-adversary. Divested of spiritual form and substance, Satan was consequently powerless to intervene in the natural world except as a tempter of mankind. In the process, witchcraft was redefined by Webster as the deeds of evil men and women who may or may not have been inspired by the Devil in the pursuit of their profane but wholly natural activities.

Despite the ecclesiastical opposition that Webster had spoken of prior to the publication of *The displaying* in the early 1670s, the work itself produced surprisingly

[41] Ibid., pp. 220, 224, 18, 152, 78–79. Webster was, however, inclined to allot a minor role to fallen angels in "the sublunary changes or motions of Meteors . . . as the Christian Philosopher Doctor Fludd hath most learnedly proved"; ibid., p. 222. For Webster's assertion that devils possess physical attributes and corporeal form, see esp. ibid., pp. 197–215.

[42] Ibid., pp. 139–140, 183, 18; cf. John Everard's statement that "in our forefather's days, we have heard that there appeared Spirits and Hobgoblins, and such kind of things; but that was in the days of Popery and blindness . . . now the light have vanished all these things"; Everard, *Some gospel-treasures opened,* London, Rapha Harford, 1653, p. 148. Webster published an 'approbration' to Everard's works, which appeared in the enlarged 1659 edition of *Some gospel-treasures opened,* and was added to Webster's own *The judgement set,* pp. 311–312. Everard does not appear, however, in the catalogue of books owned by Webster.

[43] Webster, op. cit., note 15 above, pp. 67, 78, 152 and *passim.* For Webster's general indebtedness to van Helmont in the formulation of his own scepticism, see ibid., pp. 17, 152–159, 162, 241–266.

little response from the defenders of the orthodox position. Apart from further denunciations by Glanvill and Henry More, and an attack upon Webster's intellectual inconsistency from the pen of the cleric Benjamin Camfield, Webster's views on witchcraft elicited little serious response.[44] We may assume, therefore, that the last years of Webster's life were largely untroubled by further controversy. In January 1680, he made his last will and testament (the details of which suggest a comfortable existence; see Appendix 1), and on 18 June 1682 he died, leaving behind an epitaph that he himself wrote and which now stands in the parish church of Clitheroe.[45]

[44] Joseph Glanvill, *Saducismus triumphatus . . . With a letter of Dr. H. More on the same subject*, London, J. Collins & S. Lownds, 1681; Benjamin Camfield, *A theological discourse of angels . . . Also an appendix containing some reflections upon Mr. Websters displaying supposed witchcraft*, London, Henry Brome, 1678, esp. pp. 178, 197–200.
[45] See Appendix 2.

2

THE LIBRARY OF JOHN WEBSTER

INTRODUCTION

The manuscript of the catalogue of the library of Dr John Webster of Clitheroe is to be found today in the archives of Chetham's library, Manchester (Chetham MS A.6.47). It was previously in the ownership of the celebrated Lancashire antiquarian, James Crossley, who was himself given the manuscript on 12 June 1876 by a friend, the Reverend Thomas Corser of Stand.[46] The manuscript consists of twenty-two foliated leaves bound with marbled boards and leather spine, and is almost certainly a copy of an original draft, composed by Webster himself, probably for the purpose of evaluating his estate.[47] In Webster's will, dated 3 January 1680 (see Appendix 1), the contents of the library were valued at £400, a figure roughly approximating to the more accurate catalogue evaluation of £402 6s. 10d.

The catalogue is systematically arranged according to subject and book-size and would appear to reflect the original plan of the books as they actually appeared on the shelves of Webster's library. It comprises fifteen sections (which, for the sake of convenience, I have labelled A to O) with 1501 entries in total. This figure, however, is not an accurate assessment of the number of volumes once possessed by Webster. Although it is impossible to give a precise figure,[48] a conservative estimate would indicate a total number of volumes in the region of 1662 (a figure which includes works from Section M which were not in Webster's possession at the time the catalogue was produced).

Clearly, the sheer size of Webster's library is one of its most striking features, but what else, apart from the broadest generalizations, can it tell us about the owner of this collection? The limited use of such evidence is all too obvious. For example, even if it were possible to read every work, how would this help us to understand how a seventeenth-century reader such as Webster would interpret the same information and knowledge? How can we know whether or not Webster even read some or all of these works? Many of the volumes, particularly the older ones, were almost certainly the fruits of inheritance. Others may constitute unread gifts or volumes acquired merely for the sake of collection. To make matters worse, the library itself has not survived

---

[46] Corser had originally intended to publish the catalogue, along with a "fuller life" of Webster, in the *Proceedings of the Chetham Society;* see *Pots's discovery of witches . . . reprinted from the original edition of 1613,* Publications of the Chetham Society, new series, no. 6, Manchester, 1845, Appendix ('Works suggested for publication').

[47] For evidence of Webster's authorship, see below, item 1176: "2 my owne Sermon bookes". This is presumably a reference to Webster's *The judgement set* [also item 451].

[48] Difficulties encountered in this respect are largely due to the vague descriptions that the cataloguer frequently employed in the composition of the manuscript. Item 1197, for example, is simply described as "H:N: Workes". Likewise, the use of "Opera" to describe an unknown quantity of books (e.g., item 1390: "Opera Jo: Wigandi") makes it impossible to arrive at an accurate figure for the total number of volumes in the collection. For the sake of statistical analysis, I have counted such items as comprising one volume only.

intact, nor, as far as I am aware, have individual volumes come to light, which might have provided some clues to Webster's reading habits. In the absence of annotated books in Webster's handwriting, one is bound to accept that the catalogue as it stands represents for the historian only a limited record of one man's intellectual and literary tastes.[49]

Notwithstanding the very real methodological problems and consequent limitations that beset a study such as this, it is possible to elicit much useful information which might add to our overall picture of Webster. To a very large extent, I am encouraged in my optimism by the invaluable evidence of the breadth of Webster's reading to be found in his published writings. In all but his earliest theological writings, Webster included comprehensive and often detailed citations of references which I have included in the main body of the catalogue.[50] An analysis of these suggests that in the writing of just three works (*Academiarum examen, Metallographia,* and *The displaying of supposed witchcraft*), Webster cited over two hundred authorities, or roughly fourteen per cent of the total number of items in his possession in 1682. Such a high figure (given the low sample) certainly suggests that Webster was no mere dilettante collector of books, a view confirmed by Webster himself in 1677, when he confessed to having led "a solitary and sedentary life . . . having had more converse with the dead than the living, that is, more with Books than with Men".[51]

All other arguments to one side, the sheer size and value of Webster's library is surely testament enough to his voracious appetite for the printed word. Such a collection could only have been amassed at considerable personal expense, and Webster was, after all, a man of only moderate income and wealth. Moreover, geographical isolation, particularly from the specialist book markets in the new medical and scientific literature that features so prominently in Webster's library, must have placed real constraints on Webster's ability to purchase books. Some instances of individual items will serve to illustrate the point. The most expensive item in the library, Robert Fludd's five-volume *Opera* (Oppenheim & Frankfurt, 1617–26: item 1), was valued in 1680 at the staggering figure of £9 10s. 0d. A colour edition of Gerard Mercator's *Atlas* (Amsterdam, 1636–38; 1641: item 77) was priced at £8, and a three-volume edition of Conrad Gesner's *Historia animalium* (Zurich, 1551–58: item 83) at £6 10s. 0d.

In the case of less expensive items, the greatest problem for Webster was probably inaccessibility to booksellers. This fact alone probably accounts for one of the more curious features of Webster's library, namely the virtual absence of books dating from the period after 1658–59. Although the problem of identification of editions makes it

---

[49] I hope it will be possible to locate works that once formed part of Webster's library. According to James Crossley in 1845, he had in his possession "two books which appear to have at one time formed part of his collection, from having his favourite signature, Johannes Hyphantes, in his autograph, on the title pages"; introduction to *Potts's discovery,* op. cit., note 46 above, p. 16n. The librarian of Chetham's Library, Manchester, kindly informs me that at Crossley's death he owned approximately 60,000 to 90,000 volumes which were dispersed by auction in two portions. Since the catalogues of both sales survive, it should one day prove possible to locate some of the volumes that were once in Webster's possession.

[50] In some cases, this has allowed me to identify precise editions. For the great majority of items, however, this has proved impossible.

[51] Webster, op. cit., note 15 above, sig.A1v.

impossible to speak with certainty on this issue, the fact that only a handful of items can be positively dated to the period after 1659 does seem to indicate an end to Webster's book buying shortly before the restoration.[52] The temptation to correlate this disjuncture with Webster's public recantation from the radical cause at roughly the same time (above pp. 6–7) is overwhelming. In all probability, when Webster withdrew from the radical scene in 1657–58, he also severed all links with London and its printers and booksellers, and so ceased to acquire new works of science and literature. One should not assume from this, however, that Webster's love of novelty and books ceased at the restoration. Both his later works, printed in the 1670s, carry numerous references to works of natural philosophy and other subjects which were published after 1659 and which cannot be found in his own library.[53] During this period then, Webster clearly borrowed books rather than buying them, a change of practice which does not appear to have blunted his desire to remain well-informed.

One source of new information was Martin Lister. In the abbreviated correspondence between the two men which survives, it is clear that Webster's residence in remote Clitheroe was not the barrier that it might at first seem to a man with Webster's thirst for knowledge. For example, in a letter dated 9 October 1674, Webster wrote to Lister thanking him for the loan of two books, one of which had only recently appeared at Copenhagen in the same year. The work in question was, in fact, a reply to the famous adversary of the Paracelsians, Hermann Conringius (1606–81) by the Danish scholar Olaus Borrichius (1626–90), and Webster thanked Lister for the prompt procurement of "such a peice as I have much desired to see, for of all the malicious enemyes of the Hermetick learning, I have often wished to have had Conringius undertaken, which he hath done, and performed beyond all expectation".[54]

The Webster-Lister correspondence thus helps to reinforce what is already very apparent from Webster's published works, namely an unquenchable appetite on the part of the Clitheroe physician for up-to-date scientific information. This image of Webster the bibliophile, busily accumulating works of science, medicine, and literature in the period prior to the restoration, does not exactly fit with the stereotypical image of the radical reformer. Excessive veneration of books and the knowledge that they contained was not generally a hallmark of Webster's like-minded colleagues. The chemist, John French, for example, in the preface to *A new light of alchymie* (1650),

---

[52] In the period from 1650 to 1660, I have counted 112 items that were published exclusively during these years. Of these, only five, or 4·5 per cent, appeared in the years 1659–60 [items: 26; 40; 50; 484; 665]. After 1660, only a further five, or perhaps six, items can be positively dated from this period [items: 164; 322; 467?; 694; 920; 962].

[53] This is most striking in the case of *The displaying*, since Webster possessed no personal copy of either of the tracts by Glanvill and Casaubon which had induced his reply. He also cited a number of important texts relating to the European witchcraft debate which were not in his possession, e.g. Johann Wier's *De praestigiis daemonum* and King James's *Daemonologie*. In all, I have counted only thirteen volumes in Webster's library concerned specifically with the subject of witchcraft.

[54] Bodleian Library, Oxford, Lister MS. 34, f.173. The work to which Webster referred is Borrichius, *Hermetis, Ægyptiorum, et chemicorum sapientia ab Hermanni Conringii animadversionibus vindicata*, Copenhagen, Petrus Hauboldus, 1674. Webster possessed two works by Conringius, including his full-scale assault upon the ancient origins and veracity of hermetic wisdom, *De hermetica Ægyptiorum vetere et Paracelsiorum nova medicina liber unus*, Helmstadt, Henningus Mullerus, 1648; 2nd ed., 1659 [item 343].

apologized for the publication of this translation because "there are too many books already, and the multitude of them is the greatest cause of our ignorance". In religion, similar claims were made by the spokesmen of the radical sects, yet Webster, who shared the view that book learning and other aids were irrelevant to the acquisition of grace, was simultaneously establishing a vast library that included a large percentage of orthodox theological writings.[55]

In Webster's case at least, the charge of "ignorance" which was levelled against him in the 1650s, and has been repeated since, was clearly unfounded.[56] Webster, in fact, never condemned book learning *per se*, even in his most vitriolic attacks upon the scholastic teachers of Oxford and Cambridge. The thrust of his argument was against what he perceived as the *total* reliance of the schools upon "poring continually upon a few paper Idols and unexperienced Authors: as though we could fathome the Universe by our shallow imaginations, or . . . weak brains". It was for this reason that Webster advised the adoption of Baconian inductivism in natural philosophy and other branches of learning in order to redress the balance of university studies. Henceforth students should proceed to learn about the secrets of nature through the use of "manual operation, and ocular experiment", an eventuality which would "never come to pass, unless they have laboratories as well as Libraries, and work in the fire, [rather] than build Castles in the Air."[57]

Of Webster's breadth of learning and love of books there can be little serious doubt. But what of the actual contents of his library? Classification of each entry by subject (Table 1) and language (Table 2) is an obvious starting-point, notwithstanding certain important reservations as to the reliability of the statistical evidence used to determine these categories. In the case of Table 1, the most serious caveat concerns the quite often insuperable problem of definitional status. Certain works obviously fall under more than one broad subject classification (e.g. items 102; 895; Pierre de la Primaudaye's encyclopaedic *French academy*), and these have been entered under the rather unhelpful category of 'Miscellaneous works'. Under this heading I have also included the various collected works of authors such as Aristotle [79], Plato [43;1180], Bacon [694], and Nicholas of Cusa [33], as well as a whole series of volumes on such diverse topics as hunting [194;888;1192], prophecy [406;684;1485], tobacco-smoking [945], etc. For the purposes of statistical accuracy, I have also excluded from analysis thirty-six volumes which defy classification of any kind (e.g., items 1100; 1101; 1102; 1103; 1104). Similarly, in Table 2, forty-three volumes have been omitted from the total number of works classified by language (e.g., item 1351: "4 litle books of pdestinacon & such like").

---

[55] Michael Sendivogius, *A new light of alchymie . . . translated . . . by J*[ohn] *F*[rench], London, R. Cotes, 1650, sigs. A4r-v; cf. Everard Maynwaring, *Medicus absolutus,* London, 1668, p. 135; Anon., *A rational discours touching the universal medicin,* London, 1664, p. 7.

[56] Mark Curtis, for example, has described Webster as "an ignorant and fanatical critic of the universities"; Curtis, *Oxford and Cambridge in transition, 1558—1642,* Oxford, Clarendon Press, 1959, p. 274. Of his contemporary critics, note that Webster possessed a copy of John Wilkins' and Seth Ward's reply to Webster's critique of the universities [item 446].

[57] John Webster, op. cit., note 4 above, pp. 68, 106. Webster did, in fact, possess his own laboratory in Clitheroe, which he referred to as "my Furnace house"; see Appendix 1.

TABLE I.   THE LIBRARY OF DR JOHN WEBSTER CLASSIFIED ACCORDING TO SUBJECT

Subject	Total	Percentage
Natural Philosophy	647	39·8
(i) Medicine	[242]	[14·9]
(ii) Mathematics	[79]	[4·9]
(iii) Natural science	[326]	[20·0]
Theology	397	24·4
History	169	10·4
Literature	148	9·1
Linguistics	90	5·5
Miscellaneous	69	4·25
Philosophy	56	3·45
Law and Politics	50	3·1
TOTAL	1626*	100

*Excluding 36 unidentified volumes

TABLE 2.   THE LIBRARY OF DR JOHN WEBSTER CLASSIFIED ACCORDING TO LANGUAGE

Language	Total	Percentage
Latin	967	59·7
English	405	25·0
French	87	5.4
Italian	34	2·1
Greek-Latin	26	1·6
German	19	1·2
Spanish	15	0·95
Hebrew	15	0·95
Greek	12	0·75
Dutch	2	0·1
Arabic	1	0·05
Miscellaneous (i.e., polyglot dictionaries, grammars, etc.)	36	2·2
TOTAL	1619*	100

*Excluding 43 unidentified volumes

NATURAL PHILOSOPHY

By far the largest category of books owned by Webster was that which I have classified under the general heading of natural philosophy (647 volumes or approximately forty per cent of the total number of volumes in the library). Over half (326) were concerned with what I have rather artificially termed natural science. The remaining works have been classified under the equally imprecise headings of medicine (242) and mathematics (79). Within the major sub-division of natural science are to be found volumes on a wide range of subjects including astronomy, botany, chemistry, cosmography, geography, husbandry, mineralogy, optics, psychology, witchcraft, and zoology. Not surprisingly, however, the largest group of works within this sub-division comprises those which for the sake of simplicity (if not complete accuracy) one might best describe as "occult philosophy"—i.e., alchemy, astrology, cabbalism, and natural magic. Excluding works of occult medicine, Webster owned over one hundred volumes of occult science.

Such are the bare statistics, but what of the range and content of this extraordinarily impressive collection of scientific and medical literature? One conclusion is inescapable. On the evidence of both his published writings and his library, Webster was a committed eclectic who did not appear to perceive any contradiction in the diversity of his scientific reading and interests. His critics, on the other hand, accused him of inconsistency and ignorance when in the 1650s he advocated the replacement of sterile Aristotelianism in the universities with a new curriculum based upon a wide range of modern scientific and philosophical beliefs. Alongside Robert Fludd and the Paracelsians, Webster praised the revival of Platonism (undertaken by Patrizi and Ficino), Democritean atomism (by Descartes, Regius, Holwarda, and Magnenus), and Epicureanism (by Gassendi), as well as the works of Telesio, Gilbert, and Bacon. This was not, as recently suggested, a mere exercise in name-dropping. In Webster's library are to be found works by all these authors, including a two-volume edition of Descartes' *Opera* (Amsterdam, 1650) [315] and an eight-volume edition of Bacon's *Works* (Amsterdam, 1660–63) [694].58 Of one fact we can be absolutely certain. Webster's assault on the universities in the 1650s was not simply the work of an "ignorant fanatic" hell-bent on destroying the educational *status quo*. It was rather the product of extensive reading in the literature of the new science, in all its various forms, which Webster continued to cultivate throughout the 1650s.59

Another equally important element of Webster's eclecticism was his solid grounding in the learning of the "ancients", and in particular Aristotle, whom he regarded as the root of scientific error. Webster not only possessed a large edition of Aristotle's *Works* in Greek and Latin [79], but also a whole series of learned commentaries and textbooks on Aristotelian natural philosophy. The commentary of the Jesuit, Franciscus Toletus [241], and the textbooks of Giacomo Zabarella [236] and Joannes Magirus [778; 821] were standard reading at Oxford and Cambridge in the late-sixteenth and early-seventeenth centuries, as were the commentaries of another Jesuit, Petrus Fonseca [233], and Julius Pacius [234] on Aristotle's *Metaphysics* and *Logic* respectively.60 It is possible to add to this list a whole host of lesser commentaries and manuals by Jesuit and Protestant scholars. Among the former, Webster owned three volumes of commentaries by the learned Jesuits of the university of Coimbra [237; 238; 239], two copies of Benedictus Pererius' *Physica* [788; 815], and an unspecified three–volume edition of commentaries by Antonio Ruvio [820].61 Protestant authors are represented

58 Ibid., pp. 105–106. Pride of place in this illustrious collection of scientific and philosophical investigators was reserved for the English hermeticist, Robert Fludd (1574–1637), whose "elaborate writings . . . the world never had a more rare, experimental and perfect piece". Ibid., p. 105. Admiration for Fludd was reflected in Webster's ownership of Fludd's works in five large volumes [item 1], the most valuable item in the whole library (above, p. 16).

59 Of the 154 items (178 volumes) published after 1650 in Webster's possession, 73 per cent were concerned with some aspect of natural philosophy. Again, it is impossible to discern a theme or pattern to these works, which were concerned with a whole variety of topics and scientific view-points.

60 Toletus (1532–96) was created cardinal by Pope Clement VIII in 1593, and played an important rôle in the reconversion of Henry IV of France. Zabarella (1533–89) taught at the University of Padua for twenty-six years, his lectures there forming the basis of item 236. Magirus (d. 1596) taught philosophy at the university of Marburg. For the use of the works of these authors in the English universities, see Curtis, op. cit., note 56 above, pp. 110–112; H.F. Kearney, *Scholars and gentlemen: universities and society in pre-industrial Britain, 1500—1700,* London, Faber & Faber, 1970, p. 105. Webster's concern with Aristotelian metaphysics and logic is discussed in more detail below, pp. 40, 41.

61 Pererius (1535–1610) had an international reputation in all fields of learning, including rhetoric, philosophy, and theology. Lynn Thorndike has suggested that his *Physica* was used "as a text in Jesuit schools in teaching the *Physics* and natural philosophy of Aristotle"; Thorndike, *A history of magic and experimental science,* New York, Macmillan, 1929–58, 8 vols., vol. 6, pp. 409–413. Ruvio (1548–1615) studied extensively in Mexico for twenty-five years before returning to his native Spain.

by Johann Thomas Freigius [830] and the Scottish philosopher Gilbert Jacchaeus or Jack [1120a].[62]

One possible explanation for Webster's possession of such a large and varied selection of Aristotelian works of science is that Webster, as Anthony Wood, suggested, spent some time at Cambridge in his youth (above p. 1). Even if this was the case, it is still possible that Webster continued to collect such works for the explicit purpose of composing a radical critique of the Aristotelian system as it was commonly taught in the schools. This, after all, was the chief purpose of *Academiarum examen* in which he hinted at his own complete familiarity with the writings of Aristotle:

> He [Aristotle] denies in the twelfth of his *Metaphysicks* that God takes care of minute, and small things; in his books *De Coelo* he makes the world eternal and increate; in his *Physicks* he teacheth that nothing can be made *ex nihilo*; in his books *De anima* and of *Ethicks,* he denies the possibility of the resurrection of the dead, and in many places doth deny the immortality of the soul . . . *and yet this is the man that is onely thought worthy to be the father of Christian Philosophy.*[63]

The key to Webster's rejection of the Aristotelian system is clear. As a pagan, he was not fit to carry the title of "father of Christian Philosophy", a view consistently repeated by the radical sectaries in the 1650s. Furthermore, the high proportion of Jesuit scholars in Webster's library, many of them orthodox Aristotelians, must have strengthened Webster's conviction that herein lay the route to anti-Christian ignorance.[64] To combat the continuing support for Aristotle in Protestant academic circles, Webster therefore turned to the scholars of the pansophist enlightenment for guidance and support. Undoubtedly one of the leading figures in this movement was the Italian neo-Platonist Francesco Patrizi (1529–97), who sought, in his *Nova de universis philosophia* [36] to construct a reformed Christian natural philosophy on hermetic and neo-Platonic lines. The heir to this tradition in the seventeenth century was the Bohemian Protestant and exile, Jan Amos Komenský or Comenius (1592–1670), who was himself taught by the Calvinist syncretist and encyclopaedist, Johann Heinrich Alsted (1588–1638). Webster possessed eleven volumes of Alsted's works, including a two-volume edition of the celebrated *Encyclopaedia* [232], as well as four volumes by Comenius, one of which, *Pansophiae prodromus* [686], was intended as a blueprint for pansophic reform.[65]

---

[62] Freigius (b. 1543) was a celebrated Aristotelian natural philosopher. Jacchaeus (1578?–1628) was a student of Marischal College, Aberdeen, who, after studying at Helmstadt and Herborn, was appointed to the chair of philosophy at Leyden (1604). A friend of Hugo de Groot (Grotius), he was the first to teach metaphysics at the Dutch university. For Jacchaeus, see *DNB,* vol. 10, pp. 522–523.

[63] John Webster, op. cit., note 4 above, p. 53 (my italics). Other works of Aristotelian science in Webster's possession included four lesser volumes by Henningus Arnisaeus [1467], Jacobus Cheyneius [795], Franciscus Titelman [813], and Joannes Velcurio [700].

[64] Of Jesuit natural philosophers, Webster remarked that it was "the custom of those kind of men to seem ignorant of nothing, when indeed experimentally they scarce know anything"; Webster, op. cit., note 21 above, p. 86. He nonetheless owned works by twenty-five Jesuit scholars (thirty-two volumes in all), fifteen of which were concerned specifically with some aspect of natural philosophy [items 29; 39; 87; 223; 233; 241; 295; 317; 395; 497; 788; 815; 820; 919; 959].

[65] John Webster, op. cit., note 4 above, p. 105. Of the remaining three works by Comenius, two were concerned with the reform of language teaching [862; 870] see below p. 39, and the other was an attempt to reconcile the study of nature with the truths of the Christian religion [655]. Such thinking, which lay at the root of much of Webster's own reform proposals, was shared by Comenius's English patron, Robert Greville (1608–43), whose *The nature of truth* [1365] was also in Webster's possession. An earlier example of this concern for a truly Christian natural philosophy can be found in the work of the French Huguenot, Lambert

The guiding spirit behind the work of these men was the rediscovery of the original unity between man, nature, and God, an enterprise which, if successful, would lead to an end to religious and intellectual division in Europe. One aspect of the pansophist vision was the revival of Renaissance hermeticism. For Webster and others, here lay the answer to the stale and corrupting paganism that continued to contaminate the learning of the academies in mid-seventeenth-century England. The various branches of hermetic learning are all well-represented in Webster's library, with particular emphasis upon the art of alchemy as taught by Paracelsus (1493–1541) and his followers. According to Webster in *Academiarum examen*, "the secrets of nature" were more likely to be uncovered by the study of this one subject than "by all the Peripatetick Philosophy in the world". Such faith is clearly reflected in Webster's large holding of Paracelsian literature. In all, he owned fifteen volumes [11 items] of Paracelsus' writings, in English, German, and Latin, including the most recent edition of the *Opera omnia* published at Geneva in 1658 [16].[66] In addition to this substantial body of original works, Webster owned a vast collection of medical and alchemical literature, much of it the work of Paracelsians (e.g., six volumes by Michael Maier [332; 334; 337; 385; 598; 651]) as well as earlier exponents of "mystical chymistrye" (e.g., Ramón Lull [282; 540; 575; 576], Roger Bacon [382; 383], George Ripley [466; 633], Basil Valentine [542; 544], etc.).[67]

Since Webster was also an active practitioner of alchemy (see Appendix 1 and the reference to his "furnace house"), the presence of a large number of chemistry manuals in his library takes on an added significance (e.g., those of Beguin [545], Brendel [599], Burnet [335], Davisson [552], Gesner [359; 510] and Hartmann [623]). Interest in furnace construction and the apparatus of chemistry is indicated by the possession of two other works of importance: an English translation of Johann Rudolph Glauber's up-to-date *Furni novi philosophici* (trans. John French, London, 1651) [462] and an earlier manual of alchemy in Italian by the Dominican Donato D'Eremita [23].[68] The latter is a particularly interesting work, since it provides large and detailed illustrations of alchemical instruments and furnace construction, followed by a basic introduction, with glossary, to the alchemist's art.

Webster's active involvement in alchemical experimentation–a passion which seemed to occupy much of his later years[69]—should not be allowed to disguise his

---

Daneau (1530–95) [1116]. It was also partially effected by Gulielmus Adolphus Scribonius (fl. late-sixteenth century) in his *Physica* [1122].

[66] John Webster, op. cit., note 4 above, p. 77. This edition is mistakenly referred to in *The displaying*, p. 60, as having been printed at Geneva in 1648. Virtually all of the many references to Paracelsus in Webster's final two works are taken from this particular edition.

[67] This impressive collection of Paracelsian writings includes the works and popular translations of Croll [527], Du Chesne [327], Fioravanti [308], Hartmann [312; 623], Ruland [531], Severinus [608], and Toxites [592]. Less familiar are the works of the French alchemist Pierre Jean Fabre [nine volumes: 323; 523a-h], Heinrich Khunrath [619], and Michael Potier [610]. In addition to single-author collections, Webster also owned a number of influential alchemical miscellanies including those of Lazarus Zetzner [five volumes: 536], Philipp Ulstadt [709], and Janus Lacinius [360].

[68] Johann Rudolph Glauber (1603?–70?), a native of Franconia, was the author of some thirty treatises on alchemical and related subjects. Webster possessed ten volumes by Glauber [462; 559; 626; 1184], but unfortunately only item 462 is mentioned by name in the catalogue.

[69] See, for example, Webster's correspondence with the naturalist, Martin Lister, where frequent references are to be found to Webster's request for minerals and other matters of alchemical concern. Thus in March

profound interest in other areas of occult science. Astrology, for example, which Webster described in 1654 as an art that was "high, noble, excellent . . . and no way offensive to God or true religion," also features prominently in Webster's library.[70] There are also a number of volumes on natural magic and cabbalism, the latter represented by such seminal studies as Reuchlin's *De verbo mirifico* [734] and Pistorius' *Artis cabalisticae* [27]. One might add to this list a curious little tract by the French eirenicist, Guillaume Postel (1510–81), entitled *Absconditorum a constitutione mundi clavis* [729]. An exposition of apocalyptic cabbalism, it has been described as an attempt by the author to envisage "a return to the earthly paradise of Genesis" where "mankind will be united in a common speech [Hebrew], a common government, and a common religion based on cabala".[71] The concordancy with Webster's own concerns in the 1650s is strikingly apparent (cf. above pp. 3–6).

Works on various aspects of occult philosophy occupy almost a third of Webster's collection of natural science books. Apart from the large number of works which fit no specific heading (sixty-eight; e.g. encyclopaedic compilations of natural curiosities such as Olaus Worm's *Museum* [4]), the next largest category of works in this section comprises the study of astronomy (twenty-eight volumes). Since Webster was an unqualified supporter of the heliocentric system, one would expect to find a preponderance of pro-Copernican works in his library. This, however, is not the case. For every astronomical text advocating the Copernican system, Webster owned an equivalent volume defending the traditional view of the geocentrists.[72] Neither were the latter simply the long-forgotten remnant of volumes purchased, in all likelihood, before Webster's birth. The *De universo* [290] of the Italian astronomer, Scipio Chiaramonti (1565–1653), was not published until 1644 and consisted of a comprehensive defence of the ancients from the criticisms of modern astronomers such as Tycho Brahe and Galileo. Nonetheless, the depth of Webster's interest in the new astronomical theories is clearly illustrated by his ownership of several major texts (Copernicus [211], Galileo [291], and Keppler [485]) and numerous defences of these beliefs (e.g., in works by the Catholic Ismael Boulliau or Bullialdus (1605–94) [193; 425] and the Englishman John Wilkins (1614–72) [453]). In addition, a large collection of lesser authorities, many of

---

1674, Webster informed Lister that he had prepared "a peice written of the Philosophers Universall Dissolvent, that hath laid by me above this five yeares, being unwilling to make it publike, untill I had by assured practise verified the virtues, and effects of the same"; Bodleian Library, Oxford, Lister MS. 34, f. 157. In the same letter, Webster referred to the Helmontian William Simpson, whom he claimed to have known in York "a good many yeares ago".

[70] John Webster, op. cit., note 4 above, p. 51. Webster praised the achievements of five English astronomers, Ashmole, Lilly, Booker, Sanders, and Culpeper. Of these, two are represented on Webster's shelves: Sanders' *Physiognomie* [35] and Culpeper's *English physitian* [666], both first published in 1653. Other works in defence of astrology include those of Dariot [463], Gallucci [217], Giuntini [224], Heydon [640], and Ramesey [652].

[71] William J. Bouwsma, 'Postel and the significance of renaissance cabalism', *J. Hist. Ideas*, 1954, **15**: 231. Other works of cabbalism in Webster's possession were Jacques Gaffarel's *Unheard of curiosities* [454] and Henry More's *Conjectura cabbalistica* [974].

[72] Traditional texts expounding the Ptolemaic system include those by Alfraganus [1489], Apianus [397], Christmannus [400], Metius [487], Sacro Bosco [503; 1488], Valerius [1490], and Witekind [501]. Additionally, strong support for the geocentric system can be found in such diverse works as Blundeville [1199], Hues [704], La Primaudaye [102; 895], Mazzotta [333], Saluste du Bartas, [885], and Tymme [370]. For Webster's defence of heliocentricity, see John Webster, op. cit., note 4 above, pp. 42–50.

them favourable to astronomical innovation, was available to Webster.[73]

Two further aspects of Webster's library of natural philosophy demand our attention: mathematics and medicine. From Webster's ownership of seventy-nine volumes of mathematical and related writings (e.g., works on mechanics, surveying, architecture), it is possible to gain some idea of the relative importance that he attached to this particular branch of learning. In *Academiarum examen,* Webster had reprimanded the universities for their neglect of the mathematical sciences, "the superlative excellency of which transcends the most of all other sciences". In particular, Webster lamented the failure of the universities to appreciate the academic and utilitarian value of such studies (a fault shared, of course, by Francis Bacon). Arithmetic and geometry were both worthy of serious attention, Webster claimed, echoing in the process a similar plea made by John Dee in his preface to Billingsley's edition of Euclid's *Geometry* [200].[74]

If the evidence of his library is a faithful guide, Webster's own knowledge of, and commitment to, mathematical investigation was substantial. A solid core of ancient texts[75] was supplemented by more recent works of sixteenth-[76] and seventeenth-century[77] authorities. To these one might add Webster's English contemporaries, Isaac Barrow [484], William Oughtred [410; 506], and John Wallis [1187]. The latter's *Arithmetica infinitorum,* published at Oxford in 1655, was the most important new work of its kind in the field of mathematics, and contained within it the roots of the differential calculus. Oughtred's *Clavis mathematica* [506], on the other hand, was probably the more influential work given its widespread popularity as a comprehensive and comprehensible guide to arithmetic and algebra. As Richard Greaves has noted, the fact that two of these three English mathematicians were unattached to the universities when they completed their mathematical researches tends to lend substance to Webster's view that mathematics was largely ignored in the contemporary curriculum.[78]

Webster's possession of 242 volumes concerned solely with medical practice and theory is a sufficient indication of the significance that he attached to this specialized field of learning. Webster was, of course, a medical practitioner of long experience, who, despite the lack of any formal qualification (he gained official licence to practise in 1669), was clearly well-versed in all aspects of his chosen profession. As with Webster's interest in natural science generally, so too in the field of medicine one cannot fail to admire the astonishing breadth of medical learning covered by his library. Once again, one is struck by the familiar emphasis upon works of a modernist

[73] Amongst these: Borel [683], Thomas Digges [426], Maestlin [505], and Schickard [1375], as well as an edition of Aristarchus [424]. Other favourable evaluations of the Copernican system can be found in Hill [1125], Holwarda [572], Le Roy [188], and Ridley [428]. Support for the Tychonic system is to be found in Carpenter [415] and Hopton [480].

[74] John Webster, op. cit., note 4 above, pp. 40–41.

[75] Apollonius Pergaeus [212; 218], Archimedes [210; 213; 427], Euclid [200; 220a-b; 484; 488; 491], Pappus of Alexandria [201; 424].

[76] Buteo [500], Leonard Digges [215], Finé [433; 435], Lansbergen [420], Mueller Regiomontanus [196], Vieta [195; 218].

[77] Herigone [478], Huygens [391], Napier [696], Snellius [423], Stevin [438].

[78] Richard L. Greaves, *The puritan revolution and educational thought,* New Brunswick, NJ, Rutgers University Press, 1969, p. 72.

hue, but not without due consideration to older authorities. The former trend is most noticeable in the case of works relating to recent anatomical research. Webster's defence of the Harveian circulation, for example, was almost certainly based upon first-hand acquaintance with *De motu cordis* [731].[79] Further support for the Harveian system was available to Webster in the writings of numerous distinguished continental anatomists, including Thomas Bartholin [322], Antonius Deusingius [679], and Joannes Veslingius [274]. Interest in other areas of anatomical research and innovation is suggested by a series of works relating to a number of contemporary disputes and discoveries in the field of anatomy. Webster thus possessed five volumes concerned with Jean Pecquet's recent elucidation of the operation of the thoracic duct and lacteal chyle [298; 524; 664; 730; 1188], and a further two volumes relating to the controversy between Bartholin and Rudbeck over the discovery of the lymphatic system [617; 668].[80] In addition, Webster owned the pioneering works of the English anatomists, Francis Glisson [541] and Thomas Wharton [543], on the liver and glands respectively.[81]

This fascination with novelty and medical innovation is evident throughout the catalogue. It should be stressed, however, that Webster, despite his public dismissal of Galenism, was neither ignorant of, nor unconversant with, the more traditional forms of medical theory and practice. Like Aristotle, Galen was not held entirely to blame by Webster for the excessive trust which the physicians and natural philosophers of his own day placed in his writings.[82] This no doubt helps to explain in part Webster's ownership of numerous conventional Galenic texts (including a five-volume edition of Galen's *Opera* [566] and a large folio edition of the *Methodus medendi* [37]). Less easy to account for are the large number of tracts by sixteenth- and seventeenth-century physicians of the traditional Galeno-Hippocratic school of medicine which Webster deigned to despise. Leading representatives of this tradition were Leonhard Fuchs [568; 739], Jean Fernel [21], Joannes Heurnius [7; 355], Petrus Forestus [6; 660], and Daniel Sennert [9; 297; 319], the latter including an extremely expensive three-volume edition of the *Opera omnia* [9].

In addition to these treatises of orthodox medical practice and theory, Webster owned twenty-eight volumes concerned solely with the art of surgery, an area of medicine which he almost certainly performed in the course of his own practice in Clitheroe. The most striking feature here is the high incidence of valuable folio editions, which include the works of such renowned authors as Joannes Scultetus [12], Thomas Cornacchinius [13], Wilhelm Fabricius [14], Peter Uffenbach [18], Francescus Peccettius [19], Ambroise Paré [85], and the Englishman, John Woodall [163]. Smaller

---

[79] John Webster, op. cit., note 4 above, p. 72; Webster, op. cit., note 15 above, pp. 3–4.

[80] For the controversy between Bartholin and Rudbeck over the discovery of the lymphatic system, see W. Kock, 'Anatomical science and education in the seventeenth century', *Analecta Medico-Historica*, 1968, 3: 281–292. In addition to Bartholin's *Anatomia* [322], Webster also owned two volumes of the Danish physician's *Historiarum anatomicarum rariorum* [621a-b], which were widely cited in *The displaying*.

[81] Glisson's *Anatomia hepatis* [541] also included an elaborate defence of Harveian circulation, as well as further insights into the contemporary controversy surrounding the lymphatic system. See Charles Webster, op. cit., note 4 above, pp. 317–318.

[82] See, for example, Webster's description of Galen as "industrious and sharp witted"; Webster, op. cit., note 15 above, p. 20.

in size, but equally popular, were the manuals of the medieval surgeon, Guido de Cauliaco (Guy de Chauliac) [534], the two Englishmen, Thomas Vicary [367] and Thomas Brugis [741], and the works of "that learned and experienced Chirurgion" Felix Wuertz [in German and English: 539 and 1194 respectively].[83]

Not surprisingly, however, the largest category of works in Webster's medical library falls under the heading of occult and iatrochemical medicine (sixty-eight volumes or 28·1 per cent). The vast majority of these are by authors of the Paracelsian school of medicine. In Webster's eyes, the key to medical reform lay in the study and application of Paracelsian medical methods, which would, he believed, ultimately overthrow the rotten edifice of the Galenic system. Webster was no half-hearted reformer who wished, like some, to amalgamate elements of Galenism (usually its theoretical base) with elements of Paracelsianism (chemical remedies).[84] On the contrary, he argued tirelessly for the adoption of a new theory of medicine based wholly upon the iatrochemical precepts of Paracelsus and van Helmont. Besides the medical works of Paracelsus (see above p.22), Webster owned a vast array of Paracelsian literature, much of it concerned exclusively with medicine and medical reform. Alongside familiar names such as Oswald Crollius [527], Joseph Du Chesne [327], and Petrus Severinus [608], there appear less well-known works by a variety of continental Paracelsians: Johann Ernst Burggrav [346; 561; 580], Bartholomaeus Carrichter [574], Joannes Finckius [697], Johann Pharamund Rhumel [676; 677], Angelo Sala [287; 1198], and Henningus Scheunemann [614]. To this list, which is by no means exhaustive, one must add the work of the Helmontians. Chief amongst these was the oft-quoted *Opera* of van Helmont himself [330], as well as a number of tracts by English and continental Helmontians: George Starkey [647a-b], James Thompson [663], Walter Charleton [307], and Franciscus Oswald Grembs [304].[85]

It would be a mistake, however, to view these works in isolation from those other works of occult philosophy which he owned (above pp. 22–23) and which together constitute 170 volumes or almost ten per cent of the complete contents of the library. Throughout his own published works, he continued to cite favourably authors of the occult and hermetic school of natural philosophy, in full awareness of the damaging criticisms that were consistently levelled against this form of scientific enquiry.[86] And yet this view of Webster as occult philosopher and hostile critic of traditional science is, I believe, only partially reflected in his library. In medicine, astronomy, mathematics, and various other branches of natural science, Webster was fully conversant with, and

---

[83] Webster, op. cit., note 21 above, p. 269. Webster's surgical skills were no doubt put to good use during his period of service in the armies of Parliament in 1648. When he died in 1682, he left surgical instruments to the value of £20. See Appendix 1.

[84] An example of such a compromise was item 15: Joannes Guinterius, *De medicina veteri et nova,* Basle, A. Henricpetri, 1571.

[85] Grembs, physician to the archbishop of Salzburg, is an obscure figure of whom very little is known. His *Arbor integra et ruinosa hominis* [304] consists of 512 pages outlining the various tenets of Helmontian medical theory, which are everywhere favourably compared with those of Galen.

[86] Opposition to Paracelsus is referred to, for example, in Webster, op. cit., note 15 above, pp. 60–62. Webster owned a number of works written by opponents of occult and hermetic medicine and philosophy including Meric Casaubon's exposé of John Dee [40], Conringius' diatribe against the whole edifice of the hermetic and Paracelsian system [343], anti-Paracelsian works by John Cotta [372] and Thomas Erastus [589], and an assault upon the Rosicrucians by Henricus Neuhusius [579],

appreciative of, the contribution which the "ancients" had made in all these fields of learning. Webster's library thus reveals a man of truly eclectic tastes in science who, despite his obscure background and apparent lack of academic credentials, was probably as well-qualified as anyone in England to criticize the deficiencies of contemporary scientific education.[87]

THEOLOGY

After natural science, the largest category of books in Webster's possession was devoted to theology (397 volumes or 24·4 per cent). In the light of Webster's career as non-conformist and radical critic of the national church (above pp. 1–6), one cannot fail to be impressed and somewhat surprised by the number and range of works contained in this part of the library. For the best part of twenty years, Webster's theological outlook was based upon a fundamental rejection of the premise that other men, through their writings, might act as authoritative guides in religious matters. And yet, from the evidence of his library, it is apparent that Webster was a man steeped in the accumulated wisdom of theologians, ancient and modern, particularly those of the Calvinist school. Works by learned Calvinist professors and preachers on a variety of topics dominate the collection (135 volumes or 34 per cent) and far exceed the relatively small number of works representative of what one might term the "mystical-radical" tradition (only thirty-three volumes or 8·3 per cent).[88] Indeed, works by Catholic theologians and apologists are almost as numerous as works in the latter category (thirty-one volumes or 7·8 per cent), so that one can only assume that works of this kind possessed a significance for Webster out of all proportion to their size and number. What conclusions, then, can one draw from Webster's library of theological works?

First, it would seem wholly reasonable to suppose, howsoever Webster acquired or read these works, that one of the major early theological influences upon his religious beliefs was orthodox Calvinism. In addition to five volumes of Calvin's writings [91; 156; 1253; 1269; 1301], Webster owned a whole series of doctrinal treatises, polemics, commentaries, and sermons from the pens of many of the leading Calvinists of sixteenth- and seventeenth-century Europe. Particularly prominent are works by the

---

[87] For Webster's eclecticism in practice, see above p. 10.

[88] Precise figures for this section of the library are not possible, given some of the rather vague descriptions (e.g., item 1376: "15 litle treatasies in English"). With this in mind, the theological bias of the works in this section may be categorised as follows:

Orthodox Calvinist	135
Bibles, concordances, etc.	34
"Radical-mystical"	33
Catholic	31
Lutheran and other Protestant denominations	25
Anglican (non-Calvinist)	18
Patristic	13
Medieval/scholastic	13
Miscellaneous	95
Total number of volumes	397

French Calvinists, Theodore de Bèze (Beza) (eight volumes), Lambert Daneau (six volumes), Jean Mestrezat (four volumes), and François Du Jon (Junius) (three volumes), with a noticeable emphasis upon a whole range of Huguenot writers (thirty-two volumes in total).[89] Equally prominent are works representative of the German Calvinist tradition (twenty-eight volumes). Not surprisingly, however, the works of English and Scottish Calvinists, particularly those of puritan persuasion, constitute the majority of volumes in this section (seventy), with substantial contributions from William Ames (five volumes) and Ames's teacher, William Perkins (three volumes); the Elizabethan puritans, Dudley Fenner and Thomas Cartwright (three volumes each); and the Calvinist bishop of Derry, George Downame (three volumes).

Taken as a whole, it is possible to detect recurrent themes in many of these works which may or may not suggest a preoccupation on Webster's part with certain elements of Calvinist thought. For example, there are traces of interest here in the controversy that raged amongst Protestants in Europe, but especially in England, over the threat of Arminianism. Calvinist orthodoxy was defended, amongst others, by Ames [1438; 1440], William Prynne [1223], Samuel Rutherford [1305], Matthew Slade (Sladus) [1262], William Twisse [246], and John Williams [1233]. The view of the Arminians, or Dutch Remonstrants, was expounded in at least two works in Webster's possession, John Pocklington's *Altare christianum* (a defence of altar rails) [1227], and an anonymous *Apologia* for the Remonstrants published in 1629 [1288].

The most significant aspect of this large collection of Calvinist writings is its emphasis upon works of Calvinist exegesis (thirty-four volumes, or 25 per cent of the total for Calvinist authors). Two commentators in particular seem to have excited Webster's interest: the Scottish cleric Robert Rollock (1555?–1599) (eight volumes) and the German Ramist Johann Piscator of Herborn (1546–1625) (six volumes). Both were widely cited in Webster's later published works, alongside another leading German Calvinist and prolific biblical commentator, Amandus Polanus of Basle (three volumes). Webster clearly approved of works of this kind, the Ramist nature of many (Polanus was also a Ramist) undoubtedly providing much of their appeal (cf. below p. 41). It is worth noting, however, that Webster's liking for learned scriptural analysis was not restricted to Calvinist exegetes. In all, he owned sixty-two volumes (or 15·6 per cent of the total number of theological works) of biblical commentary covering a wide spectrum of theological views from ancient patristic and scholastic sources to modern Catholic and Lutheran commentators.[90]

Leaving to one side the question of confessional allegiance and influence posed by these works, it is difficult to avoid the conclusion that writings of this kind possessed distinct appeal for Webster. Predictably perhaps, there is a discernible emphasis upon

---

[89] These were: Jean Daillé [1088], Pierre Du Moulin the Elder [684; 1445], François Hotman [1441], Pierre de la Ramée (Ramus) [1334; 1402], Jean de L'Espine [1342], Philippe de Mornay [1326], André Rivet [1282], and Daniel Tilenus [1307; 1398]. Tilenus (1563–1633), Professor of Theology at Sedan and Saumur, was later to convert to Arminianism (see, e.g., item 1419).

[90] Particular mention should be made of the seven volumes of commentaries by the Zwinglian Rudolph Walther (Gualtherus) (1518–86) [148; 1319; 1332; 1404; 1405; 1411; 1414]. Lutheran exegetes are represented by David Chytraeus (1530–1600) [1417], Solomon Gesner (1559–1605) [1408], Polycarp Leyser (1552–1610) [1286], Joannes Tarnovius (1586–1629) [1272], and Otto Brunfels (*c.* 1488–1534) [64].

commentaries on the New Testament (thirty-five volumes in all), a reflection in all probability of Webster's antinomianism (cf. above p. 3). This thirst for biblical scholarship was complemented in Webster's case by the possession of countless Bibles, concordances, and scriptural lexicons in a variety of languages (English, Latin, Greek, Hebrew, French, Italian, German, and Dutch).[91] The view that thus begins to emerge from this litany of learned sources and aids to biblical study is one of a highly educated man, immersed in the knowledge of the scriptures and fully conversant with orthodox Protestant, especially Calvinist, interpretations of the word of God. It would appear to follow, therefore, that when Webster opted to reject the orthodox Calvinism of the English church, he did so in complete understanding of the scriptural and theological foundations upon which the reformed faith in England was based. This much is evident from a cursory reading of the contents of Webster's library. What is more difficult to ascertain is the extent to which Webster's semi-mystical faith of the spirit was itself derived from conventional and orthodox sources (see below pp. 33–34).

A further clue to Webster's theological development may be found in the frequency with which certain books of the Bible recur as the object of learned discussion and commentary. Genesis, Psalms, and Revelation appear most often (five volumes apiece), with commentaries on the books of Daniel and Romans almost as popular (four volumes each). Paul's epistle to the Romans, of course, possessed a political as well as a religious significance, with the Pauline injunction to "honour the powers that be" (Romans, 13), the subject of much debate in Protestant circles throughout this period.[92] Genesis and Psalms, on the other hand, were naturally well-favoured by all literate Christians, both for study and religious edification. In the context of Webster's proven attraction to millenial ideas in the 1650s (above pp. 2–3), undoubtedly the most intriguing entries in the catalogue are the nine commentaries upon the two prophetic books, Daniel and Revelation. All were written by Protestant scholars, three explicitly associating papal rule at Rome with the biblical figure of Antichrist.[93] This was a popular theme of many other works in Webster's possession–the connexion between Pope and Antichrist was repeated, for example, by David Pareus [1435], Gabriel Powel [1331], Lambert Daneau [1350], and Andrew Willet [143]—and it fits into another recurring theme of the library, its pronounced anti-Catholic bent.[94]

[91] Webster owned fourteen Bibles (six Latin, two English, two Hebrew, and one French, Dutch, Italian and unspecified) and twelve testaments, psalters, etc. In addition, he possessed four concordances and four biblical lexicons, as well as a number of treatises designed specifically to assist with the study of the scriptures. Most were guides to the Hebrew tongue; cf. below pp. 38–39. The various Bibles and commentaries in Webster's possession were extensively cited in his later works.

[92] All four commentaries on Romans were written by Protestant scholars. The most important, in terms of its political implications, was undoubtedly that by the Silesian humanist and Calvinist Professor of Theology at Heidelberg, David Pareus (1548–1622). In his Latin commentary on Romans [243], Pareus taught the doctrine of lawful resistance against those secular authorities who failed in their religious duties to their subjects. In England, James I ordered the work to be burned. The Scottish Calvinist, John Knox (1505–72) had adumbrated a similar view, of course, in his *Appellation* [1384].

[93] These were Thomas Brightman's two commentaries on Revelation and Daniel [1293; 1468] and John Bale's *The image of bothe churches* [1356], the latter a scathing and frequently scurrilous denunciation of the Roman church, written in the form of a commentary upon the book of Revelation.

[94] Webster owned at least twenty-two volumes concerned solely with polemical or doctrinal attacks upon the Catholic church. A number of these were aimed at the Jesuits in general, and the views of Robert Bellarmine in particular.

Strangely enough, however, there is a general paucity of works of any kind that deal with millenial themes in the period of most acute crisis in Webster's life-time, the 1640s and 1650s. Only a single work, a commentary on Revelation by the puritan divine, Francis Woodcock [1216], is to be found in this category. Published in 1643, it was an attempt to explain the current turmoil in England by placing the events of the time within the framework of the eleventh chapter of Revelation. Of far greater interest (though not strictly speaking a work concerned with the biblical millennium) was Paul Felgenhauer's *Postilion* (London, 1655) [375]. Ostensibly a work of astrological prophecy, the existence of this radical tract on the shelves of Webster's library points to a continuing interest on Webster's part in the theme of millenial reform in interregnum England. Its message of impending, fundamental change in all areas of human activity, coupled with Felgenhauer's prediction that the earth and the heavens would be made anew, was wholly in keeping with Webster's earlier pronouncements in 1653.[95]

In particular, Felgenhauer's sweeping indictment of conventional wisdom and scholastic education must have elicited a sympathetic response from the disillusioned radical who, only a few years earlier, had voiced much the same opinions with respect to the English universities. Felgenhauer, for example, chastised the Aristotelians, who "thinke not that any Physicks can be learned in the Bible", and he went on to admonish such men for holding the view that "that which is true in Theology does not hold in Phylosophy". According to Felgenhauer, these men were responsible for the destruction of that essential unity that once reigned between man, nature, and God, a common theme of radical literature in the 1650s. And Webster would surely have agreed with Felgenhauer's concluding remark that: "yee Book-men . . . have filled the world full of Bookes, which are endlesse and numberlesse, nothing else but that you thereby are more and more scattered, confused and intricated".[96]

Felgenhauer's comprehensive assault upon established learning, religious hypocrisy, and traditional forms of government was just one of a number of radical tracts in Webster's library which together point to the most obvious source for Webster's own disaffection in the 1650s. In all, works of this nature total thirty-three volumes (8·3 per cent of the theological works) and cover a broad spectrum of unorthodox religious ideas and beliefs. Many obviously have a bearing on the development of Webster's own ideas. Others may help to shed light upon his subsequent disillusionment with the radical cause. It would, of course, be wrong to place too much emphasis on single works, but the fact that Webster possessed so few dating from this period, and that the majority were distinctly radical in tone, would seem to vindicate careful scrutiny of these particular volumes.[97]

[95] Felgenhauer (1593–1677) was a Bohemian exile who studied theology at Wittenberg, but thereafter (about 1620) became a self-styled prophet for Rosicrucian-Behmenist reform.

[96] Paul Felgenhauer, *Postilion, or a new almanacke,* London, H. Crips & L. Lloyd, 1655, pp. 23, 30, 36–37, 37–38. Felgenhauer also predicted a thorough reformation of the medical profession, including the discovery of a universal medicine which would cure all diseases; ibid., p. 42.

[97] It is possible that Webster's collection of radical literature was much larger in the 1650s. In *The displaying,* pp. 293–294, 300, Webster referred to the loss of a number of his papers and books some time in 1658. These were clearly confiscated as the result of a judicial inquiry or investigation into Webster's affairs at this time. Two explanations come to mind. First, on 2 November 1657, Webster appealed to an old friend and acquaintance, John Lambert, requesting assistance in a suit brought against him by one Robert Inman. Inman was claiming compensation for the loss of an animal requisitioned by Webster in 1648 during the

The single most important source for Webster's religious heterodoxy in the 1650s probably derived from his profound admiration for the writings of the Silesian mystic Jacob Boehme (1575–1624). Cited with approval on numerous occasions (see above p. 3), Webster owned eleven volumes of Boehme's writings, including a folio edition in English of the *Mysterium magnum* [69], a detailed commentary on Genesis. Moreover, if my identification of item 467 is correct ("8 volumes of ye writeings of Jacob Behmen"), then Webster's public recantation from the radical cause in about 1657–58 did not appear to dampen his enthusiasm for Behmenist literature. Whatever the case, Boehme's simple message that all men were united in the brotherhood of the holy spirit, and his belief in the superfluous nature of doctrinal and liturgical controversy, were echoed throughout Webster's early theological works. It is not surprising, therefore, that one of Webster's few known associates during the 1650s was the Welsh radical, William Erbery (1604–54), who was himself deeply imbued with Behmenist beliefs, and whose posthumous writings [452], edited by Webster in 1658, are to be found in the catalogue.[98] It is not inconceivable that Webster may also have shared the company of another Behmenist (and ranter sympathizer) John Pordage (1607–81), who knew Erbery and whose apologetic narration *Innocence appearing* (London, 1655) [168] was also to be found on Webster's shelves.[99]

Another source for Webster's aversion to doctrinal orthodoxy and religious uniformity was the German mystic Valentine Weigel (1533–88). Webster owned two curious, but very influential, tracts by Weigel [373; 1370], both of which were translated into English in the late 1640s. In *Of the life of Christ* [1370], Weigel had stressed the idea that salvation was not tied to the observation of the sacraments or other human inventions in religion, but was rather the gift of pure faith. All men, Weigel claimed, possessed access to the transforming power of faith, which was acquired through belief in the inner spiritual Christ. Most men chose to reject this free gift and opted instead to follow the path of base "Adamic man". Those, however, who opened their hearts to the principle of the "Christ Life" within them were automatically received into membership of the true church, an invisible congregation of believers united by their common faith in the inner Christ. The result was a religion devoid of doctrine and ceremonies, tolerant and unworldly, which, like that professed by Webster in the 1650s, appealed to all men. Of faith, Weigel wrote, it "comes by inward hearing". He went on:

---

second civil war. There may well have been a religious motive in the action brought by Inman against Webster, since there was a local Presbyterian clergyman of that name. Second, Webster had at about this time bought more sequestered land that was the subject of a long and acrimonious dispute in Clitheroe. The action against Webster may well have been related to this incident. See *CSPD*, 1657–58, p. 302; Marchant, op. cit., note 2 above, p. 256; Weeks, op. cit., note 4 above, pp. 68–70 and *passim*.

[98] The appearance of Erbery's works [452] in close proximity to Webster's own radical writings [443; 445; 449; 451] almost certainly confirms Webster as the identity of the editor, J.W. It is just possible that Webster may also have been the author of items 442 and 447 ("The care of ye good Samaritan etc"), which I have been unable to locate and which may no longer be extant.

[99] Pordage's *Innocence appearing*, London, Giles Calvert, 1655, is a long and detailed account of Pordage's troubled period as rector of Bradfield in Berkshire in the early 1650s. Could Webster have known Pordage? The rectory at Bradfield was, of course, a popular refuge for a variety of radical spokesmen in the 1640s and 1650s. Like Webster, Pordage had served as a physician to Parliament in the 1640s, and he also shared Webster's interest in astrology. See Hill, op. cit., note 3 above, pp. 180–181; *CSPD*, 1655, p. 160.

Good books, outward verbal ministry have their place, they testify to the real Treasure, they are witnesses to the inner Word within us, but Faith is not tied to books, it is a new nativity which cannot be found in a book. He who hath the inward Schoolmaster loseth nothing of his Salvation although all preachers should be dead and all books burned.[100]

One of the chief features of both Boehme's and Weigel's mystical reasoning was its tendency to interpret the message of the scriptures by depicting the biblical struggle between good and evil as one large allegory for the battle that took place within the hearts and souls of each and every believer. These ideas gained wide currency in England during the 1640s, and it is likely that Webster encountered them at this time and then adapted them to his own religious ends. Webster's insistence, for example, that Satan and Antichrist existed in man only as metaphors for sin and evil (cf. above pp. 2–3) may well have derived from Joseph Salmon's *Antichrist in man* (London, 1647) [1367a]. Similar ideas are to be found in the works of William Erbery and the American Familist, Samuel Gorton (d.1677). In the latter's *Incorruptible key* (London, 1647) [464], the author interpreted the biblical references to witchcraft to mean "those spiritual juglings" that the learned ministers employed "by art, and humane learning . . . in and about the word of God".[101] Webster's interest in Gorton's work was maintained until the late 1650s, since he also possessed his *Antidote against the common plague* (London, 1657) [458]. In this work (addressed to Oliver Cromwell), Gorton defended the notion that Antichrist was "not to be confined to any one particular man, or devil", and he repeated his earlier suggestion that the clergy were little better than the witches they persecuted.[102] Published in 1657, this was one of the latest radical tracts in Webster's possession, and alongside works by Erbery, Salmon, John Biddle [1189a], William Dell [450], Robert Everard [1364], and an anonymous group of Quakers [455], it provides a limited but nonetheless fascinating glimpse into the reading habits of one such radical.[103]

In the same year as Gorton's *Antidote,* the Independent minister, John Owen (1616–83), published a defence of congregationalism under the title *Of schisme* (London, 1657) [1373]. It is one of the very few works in Webster's ownership dating from this period that represents a more moderate approach to church affairs, and as

---

[100] Quoted in Rufus M. Jones, *Spiritual reformers in the sixteenth and seventeenth centuries,* London, Macmillan, 1914, pp. 146–147. Cf. Webster's view that "reason is a monster . . . but faith is that pure and divine gift and the work of God that leads the heart of man in the light and power of the Spirit of Christ"; John Webster, op. cit., note 4 above, p. 17.

[101] For Salmon, see Hill, op. cit., note 3 above,. pp. 174–176; Samuel Gorton, *An incorruptible key,* London, 1647, p. 22. Gorton, born in Lancashire, emigrated to America in 1636 where, with a faithful band of followers, he was constantly in trouble with the colonial authorities for flouting the laws and religious conventions of the time. In 1644, he returned to England in order to pursue a claim to land in Rhode Island, but was back in America by 1648 where he remained until his death in 1677. See *DNB,* vol. 12, pp. 251–253.

[102] Gorton, *An antidote against the common plague of the world,* London, A. Crook, 1657, pp. 60, 151–152; cf. Webster, above p. 3 n7.

[103] Webster later reproached the Quakers for their excessive trust in "the guidance of the Spirit", despite the fact (or because of it?) that he was himself approached by a member of that sect, Thomas Lawson, with a view to recruitment. See Webster, op. cit., note 15 above, p. 138; Friends Library, Swarthmore MSS, vol. 7, f23b. Unfortunately, the letter from Lawson to Webster is undated. Interestingly, Lawson wrote a tract in 1679 which is reminiscent in many respects of Webster's *Academiarum examen*. In *Dagon's fall before the ark,* London?, 1679, Lawson attacked the "ethnick" philosophy of Aristotle and Galen ("profess'd enemy to Christ") and advanced the cause of utilitarian university education based upon authors such as Oswald Croll and van Helmont; ibid, pp. 2–3, 44, 45–46, 52–54, 87–88.

such may well indicate a further sign of Webster's growing disillusionment with the cause of radicalism. In this work, Owen professed to hold a strong desire for religious unity and peace but concluded, in much the same way as Webster in 1658 (above pp. 6–7), that the time was not yet right. Owen therefore cautioned that it was the duty of all men to yield to the present system of church government in England, a policy born out of practical necessity and one that would sorely test the consciences of many puritan ministers in 1660. Webster, as we have seen (above pp. 6–7), was probably reconciled to this way of thinking by the late 1650s, and so had little difficulty in accepting the restored church in 1660 (note his possession of a copy of the special prayer devised to be read on the anniversary on the death of Charles I, and published in 1661 [920]).

On a superficial level at least, there seems little reason to doubt the fact of Webster's public acknowledgement of the restoration church. It is just possible, however, that Webster combined outward conformity to the church of England after 1660 with a continuing private appreciation of the merits of radical religious beliefs. This insinuation was suggested in the case of certain elements of Webster's reasoning with regard to witchcraft (above pp. 11–12). It may also be inferred from the admittedly ambiguous evidence to be found in that section of Webster's library entitled "Bookes lent & omitted in ye form^r Catologue" (Section M). Since the catalogue was probably compiled shortly before Webster's death in 1682, it is evident from the references to his own published sermons [1176], two volumes of Socinian writings [1189a-b], and the "Works" of the Familist Hendrik Niclas [1197] that radical literature was still circulating in the Clitheroe region some twenty years after the restoration. It is not beyond the bounds of possibility, therefore, that Webster continued privately to disseminate the radical message whilst at the same time maintaining a public image of conformity. After all, such expediency was a key element in the survival of Familist groups like the Grindletonians.[104]

In the last resort, the whole issue of influence, and the extent to which it can be inferred from documents such as library catalogues, is one which defies precise analysis and evaluation. In Webster's case, I have merely attempted to suggest certain lines of speculation linking his known religious views with the volumes in his library. Naturally therefore, the emphasis of my comments has focused upon those works that espoused radical theological beliefs. One should not infer from this, however, that the other works of theology in his library were entirely unrelated to the formulation of Webster's own religious outlook. It is highly probable, for example, that the large number of orthodox Calvinist and Lutheran authorities in Webster's library may have provided him with an alternative (or original) source for the view that human reason and learning were immaterial to the acquisition of grace. Uncertainty in learned Protestant circles as to the exact function and place of reason was a common theme of much Calvinist and Lutheran literature.[105] Inevitably, the doubt that this created in some minds as to the relevance of learned human authority in spiritual matters was a

---

[104] One further piece of circumstantial evidence might be added. In Webster's will dated 3 January 1680, he bequeathed 40*s*. "to the poore of the townshipp of Grindleton in Yorkshire". This bequest would seem to indicate that Webster had maintained his links with this old centre of heresy. See Appendix 1.

[105] For a recent survey of the subject, see Morgan, op. cit., note 10 above, pp. 41–78.

double-edged sword and produced a popular obscurantism that was never the object of the original authors. An example of this kind of work was Jean Daillé's *Traicté de l'employ des sainct peres* [1088] in which Daillé censured excessive reliance upon patristic and scholastic sources. Yet Webster reminds us that even sources such as these, frequently the object of Protestant scorn, were not entirely without merit. In *Academiarum examen,* for example, he repeatedly cited Saint John Chrysostom [136] as one source for the view that human learning was antithetical to true religion. One is reminded yet again of the fact that Webster was at heart a committed eclectic— a statement which applies as much to his theology as to his views on natural science.[106]

One should not exaggerate, however, the reaction against learned values and human reason in Protestant discourse which was generally outweighed by works in favour of such aids to salvation. Webster himself owned a number of the latter, including an exhaustive defence of learning and reason by the Englishman, Egeon Askew [appended to 1234], and the German Calvinist, Nicolaus Vedelius [774]. In addition to these, Webster also possessed numerous manuals for preachers, which were designed to illustrate the various uses of learning, reason, and logic in the construction of sermons (e.g., works by Bartholomew Keckermann [1410] and Niels Hemmingsen [1469]).[107] Despite protestations to the contrary, Webster almost certainly imbibed elements of much of this literature, and was indebted, to some extent, to scholastic methods of theological argument and discourse. Indeed, his inconsistency in this respect was used by his adversaries to expose the flaws in his radical arguments. George Wither pointed out in 1653 that much of Webster's phraseology in theological matters was clothed in the language and logic of those scholastic conventions that he purported to despise.[108] In theology too, then, one is faced with the paradox of a would-be reformer whose commitment to change was shaped as much by traditional, orthodox sources as it was by new ideas and beliefs.

HISTORY

The most conspicuous feature of Webster's large collection of historical works (169 volumes or 10·4 per cent) is its astonishing range. Although works of ancient history predominate (sixty-four volumes), Webster owned an impressive set of annals and histories of medieval and Renaissance Europe, as well as a substantial number of works relating to the history of the church. Most of the works relating to ancient Greece (eleven volumes) and Rome (thirty-seven volumes) can probably be accounted

---

[106] John Webster, op. cit., note 4 above, pp. 3, 5, 11, 16. Daillé (1594–1670) was a leading French Calvinist and student of the Scottish theologian, John Cameron (1579?–1625), whose *Myrothecium* [244] was also in Webster's possession. He was pastor of the Protestant churches at Saumur (1626) and Charenton (1626–70), and was a close acquaintance of many of the most learned men of his day, including Mersenne. See Brian G. Armstrong, *Calvinism and the Amyraut heresy: Protestant scholasticism and humanism in seventeenth-century France,* Madison, University of Wisconsin Press, 1969, pp. 12–13.

[107] To this list, one might add a curious little discourse written by the physician Richard Bunworth entitled *Man in paradise,* London, James Cottrel, 1656 [667], which purported to "vindicate the souls Prerogative in discerning the truths of Christian Religion with the Eye of Reason", ibid., sig.A6r-v. Published in 1656, this work may represent more circumstantial evidence for Webster's repudiation of radicalism at about this time.

[108] G[eorge] W[ither], *The modern states-man,* London, Henry Hills, 1653, pp. 113–115. Wither was attacking Webster for his use of syllogisms, queries, consectaries, and responsions in his first published work, *The saints guide.*

for by the fact that texts such as these were frequently used for instruction in the grammar schools of early modern England. Works such as Suetonius' imperial biographies [67; 257; 1053; 1138; 1475] and Caesar's *Commentaries* [746; 747; 832; 1163] were commonly appropriated for general instruction in grammar, style, etc., as well as serving as models for classical historical study. As a grammar school teacher, it is logical to assume that Webster employed them for similar purposes, alongside a whole series of equally popular texts: Appian [104; 1161], Arrianus [120], Curtius Rufus [772; 1175], Diodorus Siculus [113], Dion Cassius [755], Dionysius [1162], Florus [725; 1146], Herodian [982; 1144], Herodotus [762; 769; 949], Livy [117; 1033], Lucanus [978; 1026], Pausanias [766], Tacitus [94; 1087], Thucydides [765], Trogus Pompeius [1145], and Xenophon [95]. These were, in turn, supplemented by other works on more specific aspects of the ancient past, the products of celebrated Renaissance scholars such as Justus Lipsius [216; 1174], Paolo Manuzio [1150; 1480], and Onofrio Panvinio [75].

Webster's interest in history was not apparently restricted to works of ancient history that can only have possessed a limited appeal for the Clitheroe reformer. Possession of Bodin's *Methodus* [776] and Buchanan's *Rerum scoticarum historia* [743] indicate a wider appreciation on Webster's part of new schools of historical writing. Even greater significance may rest, however, in the large number of British histories (twenty-four volumes) in Webster's possession, a symptom no doubt of that growing sense of national pride and destiny which was shared in this period by literate Englishmen of all religious and political backgrounds. Along with the works of Camden [128; 893; 922; 1171], Cotton [971], Hakluyt [171], Holinshed [129], Speed [127], and Stow [125; 933], Webster owned a series of lesser works which together set out to emphasize the glorious antecedents of the English people, and in some cases that of their monarchy.

Two works in particular stand out for comment, not so much for any intrinsic merit that they might possess, but rather for the prominence which they gave to the ancient historical myth that the kings of England were directly descended, through Arthur, from the Trojan founder of Britain, Brutus. The first, Sir John Price's *Historiae britannicae defensio* [897] has been described as "the major scholarly affirmation of the pro-Brutus-Arthur faction".[109] The other, Thomas Heywood's *Life of Merlin* [468], reiterates the same theme, and extends the myth to include Charles I and the Stuarts (a strange work, one might think, to find in the hands of a parliamentarian). Webster's interest in such matters, however, was probably unrelated to either historical or political concerns. A much more likely explanation lies in Webster's extraordinary fondness for tales of Arthurian-style romance, which quite often took as their starting-point the Brutus-Arthur legend (see below pp. 36–37).

Despite the concentration of interest in British history, there are surprisingly few works to be found relating to recent events in Webster's own life-time in England and Scotland. The civil war, for example, features only twice, both works having been written from the royalist perspective (Bate [1470] and Wishart [754]). Seemingly of

---

[109] Peter French, *John Dee: the world of an Elizabethan magus,* London, Routledge & Kegan Paul, 1972, p. 195. French discusses this and similar works at length in the context of John Dee's thought and library, ibid., pp. 188–199.

greater interest to Webster were events in late-sixteenth- and early-seventeenth-century Europe. Besides a number of works dealing with the Thirty Years War (e.g., Gualdo Priorato [179], Lundorp [1148; 1484], and Pomo [261]), Webster owned eight volumes relating to the war between the Spanish and the Dutch in the Low Countries, most of them written from a Catholic perspective (e.g., the works of the Jesuits, Hermannus Hugo [132] and Famianus Strada [745]). The religious significance of the events portrayed in these works was clearly not lost on Webster, who also owned nineteen volumes concerned specifically with aspects of church history. Again, Catholic authors are not ignored, the most important almost certainly the massive *Epitome* by Henri de Sponde of Cardinal Caesar Baronius' *Annales ecclesiastici* [68]. This was itself intended as a counter-reformation reply to the Protestant *Magdeburg centuries* [96], edited by Matthias Flacius (1520–75) and composed "to vindicate the historical rightness of the Lutheran reform". Similar in intent, but focusing upon the events of the reformation, was the *Commentaries* of Joannes Philippson (Sleidanus), a hugely popular work in Protestant Europe [154].[110]

It is impossible in such a brief synopsis as this to provide a complete picture of the range of Webster's collection of historical works, which covered numerous topics and issues, and which spanned all periods of known history. Europe was comprehensively covered, with a noticeable emphasis upon Italian, especially Venetian, history.[111] In addition, Webster owned historical accounts of the Turkish [111; 259; 768; 1164] and Chinese [1097; 1157] nations, as well as a history in Spanish of the conquest of the new world [107]. Much supplementary historical information relating to non-European subjects was also available to Webster in the form of early travel journals, which proved highly popular in this period as general works of scholarly reference (for statistical purposes I have included these under the category of Natural Philosophy). Webster himself was greatly indebted to one such work, by the Jesuit, Joseph de Acosta (1539–1600) [919], which he cited extensively in his *Metallographia*. Equally popular were those by William Lithgow [923], George Sandys [185b], and the imperial ambassador, Gislenius de Bousbecq [1061], which all provided a wealth of miscellaneous information upon the customs and history of the Turkish people.

LITERATURE

One of the most surprising discoveries in Webster's whole library is contained in the 148 volumes that comprise works of ancient and modern literature. Of this total, more than a quarter (forty-one volumes) were prose romances and fictions, in Spanish,

---

[110] Oliver K. Olson, 'Matthias Flacius Illyricus', in Jill Raitt (editor), *Shapers of religious traditions in Germany, Switzerland and Poland, 1560—1600*, New Haven, Conn., Yale University Press, 1981, p. 14. For Philippson, see A.G. Dickens, 'Johannes Sleidan and Reformation history', in R.B. Knox (editor), *Reformation, conformity and dissent: essays in honour of Geoffrey Nuttall*, London, Epworth Press, 1977, pp. 17–43.

[111] Among those works on Italian history are Guicciardini's celebrated *History* in Italian [249], two volumes by Carlo Sigonio [97; 98] and a history of Genoa by Uberto Foglietta [99]. The proud historical traditions of republican Venice were dealt with by Contarini [1094], Justinianus [114], and Paruta [126], the latter an English translation, published during the interregnum in 1658. Webster also owned two works by Paolo Sarpi including his famous *Historie of the Councel of Trent* [118]. For discussion of many of these works, see William J. Bouwsma, *Venice and the defence of republican liberty*, Berkeley, California University Press, 1968.

French, Italian, and English, many of them not published or translated until the 1640s and 1650s. The major source for these chivalric romances was the Brutus-Arthur legend (see above p. 35), which underwent dramatic literary embellishment in the late-fifteenth and early-sixteenth centuries at the hands of unknown Spanish authors. The most famous product of this school of writing were the stories of Amadís de Gaule [105; 1095], which were to form the basis of a whole genre of later Spanish, French, and Italian adaptations [e.g., the Palmerin-Palmendos series: 912; 953; 957; 1092]. Typically, these stories were set in either England or distant and fabulous eastern kingdoms (e.g., *The historie of Trebizond* by Thomas Gainsford [934]), and they featured fantastic tales of knightly deeds and amorous adventures, interspersed with magical interludes and similar literary devices. Moreover, in the course of time, other ancient stories and legends were grafted on to the original leitmotif of the Brutus-Arthur-Amadís series, the *Ethiopian history* of Heliodorus [902; 948; 950: in French, Greek, and English respectively] proving very influential in this respect.

Works of this kind can be interpreted and understood at various levels of meaning. Many clearly read them for pure enjoyment and little else, since they were certainly amongst the most popular forms of literature in sixteenth- and early-seventeenth-century Europe.[112] A more sophisticated audience, however, was meant to perceive a didactic purpose in these stories, ranging from princely advice and chivalric instruction to the conveyance of specific moral points. Such was the purpose of John Lyly's *Euphues* [914] and Sidney's *Arcadia* [180], the latter displaying another common feature of this genre, namely its idealization of rusticity (cf., for example, the *Diana* of Jorge de Montemayor [1096]). Of course, it is impossible to say what aspects of these novels attracted Webster's attention. But the mere fact that Webster, given his religious background, collected such works is itself quite extraordinary. Books of this kind, so one is generally led to believe, were anathema to most puritans and sectaries, who felt that they tended to corrupt the minds of their readers and distract them from their godly duties. Webster, however, far from rejecting literature of this kind, was actively engaged in the collection of the latest romances and fictions in the 1640s and 1650s–in the period, that is, of his own greatest commitment to the reform of learning and religion.[113]

Webster, in fact, had little to say about popular literature, ancient or modern, in *Academiarum examen,* apart from the vaguest indictment of excessive reliance upon pagan authors, poets, and dramatists. Poetry, rhetoric, and other branches of classical literature were not condemned outright by Webster, who, unlike many of his radical colleagues, was content to allow moderate use of such studies. One of the principal benefits of this learning was its contribution to the perfection of style and eloquence which Webster almost certainly employed in his capacity as grammar school master. In

---

[112] The popularity of such works is discussed in Margaret Spufford, *Small books and pleasant histories: popular fiction and its readership in seventeenth-century England,* London, Methuen, 1981, pp. 219–237. For the importance of the Amadis stories, see John J. O'Connor, *Amadis de Gaule and its influence on Elizabethan literature,* New Brunswick, NJ, Rutgers University Press, 1970.

[113] Works of this kind dating from the 1640s and 1650s include a five-volume edition of Gautier de Costes de la Calprenède's *Cassandre* [904], an English translation of Marin Le Roy's *Polexander* in folio [187], and two Spanish romances, again in English, by Francisco de Quintana [968] and Gonzalo de Céspedes Y Meneses [969]. To these, one might also add Sir William Davenant's poetic romance, *Gondibert,* first published in 1651 [926].

all, he owned forty-eight volumes of Roman and Greek poetry, prose, and drama, with works by Cicero and Virgil (six volumes apiece) predominant. Other authors, equally popular in the grammar school curriculum, included: Ovid [56; 1040; 1041; 1043; 1191], Aulus Gellius [909; 1155; 1474] Horace [1004; 1039], Lucian [227; 1038], Sallust [723; 1991], Aesop [985; 1074], Ausonius [1077], Hesiod [1034], Juvenal [1065], Martial [1110], Petronius [1057], and Pindar [240].

Drama, always a more equivocal subject for Protestant pedagogues, is less apparent in Webster's library. He owned only three volumes of classical drama (Euripides [1049], Plautus [1015], and Terence, in English translation [1186]) with two copies of the popular school text *Terentius christianus* by Cornelius Schonaeus [1024; 1058], an attempt to "clothe in the phrase and eloquence of Terence the old Bible stories".[114] Similarly, in rhetoric, Webster owned only a handful of classical texts (Quintilian [63; 1013], Cicero [1015], Demosthenes [1007], and Isocrates [998]), but these were bolstered in part by a number of more recent compilations by Renaissance rhetoricians.[115] Interest in modern authorities, however, was most apparent in the field of poetry or poesy. Webster owned thirty-eight volumes of modern poetry and letters, including works by scholars of international repute such as the humanists Roger Ascham [1021], George Buchanan [1018], Guillaume Budé [62], and Joseph Scaliger [1016]. He also seems to have admired a number of British poets, since he collected the anthologies of Thomas Carew [979], William Davenant [926], Sir John Davies [981], Michael Drayton [174; 967], George Herbert [976], and Arthur Johnston [1059], as well as various miscellanies [955; 977]. Clearly, Webster's taste for literature was extensive and wide-ranging and hardly fits the stereotypical image of the puritan zealot and radical reformer.[116]

LINGUISTICS

From the evidence of Table 2 (above p. 19) and the ninety volumes that comprise Webster's collection of assorted dictionaries, manuals, and linguistic aids, it would seem that Webster was an able and proficient linguist. In addition to Latin, Greek, and Hebrew, he would appear to have mastered French, Italian, Spanish, and German, but not Arabic.[117] The great majority of works in this section fall into one of two categories: dictionaries and lexicons (twenty-five volumes),[118] and manuals, grammars, and other aids to language learning (fifty-five volumes).[119] Taken as a

---

[114] Foster Watson, *The English grammar schools to 1660: their curriculum and practice*, Cambridge University Press, 1908, p. 322.

[115] Clarke [866], Conti [1000], Heinsius [1003], Junius [800], Macropedius [1044], Ravisius Textor [1048], Talaeus (Talon) [1072], Vernulaeus [1107], and Wilke [1017].

[116] A further indication of the breadth of Webster's literary interests is provided by his possession of the works of Ben Jonson [170], an anonymous book of plays [916], an Italian copy of Ariosto's *Orlando furioso* [65], the works of Chaucer [115] and Thomas More [1172], a Spanish edition of Cervantes' *Don Quixote* [1098], the works of Rabelais [972], and a collection of satirical essays by George Wither [980].

[117] Webster refers to his ignorance of Arabic in op. cit., note 21 above, p. 111. He nonetheless owned one Arabic grammar by the celebrated linguist and orientalist, Thomas Erpenius (1584–1624) [853].

[118] These may be broken down as follows: multi-lingual 7, Hebrew 3, English-Latin 2, Latin-Italian 2, Latin 1, Greek 1, Italian-English 1, Latin-German 1, Latin-Greek 1, Latin-Teuton 1, Spanish-English 1, Spanish-French 1, Syriac 1, miscellaneous subject dictionaries 2.

[119] These may be broken down as follows: Hebrew 11, Latin 11, French 8, Greek 6, Italian 5, Greek-Latin 3, Spanish 3, English 2, Arabic 1, Chaldeo-Syriac 1, German 1, Latin-French 1, multi-lingual 2.

whole, the preponderance of Hebrew (fourteen volumes), Latin (twelve volumes), and Greek (seven volumes) is entirely predictable. Not only was knowledge of all three languages considered an essential accoutrement for serious biblical scholarship, but skill in these languages was also established as a staple element in the curriculum of the grammar schools. Webster must therefore have used many of these works in his teaching duties and almost certainly applied them to his interest in scriptural exegesis (cf. above pp. 28–29).[120]

On the whole, there is little that is remarkable or noteworthy about these works. The numerous Latin grammars and manuals are primarily humanistic in tone and include a number of popular educational manuals designed to assist Latin instruction for the young [e.g., Vives' *Colloquia:* 1009]. The works of Erasmus in this field were particularly favoured [881; 1027; 1028; 1029; 1035; 1036]. A hint of greater innovation is to be found in the works of Joseph Webbe [1025; 1105] and John Brinsley [1501], both of whom were applauded by Webster for their novel approaches to the teaching of Latin grammar.[121] Both men disapproved of the traditional pedantry of language instruction in the grammar schools, and Webster was particularly enamoured with the thought of Brinsley in this respect, who, he claimed, had done away with rules and method in grammar teaching.[122] This movement away from more formal methods of language instruction was epitomized by the radically new approach of Jan Amos Komenský (Comenius) [862; 870], who, in Webster's words, had attempted "to lay down a platform . . . that youth might as well in their tender years receive the impression of the knowing of matter, and things, as of words, and that with as much ease, brevity and facility".[123]

The appeal of Comenius's linguistic theories lay in the practical benefits to learning in general which such methods were purported to produce. Science, in particular, stood to gain from the implementation of the Comenian system, which attempted to substitute an emphasis on words for an emphasis on things. In England, ideas of this kind were extremely influential among the Baconian reformers, who, in some cases, extended the scope of their linguistic research to the quest for a universal language. Webster had, of course, shown a great deal of interest in such schemes in *Academiarum examen,* citing Jacob Boehme as the source of his belief that one day the universal language of nature would be rediscovered (above p. 3). According to Webster, all learning, not just science, stood to benefit from this discovery, a view which no doubt accounts for his possession of other works concerned with this subject (John Wilkins [588], Francis Lodowick [377], and Cave Beck [964]). Beck's *Universal character* (1657)

---

[120] Of Greek and Hebrew, Webster wrote "we have in our younger years both studied and taught them to others," op. cit., note 15 above, p. 106. Two of the most popular manuals for the instruction of Hebrew in schools were Buxtorf's *Epitome* [868; 879] and Martinius' grammar [844; 867; 876; 878]. See W.A.L. Vincent, *The grammar schools: their continuing tradition, 1660—1714,* London, John Murray, 1969, p. 80.

[121] John Webster, op. cit., note 4 above, pp. 23–24.

[122] For Brinsley, see esp. Rosemary O'Day, *Education and society, 1500—1800,* London, Longman, 1982, pp. 47–53; Morgan, op. cit., note 10 above, pp. 195–199 and *passim.* In praising Brinsley for his opposition to rules in grammar, Webster was accused by the Presbyterian Thomas Hall of inaccuracy and inconsistency since Brinsley's method, according to Hall, was well known "to hath reference to Rules". Thomas Hall, *Vindiciae literarum,* London, N. Webb & W. Grantham, 1654, p. 201.

[123] John Webster, op. cit., note 4 above, p. 22. See also item 1500, an English adaptation of Comenius' *Janua linguarum.*

is an especially interesting item. Not only does it hint at Webster's continuing fascination with this particular subject in the late 1650s, but Beck's use of mathematics to solve this difficult problem reflects Webster's own faith in this particular field of learning (cf. above p. 24).[124]

PHILOSOPHY (ETHICS, LOGIC, AND METAPHYSICS)

One of the smallest categories of works in Webster's library consists of the three branches of philosophy: ethics, logic, and metaphysics (fifty-six volumes). All three, to some extent, were considered in need of reform by Webster in the 1650s, with metaphysics singled out for special criticism. Metaphysics was, in fact, one of the few subjects under-represented in Webster's library (nine volumes), and most of these were wholly traditional in their adherence to Aristotelian method and form.[125] Webster seems to have attached far greater significance to the study of logic (twenty-two volumes) and ethics (twenty volumes), subjects which he considered worthy of university study once they too had been purified from the corruptions of Aristotle and the schoolmen. In both cases, however, Webster possessed a solid grounding in the works of traditional authors, which formed the basis of instruction at Oxford and Cambridge.

In ethics (twenty volumes), Webster owned a substantial body of classical texts and learned commentaries on Aristotle's *Ethica Nicomachea* [798], including those of Freigius [805], Golius [804], Lefèvre d'Étaples [1268], Magirus [822], Pavone [812], Riger [1121], and Scribonius [1115].[126] One of Webster's major criticisms of works such as these was that they based instruction in morality on pagan authors. He did, however, offer alternative sources of ancient wisdom for ethical study in the shape of Seneca [80] and Epictetus [724].[127] He also approved of the Calvinist Lambert Daneau's *Ethices christianae* [783], which, as its title suggests, was an attempt to create a system of ethical enquiry based entirely upon non-pagan sources, and he warmly applauded the ethical endeavours of Descartes and Philip Melanchthon.[128] One further source of moral instruction, unmentioned by Webster in *Academiarum examen*, was the emblem book. Webster owned five specimens of this popular, multi-purpose

---

[124] John Webster, op. cit., note 4 above, pp. 25–32. A similar concern for the universal language, and its application to occult learning, is discernible in those works of cryptography owned by Webster. These included three volumes by Johann Tritheim (1462–1516) [471; 472; 586], as well as a large folio on the subject by Gustavus Selenus (b.1579) [38]. For the latter, see especially Wayne Shumaker, *Renaissance curiosa,* Burlington, Centre for Medieval and Renaissance Studies, 1982, pp. 99–105.

[125] John Webster, op. cit., note 4 above, pp. 84–86, 107. Webster owned works on metaphysics by a number of distinguished Protestant scholars, among them Robert Baron [1118], Gilbert Jacchaeus [1120b], Bartholomew Keckermann [808], Jacob Martini [809; 827], and Christoph Scheibler [251]. In order to remedy the deficiencies of traditional studies such as these, Webster advised the study of the metaphysical works of Descartes.

[126] In addition to these works, Webster had access to further classical expositions of Aristotelian ethics in the general manuals of authors such as Eustachius [793] and Jean de Champaignac [790]. The former was commonly used as a standard text at Cambridge during the seventeenth century. See for example, Curtis, op. cit., note 56 above, pp. 110–112; Kearney, op. cit., note 60 above, p. 105.

[127] Of Epictetus' *Enchiridion* [724], a small duodecimo, Webster wrote that it contained "more pretious treasure than all the great volumes of Aristotle", op. cit., note 4 above, p. 88. Webster might also have recommended the writings of Plutarch [44, 773] and Cebes [896; 256].

[128] Ibid., pp. 86–88, 107–108.

form of literature (Alciatus [780; 1139], Boissard [429], Junius [1143], and Schoonhovius [413]), which, in its combination of poetry, art, and philosophy, possessed obvious pedagogical uses.

In the case of logic, there already existed in Webster's time a framework for wholesale reform of the Aristotelian system of logic in the shape of Ramism. Not surprisingly, Webster owned a number of Ramist texts. In addition to two copies of the *Dialectica* of La Ramée (Ramus) [801; 802], Webster possessed the Ramist manuals of Alsted [792; 826], Downame [811], Freigius [805], Granger [474], and Hotman [1129]. He was also well versed in the works of a number of Protestant theologians who applied Ramist logic to their religious studies (e.g., in England, Downame, Ames, Perkins, and Fenner; in Europe, Alsted, Piscator, and Polanus). The chief end of Ramism was to simplify the actual process of learning and to make knowledge more accessible and factual, rather than conjectural. One of the main criticisms levelled against scholastic logic (by Webster amongst others) was that it was incapable of producing new knowledge or understanding. Ramism clearly could, and one area to which it was commonly applied was the puritan sermon. Granger's *Syntagma logicam* (London, 1620) [474], for example, was a comprehensive guide to the new logic which dealt exhaustively with the various religious applications of Ramism. Interestingly, Webster had little to say about Ramus's methods in *Academiarum examen*. If this is indicative of an equivocal response on Webster's part to Ramism, then it may well have arisen because of its associations with orthodox Calvinism.[129]

In logic, as in so many other areas of learning, Webster was fully acquainted with traditional Aristotelian method. The logical works of Aristotle [234; 807] were supplemented by numerous manuals and expositions of peripatetic logic, many of which were commonly employed as standard texts in the schools and universities of seventeenth-century England (e.g., Burgersdijck [1124], Seton [1117], Stekius [777], Sturm [775], and Titelman [803]). Moreover, many of these works were prepared with the same object in mind as that of the Ramist Granger. John Case's *Summa* [473], for example, was designed specifically to accommodate Aristotelian logic to scriptural analysis (cf. Titelman [803]). A similar motive lay behind the numerous systematic treatises of the eclectic Danzig logician, Bartholomew Keckermann (1571–1609). Webster owned no less than five copies of Keckermann's *Systema logica* [787; 796; 797; 814; 1123], a work widely used for pedagogical purposes in this period and one which Webster almost certainly employed in his own teaching.[130]

LAW AND POLITICS

The final section of Webster's library, and the smallest, comprises those works concerned with law and politics (fifty volumes). In both cases, Webster's literary interest in these subjects was confined to very few books, and in the case of law presents

---

[129] I have found only two references to Ramus in Webster's writings: see ibid., p. 91, and Webster, op. cit., note 15 above, p. 344. In all, Webster owned nine volumes by Ramus, as well as the *Rhetorica* of Talaeus (Talon) [1072], which has been partially attributed to Ramus.

[130] Altogether, Webster possessed twelve volumes of Keckermann's writings, including a one-volume edition of his *Opera* [235]. Keckermann's works were popular in England, and America, where they were frequently taught at Harvard. See Morgan, op. cit., note 10 above, p. 261; Curtis, op. cit., note 56 above, p. 284n.

little of interest. Most of the law books (twenty-four volumes) were the work of English jurists and legal commentators and cover a wide range of subjects from land law, conveyancing, court administration, and wills to general compilations of the laws and statutes of England, including Magna Carta [1454]. These works would have possessed a twofold interest for Webster. First, Webster was a property owner, and a litigious one at that, who had made a number of enemies through his property transactions in delinquent land during the 1650s. And second, as resident magistrate for Clitheroe on three separate occasions, he would certainly have required some background knowledge of the English common law.[131] The remaining legal works, miscellaneous collections of practical and theoretical law, represent the work of a number of continental jurists, including such celebrated figures as François Hotman [1443; 1455], Julius Pacius [1453], and Ulrich Zasius [1478].

Webster's books on politics (twenty-six volumes) present more of a problem in that they fit no clear pattern and certainly disallow any attempt to pass judgement on Webster's own political beliefs. These were not directly alluded to by Webster in any of his published writings. It nonetheless seems logical to assume that for much of the 1640s and 1650s, Webster was actively engaged in support of Parliament in its struggle with Charles I, and thereafter backed the Cromwellian republic. In 1660, his allegiance to the monarchy was restored (above pp. 6–7), though whether through ideological commitment or political expediency is difficult to determine.

Considering Webster's support for Parliament in 1648 and his involvement in radical circles in London in 1653, one is surprised to find that Webster owned so few works of an overtly political nature. Those that he did own, moreover, display little sympathy for the parliamentarian cause and include a number of popular defences of the deposed Stuarts. Foremost among works of this kind were the anonymous *Eikon basilicon* [988], Saumaise's reply to Milton [1436], and George Bate's *Elenchus motuum nuperorum* [1470]. Equally unexpected is the presence of a number of European expositions of absolutist and divine right theories. These include the works of two French political commentators, Boitet de Frauville [1089] and Guez de Balzac [242], as well as William Barclay's *De potestate papae* [1346].[132]

From the evidence of the library catalogue, Webster was not apparently attracted to the ideas of the constitutional theorists, English or European, and apart from a few volumes advocating the virtues of republicanism as an ideal political form,[133] there is little here to indicate commitment to radical political change. Other political works include examples of the "mirror for princes" genre, which tended to reinforce political

---

[131] Weeks, op. cit., note 4 above, pp. 94–97.

[132] William Barclay (1546–1608) was Professor of Civil Law at Pont-a-Mousson and Angers. His *De potestate papae* [1346] was composed primarily to rebut the view that the Papacy possessed the right to interfere in the secular affairs of princes. In the process, he set out a strong defence of divine right monarchy and the illegality of resistance to royal authority. See J. W. Allen, *A history of political thought in the sixteenth century*, London, Methuen, 1928, pp. 390–393. Non-resistance was also taught by Lipsius in his *Politicorum* [1456].

[133] Republicanism was, of course, upheld in this way by Machiavelli [1399] and Francesco Patrizi, bishop of Gaeta (1412–94) [1132]. To these works one might also add the propagandistic defences of Venetian republicanism found in the histories of Contarini [1094] and Paruta [126]; see also above p. 36n.111. The religious duty of subjects to resist tyrants was also propounded by Knox [1384] and Pareus [243]; see above p. 29n.92. It was also the object of practical demonstration in Buchanan's Scottish history [743].

absolutism (e.g., Guevara [992], Osorio da Fonseca [1483], and James I's *Basilicon doron* [758b]). A limited interest in the field of political study is also suggested by Webster's brief comments on the subject in *Academiarum examen,* in which he recommended the writings of Bodin [776], Hobbes [989], and Machiavelli [1399]. The works of Aristotle were presumably to be relegated to a minor position in the curriculum, but not abolished altogether, since they were felt to possess some valuable insights into this particular branch of learning.[134]

CONCLUSIONS

Hugh Trevor-Roper has described John Webster as "a learned and dogmatic auto-didact . . . [and] a compulsive name dropper" who "uncritically sang the praises of all writers, who, from whatever position, had attacked . . . Aristotle . . . and Galen".[135] In the light of the preceding analysis of Webster's library, I am inclined to the view that this represents a fair assessment of Webster the man, except perhaps in one respect. If Webster did name-drop in his writings, we now know that he did so from a position of complete familiarity with the sources that he cited. Likewise, his assault on the "ancients" in general, and Aristotle in particular, was not simply the typical knee-jerk response of all radicals in this period to the traditional university curriculum. It was rather the product of a man who in all probability had received a traditional university education and who opposed the wisdom of the "ancients" from a vantage-point of knowledge rather than ignorance (cf. William Dell whose works Webster owned [450]).

The extent of Webster's knowledge, and the range of his scholarly interests, was remarkable for a man so far removed for much of his life from the mainstream of intellectual activity in England. His library, dominated by works of medicine, natural philosophy, and divinity, must have been one of the largest private collections in the north of England. Unfortunately, however, it has not survived intact, nor as yet have any of the volumes that once formed part of the library come to light. Until that time, any attempt, my own included, to evaluate the meaning of these books for their original owner must remain speculative. I am nonetheless convinced that for those more expert than myself, the catalogue of Webster's library provides a unique insight into the mind of one of the leading proponents of radical educational, religious, and scientific change in seventeenth-century England.

[134] Webster owned a single copy of Aristotle's *Politica* [794]. He also possessed an interesting commentary on Aristotle's political thought by the Englishman, John Case (d.1600). For Case's own eclecticism, based upon a firm grounding in the thought of Aristotle, see Charles B. Schmitt, 'John Case on art and nature', *Ann. Sci.,* 1976, **33**: 543–559.

[135] Hugh Trevor-Roper, 'The Paracelsian movement', in *Renaissance essays,* London, Secker & Warburg, 1985, p. 190.

INDEX TO CHAPTERS 1 AND 2

Index

Livy, 35
Lodowick, Francis, 39
logic, 6n, 20n, 21, 34, 40–41
Lombard Street, London, 3n, 4
London, 2, 3n, 4, 10n, 17, 42
Low countries, the, 36
Lucanus, Marcus Annaeus, 35
Lucian, 38
Lull, Ramón, 22
Lundorp, Michael Caspar, 36
Lutheranism, 27n, 28 & n, 33, 36
lycanthropy, 12n
Lyly, John, *Euphues,* 37
lymphatic system, 25 & n

M

Machiavelli, Niccolò, 42n, 43
Macropedius, Georgius, 38n
Maestlin, Michael, 24n
magic, natural, 10, 13, 19, 23
Magirus, Joannes, 20 & n, 40
Magna carta, 42
Magnenus, Joannes Chrysostomus, 20
Maier, Michael, 22
maleficium, 13
manuals, preaching, 34
Manuzio, Paolo, 35
Marischal College, Aberdeen, 21n
Martial, 38
Martini, Jacob, 40n
Martinius, Petrus, 39n
mathematics, 19, 24, 26, 40
Matthew, gospel of, 12
Mazzotta, Benedictus, 23n
mechanical philosophy, 9, 10 & n
mechanics, 24
medicine, 1, 5, 6n, 7, 9n, 10, 17, 19, 22, 24–27, 30n, 31n, 43
Melanchthon, Philip, 40
Mercator, Gerard, *Atlas,* 16
Mersenne, Marin, 34n
Mestrezat, Jean, 28
metaphysics, 20 & n, 21 & n, 40 & n
meteors, 13n
Metius, Adrian, 23n
Mexico, 20n
millenarianism, 2–3, 6, 7, 23, 29–30
Milton, John, 42
mineralogy, 19, 22n–23n
miracles, 12, 13
Mitton, Yorkshire, 2
Montemayor, Jorge de, *Diana,* 37
Moore, Sir Jonas, 8
More, Henry, 14
    Conjectura cabbalistica, 23n
More, Sir Thomas, 38n
Morgan, John, 4
Mornay, Philippe de, 28n
Mueller Regiomontanus, Johann, 24n
mysticism, religious, 31–32

N

Napier, John, 24n
Neile, Richard, 1

Nelson, Peter, 8 & n
neo-platonism, 20, 21
Neuhusius, Henricus, 26n
Niclas, Hendrik, 33

O

occult philosophy: *see* alchemy; astrology;
    Helmontianism; hermeticism; magic, natural;
    Paracelsism
Oldenburg, Henry, 8 & n
optics, 19
Osorio da Fonseca, Jeronimo, 43
Oughtred, William, 24
    Clavis mathematica, 24
Ovid, 38
Owen, John, 32–33
    Of schisme, 32–33
Oxford, 24
Oxford, University of, 18, 20 & n, 40

P

Pacius, Julius, 20, 42
Padua, University of, 20n
Palmendos, 37
Palmerin, 37
pansophism, 21–22
Panvinio, Onofrio, 35
Pappus of Alexandria, 24n
Paracelsians, Paracelsism, 5n, 7, 9, 12n, 17, 20, 22 & n, 26
Paracelsus, Theophrastus, 5, 10, 13, 22 & n, 26 & n
    Opera omnia, 22 & n
Paré, Ambroise, 25
Pareus, David, 29 & n, 42n
Parliament, armies of, 1, 26, 31n
    Barebones, 2
    Cavalier, 7
Parliamentarianism, 42
Paruta, Paolo, 36n, 42n
patristic learning: *see* fathers of the church
Patrizi, Francesco, Bishop of Gaeta, 42n
Patrizi, Francesco, Platonist, 20, 21
    Nova de universis philosophia, 21
Paul, Saint, 12n
Pausanias, 35
Pavone, Francesco, 40
Peccettius, Francescus, 25
Pecquet, Jean, 25
Pererius, Benedictus, 20n
    Physica, 20 & n
perfectionism, 1, 3, 4n
Perkins, William, 28, 41
Petronius, 38
Philippson Sleidanus, Joannes, *Commentaries,* 36
philosophy, 5, 10, 19, 20n, 21, 40–41
philosophy, natural, 3, 5–6, 7, 9–10, 12, 17, 19–27, 30, 36, 39, 43
Phioravant, Leonard: *see* Fioravanti, Leonardo
Pindar, 38
Pinnell, Henry, 5n

48

THE CATALOGUE OF THE LIBRARY OF JOHN WEBSTER

INTRODUCTORY NOTES

In the original manuscript of the catalogue of Webster's library (Chetham MS. A.6.47), the works have been arranged according to subject and book-size with appropriate section headings. In the transcription that follows, I have attempted to preserve the original layout of the catalogue (and by implication, the library itself), but have altered the system of numeration in order to aid easy access to particular items by use of the Index. Each item is described as follows:

(i) The catalogue description with estimated value of each item (in light type). In all cases, I have reproduced original spelling, and errors, as well as the gaps in transcription where the copier was unable to read the original manuscript (presumably in Webster's handwriting), e.g., item 1164.

(ii) A full description of the work where this is known (in bold type). In most instances, it has proved impossible to identify individual editions. Wherever possible, I have tried to indicate the full range of editions which may have included that in Webster's possession.

(iii) In the case of works published in England, or in the English language, I have included in brackets the *Short title catalogue* number (S.T.C.) as found in: A.W. Pollard and G.R. Redgrave, *A short-title catalogue of books printed in England, Scotland and Ireland, and of English books printed abroad, 1475—1640*, London, Bibliographical Society, 1926. Donald Wing, *Short title catalogue of books, printed in England, Scotland, Ireland, Wales and British America and of English books printed in other countries, 1641—1700*, New York, Columbia University Press, 1945–51, 3 vols.

Finally, I have also included in parentheses all citations by Webster of works in his possession with the appropriate page-references from the following:

AE: *Academiarum examen, or the examination of academies,* London, Giles Calvert, 1654

DS: *The displaying of supposed witchcraft,* London, J.M., 1677

JS: *The judgement set, and the bookes opened,* London, R. Hartford, 1654

M: *Metallographia, or, an history of metals,* London, Walter Kettilby, 1671

"A Catalogue of all the Bookes
late belonginge to Dr: John Webster
of Clytheroe decd: ye 18th of June
Anno Dom 1682"

SECTION A

(Works in folio)

flr

1. Opera Omnia Roberti ffludd sive de fluctibus, vols. 5
    £9 10 0

    Robert FLUDD, <u>Opera Omnia</u>, 5 vols., Oppenheim & Frankfurt,
    1617–26   folio

    (a) <u>Utriusque cosmi majoris scilicet ... (Tractatus
    secundus de naturae simia seu technia macrocosmi historia)</u>,
    Oppenheim, 1617–18 ; 2nd ed., Frankfurt, 1624
    (b) <u>Tomi secundus ... de supernaturali, naturali,
    praeternaturali et contranaturali microcosmi historia</u>,
    Oppenheim & Frankfurt, 1619–21
    (c) <u>Veritatis proscenium</u>, Frankfurt, 1621
    (d) <u>Anatomiae amphitheatrum</u>, Frankfurt, 1623
    (e) <u>Philosophia sacra et vere Christiana, seu
    Meteorologia cosmica</u>, Frankfurt, 1626

    (AE, pp. 74,105 ; DS, pp.207,222,319)

2. Parkinsons Theatrum Botanicum vols. 1   £2 15 0

    **John PARKINSON, <u>Theatrum Botanicum ; The Theatre of Plants,
    or, an Herball of large extent</u>,** London, 1640   folio

    (STC : 19302)

3. Vidi Vidij opera omnia (3 vols)   £2 08 0

    Vidus VIDIUS the Elder, <u>Opera Omnia, sive ars Medicinalis</u>,
    3 vols., Frankfurt, 1626   folio
    (Nb. An earlier edition of this work was published at
    Venice in 1611, but without the title <u>Opera Omnia</u>).

4. Musaeum Wormianum   £0 18 0

    **Ole WORM, <u>Museum Wormianum seu historia rerum rariorum
    ... quae Hafniae Danorum in aedibus Authoris servantur</u>,**
    Leyden, 1655   folio

    (M, pp. 39 and <u>passim</u>)

5.   Schuckij opera   £1 05 0

Joannes SCHENCKIUS, Observationum medicarum rariorum libri VII, in quibus nova, abdita, admirabilia, monstrosaque exempla ... proponuntur, Lyons, 1644 ; Frankfurt, 1665 folio

(DS, pp.33,86,129,247,264 ; all references are to the 1644 edition).

6.   fforesti opera omnia (2 vols)   £2 05 0

Petrus FORESTUS, Observationum et Curationum Medicinalium ac Chirurgicam Opera Omnia Quatuor Tomis Digesta, 2 vols., Rouen, 1653   folio

(DS, p.95)

7.   Heurnij opera omnia   £1 12 0

Joannes HEURNIUS, Opera Omnia ... Postrema editio, prioribus ... accuratior, Lyons, 1658   folio

(M, p.15)

8.   ffallopij opera omnia   £1 14 0

Gabriello FALLOPPIO, Opera Omnia in unum congesta, Frankfurt, 1600 ; Venice, 1606   folio

(M, p.45)

9.   Sennerti opera omnia (3 vols)   £3 00 0

Daniel SENNERTUS, Opera Omnia, 3 vols., Paris & Venice, 1641; Lyons, 1650   folio

(DS, pp.94,246 ; M, pp.14,15)

10.   Hipocratis opera omnia   £1 15 0

HIPPOCRATES, Opera Omnia, Rome, 1525 ; Basle, 1526 ; 1546 ; 1558 ; Lyons, 1564 ; Venice, 1575 ; 1610 ; 1619

(DS, p.330)

11.   Medicae artes principes post Hipoc: et Galen   £2 10 0

(Henri ESTIENNE), Medicae artis principes, post Hippocratem et Galenum, Graeci latinitate donati : Aretaeus, Ruffus Ephesius, Oribasius, Paulus Aeginata, Aetius, Alex. Trallianus, Actuarius, Nic. Myrepsus. Latini: Corn: Celsus, Scrib. Largus, Marcell. Empiricus, Geneva & Paris, 1567 folio

12.   Armamentarium Sculteti   £0 16 0

Joannes SCULTETUS the Elder, Χειροπλοθηκη , seu
Armamentarium chirurgicum, Ulm, 1655   folio

13.   Cornachini tabulae   £0 18 0

Thomas CORNACCHINIUS, Tabulae medicae in quibus ea fere
omnia quae a principibus medicis graecis, arabibus et
latinis de curationis apparatu ... sparsim reperiuntur,
methodo adeo absoluta collecta sunt, Padua, 1605 folio
(Nb. Another edition appeared under a different title
at Venice, 1609, in folio).

14.   ffabritij Hildani opera omnia   £1 10 0

Wilhelm FABRICIUS of Hilden, Opera quae extant omnia,
Frankfurt, 1646   folio

15.   Andernaci de medicina vet et nova   £0 15 0

Joannes GUINTERIUS Andernacus, De Medicina veteri et
nova tum cognoscenda, tum faciunda commentarii duo,
Basle, 1571   folio

16.   Paracelsi opera omnia Geneva excusae (2 vols)   £2 08 0

Philipp Aureol Theophrast BOMBAST VON HOHENHEIM, Opera
Omnia medico—chemico—chirurgica, 2 vols., Geneva,
1658   folio

(DS, pp. 60,162 and passim ; M, pp. 49 and passim)

17.   Paracelsi opera Germanicae (3 vols)   £1 16 0

Philipp Aureol Theophrast BOMBAST VON HOHENHEIM, Opera
(German), 3 vols., Strassburg, 1603-05 ; 1616-18 folio

      (a) Opera Bücher und Schrifften ... mit ... ihren
... eigener hangeschriebenen Originalien collacionert,
vergliechen, verbessert und durch Joannem Huserum ... in
Truck gegeben, 2 vols., Strassburg, 1603 ; 1616

      (b) Chirurgische Bücher und Schrifften ... Durch
Johannem Huserum Brisgoium, Strassburg, 1605 ; 1618

18.   Thesaurus Chirurgiae (9 vols)   £1 10 0

Peter UFFENBACH (ed.), Thesaurus Chirurgiae continens
praestantissimorum autorum utpote A. Parei, ... J. Tagaultii,
J. Hollerii, M. Sancti Barolitani, A. Bolognini, M. A. Blondi,
A. Ferrii, ... J. Dondi et G. Fabritii ... opera chirurgica
... nunc vero in unum collecta, repurgata, per
P. Uffenbachium, 1 vol., split and rebound in 9
separate volumes, Frankfurt, 1610   folio

3

19.   Peccetij Chirurgia   £1 04 0

**Francescus PECCETTIUS, Cheirurgia ... in qua omnia, tam
ad hujus artis theoriam, quam praxim spectantia traduntur
et diligentissime explicantur in quatuor libros digesta,**
Florence, 1616   folio

20.   Paracelsi Chirurgia major et minor   £0 14 0

**Philipp Aureol Theophrast BOMBAST VON HOHENHEIM,
Chirurgia magna in duos tomos digesta ... Nunc recens à
Iosquino Dalhemio ... Latinitate donata,** Basle, 1573
folio

(DS, p.330 ; M, pp. 53-54)

21.   ffernelij opera   £0 16 0

**Joannes FERNELIUS, Universa Medicina ... (De abditis
rerum causis libri duo),** Frankfurt, 1578, 1577 (Binder's
title : "Ferneli Opera")   folio
Later editions : Geneva & Lyons, 1578 ; Geneva, 1580 ;
Lyons, 1586 ; 1602 ; Geneva, 1604 ; Hanover, 1610 (all
folio)

(DS, p.324 ; reference is to the 1610 edition)

22.   Penae et Lobelij Adversaria   £0 14 0

**Petrus PENA and Matthias L'OBEL, Stirpium adversaria nova,
perfacilis vestigatio, luculentaque accessio ad priscorum,
presertim Dioscoridis & recentiorum, materiam medicam
quibus propediem accedet altera pars,** London, 1570, 1571 ;
Antwerp, 1576   folio

(STC : 19595-19595.3)

23.   Dell' Elixer vitae Italicae   £0 11 0

**Donato D'EREMITA, Dell' Elixir vitae di Fra. D. D'Eremita
... libri quattro,** Naples, 1624   folio

24.   Saltman de Mineralibus   £0 10 0

Probably a work by the Strassburg physician, **Johann
Rudolph SALTZMANN** (b. 1574).   However, I can find no latin
work of this title by this author.   It may be a reference
to the following:

**Leonhardt THURNHEISSER ZUM THURN, Zehen Bücher von kalten,
warmen und minerischen und metallischen Wassern .... Dem
eine kurtze Beschreibung des Selbacher Brunnens oder Badts
... hinzugethan. Durch J. R. Saltzman** (ed. J.L.Hauwenreuter),
Strassburg, 1612   folio

25.   Tho: Moufeti de Insectis   £0 07 0

**Thomas MOUFET, Insectorum sive minimorum animalium
theatrum : olim ab E. Wottono, C. Gesnero, T. que Pennio
inchoatum : tandem T.M. ... opera ... concinnatum, auctum,
perfectum (ed. Theodore de Mayerne)**, London, 1634 folio

(DS, p.342 ; STC : 17993)

26.   Jo: Wecker of ye secrets of art and nature   £0 07 0

**Hanss Jacob WECKER, Eighteen books of the secrets of art
and nature ... augmented by Dr. R. Read**, London, 1660 ;
1661   folio

(STC : W1236-W1236A)

27.   Pauli Ricij ars Cabalistica   £1 08 0

**Johann PISTORIUS of Nidda, Artis Cabalisticae : hoc est
reconditae theologiae et philosophiae, scriptorum,
Tomus 1 ; in quo praeter P. Ricii theologicos et
philosophicos libros sunt Latini pene omnes, et Hebraei
nonnulli praestantissimi scriptores qui artem commentariis
suis illustrarunt ex ... J. Pistorii ... bibliotheca,**
Basle, 1587   folio

28.   Wirtzungs generall practice of phisick   £0 14 0

**Christoph WIRSUNG, Praxis Medicinae universalis, or a
generall Practise of Physicke, ... translated ... by
J. Mosan**, London, 1598 ; 1605 ; 1617 ; 1654   folio

(STC : 25862-25865 ; W3100-W3101)

29.   Aguilonij optica   £1 10 0

Franciscus AGUILONIUS, F.A. ... opticorum libri sex,
Antwerp, 1613   folio

(AE, p.42 ; DS, p.268)

30.   Schindleri Lexicon   £1 06 0

**Valentin SCHINDLER, Lexicon Pentaglotton Hebraicum,
Chaldaicum, Syriacum, Talmudico-Rabbinicum, et Arabicum,**
Hanover, 1612 ; London, 1635 ; 1637 ; Frankfurt, 1653
folio

(DS, pp.107,110,113,116,120,133,134,135,338 ; STC :
21817.3-21817.7)

31.   Summae Tho: Aquinati   £1 02 0

Saint THOMAS Aquinas, Summa Theologica, Nuremburg,
1496   folio
Numerous subsequent editions in folio.

32.   Georg: Agricolae re metallica   £0 12 0

**Georgius AGRICOLA the Elder, De re metallica libri XII,
quibus accesserunt ... De animantibus subterraneis lib I;
de ortu & causis subterraneorum lib V ; de natura eorum
quae effluunt ex terra lib IV ; de natura fossilium
lib X ; de veteribus et novis metallis lib II ;
Bermannus ; sive, de re metallica, dialogus lib I,**
Basle, 1657   folio

(M, pp.70,95 and *passim* ; all references are to the 1657
edition.   Earlier editions were published at Basle in
1546, 1556 and 1561, in folio).

33.   Cardinal: Cusani opera   £1 02 0

Cardinal Nicolaus KHRYPFFS de Cusa, Opera, Basle,
1565   folio

(AE, pp.4,12)

34.   Verulamij novum organon   £0 08 0

**Francis BACON, Viscount St. Albans, Instauratio Magna
(... Novum Organum)**, London, 1620   folio

(AE, pp. 34,38,39,40,45,67-68,94 ; DS, pp.198,200 ;
STC : 1162)

---

f1v

35.   Sanders Phisiognomi Chiromancae   £0 07 6

**Richard SANDERS, Physiognomie, and Chiromancie,
Metoposcopie the symmetrical proportions and signal
moles of the body, fully and accurately handled ; with
their natural predictive significations.   Whereunto is
added the Art of Memorie (... of R. Lullius)**, London,
1653 ; 2nd ed., enlarged, London, 1670, 1671   folio
(STC : S754-S755)

36.   ffrancis Patricij philosophia platonica   £1 04 0

Francesco PATRIZI, Nova de Universis Philosophia. In qua Aristotelica methodo ... ad primam causam ascenditur Deinde propria Patricii methodo, toto in contemplationem venit divinitas ; postremo methodo Platonica, rerum universitas, a conditore Deo deducitur, Ferrara, 1591 ; enlarged, Venice, 1593   folio

(M, p.15 ; reference is to the 1593 edition)

37.   Methodus Galeni   £0 02 6

GALEN, Methodus medendi, vel de morbis curandis, Paris, 1519   folio
Numerous later editions in folio.

(DS, p.20)

38.   Gustavi Sileni Criptographia   £0 16 0

Gustavus SELENUS (i.e. AUGUSTUS II, Duke of Brunswick, Luneburg), Cryptomenytices et Cryptographiae libri IX. in quibus et planissima steganographiae a Johanne Trithemio, ... magice et aenigmatice olim conscriptae, enodatio traditur, Luneburg, 1624   folio

(AE, p.24 ; DS, p.8)

39.   Cabaei de Magnetae lib   £0 15 0

Nicolaus CABEUS, Philosophia Magnetica, in qua magnetis natura penitus explicatur, et omnium quae hoc lapide cernuntur, causae propriae afferuntur, Cologne and Ferrara, 1629   folio

(AE, p.77)

40.   Dr: Dee of Spiritts   £0 16 0

Meric CASAUBON, A True and Faithful Relation of what passed for many years between Dr. J. Dee ... and some spirits ... With a preface confirming the reality ... of this relation ... by M. Casaubon, London, 1659 folio

(DS, pp.8,292 ; STC : D811)

41.   Philosophia Telesij cum alijs   £0 13 6

Tractationum philosophicarum tomus unus : in quo continentur, I.P. Mocenici Universalium Institutionum ad hominum perfectionem Contemplationes V.   II. A. Caesalpini ... Questionum Peripateticarum libri V. III. B. Telesii ... de rerum Natura, juxta propria principia libri IX., Geneva?, 1588   folio

(AE, p.106)

42.   Plinij historia mundi naturalis   £0 16 0

Caius PLINIUS SECUNDUS, Historia mundi naturalis,
Frankfurt, 1582   folio
Although numerous editions of this work were published
in folio, the above is the only one to fit exactly the
Catalogue description, as well as correlating with the
references to it in Webster's writings, below).

(DS, pp. 69,328 ; M, pp.11,28-29,248)

43.   Platonis opera Graece et latine (2 vols)   £1 12 0

PLATO, Πλάτωνος ἅπαντα τὰ σωζόμενα. **Platonis opera**
quae extant omnia, 3 vols. in 2, Paris, 1578 (ed. J. de
Serres) ; Lyons, 1590 ; Frankfurt, 1602 (ed. M. Ficino)
folio

(AE, p.40 ; DS, p.314 ; references are to one of the
Ficino editions)

44.   Plutarchi moralia   £0 05 6

PLUTARCH, Moralia, Paris, 1521   folio
Numerous subsequent editions in folio.

45.   Burtons Melancoly   £0 07 6

Robert BURTON, The Anatomy of Melancholy, 2nd ed.,
Oxford, 1620 ... 8th ed., Oxford, 1676   folio
First edition : Oxford, 1621, in 4°.

(STC : 4160-4163 ; B6181-B6184)

46.   Brucioli Biblia Italica   £0 15 0

Antonio BRUCIOLI, La Biblia, Venice, 1532 ; 1541   folio

(DS, pp.112,114,119 ; M, pp.147,150)

47.   A french spanish & latin Dictionary   £0 07 0

Henricus HORNKENS, Recueil De Dictionaires Francoys,
Espaignolz et Latins. Recopilacion De Dictionarios
Francese, Españoles y Latinos.   Congesta
Dictionariorum Gallicorum, Hispanicorum & Latinorum,
Brussels, 1599   large 4°*
(*Nb. I have not been able to locate an edition of
this work in folio).

48.   Delle Guerre di fiandra   £0 10 0

Cardinal Guido BENTIVOGLIO, Della guerra di fiandra,
Venice, 1635 ; Paris, 1644 ; 1645 ; 1649   folio

49.   Minsius Dictionary in Spanish and English   £0 08 0

Richard PERCYVALL, A Dictionarie in Spanish and English,
first published ... by R. Percivale ... Now enlarged ...
by J(ohn) Minsheu, London, 1599 ; 1623   folio

(STC : 19620-19621b.5)

50.   Dictionarium Saxonico Latine Anglico   £0 16 0

William SOMNER, Dictionarium Saxonico-Latino-Anglicum,
Oxford, 1659   folio

(STC : S4663)

51.   A World of words by Jon: fflorio   £0 06 0

John FLORIO, A Worlde of Wordes, or most copious and exact
Dictionarie in Italian and English, London, 1598 ; 2nd ed.,
London, 1611   folio

(STC : 11098-11099)

52.   Avenarij Dictionarium Hebraicum   £0 16 0

Johann HABERMANN of Eger, Liber Radicum seu Lexicon
Ebraicum, Wittenberg, 1568 ; 1589   folio

(DS, pp.93 and chapter VI, _passim_)

53.   Hen: Stephani Concordantiae Graeco latinae   £1 02 0

Henri ESTIENNE and Robert ESTIENNE the Elder, Concordantiae
Testamenti Novi Graecolatinae, Geneva, 1594 ; 1599 ; 1624
folio

54.   Jon: Scapulae lexicon graeco latinum   £0 16 0

Joannes SCAPULA, Lexicon Graeco-Latinum Novum, Basle, 1580;
1589 ; 1605 ; 1615 ; Geneva, 1609 ; 1628 ; London, 1619 ;
1637 ; Amsterdam, 1652 ; Lyons, 1663, 1662   folio

(STC : 21805.9-21806)

55.   Ambr: Calepini Dictionarium undecem linguarum   £2 06 0

Ambrosius CALEPINUS, Dictionarium undecim linguarum ...
Respondent autem Latinis vocabulis, Hebraica, Graeca,
Gallica, Italica, Germanica, Belgica, Hispanica, Polonica,
Ungarica, Anglica, Basle, 1590   folio

(DS, p. 22-23)

56. Publij Ovidij Nasonis opera cum comentarijs   £1 08 0

Publius OVIDIUS NASO, Poetae Operum tomus primus (tertius), ... cum variorum doctorum virorum commentariis, notis, observationibus, et emendationibus, unum in corpus ... congestis, 3 vols. in 1 (?), Frankfurt, 1601 folio

57. Thresor de la langue ffrancasse   £1 02 0

Aimar de RANCONNET, Thresor de la langue Françoyse, tant ancienne que moderne ... Revue et augmenté en ceste derniere impression ... par J. Nicot ... Avec une Grammaire Françoyse et Latine, & le recueil des vieux proverbes de la France, Paris, 1606   folio

58. Sti: Hieronomi tomus octavus   £1 01 0

Saint JEROME, Opera ... Tomus Octavus, Basle 1525
folio
Volume 8 of a 9 volume edition, Basle, 1524-26, explicitly referred to by Webster, DS, p.118.
First 9 volume edition : Basle, 1516, in folio.

(AE, p.5 ; DS, pp.100,118,150)

59. Tho: Bradwardini de causa dei   £1 03 4

Thomas BRADWARDINUS, Archbishop of Canterbury, De causa Dei, contra Pelagium, et virtute causarum, ad suos Mertonenses, libri tres, London, 1618   folio

(DS, pp.186,188 ; STC : 3534)

60. Wolfangi(sic) musculi loci communes   £0 16 0

Wolfgang MUSCULUS, Loci communes in usus sacrae theologiae canditatorum parati, Basle, 1560 ; 1573 ; 1599 folio

(DS, pp.193,235)

61. Petr: Caballi resolutionum criminalium   £0 12 0

Petrus CABALLUS, Resolutionum criminalium ... centuriae duae, Florence, 1606 ; Venice, 1607 ; Florence, 1609 ; Venice, 1644.   Further editions, enlarged (**... Centuriae tertia**), Florence, 1611 ; Frankfurt, 1613 (2 vols) ; Florence, 1629 ; Venice, 1672   folio

62. G: Budaei Epistolae   £0 04 0

Guillaume BUDÉ, Epistolae, Paris, 1531 ; 1567 folio

63. M: ffabij Quintiliani institutionum oratorium   £0 03 0

Marcus Fabius QUINTILIANUS, Oratorium Institutionum lib. XII, Rome, 1470   folio
Numerous later editions in folio.

10

64.   Othonis Brunfeltij annotationes in Evangelia etc   £0 06 8

**Otto BRUNFELS, Annotationes ... in quatuor Evangelia &
Acta Apostolorum**, Strassburg, 1535   folio

65.   Orlando ffurioso Italicae   £0 06 0

Lodovico ARIOSTO, Orlando Furioso, Ferrara, 1516   4°*
(* Nb. This and all subsequent editions in Italian would
appear to have been published exclusively in quarto).
Italian.

66.   Historia de los Reyes Godos etc   £0 04 6

**Julian del CASTILLO, Historia de los Reyes Godos que
vinieron de la Scitia de Europa contra el Imperio Romano,
y a España : y la succession dellos hasta Philippe segundo
Rey de España**, Burgos, 1582 ; Madrid, 1624   folio

67.   Suetonij tranquilli cum comentarijs   £0 03 0

**Caius SUETONIUS TRANQUILLUS, C. Suetonii Tranquilli de XII
Caesaribus libri VIII.   Ejusdem de Inlustribus grammaticis
et de Claris rhetoribus.   Isaacus Casaubonus ... recensuit
et libros adjecit animadversionum.   Editio altera ...
seorsim adjecti sunt doctorum virorum in eundem Suetonium
commentarii aut aliae lucubrationes**, Paris, 1610   folio

"Shelfe 2d"

68.   Spondani Epitome Baronij   £1 15 0

**Cardinal Caesar BARONIUS, Annales ecclesiastici ex XII.
tomis Caesaris Baronii ... in epitomen redacti, opera
Henrici Spondani ... & eiusdem illustrissimi Cardinalis
auctoritate editi**, Mainz, 1614 ; 1618 ; 1623 ; Paris, 1639 fol.

69.   Jacob Behemens misterium magnum   £0 12 0

**Jacob BOEHME, Mysterium Magnum, or an Exposition of the
first book of Moses, called Genesis** (trans. J. Sparrow &
J. Ellistone) **To which is added, The life of the Author
(by D**(urant) **Hotham)**, London, 1654 ; 1656   folio

(DS, p.300 ; STC : B3411-B3411A)

70.   Crookes Anathomy   £0 18 6

**Helkiah CROOKE, Μικροκοσμογραφια . A Description of the
body of man ; together with the controversies thereto
belonging.   Collected and translated out of all the best
authors of anatomy especially out of Gasper Bauhinus and
Andreas Laurentinus**, London, 1615 ; 1631 ; 1651   folio

(STC : 6062-6063 ; C7231)

11

71.   La ffortification Jo: Errard de bar le duc   £0 14 0

Jean ERRARD de Bar le Duc, La fortification reduicte en art et demonstrée ... mis en lumière par la vefue et les deux fils de J. de Bry, Frankfurt, 1604 ; Paris, 1604 ; 1619, 1621   folio

---

f2r

72.   Jac: Bessoni il Theatro de gl' instrumenti etc   £0 12 0

Jacques BESSON, Il Theatro de gl' instrumenti & machine ... Con una brieve necesaria dichiaration dimostrativa, di M. Francesco Beroaldo. Sù tutte le figure, che vi son comprese, nuovamente di Latino in volgare Italiano tradotto & di moltissime additioni per tutto aummentato & illustrato pel signor Giulio Paschali, Lyons, 1582   folio

73.   Jac: Androvesij architectura   £0 16 0

Jacques ANDROUET DU CERCEAU, De Architectura ... opus, Paris, 1559, 1561   folio

74.   Les fortificationis et Artifices architectura etc £1 06 0

Jacques PERRET, Des Fortifications et artifices, architecture et perspective de Jacques Perret, Paris?, 1601 ; Frankfurt, 1602 ; Paris, 1620   folio

75.   Onuphrij panvinij de ludis Circencibus   £1 16 0

Onofrio PANVINIO, De Ludis Circensibus libri II. De Triumphis liber unus : quibus universa fere Romanorum veterum sacra rituos declarantur, ac figuris aeneis illustrantur, Venice, 1600 ; Padua, 1642   folio

76.   Della Architectura militare   £6 10 0

Francesco MARCHI, Della architettura militare ... libri tre. Nelli quali si descrivono li veri modo, forticare, che si usa a' tempi moderni, Brescia, 1599   folio

77.   Mercators maps in colours   £8 00 0

Gerardus MERCATOR, Atlas ; or, a Geographicke description of ... the world ... represented by new and exact maps. Translated by H. Hexham, 2 vols. in 1, Amsterdam, 1636-38 ; 1641   folio
First edition in latin : Dusseldorf, 1602

(STC : 17827-17828)

78.   Jon: Buxtorfij Concordantiae Hebraicae   £1 15 0

Johannes BUXTORFIUS the Elder, <u>Concordantiae Bibliorum Hebraice, nova et artificiosa methodo dispositae</u>, Basle, 1632   folio

(DS, chapter VI, <u>passim</u>)

79.   Aristotelis opera omnia Graecae et lat   £2 04 0

ARISTOTLE, <u>Opera Omnia</u>, 2 vols. in 1 (?), Lyons, 1590 ; Orleans, 1605 ; Paris, 1619 ; 1629 ; 1639 ; 1654   folio **Greek and latin** (all 2 vol. editions).

80.   Senecae opera omnia p(er) Lipsium   £1 08 0

Lucius Annaeus SENECA, <u>Opera, quae exstant omnia, a Justo Lipsio emendata et scholiis illustrata</u>, Antwerp, 1605 ... 4th ed., Antwerp, 1652   folio

(AE, pp.35,36,55,87,88,89,93,94,108 ; DS, p.13)

81.   Ariae Montani Biblia Hebraica   £2 10 0

Benedictus ARIAS MONTANUS, <u>Biblia Hebraica</u>, Antwerp, 1584 ; Geneva, 1609 ; 1619 ; Leipzig, 1657   folio

(DS, pp.22,84,92,93 & chapter VI, <u>passim</u> ; M, pp.2,147,148)

82.   Sti: Bernardi opera omnia   £2 15 0

Saint BERNARD, Abbot of Clairvaux, <u>Opera Omnia</u>, Paris, 1513   folio Numerous later editions in folio.

83.   Conr: Gesneri Historia animalium (3 vols)   £6 10 0

Conrad GESNER, <u>Historia animalium, cum iconibus certis suis coloribus distinctis</u>, 3 vols., Zurich, 1551-58   folio

(DS, p.22)

84.   Petr: Andraeae Mathioli opera omnia   £2 15 0

Pietro Andrea MATTIOLI, <u>Opera quae extant omnia ; hoc est, Commentarii in VI. libros P. Dioscoridis ... de medica materia</u>, Frankfurt, 1598 ; Basle, 1674   folio

(M, pp.1,28 ; reference to 1598 edition)

85.   Les oeuvres Dr Ambrose Pare   £1 02 6

Ambroise PARÉ, <u>Les Oeuvres</u>, Paris, 1575 ... 12th ed., Lyons, 1664   folio

(DS, pp.89-90,264 ; M, p.362)

86. P: Virgilij opera omnia per Jac: pontanum   £2 05 0

**Publius VIRGILIUS MARO, Symbolarum libri XVII, quibus
Bucolica, Georgica, Aeneis declarantur** (ed. Jacobus
Pontanus), Augsburg, 1599   folio

87. Cetij de mineralibus lib   £0 14 0

**Bernardus CAESIUS, Mineralogia, sive Naturalis philosophiae
thesauri**, Lyons, 1636   folio

(M, pp.30,86,129)

88. Hieronom: Zanchij opera   £0 18 0

**Hieronymus ZANCHIUS, Omnium operum theologicorum tomi
octo**, 3 vols., Geneva, 1599 ; Heidelberg & Geneva?,
1613   folio
Presumably volume 1 only, since all references below are
to Tomes 1-3, i.e. volume 1.

(DS, pp.150,208,223,224-225,228,238)

89. Hier: Zanchij tratationum Theologicarum   £0 13 4

Hieronymus ZANCHIUS, Tractationum theologicarum volumen,
Neustadt, 1597   folio

90. D: Epiphanij opera   £0 18 0

**Saint EPIPHANIUS, D. Epiphanii contra octoaginta haereses
opus ... Omnia**, Basle, 1543 ; 1545 ; Paris, 1566   folio

91. Jo: Calvini tractatus theologici omnes   £0 13 4

**Jean CALVIN, Tractatus theologici omnes. His accesserunt
eiusdem In libros Senecae de clementia commentarij** (ed.
Théodore de Bèze), Geneva, 1576 ; 2nd ed., Geneva, 1597 ;
3rd ed., Geneva, 1611   folio

92. D: Augustini de Civitate Dei   £0 15 0

Saint AUGUSTINE, Bishop of Hippo, De Civitate Dei,
Rome, 1467   folio
Numerous subsequent editions in folio.

(DS, pp.18,83,87-88,142,184,219)

93. Origenis opera omnia (2 vols)   £1 10 0

ORIGEN, Opera, 2 vols., Paris, 1512 ; 1522 ; Basle, 1536 ;
1545 ; 1571 ; Paris, 1574-72   folio

(M, p.9)

94.   Corneli taciti opera cum comentarijs   £0 10 0

Publius Cornelius TACITUS, Opera quae extant, ex J. Lipsii editione ultima : et cum ejusdem ad ea omnia commentariis, Antwerp, 1585 ; 1589 ; 1600 ; 1607   folio

95.   Xenophontis opera omnia graece et lat   £1 08 0

XENOPHON, Opera quae quidem extant, omnia tam Graeca quam Latina, Basle, 1545 ; 1555 ; Geneva, 1561 ; Basle, 1569 ; 1572   folio

96.   Centuriae Magdeburgensis volumina (2 vols)   £1 10 0

Matthias FLACIUS Illyricus, Historiae Ecclesiasticae Volumen Primum (−Secundum), 2 vols, Basle, 1624   folio (Containing Centuries I–IX of the collection more popularly known as the **Magdeburg Centuries**.)

97.   Caroli Sigonij historia de rebus Bononibusibus(sic) £0 15 0

Carlo SIGONIO, Historia de rebus Bononiensibus libri VIII., Frankfurt, 1604   folio

98.   Caroli Sigonij historia Italicae   £0 18 0

Carlo SIGONIO, C. Sigonii historiarum de regno Italiae libri quindecim, Venice, 1574 ; Frankfurt, 1575 ; Bologna, 1580.   Revised and enlarged (**... libri viginti**), Frankfurt & Venice, 1591 ; Hanover, 1613   folio

99.   Uberti ffoliete historia Genuensium   £0 10 0

Uberto FOGLIETTA, Historiae Genuensium libri XII, Genoa, 1585   folio

100.   Plutarch de vita Graecorum et Romanorum   £0 08 6

PLUTARCH, Plutarchi ... Graecorum Romanorumque illustrium vitae, Venice, 1538 ; Basle, 1552 ; Paris, 1558 ; Basle, 1564 ; 1573   folio

(DS, p.55)

101.   Josephi opera omnia latine   £0 12 0

Flavius JOSEPHUS, Opera, Augsburg, 1470 ... Frankfurt, 1580   folio

(DS, p. 84)

102.   Academie ffrancoyse   £0 13 4

**Pierre de LA PRIMAUDAYE, Academie Françoise. En laquelle
il est traicté du l'institution des moeurs & de ce qui
concerne le bien & heureusement vivre en tous estats &
conditions**, Paris, 1577 ; 3rd ed., Paris, 1581   folio

103.   Les Croniques et Annales de france   £0 12 6

**Nicole GILLES, Les chroniques et annales de France ...
continuées par D. Sauvage ... à present reveues, corrigées
et augmentées ... jusqu'au roy Charles neufième ... par
F. de Belleforest**, Paris, 1573*   folio
(* nb. Earlier editions appeared under slightly different
titles, the first at Paris, 1534).

104.   Appiani Alexandri historia   £0 08 0

APPIAN of Alexandria, Appiani ... Romanorum historiarum,
Venice, 1472 ; Paris, 1538 ; Basle, 1554   folio

105.   Amadis de Gaule Gallicae   £0 11 0

**AMADÍS de Gaula, Le premier (–dixiesme) livre de Amadis de
Gaule, ... Traduict nouvellement d'Espagnol en Francoys par
le Seigneur des Essars Nicolas de Herberay**, Paris, 1540–42
folio
Books 1–5, 7 and 9 from the original Spanish edition.

---

f2v

106.   Historia de las guerras de flandes (2 vols)   £1 00 0

**Antonio CARNERO, Historia de las Guerras Civiles, que ha
avido en los estados de Flandes des del año 1559 hasta el
de 1609, y las causas de la rebellion de dichos estados,**
originally published in 1 volume ; split and rebound in
two, Brussels, 1625   folio

107.   Historia de Mexico Hispanice   £0 16 0

**Francisco LOPEZ DE GÓMARA, La Istoria de las Indias, y
Conquista de Mexico**, Saragossa, 1552 ; Medina del Campo,
1553 ; Saragossa, 1554   folio

108.   Annales de flandes   £0 10 0

Emanuel SUEIRO, <u>Anales de Flandes</u>, 2 vols. in 1,
Antwerp, 1624   folio

109.   A large Church Bible (folio)   £2 10 0

110.   Photij Bibliotheca   £1 10 0

Saint PHOTIUS, Patriarch of Constantinople, <u>Photii
Bibliotheca : sive lectorum a Photio librorum recensio,
censura atque excerpta philologorum, oratorum,
historicorum, philosophorum, medicorum, theologorum.
Ex Graeco Latine reddita, scholiisque illustrata, opera</u>
<u>A</u>(ndreae) <u>Schotti</u>, Augsburg, 1606   folio

111.   The Turkish history   £1 06 0

Richard KNOLLES, <u>The Generall Historie of the Turkes from
the first beginning of that Nation to the rising of the
Othoman Familie ... Together with the lives and conquests
of the Othoman Kings and Emperours</u>, London, 1603 ...
London, 1638 (5th ed., updated)   folio

(STC : 15051-15055)

112.   Voiage faict pors oliver du Noort   £0 02 0

Olivier van NOORT, <u>Description du penible Voyage faict
entour de l'Univers ou Globe terrestre par O. du Nort
.... Le tout translaté du Flamand en Franchois</u>,
Amsterdam, 1602 ; 1610   folio

113.   Diodori Siculi opera   £0 12 0

Siculus DIODORUS, <u>Opera</u>, Bologna, 1472   folio
Numerous later editions in folio.

(M, pp.9,19-20,139,268)

114.   Petr: Justiniani historia Venetarum   £0 09 0

Petrus JUSTINIANUS, <u>Rerum Venetarum ab urbe condita
historia</u>, Venice, 1560 ; 1576 ; Strassburg, 1610, 1611
folio

115.   The workes of the Geofrey Chaucer   £0 14 0

Geoffrey CHAUCER, <u>The Workes of Geoffray Chaucer</u>, London,
1532 ... London, 1602   folio

(STC : 5068-5081)

17

116. Dr: Brownes Vulgar Errors   £0 07 0

**Sir Thomas BROWNE, Pseudodoxia epidemica : or,
Enquiries into very many received tenents, and
commonly presumed truths**, London, 1646 ; 2nd ed.,
enlarged, London, 1650 ; 3rd ed., London, 1658 ; another
ed., London, 1659   folio

(DS, pp.59,183 ; STC : B5159-B5163)

117. Titi livij opera cum commentarijs   £1 02 0

**Titus LIVIUS Patavinus, Historiae Romanae ... libri XLV
... Cum commentariis**, Paris, 1573   folio

118. The history of the Councell of trent   £0 18 0

**Paolo SARPI, The Historie of the Councel of Trent ...
translated ... by Nathaniel Brent**, London, 1620 ; 2nd
ed., London, 1629 ; 3rd ed., London, 1640 ; another ed.,
London, 1676   folio

(STC : 21761-21763 ; S696)

119. Pauli Jovi historia   £1 02 0

**Paolo GIOVIO the Elder, Historiarum sui temporis tomus
primus (-secundus)**, 2 vols. in 1, Florence, 1550-52 ;
Paris, 1553-54 ; 1558-60 ; 1598   folio

120. Arriani historia Graece et latine   £0 06 8

Flavius ARRIANUS, Ἀρριανου Περι ἀναβασεως Ἀλεξανδρου,
ἱστοριων βιβλια η. **Arriani ... De expedit. Alex.
Magni, historiarum libri VIII**, Geneva, 1575   folio

121. Jo: ffuncij Cronologia   £1 03 0

**Johann FUNCK, Chronologia, hoc est. Omnium temporum et
annorum ab initio mundi usque ad resurrectionem Domini
Nostri Iesu Christi, computatio ... Item commentariorum
liber unus**, Nuremburg, 1545 ; revised and updated,
Königsberg, 1552 ; Wittenberg, 1570 ; 1578 ; 1601 folio

122. Ludovicij descriptio Germaniae Inferiora   £0 18 0

**Lodovico GUICCIARDINI, Omnium Belgii, sive Inferioris
Germaniae regionum descriptio ... ex idiomate Italico
... in Latinum sermonem conversa. Regnero Vitellio
Zirizaeo interprete. Insertis ... tabulis Geographicis.
Adjectisque ... nonnullis additamentis**, Amsterdam, 1613;
1646 ; 1648   folio

123.　Tymes Storehouse　　　　　　　　　　£1 01 0

(Thomas MILLES), Αρχαιοπλουτος. **Containing, ten following bookes to the former Treasurie of Auncient and Moderne Times.** Being the learned Collections, Iudicious Readings, and Memorable Observations ... of ... Pedro Mexia, And M. Francesco Sansovino ... As also ... Anthony du Verdier ... Loys Guyon ... Claudius Gruget, London, 1619　　　　　　　　folio
(Engraved title-page reads "Times Storehouse").

(STC : 17936.5)

124.　The Imperiall history　　　　　　　　£1 00 0

Pedro MEXIA, The Imperial Historie : or, the lives of the Emperours, from Julius Caesar, unto this present yeare ... Translated ... by W. T. and now corrected and continued to these times by E. Grimeston, London, 1623　folio

(STC : 17852)

125　Jo: Stowes Annals of England　　　　　£1 06 8

John STOW, The Annales, or Generall Chronicle of England, begun ... by maister John Stow, and after him continued ... by E. Howes, London, 1615 ; 1631　　folio

(DS, pp.126,245,271 ; STC : 23338 ; 23340)

126.　The history of Venice　　　　　　　　£1 05 0

Paolo PARUTA, The History of Venice ... written originally in Italian, ... likewise the wars of Cyprus ... Made English, by Henry Earl of Monmouth, London, 1658　folio

(STC : P636)

127.　Speeds Cronickle　　　　　　　　　　£1 08 0

John SPEED, The History of Great Britaine under the conquests of ye Romans, Saxons, Danes, and Normans ... from Julius Caesar to our most gracious soveraigne King James, London, 1611 ; 2nd ed., London, 1623 ; 3rd ed., London, 1631 ; "3rd ed.", London, 1650　　　folio

(STC : 23045-23049 ; S4880)

128.　Cambdens Britania　　　　　　　　　　£1 10 0

William CAMDEN, Britain ; or a chorographicall description of England, Scotland and Ireland (trans. P. Holland), London, 1610 ; 1637　　　　folio

(M, pp.19,20,244,280,289,332 ; STC : 4509-4510)

129. Hollingshead Cronickle   £1 07 6

Raphael HOLINSHED, The first volume of the cronicles
of England, Scotlande, and Irelande, conteyning the
description and chronicles of England, London, 1577 ;
3 vol. ed., London, 1587   folio

(DS, pp.271,294 ; M, p.20 ; STC : 13568-13569)

130. Ludolphus de vita Christi   £0 05 0

LUDOLPHUS de Saxonia, Vita Jesu Christi, Strassburg,
1474 ... Lyons, 1642   folio

131. Coccij Sabellici AEneades   £0 15 0

Marcus Antonius COCCIUS Sabellicus, Enneades, Paris,
1513-17 ; Lyons, 1535   folio

132. Hermanni Hugonij Obsidio Breddana   £0 03 6

Hermannus HUGO, Obsidio Bredana armis Philippi IIII.
auspiciis Isabellae ducta A. Spinolae perfecta,
Antwerp, 1626   folio

133. Genealogie et lauriers des Comtes de Nassue   £1 04 0

Jan ORLERS, La genealogie des illustres Comtes de Nassau
... avec la Description de toutes les victoires
lesquelles Dieu a octroiées aux ... Estats des Provinces
Unies du Pais-bas, sous la conduite & gouvernement de
Maurice de Nassau, Leyden, 1615 ; Amsterdam, 1624
folio
(Half-title reads "Genealogie, et lauriers ... des
Comtes de Nassau").

134. Natalis Comitie universae historiae   £1 02 0

Natale CONTI, Natalis Comitis Universae historiae sui
temporis libri triginta ab anno salutis nostrae 1545.
usque ad annum 1581. Cum duobus indicibus Laurentij
Gottij, Venice, 1581 ; Strassburg, 1612   folio
First edition : Venice, 1572, in 4°.

135. Sebastiani Castalioni Biblia   £1 00 0

Sébastien CHÂTEILLON, Biblia, interprete Sebastiano
Castalione. Una cum eiusdem annotationibus, Basle,
1551 ; 1554 ; 1556 ; 1573   folio

(M, pp.2,146)

136. Jo: Chrysostomi tomus quartus   £0 10 0

Saint JOHN Chrysostom, Patriarch of Constantinople,
Opera ... Tomus Quartus (Omnium Divi Pauli Epistolarum
enarrationes), 1st ed., 5 vols., Basle, 1530 ...
Antwerp, 1614   folio

(AE, pp.3,5,11,16 ; DS, pp.53,88,186,223)

137. Oraison militaires et Harangues D'Embassadears
                                               £1 02 0

Francois de BELLEFOREST, Harangues militaires, et
concions de princes, embassadeurs, et autres manians
tant la guerre que les affaires d'Estat ... Recueilles
& faictes Françoyses, par Francoys de Belle-Forest,
Paris, 1572 ; 1588   folio

138. Origenis opera imperfecta   £0 14 0

ORIGEN, Opera (incomplete).   See Item no. 93 above.

139. The Workes of Bishop Jewell   £1 15 0

John JEWEL, Bishop of Salisbury, The Works ... of John
Jewel newly set forth with some amendments of divers
quotations : And a briefe discourse of his life (by D.
Featley), London, 1609 ; 1611   folio

(DS, p.46 ; STC : 14579-14580)

140. Destractorium vitiorum   £0 16 6

ALEXANDER Anglus, Destructorium viciorum, Cologne,
1480 ; 1485 ; Nuremburg, 1496 ; Paris, 1497 ; 1516 ;
1521   folio

141. Lyra sup novum Testamentum   £0 08 0

NICOLAUS de Lyre, Nicolai de Lyra Postilla super Novum
Testamentum, n.p., n.d.   folio

---

f3r

142. Theophilacti opera   £0 06 8

THEOPHYLACT, Archbishop of Achrida, Theophylacti ... in
quatuor Evangelici enarrationes ... Ioanne Oecolampadio
interprete, Basle, 1525 ; Cologne, 1531 ; Basle, 1541 ;
1570   folio

(DS, pp.52,73,100)

21

143.   Dr: Willets Synopsis papismi   £0 10 0

**Andrew WILLET, Synopsis Papismi, that is a generall
viewe of Papistry : wherein the whole mysterie of
iniquitie, and summe of Antichristian doctrine is set
downe, which is maintained this day by the Synagogue
of Rome**, 3rd ed., London, 1600 ; 4th ed., London,
1613 ; 5th ed., London, 1634   folio
First and second editions : London, 1592, 1594 in 4°.

(STC : 25698–25700a.7)

144.   Jo: Viguerij Theologia Scholastica   £0 11 0

**Joannes VIGUERIUS, Ad naturalem et christianam
philosophiam, maxime vero ad scholasticam ... theologiam,
institutiones, sacrarum literarum universaliumque
conciliorum authoritate, necnon doctorum ecclesiasticorum,
praesertim d. Thomae Aquinatis eruditione confirmatae,**
Paris, 1554 ; 1558 ; Antwerp, 1558 ; 1565 ; Lyons,
1571 ; Antwerp, 1572   folio

145.   The booke of homilies   £0 06 0

CHURCH OF ENGLAND, Certain Sermons or Homilies, London,
1623 ; 1633, 1635 ; 1640   folio

(STC : 13659–13662 ; 13675–13677)

146.   Pelacheri analysis tipyca   £0 06 0

**Moses PFLACHER, Analysis typica omnium cum veteris tum
novi Testamenti Librorum Historicorum**, Basle, 1587
folio

147.   Missale (folio)   £0 05 0

148.   Rodulphi Gualteri in Epist: ad Corintios   £0 06 8

**Rudolph WALTHER, In posteriorem D. Pauli Apostoli ad
Corinthios Epistolam homiliae**, Zurich, 1572 ; 1578 ;
1588   folio

149.   Dr: Cirilli Alexandrini tomus secundus et tertius
        £0 12 0

**Saint CYRIL, Patriarch of Alexandria, Opera ... Tomus
Secundus et Tertius**, 2 vols. in 1, 1st ed., 4 vols.,
Basle, 1546 ; another ed., 5 vols., Basle, 1566 folio

150.   D: Jac: Pares de volentia opera   £0 10 0

      Jacobus PEREZ DE VALENCIA, Commentaria in Psalmos,
Valencia, 1484 ; 1486 ; Barcelona, 1506 ; Paris, 1509 ;
1518 ; 1521 ; 1533   folio

151.   D: Augustini in Psalmos   £0 10 0

      **Saint AUGUSTINE, Bishop of Hippo, Divi Aurelii
Augustini Psalmorum explanatio**, Basle, 1489 ; Venice,
1493 ; Basle, 1497 ; Lyons, 1519 ; Paris, 1529 ;
Antwerp, 1662   folio

      (AE, p.4 ; DS, pp.19,77)

152.   An ould lattin bible (folio)   £0 05 6

153.   A peece of St: Austins workes   £0 02 6

      Part of an unidentified work by **Saint AUGUSTINE, Bishop
of Hippo**, in folio.

154.   Sleidanes Comentaryes   £0 08 0

      **Joannes PHILIPPSON Sleidanus, A Famous Cronicle of oure
time, called Sleidanes Commentaries, concerning the
state of Religion and common wealth, during the raigne
of the Emperour Charles the fift ... Translated out of
Latin into Englishe, by John Daus**, London, 1560   folio

      (STC : 19848)

155.   Part of Dr: Luthers workes in 2 vollumes   £1 08 0

      Part of an unidentified work by **Martin LUTHER** in two
volumes (folio).

156.   Mr: Calvines sermons upon Dutronomie   £0 11 6

      **Jean CALVIN, The Sermons of M. Iohn Calvin upon the
fifth booke of Moses called Deuteronomie ... Translated
out of French by Arthur Golding**, London, 1583   folio

      (STC : 4442-4443)

157.   A peece of ye workes of Gregorie Nazianzene   £0 02 0

      Part of an unidentified work by **Saint GREGORY of
Nazianzus, Patriarch of Constantinople**, in folio.

158.   Petr: Comestoris historia Scholastica   £0 08 0

      PETRUS Comestor, Historia Scholastica, Strassburg,
1470?   folio
Numerous subsequent editions in folio.

159. Bishop Babingtons workes   £0 15 0

**Gervase BABINGTON, Bishop of Llandaff, Exeter &
Worcester, The Workes of the Right Reverend Father in
God Gervase Babington**, London, 1615 ; 1622 ; 1637
folio

(STC : 1077-1080)

160. Erasmus upon ye 4 Evangalists & ye Acts   £0 08 6

**Desiderius ERASMUS, The first (-second) tome or volume
of the Paraphrase of Erasmus upon the newe testamente**
(trans. N. Udall), London, 1548, 1549 ; 1551, 1552
folio

(STC : 2854 ; 2866)

161. A peece of Tho: Aquinas summus (folio)   £0 02 6

Part of **Saint THOMAS Aquinas, Summa Theologica**.   See
Item no. 31 above.

"Upon ye 2d & lower Shelves in ye further Chambr:"

162. Martins Cronickle   £0 05 6

**William MARTYN, The Historie, and Lives, of twentie
Kings of England**, London, 1615 ; 1628 ; 1638   folio
(STC : 17526-17529)

163. The Surgions Mate   £0 13 6

**John WOODALL, The Surgeons Mate ; or, military &
domestique surgery**, London, 1639 ; 1655   folio
First edition : London, 1617, 4°.
(STC : 25963 ; W3421)

164. Remalinis Anathomie   £0 16 0

**Johann REMMELIN, A survey of the microcosme. Or the
anatomie of the bodies of man and woman ... By
Michael Spaher and Remilinus. Englished by John
Ireton**, London, 1675   folio
(nb. The attribution to Spaher is erroneous).

(Not entered in Wing. The above copy is to be found
in the Library of the Wellcome Institute for the
History of Medicine, London).

165.   Chr: Helvici Cronologia   £0 12 0

Christophorus HELVICUS, Theatrum Historicum, sive Chronologiae systema novum aequalibus centuriarum et decadum intervallis, cum assignatione imperiorum, regnorum, ... virorum celebrium ... ita digestum ut universa temporum et historiarum series a mundi origine ad annum 1609, Giessen, 1609 ... Frankfurt, 1666   folio

(STC : Oxford, 1651 and 1662 eds. : H1412–H1413)

166.   Luthers Dutch bible   £0 14 0

Martin LUTHER, Den Bibel, Antwerp, 1532 ; Emden, 1558 folio

(DS, pp. 21,93,111,115,118,211 ; M, pp.147,150)

167.   Historia Ecclesiastica Hispanice   £0 16 0

Almost certainly the following:

Pamphili EUSEBIUS, Bishop of Caesarea in Palestine, Historia dela Yglesia, que Ilamã Ecclesiastica y tripartita, Coimbra, 1554   folio
(A Spanish edition of Eusebius' **Historia Ecclesiastica**).

There are at least three other works, however, which fit the catalogue description:

       (a) **Alonzo FERNÁNDEZ, Historia Ecclesiastica de nuestros tiempos**, Toledo, 1611   folio
       (b) **Juan de MARIETA, Historia Ecclesiastica de todos los Santos de España**, Cuenca, 1596   folio
       (c) **Francisco de PADILLA, Historia Ecclesiastica de España**, Malaga, 1605   folio

168.   Dr Pordages defence   £0 02 6

John PORDAGE, Innocence appearing, through the dark Mists of pretended Guilt ; or, a full and true narration of the unjust ... proceedings of the Commissioners of Berks ... against J. Pordage of Bradfield, London, 1655   folio

(STC : P2967)

169.   The English Creed by Thomas Rogers   £0 01 6

Thomas ROGERS, Chaplain to Archbishop Bancroft, The English Crede consenting with the true, auncient, catholique and apostolique Church ... The first parte, London, 1585 ; **The second parte**, London, 1587   folio

(STC : 21226–21227)

170.   The workes of Ben: Johnson   £0 08 6

Ben JONSON, The Workes of Beniamin Jonson, London, 1640   folio

(STC : 14751–14754)

171.   Hackluits Voages   £0 06 8

Richard HAKLUYT, The principall navigations, voiages and discoveries of the English nation, made by sea or over land ... within the compass of these 1500 yeares, London, 1589 ; 3 vol. ed., London, 1598–1600   folio

(STC : 12614 ; 12626)

172.   The life & death of Hecter by Jo: Lidgate   £0 03 0

John LYDGATE, The Life and Death of Hector, London, 1614   folio
A modern version by **Thomas HEYWOOD** of Lydgate's original poem.

(STC : 13346a)

173.   The triumphs of Nassau   £0 07 6

Jan ORLERS and Henrik van HAESTENS, The triumphs of Nassau : or, A Description and representation of all the victories ... granted by God to ... the Estates generall of the united Netherlands Provinces. Under ... Prince Maurice of Nassau. Translated out of French by W. Shute, London, 1613   folio

(STC : 17676–17677)

174.   Draytons Poliolbion   £0 06 0

Michael DRAYTON, Poly–olbion, or a chorographicall description of Great Britain, London, 1612 ; **Part 2**, London, 1622   folio

(STC : 7226–7228 ; 7229–7230)

175.   Camerarius Meditations   £0 05 6

Philippus CAMERARIUS, The Walking Librarie, or Meditations and observations historical, natural, moral, political, and poetical ... done into English by Iohn Molle (ed. Richard Baddeley), London, 1621 ; 2nd ed., London, 1625   folio

(DS, pp.69,91 ; STC : 4528–4530)

176.   The Romance of Romants   £0 08 0

**Gilbert SAULNIER, Sieur du Verdier, The Love and Armes
of the Greeke Princes. Or the Romant of Romants.
Written in French by Monsieur Verdere, and translated
for ... Philip, Earle of Pembroke**, London, 1640 folio

(STC : 21775)

177.   Nobillitas Politica by Tho: Milles   £0 10 0

**Robert GLOVER, Nobilitas politica et civilis. Personas
scilicet distinguendi et ab origine inter gentes, ex
Principum gratia nobilitandi forma** (edited from the
manuscript of Robert Glover by Thomas Milles), London.
1608   folio

(STC : 11922)

f3v

178.   The Reception of Lady Eliz   £0 05 6

I have not been able to trace any work in English with
this title.   It is almost certainly a tract relating
to the arrival of Princess Elizabeth, daughter of
James I and wife of Frederick, Elector Palatine, in
Germany following her marriage to the latter in 1613.
This may well be a reference, therefore, to the
following anonymous work published in German with
accompanying coloured illustrations:

**Beschreibung der Reiss ... Volbringung des Heyraths :
und glücklicher Heimführung ... des ... Herrn
Friederichen dess Fünften ... mit der Princessin
Elisabethen ... Mit schönen Kupfferstücken gezieret,**
Heidelberg, 1613   4°

179.   The late warrs of Christendome   £0 08 0

**Count Galeazzo GUALDO PRIORATO, An History of the late
Warres And other state affaires of the best part of
Christendom, Beginning with the King of Swethlands
entrance into Germany, and continuing to the yeare 1640.
Written in Italian ... And in English by ... Henry
Earle of Monmouth**, London, 1648   folio

(STC : G2167)

180.   The Countess of Pembrokes Arcadia   £0 08 6

Sir Philip **SIDNEY**, **The Countesse of Pembrokes Arcadia,**
London, 1593 ... London, 1674 (13th ed.)   folio
First edition : London, 1590, 4°.

(STC : 22540-22550 ; S3768-S3770)

181.   The welcome of Kg: James into Scotland   £0 03 6

John **ADAMSON**, Principal of the University of
Edinburgh, Τα Των Μουσων Εισοδια . **The Muses Welcome**
to the High and Mightie Prince James ... King of Great
Britaine ... at his Majesties happie Returne to his ...
Kingdome of Scotland ... in anno 1617, Edinburgh, 1618
folio

(STC : 140)

182.   The ffrench Cronickle   £0 03 0

I have not been able to trace any work in English with
this title.   Two possible works are suggested: ⸺

      (a) **Philippe de COMINES, The historie of Philip de**
de Comines (trans. Thomas Danett), London, 1596 ; 1601 ;
1614 ; 1674   folio
      (b) **Jean de SERRES, A general inventorie of the**
History of France (trans. E. Grimeston), London, 1607 ;
1611 ; 1624   folio

183.   Edmonds observacons upon Caesars comentaries   £0 08 6

Clement **EDMONDES, Observations upon the five first**
bookes of Caesars Commentaries, London, 1600 ; 1604 ;
1609 ; 1655 ; 1677   folio

(STC : 7488-7492 ; C199-C200)

184.   A revew of ye Councell of trent   £0 07 0

Guillaume **RANCHIN, A review of the Councell of Trent ...**
First writ in French by a learned Roman Catholique ...
Now translated ... by G. L(angbaine), Oxford, 1638
folio

(STC : 20667)

185.   Herberts and Sands travailes   £0 18 0

Two separate works bound together in 1 volume:

      (a) **Sir Thomas HERBERT, A Relation of some yeares**
travaile, begunne Anno. 1626 into Afrique, and the greater
Asia, especially the Territories of the Persian Monarchie,
and some parts of the orientall Indies, London, 1634 ;
1638 ; 1639 ; 1664 ; 1665 ; 1677   folio

(DS, p.281 ; STC : 13190-13192 ; H1533A-H1536)

(b) **George SANDYS**, <u>Sandys Travailes : containing a</u> <u>history of the originall and present state of the Turkish</u> <u>Empire</u>, 5th ed., London, 1652 ... 7th ed., London, 1673   folio
(Nb. Earlier editions of this work appeared under the title, **A Relation of a Journey begun ... 1610**, London, 1615 ; 1621 ; 1627 ; 1632 ; 1637, all in folio).

(STC : 21726-21730 ; S677-S680)

186.   Annales of England by ye Bishop of Hereford   £0 06 8

Francis GODWIN, Bishop of Llandaff and Hereford, <u>Annales</u> <u>of England ; containing the Reignes of Henry the Eighth,</u> **Edward the Sixt, Queene Mary. Written in Latin ...** <u>Englished, corrected and inlarged ... by M</u>(organ) <u>Godwyn</u>, London, 1630   folio

(STC : 11947)

187.   Polexander   £0 10 0

Marin LE ROY, Sieur de Gomberville, <u>The History of</u> <u>Polexander Done into English by W. Browne</u>, London, 1647 ; 1648   folio

(STC : G1025-G1026)

188.   Of ye interchangable variety of things   £0 02 0

Louis LE ROY, <u>Of the interchangeable course or variety</u> <u>of things in the whole world, and the concurrence of</u> <u>Armes and Learning through the first and famousest</u> <u>nations from the beginning of Civility, and the Memory</u> <u>of Man, to this present ... Written in French ...</u> <u>translated ... by R</u>(obert) <u>A</u>(shley), London, 1594 folio

(STC : 15488)

"Mathematicall bookes"

189.   A new booke of Mapps   £0 02 6

Thomas JENNER, <u>A new booke of mapps exactly describing</u> <u>Europe both the present ... and auncient state thereof</u>, London, 1645?   folio

(STC : J667A)

190.   Andreae Schoneri Gnomonice   £0 04 0

Andreas SCHOENER, <u>Gnomonicae ... hoc est : De</u> <u>descriptionibus horologiorum sciotericorum omnis generis</u> <u>... libri tres</u>, Nuremburg, 1562   folio

191. Musters(sic) Cosmographie ffrench   £0 18 0

Sebastien MUENSTER, La Cosmographie Universelle,
contenant la situation de toutes les parties du monde
avec leurs proprietez & appartenances, Basle, 1552 ;
1556 ; 1565 ; Paris, 1575   folio

(M, p.38)

192. Thaumaturgus opticus   £1 03 0

Jean François NICERON, Thaumaturgus Opticus, seu
Admiranda Optices, ... Catoptrices, ... et Dioptrices
Pars prima, Paris, 1646   folio

(DS, p.268)

193. Ismaelij Bulialdi Astronomia Philolaica   £1 04 0

Ismael BOULLIAU, Astronomia Philolaica.   Opus novum,
in quo motus planetarum per novam ac veram hypothesim
demonstrantur ... Superque illa hypothesi tabulae
constructae omnium quotquot hactenus editae sunt,
facillimae, Paris, 1645   folio

194. Venationes ferrarum, avvium, pisium(sic), etc £0 12 0

Jan van der STRAET, Venationes Ferarum, avium, piscium,
pugnae bestiariorum et mutuae bestiarum.   Depictae a
J. Stradano, editae a P. Gallaeo, carmine illustratae a
C. Kiliano, Antwerp, 1566? ; 1630   folio

195. ffran: Vietae Algebra nova   £0 06 8

Franciscus VIETA, Opus restitutae mathematicae analyseos,
seu Algebra nova, Paris, 1624   folio

196. Jo: Regiomontani de triangulis etc   £0 16 0

Johann MUELLER Regiomontanus, De Triangulis omnimodis
libri quinque.   Accesserunt ... Nicolai Cusani de
quadratura circuli ... Omnia recens in lucem edita (per
J. Schoener), Nuremburg, 1533 ; later eds (ed. D.
Santbech), Basle, 1541 ; 1561   folio

197. Guidi Ubaldi perspectivae lib 6   £0 13 4

Guidubaldo de MONTE, Perspectivae libri sex, Pesaro,
1600   folio

198. Alhazeni et vitelonis opera optica   £2 00 0

HASAN IBN HASAN, called Ibn Al-Haitham, <u>Opticae</u>
<u>Thesaurus Alhazeni Arabis libri septem nunc primum editi.</u>
<u>Eiusdem libri de Crepusculis et Nubium ascensionibus ...</u>
<u>Item Vitellonis Thuringopoloni libri X. (de Optica).</u>
<u>Omnia instaurati, figuris illustrati & aucti, adjectis</u>
<u>etiam in Alhazenum commentariis a F. Risnero</u>, Basle,
1572   folio

199. Jo: ffernelij de proportionibus lib   £0 02 6

Joannes FERNELIUS, <u>De proportionibus libri duo. Prior,</u>
<u>qui de simplici proportione est, et magnitudinem et</u>
<u>numerorum ... rationes edocet.   Posterior, ipsas</u>
<u>proportiones comparat: earumque rationes colligit</u>,
Paris, 1528   folio

200. Euclid in English wth: Billingsleys annotations &
      Dr: Dees notes   £2 15 0

EUCLID, <u>The Elements of Geometrie of</u> ... <u>Euclide</u> (Books
1-15) <u>now first translated into the Englishe toung, by</u>
<u>H. Billingsley</u> ... <u>Whereunto are annexed certaine ...</u>
<u>annotations ... of the best Mathematiciens ... With a</u>
<u>preface ... by M. J. Dee</u>, London, 1570   folio

(AE, pp.20,51,56 ; DS, p.7 ; STC : 10560)

201. ffrederici Commandini Comentaria in Pappi
      Alexandrini etc   £1 10 0

PAPPUS of Alexandria, <u>Pappi Alexandrini Mathematicae</u>
<u>Collectiones</u> (Books 3-8) <u>a F. Commandino Urbinate in</u>
<u>Latinum conversae, et commentariis illustratae</u> (ed.
V. Spacciuoli), Pesaro, 1588 ; Venice, 1589 ; Pesaro,
1602 ; Bologna, 1660   folio

202. Jon: Baptist Benedicti Speculationum lib   £0 16 0

Giovanni Battista BENEDETTI, <u>Diversarum speculationum</u>
<u>mathematicarum, & physicarum liber</u>, Turin, 1585 ; Venice,
1586 ; 1599   folio
(Nb. The 1599 edition was simply entitled <u>Speculationum</u>
<u>liber</u>).

(AE, p.52)

203. La Practica perspectiva   £0 06 8

Daniello BARBARO, Patriarch of Aquileia, <u>La Pratica</u>
<u>della perspettiva</u>, Venice, 1568 ; reissued, 1569 folio

204.   Alberti Dureri Geometria   £0 12 0

Albrecht DUERER, A. Durerus ... versus e Germanica
lingua in Latinam pictoribus, fabris erariis ac lignariis
... prope necessarius, adeo exacte quatuor his suarum
institutionum geometricarum libri lineas superficies et
solida corpora tractavit, Paris, 1532 ; 1534 ; 1535 ;
Arnhem, 1606   folio

205.   Geor: Agricolae de ponderibus lib   £0 12 0

Georgius AGRICOLA the Elder, De mensuris & ponderibus
Romanorum atque Graecorum lib.V., Basle, 1550   folio

206.   Reigles Militaires   £0 12 0

Lodovico MELZO, Reigles militaires du chevalier frère
Luis Melzo ... sur le gouvernement et service
particulier et propre de la cavalerie, traduits
d'Italien en françois par Paul Varroy, Antwerp, 1615
folio

207.   Guidi Ubaldi mechanicorum lib   £0 14 0

Guidubaldo del MONTE, Mechanicorum liber, Pesaro,
1577 ; Venice, 1615   folio

208.   Artillerie per Dego Ufano Gallice   £0 16 0

Diego UFANO, Artillerie, c'est à dire, vraye
Instruction de l'artillerie et de toutes ses
Appartenances.   Avec un enseignement de preparer
toutes sortes des feux artificiels. ... Le tout ...
publié en langue Espagnolle ... traduit ... & orné de
... figures par J. T. de Bry, Frankfurt, 1614 ;
Zutphen, 1621 ; Rouen, 1628   folio

209.   L'art militaire per Jean Jaques   £0 14 0

Johann JACOBI of Wallhausen, L'art militaire pour
l'infanterie ... le tout representé par belles figures
descrit en ... Allemand par J.J. ... traduit ... en
François (ed. J. T. de Bry), Oppenheim, 1615   folio

210.   Archimedii opera per frederic Commandinum £1 15 0

ARCHIMEDES, Archimedis opera non nulla a Federico
Commandino ... nuper in Latinum conversa, et commentariis
illustrata, Venice, 1558   folio

211.   Nicholai Copernici opera   £1 02 0

Nicolaus COPERNICUS, De revolutionibus orbium coelestium,
libri VI., Nuremburg, 1543 ; Basle, 1566   folio

(AE, p.103)

212. Apollonij Pergaei opera   £3 00 0

APOLLONIUS Pergaeus, <u>Opera per doctissimorum</u>
<u>philosophum Ioannem Baptistam Memum ... de Graeco in</u>
<u>Latinum traducta & noviter impressa</u>, Venice, 1537
folio

---

f4r

213. Guidi Ubaldi Equiponderantium lib   £0 13 4

ARCHIMEDES, <u>Guidiubaldi e Marchionibus Montis in duos</u>
<u>Archimedis aequaeponderantium libros paraphrasis</u>
<u>scholijs illustrata</u>, Pesaro, 1588   folio

214. The Surveyor by Aaron Rathborne   £0 05 6

Aaron RATHBORNE, <u>The Surveyor, in Foure bookes</u>,
London, 1616   folio

(STC : 20748)

215. Tho: Digges booke of Geometry   £0 08 0

Leonard DIGGES the Elder, <u>A Geometrical Practise,</u>
<u>named Pantometria ... lately finished by Thomas Digges</u>
<u>his sonne. Who hath also thereunto adioyned a</u>
<u>Mathematicall treatise of the five regulare Platonicall</u>
<u>bodies</u>, London, 1571   4°
(Nb. A later, expanded edition of this work appeared at
London, 1591, in folio. It is not possible to confirm
this edition as the correct one, however, since at this
point in the catalogue the last ten items in this
particular section were all published in quarto).

(STC : 6858-6859)

216. Justi Lipsi de militia Romana   £0 12 0

Justus LIPSIUS, <u>Iusti Lipsi de militia Romana libri</u>
<u>quinque, commentarius ad Polybium</u>, Antwerp, 1595, 1596 ;
1598 ; 1602 ; 1614 ; 1630   4°

217. Jo: Pauli Gallucij Theatrum mundi et temporis £0 10 0

Giovanni Paolo GALLUCCI, <u>Theatrum mundi et temporis,</u>
<u>in quo ... praecipuae horum partes describuntur & ratio</u>
<u>medendi eas traditur ... astrologiae principia cernuntur</u>
<u>ad medicinam accomodata, geographica ad navigationem</u>,
Venice, 1588 ; 1589   4°

33

218.   Jo:(sic) Vietae Apollonius Gallus   £0 02 0

APOLLONIUS Pergaeus, Francisci Vietae Apollonius
Gallus, seu, exsuscitata Apollonii Pergaei Περι
ἐπαφων geometria, Paris, 1600   4°

219.   Modelles Artifices de feu   £0 05 0

Joseph **BOILLOT**, **Modelles, Artifices de Feu, et divers**
Instrumés de Guerre, avec les moyens de s'en prevaloir :
pour assieger, battre, surprendre et deffendre toutes
places, Chaumont, 1598   4°

220.   Euclidis rudimenta musices et optices Theodg
        Sphaebricorum   £0 07 6

Three separate works bound together in 1 volume:

        (a) **EUCLID**, Εὐκλειδου Εἰσαγωγη ἁρμονικη.
Του αὐτου κατατομη κανονος . **Euclidis Rudimenta**
musices. Ejusdem sectio regulae harmonicae. E regia
bibliotheca desumpta, ac nunc primum Graecae et Latine
excusi. I. Pena ... interprete, Paris, 1557   4°

        (b) **EUCLID**, Εὐκλειδου ὀπτικα και κατοπτρικα.
Euclidis Optica et catoptrica, nunquam antehac Graece
aedita : eadem Latine reddita per J. Penam ... His
praeposita est ejusdem J. Penae de usu optices
praefatio, Paris, 1557   4°

        (c) **THEODOSIUS** of Tripoli, Θεοδοσιου Τριπολιτου
σφαιρικων βιβλια γ. **Spharicorum libri tres nunquam**
antehac Graece excusi ... latine reddite per J. Penam,
Paris, 1558   4°

221.   Petr Rami Arithmeticae et Geopeetriae(sic) lib
        £0 05 0

Pierre de **LA RAMÉE**, **P. Rami Arithmeticae libri duo :**
geometriae septem et viginti, Basle, 1569 ; 1580 ;
Frankfurt, 1599 ; 1627   4°

(DS, p.344)

222.   ffl: Vegetij cum alijs de re militari lib   £0 12 0
Flavius **VEGETIUS RENATUS**, **De re militari**, Utrecht,
1475?   4°
Numerous subsequent editions were published in quarto,
all including works by other authors.

223.   Chr: Chavij(sic) Geometria practica   £0 06 0
Christophorus **CLAVIUS**, **Geometria practica**, Rome, 1604 ;
Mainz, 1606   4°

224.   ffrancisci Junctini Astrologia   £0 07 6

Francesco GIUNTINI, Speculum Astrologiae, quod
attinet ad iudicarum rationem nativitatum atque annuarum
revolutionum : cum nonnullis astrologorum sententiis,
Lyons, 1573   4°

225   Le Capitainie   £0 01 6

Girolamo CATANEO, Le Capitaine ... contenant la
maniere de fortifier places, assaillir, & defendre ...
Le tout reveu, corrigé, & augmenté en plusieurs lieux
par l'auteur, & depuis mis en françois (by Jean de
Tournes), Lyons, 1574 ; 1593   4°

SECTION B

"Libri de varijs subjectis in fol
minore vel in quarto maximo"

(Most of the items in this section
fall into the latter category)

226.   Les Estates Empires principaute du monde   £0 16 0

(Pierre d'AVITY), Les Estats, empires et principautez
du monde : representez par la description des pays,
moeurs des habitans, richesses des provinces, les forces,
le gouvernement, la religion, et les princes qui ont
gouverné chacun estat ... Par le Sr. D.T.V.Y., Paris,
1619 ... Rouen, 1649   4°
This work first appeared under a different title at St.
Omer in 1614 (4°).   There were also numerous editions
published in folio : Paris, 1625 ; 1635 ; 1655 ;
Geneva, 1655 ; Lyons, 1659.

227.   Les Oeuvres de Lutian de Samosate Autheur Grec
       £0 14 0

LUCIAN of Samosata, Les Oeuvres de Lucian de Samosate
autheur grec, de nouveau traduites en françois et
illustrées d'annotations et de maximes politiques en
marge par J(ean) **B**(audoin), Paris, 1613   4°

228.   Osiandri(sic) Strategicus cum Nic Rigaltio   £0 04 0

ONOSANDER, Ὀνασάνδρου Στρατηγικος. Onosandri
Strategicus, sive de Imperatoris Institutione.
Accessit Οὐρβικιου Ἐπιτηδευμα.N. Rigaltius nunc
primum ... Latina interpretatione et notis illustravit,
Paris, 1598, 1599 ; Heidelberg, 1600 ; 1604 ; 1600,
1605   4°

229. Ritratti di Cento Capitani illustri   £0 08 0

**Aliprando CAPRIOLO, Ritratti di cento capitani
illustri.   Intagliati del Aliprando Capriolo.   Con li
lor fatti in guerra da lui brevemente scritti**, Rome,
1596   4°

230. Salazar de Mendoza ponses de Leon   £0 05 6

**Pedro SALAZAR DE MENDOZA, Cronico de la excellentissima
Casa de los Ponces de Leon**, Toledo, 1620   4°

231. Des Enterprises et Ruses de Guerre   £0 02 6

**Bernardino ROCCA, Des Enterprises et ruses de guerre
et des fautes qui parfois surviennent ès progrès et
exécution d'icelles, ou le Vrai portrait d'un parfait
général d'armée, tiré de l'Italien du sieur Bernardin
Roque, ... par le Seigneur de la Popellinière, Lancelot
Du Voesin**, Paris, 1571   4°

232. Jo: Hen: Alstedij Encyclopaedia in 2 vols   £0 18 0

**Johann Heinrich ALSTED, Cursus philosophici
Encyclopaedia libri XXVII complectens universae
philosophiae methodum, serie praeceptorum, regularum
& commentariorum perpetua**, 2 vols., Herborn, 1620 4°
Later editions in folio : Herborn, 1630 (2 vols) ;
Lyons, 1649 (4 vols).

233. Petr: ffonsaeca in metaphys: Aristotelis   £0 10 0

**ARISTOTLE, Commentariorum Petri Fonsecae in libros
Metaphysicorum Aristotelis tomus primus (–secundus)**,
2 vols. in 1, Rome, 1577, 1580, 1589   4°
All later editions of this work (Greek–Latin) were
published in 2 volumes : Lyons, 1591, 1590 ; Frankfurt,
1599, 1605 ; Cologne, 1615, 1629 (all in 4°).

234. Aristotelis organum per Jul: pacium   £0 10 0

**ARISTOTLE, Ἀριστοτελους Ὀργανον. Aristotelis ...
Organum, hoc est libri omnes ad logicam pertinentes,
Graece & Latine.   Iul. Pacius recensuit : e graeca in
latinam linguam convertit**, Morges, 1584 ; Frankfurt,
1597 (2 vols) ; Geneva, 1605 ; Lyons, 1606 (2 vols) 4°

235. Barth: Keckermanni opera 1 vol   £0 10 0

**Bartholomaeus KECKERMANNUS, Operum omnium quae extant
tomus primus (–secundus)**, 2 vols. in 1, Geneva, 1614
folio

36

236. Jac: Zabarellae de rebus naturalibus libri xxx
£0 04 6

**Count Giacomo ZABARELLA the Elder, De rebus
naturalibus libri XXX quibus quaestiones, quae ab
Aristotelis interpretibus hodie tractari solent ...
discutiuntur**, Cologne & Venice, 1590 ; Treviso,
1604   folio*
(*Nb. All other editions appear to have been published
in quarto : Cologne, 1594 ; 1597 ; 1601 ; 1602 ;
Frankfurt, 1597 ; 1607 ; 1617).

(M, pp.27,357)

237. Collegij Conimbrisensis Comm: in lib Aristot: de anima
£0 03 6

**ARISTOTLE, Commentarii collegii Conimbricensis
societatis Iesu, in tres libros de anima Aristotelis,**
Coimbra, 1598 ... Cologne, 1629   4°
Greek–Latin.

238. Coll Conimbricensis Comm: in lib Arist phisicorum   £0 04 6

**ARISTOTLE, Commentariorum collegii Conimbricensis
societatis Iesu, in octo libros Physicorum Aristotelis
... prima (–secunda) pars,** Coimbra, 1592 ... Lyons and
Cologne, 1625   4°
Greek–Latin.

239. Coll Conimbrisensis comment in 4 lib Arist de celo £0 03 0

**ARISTOTLE, Commentarii Collegii Conimbricensis
Societatis Iesu in quatuor libris de coelo Aristotelis,**
Coimbra, 1592 ... Cologne, 1631*   4°
(*Nb. Some editions of this work also included
Aristotle's **Meteorologica** and **Parva Naturalia**).
Greek–Latin.

240. pindari opera graece et lat   £0 06 8

PINDAR, Πινδαρου 'Ολυμπια. Πυθια. Νεμεα. 'Ισθμια. Μετα
'Εξηγησεως Παλαιας. **Pindari Olympia, Pythia, Nemea,
Isthmia. Adjuncta est interpretatio Latina,** Geneva,
1599 ; Wittenberg, 1616 ; Saumur, 1620   4°

241. ffran: Toleti in lib Phisicorum Arist coment   £0 05 0

**Cardinal Franciscus TOLETUS, Commentaria in octo libros
Aristotelis de Physica Auscultatione. Item, in librum
Aristotelis de Generatione et Corruptione,** Cologne, 1575 ;
1585 ; 1593   4°

242.   Le prince de Balzack   £0 05 6

Jean Louis GUEZ, Sieur de Balzac, Le Prince, Paris,
1631 ; 1632   4°

243.   David: Parei in Epist: ad Rom: coment   £0 06 8

**David PAREUS, Davidis Parei in divinam ad Romanos
S. Pauli Apostoli Epistolam commentarius. Quo ...
antiqua Romanorum fides adversus nunc–Romanistarum
opiniones, praecipue Roberti Bellarmini Jesuitae
argutias, & Thomae Stapletoni Antidota : nec non
Socini, Eniedini, Osterodii haereticorum
Samosatianorum blasphemias vindicatur**, Frankfurt,
1608 ; Heidelberg, 1613 ; 1620   4°

244.   Jo: Cameronis Myrothecium cum alijs   £0 06 0

**John CAMERON, Myrothecium Evangelicum. Hoc est,
Nova Testamenti loca quamplurima ab eo, post aliorum
labores ... vel illustrata, vel explicata, vel vindicata.
Quibus ... adiectum est Lud. Cappelli Spicilegium,
eiusdem argumenti, & Diatribae duae I. De interpretatione
loci Matth. xv. 5. II. De voto lephtae**, Geneva,
1632 ; Saumur, 1677   4°

(DS, p. 178)

245.   Jo: Hen: Alstedij Theol: prophetica. Theol: natural.
Theolog Catechetica. et Theol: Scholastick: Didactica
in 4 vol   £1 04 0

Four separate works (originally published as part of an
8 volume series at Frankfurt, 1614-16) by **Johann
Heinrich ALSTED**:

      (a) **Theologia prophetica, exhibens I. Rhetoricam
ecclesiasticam, in qua proponitur ars concionandi ...
II. Politiam ecclesiasticam**, Hanover, 1622   4°
      (b) **Theologia naturalis exhibens augustissimam
naturalae Scholam ; In qua creaturae Dei commune sermone
ad omnes pariter docendos utuntur ; Adversus atheos,
epicureos, et sophistas huius temporu. Duobus libris
pertractata**, Hanover, 1623   4°
      (c) **Theologia catechetica exhibens sacratissimam
novitiolorum christianorum scholam ... 3 in partes
tributa**, Hanover, 1622   4°
      (d) **Theologia scholastica didactica exhibens locos
communes theologicos methodo scholastica**, Hanover,
1618   4°

246.   Gulielm: Twissi Vindiciae gratiae   £0 08 6

**William TWISSE, Vindiciae Gratiae, Potestatis, ac
Providentiae Dei : hoc est, ad examen libelli Perkinsiani
de Praedestinationis modo est ordine, institutum a J.
Arminio, responsio scholastica, tribus libris absoluta**,
Amsterdam, 1632   4°

(DS, pp.188,189,190)

247.   Paul: Soncinnatis Question: metaphysicae   £0 04 6

Paulus BARBUS Soncinas, Quaestiones metaphysicales,
Ursel, 1622   4°
Earlier editions in folio : Venice, 1498 ; 1526 ;
Lyons, 1579 ; Venice, 1588.

---

f4v

248.   Mar: ffrederici wendelini Contemplation Physicarum
       lib   £0 07 0

**Marcus Frederik WENDELIN, Contemplationum physicarum
sectiones tres**, Cambridge, 1648   4°
First edition : Hanover, 1625, 1628 (8°).

(STC : W1349)

249.   ffranc: Guicciardini la historia D Italia   £0 05 0

**Francesco GUICCIARDINI, La Historia di Italia di M.
Francesco Guicciardini**, Venice, 1563   4°
Numerous subsequent editions in 4°. First edition :
Florence, 1561, in folio.

250.   fflores Theologic: questionum   £0 03 0

**Josephus ANGLES, Flores theologicarum quaestionum in
secundum librum sententiarum**, Madrid, 1586   4°
Later editions, enlarged (**... in quartum librum
sententiarum**), Lyons, 1587 ; 1593   4°

251.   Chr Scheibleri metaphysaca   £0 10 0

**Christoph SCHEIBLER, Metaphysica, duobus libris
Universum hujus scientiae Systema comprehendens,**
Geneva, 1636 ; Marburg & Oxford, 1637 ; Oxford, 1638 ;
Geneva, 1650 ; Giessen, 1657 ; Oxford, 1665   4°
First edition : Giessen, 1622 (8°).

(DS, p.212 ; STC : 21812-21813 ; S853)

252.   Jo: Casi Spaera Civitatis   £0 04 6

**John CASE, Fellow of St. John's College, Oxford,
Sphaera Civitatis**, Oxford, 1588   4°

(STC : 4761)

253. Guilielm: Peraldi Summa virtutum ac Vitiorum £0 07 0

Gulielmus PERALDUS, Summae Virtutum ac Vitiorum,
Brescia, 1494 ... Lyons, 1668   4°

254. De Generibus Carminum gracorum   £0 01 0

Renatus GUILLONIUS, De generibus carminum Graecorum,
Paris, 1548 ; 2nd ed., Paris, 1560   4°

255. Theses Academicae lib 16 in 4to   £0 05 4

256. Augustini mascardi Discorsi morali   £0 04 6

**Agostino MASCARDI, Discorsi morali ... su la Tavola di
Cebete Tebano (La Tavola ... vulgarizata da A.
Mascardi)**, Venice, 1627 ; 1638 ; 1642   4°

257. Suetonij Tranquilli de 12 Caesaribus Gallice cum
Annotat   £0 08 0

**Caius SUETONIUS TRANQUILLUS, Suétone Tranquile. De la
Vie des XII. Césars**, Lyons, 1556 ; Paris, 1569 (trans.
George de la Boutière) ; Paris, 1611, 1616 (trans. anon);
Paris, 1621 (trans J. Baudoin) ; Paris, 1641 ; 1661
(trans. Du Teil)   4°

258. Jo: Rosini Antiquitatum Romanorum lib   £0 10 0

**Joannes ROSINUS, Romanorum Antiquitatum libri decem, ex
variis scriptoribus ... collecti**, Geneva?, 1611 ;
Cologne, 1613 ; 1619 ; Geneva, 1620 ; 1632 ; 1640 ;
Cologne, 1645 ; Leyden, 1663   4°
First edition : Basle, 1583, in folio.

259. Historia universale dell origine et imperio de Turchi
£0 05 0

**Francesco SANSOVINO, Dell' Historia Universale dell'
origine et imperio de' Turchi**, Venice, 1560, 1561 ;
1568 ; 1582 ; 1600 ; 1654   4°

260. Selva rinovata di varia lettione   £0 05 6

**Pedro MEXIA, Selva rinovata di varia lettione di P.
Messia ... di M. Roseo. F. Sansovino divisa in cinque
parti ; dove si leggono historie particolari ... dal
principio del mondo ... aggiuntovi di nuova alcuni
raggionamenti filosofici in dialogo ... con la nuova
seconda selva**, Venice, 1638 ; 1658   4°

261.   Guerre di Germania in 2 vols   £0 05 0

**Pietro POMO, De Saggi d'Historia ... parte prima
(-secunda) in cui si descrivono le attioni seguite
dell' invasione del Re di Suetia in Germania** (running
title : "Guerre di Germania"), Venice, 1640   4°
Two parts, with separate pagination, presumably split
and rebound in two volumes.

262.   Nicho: Causini Symbolica AEgiptiorum Sapientia
£0 06 8

**Nicolas CAUSSIN, De Symbolica AEgyptiorum sapientia
(Polyhistor symbolicus, electorum symbolarum, &
parabolarum historicarum stromata)**, Paris, 1618 ;
1647   4°

263.   Guidon: Pancirolli rerum memorabilium etc   £0 06 8

**Guido PANCIROLI, Rerum memorabilium sive deperditarum
pars prior (posterior)**, Frankfurt, 1629, 1631 ; 1646
(2 vols)   4°
First edition : Hamburg, 1599 (8°).

(DS, p.17 ; M, pp. 248,249,341)

264.   Biblium Haebreum   £0 10 0

A **Hebrew Bible** (in folio or quarto).

265.   Cubus Haebreus   £0 01 6

**Elias HUTTER, Cubus alphabeticus sanctae ebraeae
linguae vel lexici ebraici novum compendium** τετραγωνου,
in tabulas alphabeticas ita digestum, Hamburg, 1588
folio

266.   Historia Cronologica Pannoniae   £0 03 6

**Pannoniae Historia Chronologica : res per Ungariam,
Transylvaniam iam inde a constitutione regnorum illorum
... maxime vere hoc bello gestae**, Frankfurt, 1596 ;
1608   4°
Translated from an anonymous German manuscript by
Johan Adam Lonicer, with drawings by Jacques Boissard.

267.   Rich:(sic) monachi descriptio terrae sancta £0 02 6

**BROCARDUS de Monte Sion, Descriptio Terrae Sanctae et
regionum finitimarum, auctore Brochardo, ... Item
Itinerarium Hierosolymitanum Bartholomaei de Saligniaco**
(i.e. Reinerus Reineccius Steinhemius), Magdeburg,
1587 ; 1593, 1587   4°

268. Hen Ranzovij commentar: bellicus   £0 04 0

Heinrich **RANTZAU**, Governor of Sleswick–Holstein,
**H. Ranzovii ... Commentarius Bellicus ... praecepta,
consilia et stratagemata pugnae terrestris ac navalis,
ex variis ... collecta scriptis, complectens**, Frankfurt,
1595   4°

269. Les Vrais Pourtraits des hommes illustres   £0 02 0

Théodore de **BÈZE**, **Les Vrais pourtraits des hommes
illustres en piete et doctrine**, Geneva, 1581   4°

270. The passenger of Benvenuto Italian   £0 03 6

BENVENUTO Italiano, **Il passagiere, i.e. the passenger,
or dialogues in Italian and English**, London, 1612   4°

(STC : 1895–1896)

271. fflorios second fruits   £0 02 0

John **FLORIO**, **Florios Second Frutes ... To which is
annexed his Gardine of Recreation, yeelding six
thousand Italian Proverbs**, London, 1591   4°

(STC : 11097)

272. Series historiae sacrae et not sacrae   £0 01 6

Franciscus **VERHAER**, **F. Haraei Olympiades et Fasti
concordi serie Historiae Sacrae et non Sacrae usque ad
Christum passum, in quo complentur Septuaginta
Hebdomadae apud Danielem cap. 9 predictae**, Cologne,
1602   4°

SECTION C

"Liber medici et chimesi
cum alijs in 4to: maximo"

**(Primarily books concerned with
medicine, natural philosophy and
alchemy in quarto)**

273. Vita Tichonis Brahei, Nich: Copernici et aliorum
      £0 10 0

Pierre **GASSENDI**, **Tychonis Brahei ... vita ... Accessit
N. Copernici, G. Peurbachii, et Joannis Regiomontani
vita**, Paris, 1654 ; 2nd ed., Hague, 1655   4°

274.   Jo: Veslingij Syntagma Anatomicum   £0 14 0

Joannes VESLINGIUS, Syntagma Anatomicum ... Auctum, emendatum, novisque iconibus ... exornatum, Paris, 1647 ; Padua, 1651 ; Amsterdam, 1666   4°
First edition : Padua & Frankfurt, 1641 (8° and 12° respectively).

275.   opera paracelsi lat 2 vols   £1 02 0

Two volumes of the writings of **Philipp Aureol Theophrast BOMBAST VON HOHENHEIM**, in quarto. I can find no edition of Paracelsus' Works in latin, published in quarto. This may, therefore, be a reference to a two volume edition published at Basle, 1575, in octavo.

276.   Jo: Jac: Weckeri Antidotarium   £0 13 0

Hanns Jacob WECKER, Antidotarium Speciale, ex optimorum authorum ... scriptis fideliter congestum, methodiceque digestum, Basle, 1574 ; 1577 ; 1581, 1585 ; 1595 ; 1601   4°

277.   Nichol: Taurelli medicae praedictionis methodus
£0 06 0

Nicolaus TAURELLUS, Medicae Praedictionis methodus, hoc est recta brevisque ratio coram aegris praeterita, praesentia, futuraque praedicendi, morbos scilicet, morborumque causas, Frankfurt, 1581   4°

278.   Duncani Liddelij oppera medica   £0 13 0

Duncan LIDDEL, Operum omnium Iatro—Galenicorum ... tomus unicus, ... repurgatus, ... notatiunculis aliquot ... illustratus, opera ... L. Serrani, Lyons, 1624   4°

279.   Anselmij Boetij de Boodt Gemmarum et lapidum historia
£0 08 0

Anselmus Boëtius de BOODT, Gemmarum et lapidum historia ... Cum variis figuris, Hanover, 1609   4°

(M, p.225)

280.   Andreae Libavij Alchemia   £0 05 6

Andreas LIBAVIUS, Alchemia ... opera e diversis passim optimorum autorum, veterum et recentium exemplis potissimum ... collecta ... explicata et in integrum corpus redacta, Frankfurt, 1597   4°

(M, pp.12,13,14,31,56,153)

281. Vincentij alsari Crusij Vesuvius ardens   £0 07 0

**Vincenzo ALSARIO DALLA CROCE, Vesuvius ardens, sive
exercitatio medico–physica ad Ριγοπυρετον, id est,
motum & incendium Vesuvij montis,** Rome, 1632   4°

---

f5r

282. Remudi Lillij(sic) arbor scientiae   £0 10 0

**Ramón LULL, Arbor scientiae venerabilis et caelitus
illuminati patris Raymundi Lullii Maioricensis, liber ad
omnes scientias utilissimus,** Lyons, 1515 ; 1635   4°
First edition : Barcelona, 1482, in folio.

283. Pauli Renealmi Specimen historiae plantarum   £0 05 6

**Paul RENEAULME, Specimen Historiae Plantarum ; plantae
typis aeneis expressae,** Paris, 1611   4°

284. Lazari Meysonnerij Pentagonum Phylosoph medicum
£0 08 6

**Lazare MEYSSONNIER, Pentagonum Philosoph.–medicum,
sive Ars nova Reminiscientiae,** Lyons, 1639   4°

285. Jac: Hollerij opera omnia practica   £0 12 0

**Jacobus HOLLERIUS, Omnia opera practica. Doctissimis
eiusdem scholiis ... illustrata : deinde L. Dureti ...
enarrationibus ... et A. Valetii exercitationibus ...
Accessit etiam ... Therapia puerperarum J. Le Bon,**
Geneva, 1623   4°

286. Tho: Whitae Dialogi de mundo   £0 10 0

**Thomas WHITE (called Thomas Blacklow), De mundo dialogi
tres ; quibus materia ... forma, ... caussae, ... et
tandem definitio rationibus pure e natura depromptis
aperiuntur, concluduntur,** Paris, 1642   4°

(AE, pp.45,48,50,78)

287. Angeli Salae opera medico Chimica omnia   £0 10 0

Angelo SALA, Opera medico–chymica quae extant omnia,
Frankfurt, 1647 ; Rouen, 1650   4°

(M, pp.184,333)

288.   Conradi Khunrathi medulla destillatoria et medica
£0 12 0

**Conrad KHUNRATH, <u>Medulla destilatoria et medica. Das
ist, Wahrhafftiger ... Bericht, wie man den spiritum
Vini ... item die Perlen, Corallen, &c. kunstlich
destilleren ... soll item etzlicher herlicher Wundt
Balsam ... Praeparationes ... durch C.L.</u>**, Schleswig,
1594 ; Hamburg, 1601 ; 1605 ; 1621 ; 1623 ; 1638   4°

289.   Tho: Campanellae medicinalium lib   £0 10 0

**Tommaso CAMPANELLA, <u>Medicinalium iuxta propria principia
libri septem</u>** (ed. Jacques Gaffarel), Lyons, 1635   4°

290.   Scipionis Claramontis de universo lib   £0 07 6

Scipione CHIARAMONTI, <u>De Universo</u>, Cologne, 1644   4°

291.   Galilaei Galilaei Systema Cosmicum   £0 07 6

**Galileo GALILEI, <u>Systema Cosmicum ... in quo quatuor
dialogis de duobus maximis Mundi systematibus, Ptolemaico
et Copernicano, utriusque rationibus philiosophicis ac
naturalibus indefinite propositis, disseritur.   Ex
Italica lingua Latine conversum</u>** (ed. M. Berneggerus),
Trier, 1635 ; Lyons, 1641   4°

(AE, p.44)

292.   Gulielm: Gilberti de magnete   £0 07 6

**William GILBERT, <u>Tractatus, sive Physiologia nova de
Magnete, magneticisque corporibus et magno magnete tellure
sex libris comprehensus a Gulielmo Gilberto</u>**, Sedan,
1628 ; Frankfurt, 1629 ; Sedan, 1633   4°
First edition : London, 1600, in folio.

(AE, pp.44,77,106)

293.   P: Alpini de medicina AEgiptiorum et Jac: Bontij de
Indorum medic: £0 13 0

**Prosper ALPINUS and Jacobus BONTIUS, <u>P. Alpini De
medicina Aegyptiorum, libri quatuor, & Jacobi Bontii De
medicina Indorum</u>**, Paris, 1645   4°

294.   Julij Caesari Claudini Responsiones et consultationes
medicinal.   £0 10 0

**Julius Caesar CLAUDINUS the Elder, <u>Responsionum et
Consultationum medicinalium tomus unicus</u>**, Hanover, 1628 ;
Venice, 1646   4°
First edition : Venice & Frankfurt, 1607 (folio and 8°
respectively).

295. Pauli Casati de vacuo lib   £0 06 0

Paolo CASATI, Vacuum proscriptum.   Disputatio physica
... in quâ nullum esse in rerum naturâ vacuum
ostenditur, Genoa, 1649   4°

296. Jo: Chicotij Epistolae et disertationes medicae
£0 07 6

Joannes CHICOTIUS, Epistolae et dissertationes medicae
... Accessit manuductio ad medicinam faciendam, Paris,
1656   4°

297. Dan Sennerti de consensu ac dissensu Chimicorum et
Galenic   £0 06 0

Daniel SENNERTUS, De Chymicorum cum Aristotelicis et
Galenicis consensu ac dissensu liber I, Wittenberg,
1629 ; Paris, 1633 ; Frankfurt & Wittenberg, 1655 4°

298. Petr: Guiffarti de cordu officio lib   £0 04 6

Pierre GUIFFART, Cor vindicatum, seu tractatus de cordis
officio ... Item tractatus de proxima lactis materia,
Rouen, 1652   4°

299. Hieronomi Rubaei de destillationae lib   £0 03 4

Hieronymus RUBEUS, De Destillatione liber In quo
Stillatitiorum liquorum, qui ad medicinam faciunt, methodus
ac vires explicantur ; et chemice artis ventas ratione
et experimento ... comprobatur, Ravenna, 1582 ; Venice,
1604   4°

300. Hieronomi Jordani cum alijs de eo qd divinum est in
morbis   £0 08 0

Hieronymus JORDAN, De eo, quod Divinum, aut supernaturale
est in morbis humani corporis, ejusque curatione liber.
1. Accesit Consilium pro nobili foemina rarissimo cordis
affectu laborante.   2. Morbi D. Joachimo Lager, rari,
admirandi ac plusquam ferini, Veneficio illati, historia.
3. Discursus D. Hermanni Conringii de angelis, Frankfurt,
1651   4°

(DS, p.342)

301. Cesalpinus de mettalis lib   £0 07 0

Andreas CAESALPINUS, De metallicis, libri tres, Rome,
1596 ; Nuremburg, 1602   4°

(M, pp.30,114,235,271)

302. Jo: Lazari Guitterij de fascino lib   £0 06 0

Joannes Lazarus GUTIERREZ, Opusculum de fascino,
Lyons, 1653   4°

(DS, pp.26,79,181,241)

303. Guilielmi Giberti(sic) Phylosophia novo   £0 07 0

William GILBERT, De mundo nostro sublunari
philosophia nova. Opus posthumum, ab authoris fratre
collectum pridem & dispositum, nunc ex duobus mss.
codicibus editum. Ex museo viri per illustris
Guilielmi Boswelli, Amsterdam, 1651   4°

(AE, p.44)

304. ffranc: Oswaldi Grembs arbor integra et ruinosa
hominis   £0 10 0

Franciscus Oswaldus GREMBS, Arbor integra et ruinosa
hominis, id est : Tractatus medicus theoretico-
practicus, Frankfurt & Munich, 1657   4°

305. Gyneciorum lib a diversis Authoribus   £0 07 0

Kaspar WOLF (ed.), Gynaeciorum, hoc est de Mulierum tum
aliis, tum gravidarum, parientium et puerperarum
affectibus et morbis libri veterum ac recentiorum
aliquot, partim nunc primum editi, partim multo quam
antea castigatiores, Basle, 1566 ; 1586 (3 vols) 4°

306. Jo: Danielij Horstij observationes   £0 03 6

Johann Daniel HORST, Observationum anatomicarum decas.
Additae sunt epistolae quibus singularia scitu digna
lactearum nempe thoracicarum, et vasorum lymphaticorum
natura, embryonisque per os nutritio ... exponuntur,
Frankfurt, 1656   4°
First edition : Frankfurt, 1654 (8°).

307. A ternary of paradoxes   £0 03 0

Jan Baptista van HELMONT, A Ternary of Paradoxes of the
Magnetic Cure of Wounds, the nativity of tartar in wine
and the image of God in Man ... translated, illustrated,
and ampliated by W(alter) Charleton, London, 1650 4°

(STC : H1401-H1402)

308. Leonard Phioravvant his secrets & chirurgery wth others
£0 07 6

Leonardo FIORAVANTI, Three exact pieces of L. Phioravant,
... viz. his rationall secrets, and chirurgery, reviewed
and revived ... Whereunto is annexed Paracelsus his one
hundred and fourteen experiments, with certain excellent
works of B.G. à Portu Aquitano, ..., London, 1652 4°

(STC : F953)

309.   Jo: Wieri observaconum medicarum libr   £0 02 0

Johann **WIER, J. Wieri medicarum Observationum rararum liber I. De scorbuto. De Quartana. De pestilentiali angina, pleuritide, & peripneumonia. De hydropsis curatione meatuum naturalium clausorum & quibusdam aliis**, Basle, 1567   4°

310.   Jo: Langij Epistolarum medicinalium libr   £0 03 6

Joannes **LANGIUS**, Physician of Lemberg, **Medicinalium Epistolarum miscellanea**, Basle, 1554 ; 1560   4°

311.   The workes of Mr Jo: Vigo   £0 12 0

Joannes de **VIGO, The whole worke of that famous chirurgion Maister Iohn Vigo : newly corrected ... Whereunto are annexed certain works, compiled and published by Thomas Gale** (eds. G. Baker and R. Norton), London, 1586   4°
First edition : London, 1543, in folio.

(STC : 24723)

312.   Jo: Hartmanius disputationes Chimico medicae   £0 04 6

Johann **HARTMANN**, Prof. of Chemistry at Marburg, **Disputationes chymico–medicae : pleraeque ... ab aliquot medicinae candidatis ... publicae censurae expositae**, Marburg, 1611 ; 1614   4°

313.   Gebri Arabis opera cum alijs multis   £0 06 0

JĀBIR IBN HAIYĀN Al Tarsūsī (called Geber), **In hoc volumine de alchemia, continentur haec : Gebri ... De investigatione perfectionis metallorum ... Summae perfectionis metallorum ... De inventionis veritatis ... De fornacibus construendis ... Item, Speculum alchemiae ... Rogerii Bachonis. Correctorium alchemiae ... Richardi Anglici. Liber secretorum alchemiae Calidis filii Iazichi Judaei. Tabula smaragdina de alchemia. Hermetis Trismegisti. Hortulani ... super Tabulam smaragdinam** (ed. C. Polydorus), Nuremburg, 1541 ; Berne, 1545   4°

(M, frontispiece & pp.74,162,165,180,294,295,373,377)

314.   Hen: Regij ffundamenta Physices   £0 08 0

Henricus **REGIUS**, Prof. of Medicine at Utrecht, **Fundamenta Physices**, Amsterdam, 1646   4°

(AE, pp.78,105 ; DS, p.5)

315. Renati des Chartes opera in 2 vols   £1 01 0

**René DESCARTES, Opera philosophica. Editio secunda ab
auctore recognita (Principia philosophiae – Specimina
philosophiae : seu Dissertatio de methodo)**, 2 vols.,
Amsterdam, 1650   4°

(AE, pp.9,11,85,89,107 ; DS, p.209)

316. Jo: Antonidae vader(sic) linden selecta medica £0 13 0

**Joannes Antonides van der LINDEN, Selecta Medica, et ad
ea Exercitationes Batavae**, Amsterdam, 1656   4°

317. Athanasij Kircheri de arte magnetica lib   £0 16 0

**Athanasius KIRCHER, Magnes ; sive de arte magnetica
opus tripartitum**, Rome, 1641 ; 2nd ed., Cologne, 1643 4°

(AE, pp.77,78 ; DS, pp.28,342)

318. Jo: Baptist: Birelli Alchimia nova Germanicae £0 10 0

**Giovanni Battista BIRELLI, Alchimia nova. Das ist, die
güldene Kunst, oder alter Künsten Gebärerin, sampt dero
heimlichen Secreten ... Auss dem Italienischen ... auff
das fleissigst verteutscht durch Petrum Uffenbachium
... Mit ... Figuren**, Frankfurt, 1603 ; Copenhagen and
Frankfurt, 1654   4°

---

f5v

319. Tractatus varij de Scorbuto   £0 08 0

**Daniel SENNERTUS (ed.), De Scorbuto tractatus. Cui
accesserunt ejusdem argumenti tractatus et epistolae
B. Ronssei, J. Echthii, J. Wieri, J. Langii, S. Alberti,
M.Martini. Editio secunda**, Frankfurt & Wittenberg,
1654   4°
First edition : Wittenberg, 1624 (8°).

320. Chr: Guarinonij rerum memorabilium lib   £0 05 0

**Christophorus GUARINONIUS, Rerum naturalium, memorabilium,
rararum, et maxime scientibilium, libri quatuor. I. De
methodo doctrinarum ; II. De natura humana ; III. De
anima. IV. De animalibus**, Frankfurt, 1606   4°

321.　Marcelli Donati de re medica historia mirabili
£0 11 0

**Marcellus DONATUS of Mantua, De medica historia
mirabili libri sex nunc primum editi**, Venice, 1588 ;
1597　　　　　　　　　　　　　　　　　　　　　4°

(DS, pp.35,325)

322.　Tho: Bartholini Anathomia　　　　　　　　£0 12 0

**Thomas BARTHOLINUS, Prof. of Anatomy at Copenhagen,
Anatomia ... Nuncque iterum ad Circulationem Harvejanam
& Vasa Lymphatica renovata.　Cum iconibus novis &
Indicibus**, Lyons, 1676　　　　　　　　　　　4°
First edition : Leyden, 1641 (8°).　All other editions
would appear to have been published in 8°.

323.　Petr: Jo: ffabri sapientia universalis　　£0 08 6

**Pierre Jean FABRE, Sapientia Universalis quatuor libris
comprehensa.　Videlicet　1. Quid sit sapientia, et de
mediis ad eam perveniendi.　2. De cognitione hominis.
3. De medendis morbis hominum.　4. De meliorandis
metallis**, Frankfurt, 1656　　　　　　　　　4°

324.　Phil: Grulingij fflorilegium Hipocratea Galeno Chymicum £0 07 0

**Philippus GRUELINGIUS, Florilegium Hippocrateo—Galeno—
chymicum novum longe pluris priore auctem in quo
praescribitur plurimorum medicamentorum tum chymicorum
è metallis, mineralibus, & vegetabilibus**, Leipzig,
1644 ; 2nd ed., Leipzig, 1645 ; 3rd ed., Leipzig,
1665　　　　　　　　　　　　　　　　　　　　　4°

325.　Jac: Primrosij de mulierum morbis　　　　£0 06 6

**Jacobus PRIMEROSIUS, De mulierum morbis et symptomatis
libri quinque.　In quibus plurimi tum veterum tum
recentiorum errores breviter indicantur et explicantur**,
Rotterdam, 1655　　　　　　　　　　　　　　　4°

326.　Hen: Petraei Nosologia Harmonica　　　　£0 12 0

**Henricus PETRAEUS of Marburg, Nosologia Harmonica
dogmatica et hermetica : dissertationibus quinquaguita
in ... Academia Mauritania, quae est Marpurgi ...
discepta**, Marburg, 1615, 1616 ; Marburg, 1615, 1623　4°

327.　Joseph: Quercetani opera omnia　　　　　£0 18 0

**Joseph DU CHESNE, Quercetanus redivivus, hoc est, Ars
medica dogmatico—hermetica ex scriptis Josephi
Quercetani tomis tribus digesta ... opera Joannis
Schröderi**, Frankfurt, 1648 ; 1667 ; 1679　　　4°

(DS, p.244 ; M, pp.224,317,318)

328.　Guerneri Rolfincij dissertationes Anatomicae　£0 15 0

Guerner ROLFINCK, Dissertationes anatomicae, methodo synthetica exaratae ... observationibus illustratae, Nuremburg, 1656　4°

329.　Matthiae Untzeri opera omnia　£0 16 0

Matthias UNTZER, Opus Chymico—Medicum, in quo Anatomia Spagirica trium principiorum, nec non corporis humani affectus, ... explicantur, Halle, 1634　4°

(DS, p.245 ; M, pp.314,318)

330.　Jo: Baptist: van: Helmont opera　£0 18 0

Jan Baptista van HELMONT, Ortus Medicinae, Amsterdam, 1648 ; 1652　4°

(AE, pp.10,12,37,65,66,71,75,76 ; DS, pp.17,199-200, 210 and passim ; M, pp. 18,52-53,78,80,169 and passim.

331.　Nichol: Claudij fabritij de Peiresc vita per Petr: Gassendum　£0 05 0

Pierre GASSENDI, Viri illustris N.C. Fabricii de Peiresc ... vita, Paris, 1641 ; Hague, 1655　4°

332.　Michael Majeri Atalanta fugiens　£0 06 0

Michael MAIERUS, Atalanta fugiens ; hoc est, Emblemata nova de Secretis Naturae chymica, accommodata partim oculis et intellectui, figuris cupro vicisis, ... partim auribus ... figuris musicalibus trium vocum, Oppenheim, 1617 ; 1618　4°

333.　Mazzotta de triplici Philosophia　£0 07 6

Benedictus MAZZOTTA, De triplici philosophia, naturali, astrologica et minerali, Bologna, 1653　4°

334.　Michael: majeri Septimana Philosophica　£0 07 0

Michael MAIERUS, Septimana Philosophica, qua Aenigmata Aureola de omni naturae genera a Salomone Israëlitarum ... Rege, et Arabiae Regina Saba, nec non Hyraemo, Tyri Principe, sibi invicem in modum coloquii proponuntur et enodantur, Frankfurt, 1620　4°

335. Duncani Bornetti Iatrochimicus   £0 03 6

Duncanus BURNET, Iatrochymicus, sive de praeparatione
et Compositione medicamentorum chymicorum artificiosa
tractatus Duncani Bornetti ... Studio ac opera Ioannis
Danielis Mylii, Frankfurt, 1616 ; 1621 ; Lucca, 1621
4°

336. Jo: Schroderi Pharmacopoeia medica chymica   £0 10 0

Johann SCHROEDER, Pharmacopoeia medico—chymica ; sive,
Thesaurus pharmacologicus, quo composita quaeque
celebriora, hinc mineralia, vegetabilia & animalia
chymico—medico describuntur, atque insuper principia
physicae Hermetico—Hippocraticae ... exhibuntur, Ulm,
1641 ... Lyons, 1681   4°

(DS, p.158 ; M, pp.88—89,112,121,318,333,349)

337. Michaell: Majeri Symbola aureae mensis   £0 08 0

Michael MAIERUS, Symbola Aureae Mensae duodecim
Nationum. Hoc est Hermea seu Mercurei Festa ab
Heroibus duodenis selectis, artis chymicae usu,
sapientia et authoritate paribus celebrata ; ubi et
artis continuatio et veritas ... 36 rationibus, et
experientia librisque authorum plusquam trecentis
demonstrantur, Frankfurt, 1617   4°

(M, p.15)

338. Tho: Campanellae Prodromus Phylosophiae   £0 01 8

Tommaso CAMPANELLA, Prodromus philosophiae instaurandae,
id est, Dissertationis de natura rerum compendium
secundum vera principia, ex scriptis Thomae Campanellae
praemissum. Cum praefatione ad philosophos Germaniae
(by Tobias Adami), Frankfurt, 1617   4°

339. Mar: Aurelij Severini de venae Salvatellae usu et abusu
      £0 06 0

Marco Aurelio SEVERINO, Seilo—Phlebotomè castigata :
sive de venae salvatellae usu et abusu, Hanover, 1654
4°

340. Roberti fflud monochordum mundi Symphoniacum £0 01 8

Robert FLUDD, Monochordum Mundi Symphoniacum, seu
Replicatio R.F. ... ad Apologiam ... J. Kepleri
adversus demonstrationem suam analyticam nuperrime
editam in qua Robertus validioribus Joannis
objectionibus Harmoniae suae legi repugnantibus,
comiter respondere aggreditur, Frankfurt, 1622   4°

341.   Jo: Guidi de Mineralibus lib   £0 03 6

**Joannes GUIDIUS the Elder, De mineralibus, tractatus
in genere ... opus ... nunc .. prima vice ...
editum** (by J. Guidius the Younger), Venice, 1625 ;
Frankfurt, 1627   4°

342.   Mysterium Sigillorum herbarum et lapidum   £0 04 0

**Israel HIBNER, Mysterium Sigillorum, Herbarum et
Lapidum, oder vollkommene Cur und Heilung aller
kranckheiten Schäden und Leibes–auch Gemüths–
Beschwerungen ... ohne Einnehmung der Artzney**, Erfurt,
1651   4°

(DS, p.158)

343.   Hermanni Conringij de veteri et nova medicina £0 05 0

**Hermannus CONRINGIUS, De Hermetica Aegyptiorum vetere
et Paracelsiorum nova medicina liber unus. Quo simul
in Hermetis Trismegisti omnia, ac universam cum
AEgyptiorum tum chemicorum doctrinam animadvertitur**,
Helmstadt, 1648 ; 2nd ed., Helmstadt, 1659   4°

(M, pp.8,11,13)

344.   Andreae van Berlicom de rerum naturalium gravitate etc
        £0 05 6

**Andreas van BERLICOM, Elementorum de rerum naturalium
gravitate, pondere, impulsu, motu, loco, et motuum,
et actionum caussis, rationibus, ac modis ... libri
XII.**, Rotterdam, 1656   4°

345.   Hermanni Conringij de Calido innato lib   £0 04 0

**Hermannus CONRINGIUS, De calido innato, sive igne
animali liber unus**, Helmstadt, 1647   4°

346.   Jo: Ernesti Burgravij Introductio in vitalem philosophiam
        £0 03 6

**Johann Ernst BURGGRAV, Introductio in vitalem
philosophiam. Cui cohaeret omnium morborum astralium &
materialium ... explicatio atque curatio**, Frankfurt,
1623 ; Hanover, 1643   4°

347.   Jo: Stephani Strobelgeri tractatus novus etc £0 03 0

**Johann Stephan STROBELBERGER, Tractatus novus de Cocco
Baphica, et ... confectionis Alchermis recto usu ...
Cui insertus est L. Catelani genuinus ejusdem confectionis
apparandae modus ... in Latinum sermonem è Gallico ...
conversus. Cum censura et approbatione J. ab Oberndorff**,
Jena, 1620   4°

348.   M: ffriderici Helbachij Olivetum   £0 02 6

Friedrich HELBACH, Olivetum, das ist Kunstbuch,
darinnen gründtlicher und aussführlicher Berricht
gezeigt wird, wie man auss allen Erdtgewächsen,
Metallen, und andern natürlichen dingen, die zwey
edelstenstück in der Artzney, als Oel und Saltz,
nach alchymisticher Arth extrahiren und machen könne,
Frankfurt, 1605   4°

349.   Jo: Baptist portae de destillationibus lib ix £0 03 6

Giovanni Battista PORTA, De Destillationibus libri IX.
Nunc primum in Germania typis evulgati, Strassburg,
1609   4°
First edition (slightly different title) : Rome, 1608
(4°).

350.   Nichol: ffontani observat: rariorum Analecta £0 03 6

Nicolaus FONTANUS, Observationum rariorum analecta,
Amsterdam, 1641   4°

351.   Dodoneus his herball in English   £0 06 0

Rembert DODOENS, A Niewe Herball or historie of plantes
... First set foorth in the Doutche or Almaigne tongue
... nowe first translated ... into English by H. Lyte,
London, 1586 ; 1595   4°
First edition : London, 1578, in folio.

(STC : 6985–6986)

352.   Dr: Reads booke of Anatomy & Chyrurgicall instrumts:
        £0 05 0

Alexander READ, Σωματογραφια ἀνθρωπινη**, or, a**
Description of the Body of Man. With the Practise of
chirurgery and the use of three and fifty instruments
(gathered out of Ambrosius Pareus ... and done into
English ... by H(elkiah) **C**(rooke) **),** London, 1634
large 8°*
(*Nb. There does not appear to have been an edition
published in 4°).

(STC : 20783)

353.   Dr: Reads booke of wounds Tumors & Ulcers   £0 05 6

Two separate works bound together in 1 volume:

        (a) **Alexander READ, A Treatise of the first part**
of chirurgerie ... Containing the methodical doctrine
of wounds : delivered in lectures in the Barber-
Chirurgeons Hall, London, 1638   4°

(STC : 20786)

(b) **Alexander READ**, <u>The Chirurgical Lectures of</u>
<u>Tumors and Ulcers delivered ... in the Chirurgeans Hall</u>
<u>... 1632, 1633 and 1634</u>, London, 1635   4°

(STC : 20781)

354.   Pharmacopoeia Londinensis in fol   £0 03 6

ROYAL COLLEGE OF PHYSICIANS OF LONDON, <u>Pharmacopoea</u>
<u>Londinensis in qua medicamenta antiqua et nova</u>
<u>usitatissima, sedulo collecta, accuratissime examinata</u>
<u>... describuntur. Opera Medicorum Collegii Londinensis</u>,
London, 1618   folio
Numerous later editions in folio, including two English
translations by Nicholas Culpeper (London, 1653 ; 1661).

(STC : 16772-16776 ; R2111)

---

f6r

355.   Jo: Heurni praxis   £0 05 0

Joannes HEURNIUS, <u>Praxis medicinae nova ratio : qua,</u>
<u>libris tribus methodi ad praxin medicam, aditus</u>
<u>facillimus aperitur ad omnes morbos curandos</u>, Leyden,
1587 ; 1590   4°

356.   Antonij Musae et L: Apulei de medicaminibus herbarum lib
£0 02 6

Antonius MUSA, <u>In hoc opera contenta : A. Musae de</u>
<u>herba vetonica liber I, L. Apulei de medicaminibus</u>
<u>herbarum liber I. Per G. Humelbergium ... recogniti &</u>
<u>emendati, adiuncto Commentariolo ejusdem</u>, Zurich, 1537
4°

357.   Hen Smetij miscellania medica   £0 05 0

Henricus SMETIUS, <u>Miscellanea Medica H. Smetii ... cum</u>
<u>quinque medicis ... T. Erasto ... H. Brucaeo ...</u>
<u>L. Batto ... J. Weyero ... H. Weyero ... Communicata,</u>
<u>et in libros XII digesta</u>, Frankfurt, 1611   4°

(DS, p.332)

358.   The Secrets of Alexis compleat   £0 06 0

ALESSIO Piemontese (i.e. Girolamo RUSCELLI), **The Secrets
of Alexis ... Newly corrected and amended, and also
somewhat more enlarged** (Parts 1-5), London, 1615   4°

(STC : 299)

359.   Bakers booke of distillacons   £0 03 6

Conrad GESNER, **The newe jewell of health, wherein is
contayned the most excellent secretes of phisicke and
philosophie ... treating very amplye of all dystillations
... faithfully corrected and published in Englishe, by
George Baker**, London, 1576 ; 1599   4°

(STC : 11798-11799)

360.   Chymiae Collectannea per Janum Lacinium   £0 02 6

Janus Therapus LACINIUS, **Praeciosa ac nobilissima artis
chymiae collectanea de occultissimo ac praeciosissimo
Philosophorum Lapide ... Nunc primum in lucem audita**,
Nuremburg, 1554   4°

361.   The Art of Gardeninge wth many other things by Th: Hill
£0 05 6

Thomas HILL, Londoner, **The profitable Arte of Gardening.
Whereunto is added a treatise of the Arte of graffing
and planting of trees**, London, 1574 ; 1579 ; 1586 ;
1593 ; 1608   4°
First edition : London, 1568 (8°).

(STC : 13493-13497)

362.   Via recta ad vitam longam by Dr: Venner   £0 02 0

Tobias VENNER, **Via recta ad vitam longam, or a plaine
philosophical discourse of the nature ... and effects
of all such things, as by way of nourishments and
dieteticall observations make for the preservation of
health ... Wherein also ... the true use of our famous
Bathes of Bathe is ... demonstrated**, London, 1620 ; 1622 ;
1628 ; 1637 ; 1650 ; 1660   4°

(STC : 24643-24647 ; V195-V196)

363.   4 bookes of husbandry by M: Conradus Heresbachius £0 02 6

Conrad HERESBACH, **Foure Bookes of Husbandry ... Conteyning
the whole arte and trade of Husbandry, with the antiquitie
and commendation thereof. Newly Englished, and increased,
by B. Googe, Esquire**, London, 1577 ; 1579 ; 1586 ; 1596 ;
1601   4°

(STC : 13196-13200)

364. of things bought from the West Indes by Dr: Monardes
£0 02 0

Nicolas MONARDES, Ioyfull Newes out of the newe founde worlde, wherein is declared the rare and singuler vertues of diverse and sundrie Hearbes, Trees, Oyles, Plantes, and Stones ... Also the portrature of the saied hearbes ... Englished by J. Frampton, London, 1577 ; 1580 ; 1596   4°

(STC : 18005-18007)

365. The Breviary of Health by Andrew Boord   £0 01 8

Andrew BOORDE, The Breviary of Helthe ... Expressynge the obscure termes of Greke, Araby, Latyn, and Barbary in to englysh concerning phisicke and cheirurgye, London, 1547 ; 1552 ; 1557 ; 1575 ; 1587 ; 1598   4°

(STC : 3374-3378 ; 1547 edition unnoticed)

366. Dr: Jordan of naturall Bathes   £0 01 6

Edward JORDEN, A Discourse of naturall Bathes, and minerall Waters, ... especially of our Bathes at Bathe in Sommerset-shire, London, 1631 ; 2nd ed., enlarged, London, 1632 ; 3rd ed., much enlarged, London, 1633 4°

(M, pp.20,40,43,44,61 and *passim* ; STC : 14791-14793)

367. The Englishmans Treasure by Tho: Vicery   £0 01 0

Thomas VICARY, The Englishmans Treasure, or Treasor for Englishmen : with the true Anatomye of Mans Body ... Whereunto are annexed many secrets appertaining to Chirurgery ... Also the rare treasor of the English Bathes, ... by W. Turner Gathered and set forth ... by W. Bremer, London, 1585? ... London, 1641 (9th ed.) 4°

(STC : 24707-24712 ; V334 ; 1585? edition unnoticed)

368. The Castle of Health by Tho: Eliot   £0 0 10

Sir Thomas ELYOT, The Castel of Helth gathered and made by Syr Thomas Elyot ... out of the chiefe Authors of Physicke, wherby every manne may knowe the state of his owne body, the preservation of helth, and how to instructe welle his physytion in sycknes that he be not deceyved, London, 1541 ; 1595 ; 1610   4°
First edition : London, 1539 (8°).

(STC : 7644 ; 7656 ; 7657)

369. Magneticall Advertismts: by Wm: Barlow   £0 01 6

William BARLOW, Archdeacon of Salisbury, Magneticall Advertisements : or, divers pertinent observations, and approved experiments concerning the nature and properties of the Load-Stone, London, 1616 ; 2nd ed., London, 1618 4°

(AE, p.77 ; STC : 1442 ; 1444)

370. A Phylosophicall Dialogue   £0 01 4

**Thomas TYMME, A Dialogue Philosophicall. Wherein
Natures secret closet is opened, and the cause of all
motion in Nature shewed out of Matter and Forme ...
Together with the wittie invention of an Artificiall
perpetuall motion** (by Cornelius Drebbel), London,
1612   4°

(STC : 24416)

371. A Defence agst: the plauge   £0 00 8

**Simon KELLWAYE, A defensative against the plague ...
Whereunto is annexed a short treatise of the small
poxe**, London, 1593   4°

(STC : 14917)

372. Cotta contra Antonium   £0 01 6

**John COTTA, Cotta contra Antonium : or, an Ant-Antony
... manifesting Doctor Antony his Apologie for Aurum
potabile, in true and equall ballance of right reason,
to be false and counterfait**, Oxford, 1623   4°

(STC : 5832)

373. Astrologie Theologized   £0 01 0

**Valentin WEIGEL, Astrologie Theologized : wherein is set
forth, what Astrologie, and the light of nature is ;
what influence the stars naturally have on man, and how
the same may be diverted and avoided**, London, 1649 4°

(STC : W1255)

374. Magick & Astrology vindicated   £0 00 8

**Hardick WARREN, Magick and Astrology vindicated from
false aspersions and calumnies**, London, 1651   4°

(STC : W971)

375. Postillion or a new Almanack   £0 01 0

**Paul FELGENHAUER, Postilion, or a New Almanacke and
Astrologicke prophetical prognostication calculated for
the whole world, and all creatures : and what the issue
or event will be of the English warres, and of the Roman
Empire, and that aboundance of calamities is yet to
come**, London, 1655   4°

(STC : A1658)

376.   2 Sermons of Dr: Gells   £0 01 2

Two books of sermons written by **Robert GELL**. Three
such works are listed in Wing:

(a) Ἀγγελοκρατια θεου, **or a sermon touching
Gods Government of the World by Angels**, London, 1650   4°
  (b) **Noahs flood returning, a sermon**, London, 1655   4°
  (c) **Stella nova ... a sermon**, London, 1649   4°

(STC : G468-G468A ; G471 ; G473)

377.   A Common Writeinge   £0 00 6

**(Francis LODOWYCK), A Common Writing : whereby two,
although not understanding one the others language, yet
by the helpe thereof, may communicate their minds one to
another**, London, 1647   4°

(STC : L2814)

378.   Parmacopoeia pinax   £0 00 4

D. GORDON, Apothecary, **Pharmaco-Pinax, or a table and
taxe of the pryces of all usuall medicaments ... in D.
Gordons apothecarie and chymicall shop**, Aberdeen, 1625   4°

(STC : 12070)

379.   A treatise of Blazeinge Starrs   £0 00 6

Fredericus NAUSEA, Bishop of Vienna, **A Treatise of
Blazing Starres in Generall. As well supernaturall as
naturall : to what countries or people soever they
appear in the spacious world** (trans. Abraham Fleming),
London, 1618   4°

(STC : 18413.3-18413.7)

380.   500 points of good husbandry   £0 00 8

**Thomas TUSSER, Five hundreth points of good husbandry
... lately augmented with diverse approved lessons
concerning hopps and gardening, and other needeful
matters, together with an abstract before every moneth,
conteining the whole effect of the sayd moneth**, London,
1573 ... London, 1672   4°

(STC : 24377-24392 ; T3368-T3369)

381.   Rare Inventions   £0 01 2

**John SHAW, Soli gloria Deo. Certaine rare and new inventions
for the manuring and improving of all sorts of ground**,
London, 1636   4°

(STC : 22391.6)

382.   Rogerij Baconis de retardandis senectutis accidentibus
       £0 02 0

       **Roger BACON, De retardandis senectutis accidentibus,
       & de sensibus conservandis ... Item, Libellus Ursonis
       medici, De primarum qualitatum arcanis & effectibus
       Uterq; affixis ad marginem notulis illustratus, &
       emendatus ... operâ Iohannis Williams**, Oxford, 1590   8°*
       (*Nb. I can find no edition of this work in 4°).

       (STC : 1181)

383.   Roger Bacons secret of Alchimye etc   £0 01 0

       **Roger BACON, The Mirror of Alchimy ... With certaine
       other worthie treatises of the like argument** (including
       **The Booke of the Secrets of Alchimie, ... by Galid the
       sonne of Iazich**), London, 1597   4°

       (STC : 1182)

384.   A discourse of ye nature of Episcopacy   £0 01 6

       **Robert GREVILLE, 2nd Baron Brooke, A discourse, opening
       the nature of that episcopacie which is exercised in
       England**, London, 1641 ; 2nd ed., London, 1642   4°

       (STC : B4911-B4912)

385.   Mich: Majeri Lusus serius   £0 02 0

       **Michael MAIERUS, Lusus Serius ; quo Hermes, sive
       Mercurius, Rex mundanorum omnium sub homine existentium,
       post longam disceptationem in Concilio Octovirali
       habitam, ... judicatus et constitutus est**, Oppenheim,
       1616   4°

386.   Martini Biermanni de Magicis actionibus   £0 00 8

       Martinus BIERMANNUS, De magicis actionibus ἐξετασις
       succincta : sententiae Iohannis Bodini ... opposita,
       Helmstadt, 1590 ; Frankfurt, 1629   4°

       (DS, p.26)

387.   Newes out of Yorkeshire   £0 00 4

       **M(ichael) ST(ANHOPE), Newes out of York-shire : or, an
       account of a journey, in the true discovery of a
       soveraigne minerall water ... neere ... Knaresbrough,
       not inferiour to the Spa in Germany**, London, 1627   4°

       (STC : 23228)

388.   Hocus pocus Junior   £0 01 6

**Hocus Pocus Junior. The Anatomie of Legerdemain.
Or the art of iugling set forth in his proper colours**,
London, 1634 ; 1635 ; 1638 ; 1654 ; 1658 ; 1671   4°

(DS, p.270 ; STC : 13543–13544 ; H2279A–H2281A)

389.   ffra: Antonij apologia pro Auro potabili   £0 0 10

**Francis ANTHONIE, Apologia veritatis illucescentis,
pro auro potabili**, London, 1616   4°

(STC : 667)

---

f6v

SECTION D

"Mathemathicall & other
miscelanious bookes in 4tos:"

390.   Sr: Kenelme Digby of bodyes & spiritts   £0 07 6

**Sir Kenelm DIGBY, Two Treatises. In the one of which,
the nature of bodies ; in the other, the Nature of mans
soule ; is looked into : in way of discovery, of the
immortality of reasonable soules**, London, 1645 ; 1658 ;
1665 ; 1669   4°

(AE, p.25 ; reference is probably, therefore, to the
first edition of 1645).

391.   Chr Hugenij de circuli magnitudine   £0 02 6

**Christiaan HUYGENS van Zuylichem, De Circuli Magnitudine
inventa. Accedunt ejusdem problematum quorundam
illustrium constructiones**, Leyden, 1654   4°

392.   Rogerij Baconis perspectiva   £0 04 6

**Roger BACON, Perspectiva ... Nunc primum in lucem edita
opera & studio Iohannis Combachii**, Frankfurt, 1614 4°

393.   Cl: Eliani et Leonis imperat: Tactica Graecae et lat
£0 08 0

**Tacticus AELIANUS, Claudi AEliani et Leonis Imp. Tactica ;
sive, de instruendis aciebus, quorum hic graece primum
opera Iohannis Meursii, ille ex Sixti Arcerii nova
interpretatione Latina**, Leyden, 1613   4°

61

394. Jo: Hartmanni Stereometriae lib   £0 04 6

Johannes Hartmannus BEYER, **Stereometriae inanium nova
et facilis ratio geometricis demonstrationibus confirmata**,
Frankfurt, 1603   4°

395. Jo: Marianae de ponderibus lib   £0 02 0

Juan de MARIANA, **De ponderibus et mensuris**, Toledo,
1599   4°

396. Theodotij Tripolicae Spaericorum lib 3 per Chr: Clavium
      £0 07 6

THEODOSIUS of Tripoli, **Theodosii Tripolitae sphaericorum
libri III. a C. Clavio ... perspicuis demonstrationibus
... illustrati. Item ejusdem C. Clavii sinus, lineae
tangentes, et secantes, triangula rectilinea, atque
sphaerica**, Rome, 1586   4°

397. Cosmographia Gemmae ffrisij   £0 01 0

Petrus APIANUS, **Cosmographicus liber ... studiose
correctus, ac erroribus vindicatus per Gemmam Phrysium**,
Antwerp, 1529 ... Antwerp, 1584   4°

398. De Agorum(sic) limitibus p(er) diversos Authores £0 03 6

Petrus GALLANDIUS and Adrianus TURNEBUS (eds.), **De agrorum
conditionibus, & constitutionibus limitum, Siculi Flacci
lib I.   J. Frontini lib I.   Aggeni Urbici lib II.
Hygeni Gromatici lib II.   Variorum auctorum ordines
finitionum. De jugeribus metiundis, etc.**, Paris, 1554   4°

399. ffriderici Risneri opticae lib 4to   £0 04 6

Fridericus RISNERUS, **Opticae libri quatuor ex voto Petri
Rami novissimo per Fridericum Risnerum** (ed. N. Crugius),
Cassel, 1606 ; 1615   4°

400. Jac: Christmanni observation: solarium lib   £0 03 6

Jacobus CHRISTMANNUS, **Observationum solarium libri tres,
in quibus explicatur verus motus solis in Zodiaco : &
universa doctrina triangulorum, ad rationes apparentium
coelestium accommodatur**, Basle, 1601   4°

401. Opere Del Nicolo Tartaglia Italicae   £0 05 0

Niccolò TARTAGLIA, **Opere, ... cioè : Quesiti, Travagliata
Inventione, Nova Scientia, Ragionamenti sopra Archimede,
nelle quali ... si spiega, l'arte di guerreggiare cose in
mare, come in terra, col modo appresso di diffendere,
offendere, & espugnare ogni gran Forterezza**, Venice,
1606   4°

402.   Conformatio Horologiorum   £0 01 0

Hermann WITEKIND, Conformatio horologiorum sciotericorum
in superficiebus planis utcunque sitis, jacentibus,
erectis, reclinatis, inclinatis et quocumque spectantibus,
compendiaria et facilis, cum quadrantis horologici et
geometrici conformatione et usibus ac tabulis sinuum,
Hermanni Witekindi, Heidelberg, 1576   4°

403.   The Jewell of Arithmetiq   £0 01 6

Jo. HARPUR, The Jewell of Arithmetic : or, the
explanation of a new invented arithmeticall table,
London, 1617   4°

(STC : 12796)

404.   Portuum Investigandorum ratio   £0 00 8

Simon STEVIN, Λιμενευρετικη, sive, Portuum
investigandorum ratio. Metaphraste Hug. Grotio Batavo,
Leyden, 1599   4°

405.   De Sydere novo   £0 00 6

Elias MOLERIUS, De Sydere Novo, Seu de nova Stella :
quae ab 8. die Octobris anni .... Enarratio Apodeictica,
Geneva?, 1606   4°

406.   Artemidori de Somniorum interpretatione   £0 02 6

ARTEMIDORUS Daldianus, De somniorum interpretatione,
libri quinq, iam primum a Iano Cornario ... latina lingua
conscripti, Basle, 1539 ; 1544 ; 1546 ; Paris, 1603
large 8°*
(*Nb. I can find no edition of this work in 4°).

407.   Barthol Pitisci opera   £0 08 0

Bartholomaeus PITISCUS, Trigonometriae sive de dimensione
triangulor, libri quinque. Item problematum variorum
nempe Geodaeticorum, Altrimetricorum, Geographicorum,
Gnomonicorum, et Astronomicorum libri decem, Augsburg,
1600 ; 2nd ed., Augsburg, 1608 ; 3rd ed., Frankfurt,
1612   4°

408.   The Seamans Kallendar   £0 07 0

John TAPP, The Seamans Kalender ; or an Ephemerides
of the Sun, Moone, and certaine of the most notable
fixed Starres ... By J. T(app), London, 1602 ...
Amsterdam, 1676   4°

(STC : 23679-23682.7 ; T160-T164 ; 2537A ; 2537B)

409.   A Catolouge of Mr: Puleynes bookes   £0 01 6

Octavian PULLEYN, Catalogus librorum in omni genere
Insignium, Quorum Copia Suppetit Octaviano Pulleyn,
Bibliopolae Ad Insigne Rosae in Caemiterio Paulino
juxta Cochleam, London, 1657   4°

(STC : P4201)

410.   Gulielmi Oughtred: Trigonometria   £0 05 6

William OUGHTRED, Trigonometria : hoc est, modus
computandi triangulorum latera et angulos : ... una
cum tabulis sinuum tangent : et secant (eds. R. Stokes
and A. Haughton), London, 1657   4°

(STC : O589)

411.   Petr: Borelli de vero Tellescopij inventore   £0 03 6

Pierre BOREL, De vero telescopii inventore, cum brevi
omnium conspiciliorum historia ... Accessit etiam
Centuria Observationum microscopicarum, Hague, 1655 4°

412.   Petr: Gassendi Institutio Astronomica   £0 06 6

Pierre GASSENDI, Institutio Astronomica iuxta
hypotheseis tam veterum, quam Copernici, et Tychonis.
Dictata à Petro Gassendo ... Eiusdem Oratio Inauguralis
iterato edita, Paris, 1647 ; Hague, 1656 ; Amsterdam,
1680   4°

413.   fflorentij Schoonhovij Emblemata   £0 04 6

Florentius SCHOONHOVIUS, Emblemata F. Schoonhovii
partim moralia partim etiam civilia. Cum latiori
eorundem ejusdem Auctoris interpretatione. Accedunt et
alia quaedam poematia in aliis poëmatum suorum libris
non contenta, Gouda, 1618 ; Leyden, 1626 ; Amsterdam,
1648   4°

414.   Dell' Imprese di Scipion Bargagli   £0 07 0

Scipione BARGAGLI, Dell' imprese di Scipion Bargagli.
Dove ; dopo tutte l'opera cosi a penna, come a stampa,
ch' egli ha potuto vedere di coloro, che della materia
dell' imprese hanno parlato ; della vera natura di
quelle si ragiona, Sienna, 1578 ; Venice, 1589-94 (Parts
1-3)   4°

415.   Geography by Nat: Carpenter   £0 04 6

Nathanael CARPENTER, Geography delineated forth in two
bookes. Containing the sphaericall and topical parts
thereof, Oxford, 1625 ; 2nd ed., Oxford, 1635   4°

(AE, p.50 ; STC : 4676-4677)

416.   Jo: Mar: Marci, de proportione motus lib   £0 05 6

One of two works, or both bound together in 1 volume,
by **Joannes Marcus MARCI A KRONLAND:**

(a) **De proportione motus figurarum rectilinearum,
et circuli quadratura ex motu**, Prague, 1648   4°
(b) **De proportione motus, seu regula sphygmica
ad celeritatem et tarditatem pulsuum ex illius motu
ponderibus geometricis librato absque errore metiendam**,
Prague, 1639   4°

417.   Jo: Dee de Prestant quibusdam naturae virtutibus   £0 02 0

John **DEE**, Προπαιδευματα ἀφοριστικα   Ioannis Dee ...
**de praestantioribus quibusdam naturae virtutibus, ad
Gerardum Mercatorem**, London, 1558 ; 1568   4°

(STC : 6463-6464)

418.   Jo: Hen: Alstedij Elementale mathematicum   £0 05 0

**Johann Heinrich ALSTED, Elementale mathematicum ...
Continentur ... hoc Elementali   I. Arithmetica.   II.
Geometria.   III. Geodaesia.   IV. Astronomia.   V.
Geographia.   VI. Musica.   VII. Optica**, Frankfurt, 1611   4°

419.   Heronis Allexandrini Spiritalium lib   £0 06 0

**HERO of Alexandria, Heronis Alexandrini Spiritalium
Liber, a F. Commandino ex Graeco in Latinum conversus**
(ed. V. Spacciuoli), Urbino, 1575 ; Paris, 1583 ;
Amsterdam, 1680   4°

(DS, p. 268)

420.   Phil: Lansbersi triangulorum   £0 04 0

**Philippus van LANSBERGEN, Triangulorum Geometriae libri
quatuor**, Leyden, 1591 ; 2nd ed., Amsterdam, 1631   4°

---

f7r

421.   Phil: Horcher de Constructione Circini proportionum
£0 03 6

**Philippus HORCHER, P.H. ... libri tres, in quibus primo
constructio circini proportionum edocetur.   Deinde
explicatur, quomodo eodem mediante circino, tam
quantitates continuae, quam discretae, inter se addi,
subduci, multiplicari, et dividi ... brevissimo
compendio possint**, Mainz, 1605   4°

422.   Archiepiscopi Cartuariensis perspectiva lib 3   £0 02 6

Joannes PECKHAM, Archbishop of Canterbury, Perspectiva tribus libris succinctis denuo correcta, et figuris illustrata, per Pascasium Hamellium, Paris, 1556 ; Cologne, 1580 ; 1592   4°

423.   Willebordi Snelli Geometria resuscitata   £0 01 0

Willebrodus SNELLIUS, ... Περὶ λόγου ἀποτομῆς καὶ περὶ χωρίου ἀποτομῆς **resuscitata geometria**, Leyden, 1607 4°

424.   Aristarchi de magnitudinibq et distantis solis et Lunae
£0 02 6

Samius ARISTARCHUS, Aristarchi De magnitudinibus & distantiis solis et lunae liber, cum Pappi Alexandrini explicationibus quibusdam : a Federico Commandino in Latinum conversus ac commentariis illustratus, Pesaro, 1572   4°

425.   Philolai sive de vero systemate mundi lib 4to   £0 03 6

Ismael BOULLIAU, Philolai, sive dissertationis de vero systemate mundi, libri IV., Amsterdam, 1639   4°

(AE, p.48)

426.   Alae seu Scalae Mathematicae p(er) Tho: Diggesaeum
£0 01 8

Thomas DIGGES, Alae seu Scalae Mathematicae, quibus visibilium remotissima Coelorum Theatra conscendi, & Planetarum omnium itinera novis & inauditis Methodis explorari, London, 1573   4°

(STC : 6871)

427.   Archimedis de insidentibq aquae lib   £0 01 8

ARCHIMEDES, Archimedis De insidentibus aquae, Venice, 1565   4°

428.   A treatise of magneticall bodys & motions by Marke Ridley   £0 03 6

Mark RIDLEY, A short Treatise of magneticall bodies and motions, London, 1613   4°

(AE, p.77 ; STC : 21045-21045.5)

429. Jani: Jac: Boissardi Emblemata   £0 02 0

Jean Jacques BOISSARD, <u>Emblematum liber. Ipsa emblemata</u>
<u>ab auctore delineata, a Theodoro de Bry sculpta et nunc</u>
<u>recens in lucem edita</u>, Frankfurt, 1593 ; 1596 ; 1600 4°

430. Pallas Armata   £0 01 6

Sir Thomas KELLIE, <u>Pallas Armata, or Militarie</u>
<u>Instructions for the Learned, and all generous spirits</u>
<u>who affect the profession of Armes. The first part</u>
<u>containing the Exercise of Infanterie, as well ancient, as</u>
<u>moderne</u>, Edinburgh, 1627   4°

(STC : 14906)

431. Conformatio Horologiorum   £0 01 4

Another copy of Item no. 402, above.

432. Hen: Woolphij Cronologia   £0 02 0

Henricus WOLPHIUS, <u>Chronologia sive de tempore et ejus</u>
<u>mutationibus ecclesiasticis tractatio theologica</u>,
Zurich, 1585   4°

433. Orontij ffinaei de Spaera etc   £0 02 0

Oronce FINÉ, <u>Sphaera mundi, sive cosmographia, quinque</u>
<u>libris recens auctis et emendatis absoluta, in qua tum</u>
<u>prima astro-nomiae pars, tum geographiae ac hydrographiae</u>
<u>rudimenta pertractantur</u>, Paris, 1551 ; 1555   4°

434. Jac: Peletarij de contactu liniarum   £0 00 8

Jacques PELETIER, <u>De Contactu linearum commentarius</u>,
Paris, 1581   4°

435. Orontij finaei praxis Geometrica   £0 02 0

Oronce FINÉ, <u>De re & praxi geometrica libri tres,</u>
<u>figuris & demonstrationibus illustrati : ubi de quadrato</u>
<u>geometrico, & virgis seu baculis mensoris, necnon aliis</u>
<u>cum mathematicis tum mechanicis</u>, Paris, 1556 ; 1586 4°

436. Hen: Glareani Geographia   £0 01 0

Henricus LORITUS Glareanus, <u>De geographia liber unus</u>,
Basle, 1527 ... Paris, 1577   4°

437. Jac Alealmi confutatio etc   £0 00 8

**Jacques ALEAUME, <u>Confutatio problematis ab Henrico</u>
<u>Monantholio ... propositi, quo conatus est demonstrare</u>
<u>octavem partem diametri circulis aequalem esse lateri</u>
<u>polygoni aequilateri et aquianguli eidem circulo</u>
<u>inscripti, cujus perimeter ad diametrum rationem habet</u>
<u>triplam sesquioctavam</u>**, Paris, 1600   4°

438. Simonis Stevinij Problematum Geometricorum lib   £0 02 0

Simon STEVIN, <u>Problematum Geometricorum ... libri V</u>,
Antwerp, 1583   4°

439. Levini Hulsij Usus Quadrati et Quadrantis Geometrici
      £0 02 0

**Levinus HULSIUS, <u>De usu quadrati et quadrantis geometrici</u>
<u>ac chronologici</u>**, Nuremburg, 1596   4°

440. Vincentij contareni de frumentaria Romanorum largitione lib
      £0 01 6

**Vincenzo CONTARINI, <u>De frumentaria Romanorum largitione</u>
<u>liber, in quo ea praecipuè, quae sunt à Iusto Lipsio cum</u>
<u>in electis, tum in admirandis de eadem prodita, examinantur.</u>
<u>Eiusdem de militari Romanorum stipendio commentarius</u>**,
Venice, 1609   4°

441. Nicol: Raimari de Hipothesibus Astronomicis   £0 02 0

**Nicolaus Raimarus URSUS, <u>De Astronomicis hypothesibus,</u>
<u>seu Systemate mundano, tractatus astronomicus et</u>
<u>cosmographicus</u>**, Prague, 1597   4°

442. The care of ye good Samaritan etc   £0 01 0

      I have not been able to locate this work.

443. Academiarum Examen   £0 01 6

**John WEBSTER, <u>Academiarum Examen : or, the Examination</u>
<u>of Academies</u>**, London, 1654   4°

      (STC : W1209)

444. A Candle in ye darke   £0 02 0

**Thomas ADY, <u>A Candle in the Dark ; or, a treatise</u>
<u>concerning the nature of witches & witchcraft. Being</u>
<u>advice to Judges, Sheriffes</u>**, London, 1655 ; 1656 ; and
with different title, London, 1661   4°

      (DS, p.26,106,124,126-127,133 ; STC : A673-A674 ; A676)

445. Academiarum Examen   £0 01 6

Another copy of Item no. 443, above.

446. Vindiciae Academiarum   £0 01 0

(Set)H (WAR)D and (Joh)N (WILKIN)S, Vindiciae Academiarum :
Containing some briefe animadversions upon Mr. Websters
book, stiled, The Examination of Academies. Together with
an appendix concerning what M. Hobbs, and M. Dell have
published on this argument, Oxford, 1654   4°

(STC : W832)

447. The Care of ye good Samaritan   £0 00 6

Another copy of Item no. 442, above.

448. The Art of Diallinge   £0 01 6

One of at least four possible works with this title in 4°:

    (a) John BLAGRAVE, The Art of Dyalling, London, 1609
    (b) Thomas FALE, Horologiographia. The Art of
Dialling, London, 1593 ; 1626 ; 1633
    (c) Samuel FOSTER, The Art of Dialling, London, 1638
    (d) William LEYBOURN, The Art of Dialling, London, 1669

(STC : (a) 3116 ; (b) 10678-10681 ; (c) 11201 ; (d)
L1900-L1901)

449. The Sts: Guide   £0 01 4

John WEBSTER, The Saints Guide : or, Christ the Rule and
Ruler of Saints ; manifested by way of positions,
consectaries, and queries, London, 1653 ; 2nd ed., London,
1654   4°

(JS, p.285 ; STC : W1212-W1213)

450. Mr Dells workes   £0 05 0

William DELL, Several Sermons and Discourses of William
Dell ... now gathered in one volumn, London, 1652   4°

(STC : D929)

451. The Judgmt: sett   £0 06 0

John WEBSTER, The Judgement Set and the bookes opened ;
religion tried whether it be of God or of men ; ... in
several sermons at Alhallows Lumbard Street, London,
1654   4°

(STC : W1210)

452.   The Testimony of Wm: Erbery   £0 03 0

William ERBERY, The testimony of W.E. left upon record
for the saints of succeeding ages. Being a collection
of the writings of the aforesaid authour ... Whereunto
is added The honest Heretick, being his tryal at
Westminster, a piece never printed before (preface by
J.W., i.e. John Webster), London, 1658   4°

(STC : E3239)

453.   Dr: Wilkins his 2 bookes of ye moone & ye Earth   £0 03 0

John WILKINS, A Discourse concerning a new World and
Another Planet. In 2 bookes, London, 1640   8°*
(* Nb. I can find no edition of this work in 4°).

(STC : 25641)

454.   Unheard of Curiosityes by James Gafferell   £0 04 0

Jacques GAFFAREL, Unheard of curiosities concerning the
talismanical sculpture of the Persians ... Englished by
E. Chilmead, London, 1650   8°*
(* Nb. I can find no edition of this work in 4°).

(DS, p.156 ; STC : G105)

455.   Some writeings of ye Quakers   £0 03 0

A collection of Quaker tracts in 4°.

456.   An English bible   £0 06 8

457.   A Lattine bible   £0 05 6

---

f7v

458.   An Antidote agst the Common plauge of ye World
       by Sam: Gorton   £0 03 0

Samuel GORTON, An Antidote against the Common Plague of
the World. Or, an answer to a small treatise ...
intituled Saltmarsh returned from the dead, London,
1657   4°

(STC : G1305)

459.   The lives of ye ffathers by Samuell Clarke   £0 04 0

Samuel CLARKE, Minister of St. Bennet Fink, The Marrow
of Ecclesiastical Historie, conteined in the Lives of
the Fathers, and other learned men, and famous divines,
which have flourished in the church since Christs time,
to this present age ... Together with the livelie
effigies of most of the eminentest of them cut in
copper, London, 1650 ; 1654   4°

(STC : C4543-C4544A)

460.   Theatrum Chemicum Bretanicum by Elias Ashmole Esqe
        £0 05 6

Elias ASHMOLE, Theatrum Chemicum Britannicum ; containing
severall poeticall pieces of our famous English
philosophers, who have written the Hermetique Mysteries
in their owne ancient language. Faithfully collected ...
with annotations thereon, by E. Ashmole, London, 1652 4°

(M, pp.284,285,297-298,365 ; STC : A3987)

461.   of Art & nature by Jo: Baite   £0 02 6

John BATE, The Mysteries of Nature and Art ; conteined
in foure severall Treatises, the first of Water workes,
the second of Fyer workes, the third of Drawing, Colouring,
Painting, and Engraving, the fourth of divers Experiments,
London, 1634 ; 2nd ed., London, 1635 ; 3rd ed., London,
1654   4°

(STC : 1577-1578 ; B1092)

462.   Philosophicall ffurnaces by Jo: Rudolph: Glauber   £0 05 6

Johann Rudolph GLAUBER, A description of new Philosophical
Furnaces, or a new art of distilling, divided into five
parts ... Whereunto is added a description of the Tincture
of Gold, ... also, the first part of the Mineral Work.
Set forth in English by J(ohn) F(rench) D(octor of)
M(edicine), London, 1651   4°

(STC : G846)

463.   Dariots Juditiall Astrologie   £0 05 6

Claude DARIOT, A breefe and most easie Introduction to the
Astrologicall iudgement of the Starres. ... Translated by
Fabian Wither, London, 1583? ; 1598 ; 1653   4°

(STC : 6275-6276 ; D257)

464.   An incorruptable key by Samuell Gorton   £0 03 0

Samuel GORTON, An Incorruptible Key, composed of the CX.
Psalme, wherewith you may open the rest of the Holy
Scriptures, London, 1647   4°

(STC : G1306)

465.   Arcula Gemmea by Tho: Nichols   £0 02 6

**Thomas NICOLS of Jesus College, Cambridge, Arcula
Gemmea : or, a Cabinet of Jewels. Discovering the
nature, vertue, value of pretious stones, with
infallible rules to escape the deceit of all such as
are adulterate and counterfeit,** London, 1653   4°
First published under the title, **A Lapidary**, Cambridge,
1652 (4°).

(STC : N1143)

466.   The compound of Alchimie by Geo: Ripley   £0 01 6

**George RIPLEY, Canon of Bridlington, The Compound of
Alchymy, or the ancient hidden art of Archemie :
conteining the ... meanes to make the Philosophers
Stone ... first written by ... G. Ripley ... Whereunto
is adjoyned his Epistle to the King ... set foorth by
R. Rabbards,** London, 1591   4°

(STC : 21057)

467.   8 volumes of ye writeings of Jacob Behemen   £1 02 0

Although this could be a random selection of works by
Jacob BOEHME, in all probability it is the eight volumes
published by Giles Calvert in London in 1661 (all in 4°):

        (a) **An Apologie concerning perfection**
        (b) **An apology or defence for the requisite refuting**
        (c) **Considerations upon the book of Esaias Stiefel**
        (d) **The first apologie to Balthazar Tylcken**
        (e) **Of the four Complexions**
        (f) **The second apologie to Balthazar Tylcken**
        (g) **Several Treatises**
        (h) **Theosophick Letters**

(STC : (a) B3395 ; (b) B3396 ; (c) B3401 ; (d) B3406 ;
(e) B3414 ; (f) B3416 ; (g) B3418 ; (h) B3420)

468.   The life of Merlin   £0 02 6

**Thomas HEYWOOD, The life of Merlin, sirnamed Ambrosius.
His prophecies and predictions interpreted ; and their
truth made good by our English Annalls. Being a
chronographicall history of all the kings and memorable
passages of this kingdome from Brute to the reigne of
... King Charles,** London, 1641 ; 1651   4°

(STC : H1786 ; 1651 edition unnoticed)

469.   Hen: Cornelius Agrippas 4th booke wth othrs: £0 03 0

**Henricus Cornelius AGRIPPA*, Henry Cornelius Agrippa
his Fourth Book of Occult Philosophy. Of geomancy.
Magical elements of Peter de Abano. Astronomical
geomancy** (by Gerardus Cremonensis). **The nature of spirits**
(by G. Pictorius) **Arbatel of Magick. Translated into
English by Robert Turner,** London, 1655 ; 1665   4°
(* falsely ascribed to Agrippa).

(STC : A785-A786A)

470.   Scotts discovery of Witchcraft   £0 10 0

Reginald SCOT, The discoverie of witchcraft, London,
1584 ; 1651 ; 1654   4°

(DS, sig.A3r, pp. 9,26,83 and *passim* ; STC : 21864 ;
S943-S944)

471.   Joh: Tritemij Steganographia   £0 06 0

**Johann TRITHEIM, Steganographia : hoc est : Ars per
occultam scripturam animi sui voluntatem absentibus
aperiendi certa ... Praefixa est huic opera sua clavis
... ab ipso Authore concinnata**, Frankfurt, 1606 ;
Darmstadt, 1621   4°

(AE, p.24)

472.   Declaratio Stegano Trithemi p(er) Jo: Claramuell
£0 03 6

**Johann TRITHEIM, Steganographiae nec non Claviculae
... J. Trithemii declaratio ... A.J. Caramuel
... concinnabatur**, Cologne, 1635   4°

(AE, p.24)

473.   Jo: Casei in Aristot Dialecticarum lib   £0 03 6

**John CASE, Fellow of St. John's College, Oxford,
Summa veterum interpretum in universam Dialecticam
Aristotelis**, London, 1584   4°

(STC : 4762)

474.   Syntagma Logicum by Tho: Granger   £0 04 0

**Thomas GRANGER, Syntagma Logicam. Or, the Divine
Logicke. Serving especially for the use of Divines in
the practise of preaching**, London, 1620   4°

(STC : 12184)

475.   Logick in English   £0 01 6

Probably one of two works, both published in 8°:

      (a) **Zachary COKE, The art of Logick ; or the
entire body of logick in English**, London, 1654 ; 1657
      (b) **Thomas SPENCER, Gent., Logicke Unfolded : Or,
The Body of Logicke in English, made plaine to the
meanest capacity**, London, 1656

(STC : (a) C4986-C4987 ; (b) S4962)

476. Cleonards Greeke grammer at large   £0 01 4

An incomplete copy of:

Nicolaus CLENARDUS, Institutiones in linguam graecam,
Paris, 1540 ... Paris, 1668   8°*
(*Nb. There do not appear to be any editions of this
work in 4°. Editions after 1619 were simply entitled
Grammatica graeca).

477. Theses Academicae (4° or 8°)   £0 00 4

SECTION E

"Libri Mathematici
in 4to: minore"

**(Works on mathematics
in octavo)**

478. Petr: Herigoni Cursus Mathematicus in 4to: vol £1 10 0

**Pierre HERIGONE, Cursus Mathematicus, nova ... methodo
demonstratus ... Cours mathématique,** 6 vols. in 4,
Paris, 1634-44   8°
Latin—French.

(AE, p.24)

479. Petr: Rami Arithmetica   £0 00 6

**Pierre de LA RAMÉE, P. Rami ... arithmeticae libri
duo, a J. Studio ... recogniti et illustrati,** Paris,
1581 ; 1612 ; ?, 1613   8°

480. A Concordancy of yeares by Arthur Hopton   £0 01 6

**Arthur HOPTON, A Concordancy of Yeares. Containing a
most exact computation of time, according to the
English account. Also the use of the English and
Roman Kalender, with notes ... and tables,** London, 1612 ;
1615 ; 1616 ; 1635   8°

(STC : 13778-13781)

481. Discorsi Millitarie   £0 01 0

**FRANCIS MARY II della Rovere, Duke of Urbino, Discorsi
militari ; ... nei quali si discorrono molti avantaggi,
e disavantaggi della guerra** (ed. D. Mammarelli),
Ferrara, 1583   8°

482.   Gaeographiae lib (8°)   £0 01 0

483.   Traite Des ffeux artificiels   £0 03 0

Francis **MALTHUS**, <u>Traité des Feux artificiels pour la</u>
<u>Guerre et pour la Récréation, avec plusieurs belles</u>
<u>observations, abbrégez de Géométrie, Fortifications</u>
<u>et Exemples d'Arithmetique</u>, Paris, 1629 ; 1632 ;
1633 ; 1640   8°

484.   Euclids Elementorum lib xv p(er) Js: Barrowe   £0 03 6

EUCLID, <u>Euclidis elementorum libri XV breviter</u>
<u>demonstrati, opera J. Barrow</u> (i.e. Isaac Barrow),
London, 1659 ; Osnabruck, 1676, 1675 ; London, 1678 8°
First edition : Cambridge, 1655 (12°).

(STC : E3393-E3394)

485.   Jo: Kepleri Epitomie Astronomiae Copernicanae £0 05 0

Johann **KEPPLER**, <u>Epitome Astronomiae Copernicanae</u>
<u>usitata forma quaestionum et responsionum conscripta</u>,
Frankfurt, 1618, 1622 ; 1635   8°

(AE, pp.48,78)

486.   Barthol: Keckermanni Systema totius mathematices
£0 03 6

Bartholomaeus **KECKERMANNUS**, <u>Systema compendiosum totius</u>
<u>mathematices ; hoc est, geometriae, opticae, astronomiae</u>
<u>et geographiae, publicis praelectionibus, anno 1605, in</u>
<u>Gymnasio Dantiscano propositum</u>, Hanover, 1617 ; 1621 ;
Oxford, 1661   8°

(STC : K123)

487.   Adriani metij institution: Astronomicor: tomi 3
£0 04 6

Adriaan Adriaansz **METIUS**, <u>Institutionum astronomicarum</u>
<u>tomi tres, in quibus praecepta & praxis per sphaeram,</u>
<u>cum solidam ac planam ; tum triangulorum doctrinam partim</u>
<u>in planisphaerio ... partim numeris exhibitam,</u>
<u>declarantur</u>, Franeker, 1608 ; Amsterdam, 1626   8°

488.   Euclids Elementorum libr 15 Graecae et lat   £0 02 0

EUCLID, <u>Euclidis elementorum libri XV. Graece et</u>
<u>Latine</u> (preface by S. Gracilis), Paris, 1557 ; Cologne,
1564 ; Paris, 1573 ; 1598   8°

489.　Caroli Bovilli Geometriae libr　　　　　£0 01 6

**Charles de BOUELLES, Geometricum opus duobus libris
comprehensum**, Paris, 1557　　　　　　　　　　8°

490.　Jo: Baptisti Portae Phisiognomoniae Celestis libr 6
　　　£0 02 0

**Giovanni Battista della PORTA, Coelestis
physiognomoniae libri sex, in quibus non solum,
quomodo quis facile ex humani vultus extima inspectione
ex conjectura, praesagire futura possit, docetur ; sed
etiam Astrologia refellitur, et inanis et imaginaria
demonstrantur**, Strassburg, 1606 ; Rome, 1650　　8°
First edition : Naples, 1603 (4°).

491.　Chr: Clavij in 9 posteriores Elem: Euclidis libr:
　　　Commentar:　　　　　　　　　　　£0 06 0

**EUCLID, Euclidis Posteriores libri sex a X. ad XV.
Accesit XVI. de solidorum regularium comparatione.
Omnes demonstrationibus accuratisque scholiis illustrati,
auctore C. Clavio** (i.e. Christophorus Clavius), Rome,
1574 ; 2nd ed. (2 vols.), Rome, 1589　　　　8°

492.　Jo: Anton: Valtrini de re militari vetterum Romanorum
　　　lib 7　　　　　　　　　　　　£0 02 6

**Joannes Antonius VALTRINUS, De re militari veterum
Romanorum libri septem**, Cologne, 1597　　　8°

---

f8r

493.　Petr: Rami de millitia Julij Cesaris　　£0 01 6

**Pierre de LA RAMÉE, Liber de Caesaris militia, ad
Carolum Lotharingum cardinalem**, Paris, 1559 ; Basle,
1574　　　　　　　　　　　　　　　　8°

494.　Cunradi Dasypodij institut mathemat: lib　£0 02 6

**Conradus DASYPODIUS, Institutionum mathematicarum
voluminis primi Erotemata logisticae, geometriae,
sphaerae, geographiae**, Strassburg, 1593　　　8°
An appendix to this work appeared at Strassburg in
1596 (8°).

495. Alex: Piccolominaei in question: mecanicas Aristot
Coment   £0 02 0

**ARISTOTLE (suppositious), <u>Alexandri Piccolominei in
Mechanicas Quaestiones Aristotelis paraphrasis paulo
quidem plenior</u>**, Venice, 1565   8°
First edition : Rome, 1547 (4°).

496. Le Arithmetique   £0 02 6

497. Chr: Clavij Epitomae Arithmeticae   £0 01 6

Christophorus CLAVIUS, <u>Epitome arithmeticae practicae</u>,
Rome, 1583 ; 1585 ; Cologne, 1601 ; 1607 ; 1614   8°

498. Gemmae ffrisij Arithmetica   £0 01 6

**Reinerus GEMMA Frisius, <u>Arithmeticae practicae methodus
facilis</u>**, Wittenberg, 1542 ; Paris, 1543 ; Wittenberg,
1548 ; Antwerp, 1552 ; Leipzig, 1607   8°
Numerous editions were also published with the
annotations of Jacobus Peletarius : Paris, 1545 ...
Wittenberg, 1604 (8°).
First edition : Antwerp, 1540 (4°).

499. Petr: Rami Arithmetica   £0 01 6

Another copy of Item no. 479, above.

500. Jo: Buteonis de quadratura Circuli   £0 01 6

**Joannes BUTEO (i.e. Jean BORREL), <u>De quadratura circuli
libri duo, ubi multorum quadraturae confutantur, & ab
omnium impugnatione defenditur Archimedes. Eiusdem
annotationum opuscula in errores Campani, Zamberti ...
Io. Penae interpretum Euclidis</u>**, Lyons, 1559   8°

501. Hermanni Witekindi de Sphaera mundi   £0 02 0

**Hermann WITEKIND, <u>De Sphaera Mundi ; et temporis
ratione apud Christianos</u>**, Neustadt, 1590   8°

502. Gemmae frisij principijs Astronomiae   £0 01 6

**Reinerus GEMMA Frisius, <u>De principiis astronomiae et
Cosmographiae, deque usu globi cosmographici ab eodem
aediti. De orbis divisione, et insulis, rebusque
nuper inventis. Ejusdem de annuli astronomici usu.
Joannis Schoneri de usu globi astriferi opusculum</u>**,
Antwerp, 1548 ; 1553 ; Paris, 1556   8°
First edition : Antwerp, 1530 (4°).

503.   Sphaera Jo: de Sacra bosco   £0 01 0

    Joannes de SACRO BOSCO, Sphaera liber, Wittenberg,
1538 ... Leyden, 1647   8°
First edition : Milan & Venice, 1478 (4°).

504.   Traite de la Sphere du monde   £0 01 0

    **Jean BOULANGER, Traicté de la sphère du monde, divisé
en quatre livres, ausquels est adiousté le cinquiesme
de l'usage d'icelle,** Paris, 1620   8°

505.   Michael Maestlini Epitome Astronomiae   £0 02 6

    **Michael MAESTLIN, Epitome astronomiae, qua brevi
explicatione omnia tam ad sphaericam quam theoricam
ejus partem pertinentia, ... per questiones traduntur,
... conscripta per M. Michaelem Maestlinum,** Tubingen,
1588 ; 1597 ; 1598 ; 1610 ; 1624   8°

506.   Clavis mathematices   £0 01 0

    **William OUGHTRED, Clavis mathematicae denuo limata,
sive potius fabricata,** London, 1648 ; 3rd ed., Oxford,
1652 ; 4th ed., Oxford, 1667   8°
First published as Arithmeticae in numeris et speciebus
institutio, London, 1631 (8°).

    (STC : 18898 ; 0573-0575)

507.   Barthol: Keckerm: Systema Astronom: £0 01 4

    **Bartholomaeus KECKERMANNUS, Systema astronomiae
compendiosum in gymnasio dantiscano olim praelectum
et 2 libris adornatum, quorum prior de motu stellarum,
tum communi, tum proprio, posterior de temporis
distinctione a motu isto pendente,** Hanover, 1611 ;
1613   8°

508.   Hieronomi Cardani in Cl: Ptolomaeum Comentaria   £0 03 6

    **Claudius PTOLEMAEUS, Hieronymi Cardani ... in Cl.
Ptolemaei Pelusiensis IIII de Astrorum Iudicis, aut
ut vulgo vocant quadripartite Constructionis libros
commentaria,** Lyons, 1555   8°
First edition : Basle, 1554 (4°).

509.   A litle map of ye Netherlands (8°)   £0 01 2

"Libri Medici Chymici
et alij in 8°: majore"

(Works on medicine,
alchemy, etc. in octavo)

510.   Conradi Gesneri Euonymus   £0 02 6

EUONYMUS Philiatrus (i.e. Conrad GESNER), Thesaurus
Euonymi Philiatri. De remediis secretis liber physicus,
medicus et partim etiam chymicus et oeconomicus ... Nunc
primum in lucem editus, Zurich, 1552 ; 1554 ; Lyons,
1555 ; Venice, 1556 ; Zurich, 2 vols., 1569   8°

511.   Jo: Rupescissae opera cum alijs   £0 02 6

JOANNES de Rupescissa, Joannis de Rupescissa qui ante
CCCXX. annos vixit, de Consideratione Quintae Essentie
rerum omnium, opus ... egregium. Arnaldi de Villanova
Epistola de Sanguine humano distillato. Raymundi
Lulli Ars operativa : et alia quaedam (ed. G. Gratarolus),
Basle, 1561 ; 1597   8°

512.   Congeries Paracelsica   £0 03 0

Philipp Aureol Theophrast BOMBAST VON HOHENHEIM,
Congeries paracelsicae chemiae de transmutationibus
metallorum, ex omnibus quae de his ab ipso scripta
reperire licuit hactenus. Accessit genealogia
mineralium, atq. metallorum omnium, eiusdem autoris
... Gerardo Dorneo interprete, Frankfurt, 1581   8°

513.   Jo: Baptist: Montani opera in 2 vol   £0 08 0

Joannes Baptista MONTANUS, Opuscula varia ac praeclara :
in quibus tota fere Medicina methodice explicatur ...
H. Donzellini ... opera ab infinitis prope mendis
vindicata, atque in duo volumina digesta, 2 vols.,
Basle, 1558   8°

514.   Rodulphi Goclenij de magneticorum vulner: Curat: £0 01 6

Rudolphus GOCLENIUS the Younger, Tractatus de magnetica
curatione vulneris citra ullam & superstitionem, &
dolorem, & remedii applicationem, orationis forma
conscripta, apriori tum ob rerum & causarum, tum
exemplorum etiam augmentum longe diversis, Marburg,
1608 ; Frankfurt, 1613   8°

(JS, p.287)

515.   In Aphorismos Hipocrat Comment Galeni   £0 02 6

**HIPPOCRATES, Hippocratis Aphorismi, cum Galeni
commentariis** (ed. Nicolao Leoniceno), Paris, 1526 8°
Numerous later editions in octavo, with various editors.

516.   Hieron: ffabrit: ab aquapendente Chirurgia   £0 03 6

**Hieronymus FABRICIUS ab Aquapendente, Opera chirurgica
... in duas partas divisa : quarum prior operationes
chirurgicas per totum corpus humanum ... comprehendit
... Altera, libros quinque chirurgiae jam ante in Germania
impressos & sub nomine Pentateuchi chirurgici divulgatos
complectitur**, Lyons, 1628   8°

(M, p.357)

517.   Jo: Langij Epist Medicinal: lib   £0 05 6

**Joannes LANGIUS, Physician of Lemberg, Epistolarum
medicinalium volumen tripartitum, denuo recognitum,
... auctum** (ed. G. Wirthius, with a preface by
N. Reusnerus), Frankfurt, 1589 ; Hanover, 1605   8°

(DS, p.330 ; M, p.15)

518.   Gulielmi Rondeletij methodus   £0 03 6

**Gulielmus RONDELETIUS, Methodus curandorum omnium
morborum ... in tres libros distincta ... Omnia nunc
castigatus edita**, Lyons, 1586 ; Frankfurt, 1592   8°

519.   Davison de Sale   £0 01 6

**Willielmus DAVISSONUS, Oblatio salis sive Gallia lege
salis condita. Tractatus salis naturam**, Paris, 1641 8°

520.   Camilli Speculum   £0 04 6

**Camillus LEONARDUS, Speculum lapidum. Cui accessit
sympathia septem metallorum ac septem lapidum ad
Planetas P. Arlensis de Scudalupis**, Paris, 1610   8°

521.   Casmanni nucleus   £0 03 0

**Otho CASMANNUS, Nucleus mysteriorum naturae enucleatus
laboribus aliquando scholasticis ...methodiceque
digestus**, Hamburg, 1605   8°

522.   ffelici Plateri praxis   £0 03 0

**Felix PLATERUS the Elder, Observationum in hominis
affectibus plerisque ... libri tres.**   Totidem Praxeos
ejusdem tractatibus ... respondentes ... Secunda nunc
typis mandati ... emendati ... indice ... locupletiores,
opera ... Felicis ... nepotis, Basle, 1641   8°
First edition : Basle, 1625 (4°).   The work itself was
first published in three separate volumes at Basle,
1608, 1609.

523.   Melchior Adami vitae German: medicorum   £0 04 6

**Melchior ADAMUS, Vitae Germanorum medicorum ; qui
seculo superiori, et quod excurrit clarverunt,**
Heidelberg, 1620   8°

(DS, pp. 9,59,60,292 ; M, pp.36,37)

524.   Jo: Riolani Responsiones   £0 02 0

**Jean RIOLAN the Younger, Responsiones duae : prima, ad
experimenta nova J. Pecqueti ... altera, ad Pecquetianos
duos doctores Parisienses, adversus sanguificationem in
corde sive Refutatio panegyreos apologeticae pro
Pecqueto, adversus Riolanum,** Paris, 1655   8°

(DS, p.3)

525.   Donat: Anton: ab alto mari Ars medica   £0 05 6

**Donatus Antonius ab ALTOMARI, De medendis humani
corporis malis : ars medica,** Lyons, 1559 ; 1560 ;
1563 ; Harderwijk, 1656   8°
First edition : Naples, 1553 (4°).

(DS, p.94)

526.   Mariani Sancti de lapidae vesicae   £0 01 0

**Marianus SANCTUS, M. Sancti Barolitani ... de lapide
renum ... opusculum ... Ejusdem de lapide vesiçe per
incisionem extrahendo sequitur aureus libellus,**
Venice, 1535   8°

527.   Oswaldi Crollij Basilica Chymica   £0 03 6

**Oswaldus CROLLIUS, Basilica chymica ... in fine libri
additus est autoris ejusdem Tractatus novus de
signaturis rerum internis,** Frankfurt, 1620 ; Geneva,
1624 ; 1631 ; 1635 ; 1643 ; Venice, 1643 ; Geneva, 1658 8°
First edition : Frankfurt, 1608 (4°).

(DS, p.9 ; M, 318)

---

528. Petr: Poterij opera omnia   £0 05 6

Pierre POTIER, Opera omnia medica, et chymica, Lyons,
1645 ; Frankfurt, 1666   8°

529. Marc: Marci Idearum operatricium Idea   £0 07 0

**Joannes Marcus MARCI A KRONLAND, Idearum Operatricium
Idea, sive Hypotyposis et detectio illius occulto
virtutis quae semina foecundat, et ex iisdem corpora
organica producit**, Prague, 1635 ; Frankfurt, 1676   4°*
(*Nb. I can find no edition of this work in 4°).

(DS, pp.284,287 ; M, p.357)

530. Petr: Borelli observacones   £0 05 6

**Pierre BOREL, Historiarum, et observationum
medico–physicarum, centuriae IV ... Accesserunt
D. Isaaci Cattieri ... Observationes medicinales rarae
... et Renati Cartesii vita, eodem P. Borello autore**,
Paris, 1656 ; Frankfurt, 1670 ; 1676 ; Leipzig, 1676 8°
First edition : Castres, 1653 (12°).

(DS, p.319)

531. Martini Rulandi Curationum Empiricarum Centuriae 10
£0 06 8

**Martin RULAND the Elder, Curationum Empyricarum ...
centuriae decem, quibus adjuncta de novo eiusdem
authoris Medicina Practica**, Lyons, 1628 ; Rouen, 1650 8°

(DS, p.247)

532. Petr: Jo: ffabrij opera in 8 vols   £1 06 8

Pierre Jean FABRE, Opera, 8 vols., Toulouse, 1623–46 8°

    (a) **Myrothecium spagyricum**, 1623 ; 1628 ; 1646
    (b) **Palladium Spagyricum**, 1624 ; 1638
    (c) **Chirurgia spagyrica**, 1626 ; 1638
    (d) **Alchymista Christianus**, 1632
    (e) **Hercules piochymicus**, 1634
    (f) **Hydrographum Spagyricum**, 1639
    (g) **Propugnaculum alchymiae**, 1645
    (h) **Panchymici seu Anatomiae universi**, 2 vols in 1,
1646

(M. pp.173,304 ; reference is to (f))

533. Riverij Praxis et observacones medicae in 2 vols
£0 07 0

Two volumes by **Lazarus RIVERIUS**, published by Adrian
Vlacq at Delft and the Hague, 1651-62:

(a) **Praxis Medica**, Hague, 1651 ; 1658 ; 1662   8°

(b) **Observationes medicae & curationes insignes**,
Delft, 1651 ; Hague, 1656   8°

(DS, p.157 ; reference is to (b))

534. Guidonis de Cauliaco Chirurgia   £0 03 6

GUIDO de Cauliaco, **Chirurgia**, Lyons, 1537 ; 1559 ;
1572   8°
First edition : Venice, 1498, in folio.

535. Chelmitei Chirurgia   £0 03 6

Antonius **CHALMETEUS**, **Enchiridion chirurgicum, externorum
morborum remedia ... complectens. Quibus, morbi
venerei curandi methodus ... accesit**, Paris, 1560   8°

536. Theatrum Chimicum in 5 vols   £1 05 0

Lazarus **ZETZNER (ed.)**, **Theatrum chemicum, praecipios
selectorum auctorum tractatus de chemiae et lapidis
philosophici antiquitate, veritate, jure, praestantia,
& operationibus**, 5 vols., Strassburg, 1613-22 ;
1659-60   8°

(DS, pp.6,268,269 ; M, pp.109,127,164,181,182,222,316,
366 and passim)

537. Marci Antonij Zimarae Antrum magico medicum   £0 07 6

Marco Antonio **ZIMARA**, **Antrum Magico-Medicum, in quo
Arcanorum Magico-Phisicorum, sigillorum, signaturarum,
et imaginum magicarum ... ut et curationum magneticarum
... thesaurus ... reconditus**, Frankfurt, 1625, 1626 8°

538. Hen: Nollij naturae Sanctuarium   £0 05 6

Heinrich **NOLLE**, **Naturae Sanctuarium : quod est,
Physica Hermetica, ... ad promovendam rerum naturalium
veritatem ... et admirandorum secretorum in naturae
abysso latentium philosophica explicatione : ... in
undecim libris tractata**, Frankfurt, 1619   8°

(M, pp.32,74,75,76,199-200)

539. ffelicis Wurtzij opera Germanicae   £0 05 0

Felix WUERTZ, Practica der Wundartzney, was für
schädliche Miszbrauch bey der Wundartzney in gemeinem
Schwanck und warumb die abzuschaffen seind ... Alles
nach newer Form und Art ... durch Felix Wurtz, Basle,
1563 ... Stettin & Breslau, 1659   8°

540. Raymundi Lullij opera cum alijs   £0 06 6

Ramón LULL, Opera ea quae ad adinventam ab ipso artem
universalem ... pertinent. Ut et in eandem quorundam
interpretum scripti commentarii quae omnia ... hoc demum
tempore conjunctim ... emendatiora ... edita sunt
(including the commentaries of Giordano Bruno and
Cornelius Agrippa von Nettesheim), Strassburg, 1598 ;
1609 ; 1617 ; 1651   8°

541. ffranc: Glissonij Anatomia hepatis   £0 04 6

Francis GLISSON, Anatomia hepatis ; cui praemittuntur
quaedam ad rem anatomicam universe spectantia, London,
1654 ; Amsterdam, 1659   8°

(STC : G853)

542. ffra: Basilij Valentini Currus triumphatis Antimonij
      £0 04 6

BASILIUS VALENTINUS, Currus triumphalis antimonij
... Opus antiquioris medicinae & philosophiae
Hermeticae ... E Germanico in Latinum versum operâ,
studio & sumptibus Petri Ioannis Fabri, Toulouse,
1646   8°

(M, p.333)

543. Tho: Whartoni Glandulorum descriptio   £0 03 6

Thomas WHARTON, Adenographia, sive glandularum totius
corporis descriptio, London, 1656 ; Amsterdam, 1659 8°

(STC : W1576)

544. ffranc: Basilij Valentini opera Germanicae   £0 04 0

BASILIUS VALENTINUS, Geheime Bücher oder letztes
Testament. Vom grossen Stein der Vralten Weisen und
andern verborgenen Geheimnussen der Natur. Auss dem
Original ... nach geschrieben. Und nunmehr ... neben
angehenckten zwölff Schlüsseln ... aus Liecht gebracht,
Strassburg, 1645 ; 1651 ; 1667   8°

(M, pp.115,144,145-146 and passim).

545.   Jo: Beguini Tirocinium Chimicum cum Barthij notis etc
£0 03 0

Jean BEGUIN, Secreta Spagyrica revelata, sive
Tyrocinium chymicum ... recognitum ... ê Gallico, in
Latinum translatum, atque ... notarum et praeparatationum
auctario locupletatum, a Jeremia Barthio, ?, 1618 ;
Wittenberg, 1640 ; Venice, 1643 ; Wittenberg, 1650 ; 1656 8°

(AE, p.77 ; M, p.9,318)

546.   Tobiae Tandleri dissertationes phisicae medicae cum
alijs   £0 02 6

Tobias TANDLERUS, Dissertationes physicae—medicae :
I. De spectris ... II. De fascino & incantatione. III.
De melancholia ... IV. De melancholicorum vaticiniis ...
V. De noctisurgio ... Quibus accesserunt ... Hieron.
Nymanni VI. De imaginatione oratio, & D. Martini
Biermanni VII. De magicis actionibus ἐξετασις. **Cum**
indice questionum, Wittenberg, 1613   8°

(DS, sig.A3r ; pp.26,327)

547.   Bickeri Hermes Redivivus   £0 03 0

Johannes BICKERUS, Hermes redivivus, declarans hygieinam,
de sanitate vel bona valetudine hominis conservanda,
Giessen, 1612 ; Hanover, 1620   8°

548.   Baccij de Gemmis lib   £0 01 8

Andrea BACCI, De gemmis et lapidibus pretiosis ...
tractatus ... non solum in latinum sermonem conversus
verum etiam ... observationibus auctior redditus, a
Wolfgango Gabelchovero, Frankfurt, 1603 ; 1643   8°

(M, p.29)

549.   Servij de odoribus etc   £0 02 6

Petrus SERVIUS, Dissertatio philologica de Odoribus,
Rome, 1641   8°

550.   Strozzij Cicognae magiae omnifariae lib   £0 03 0

Strozzi CIGOGNA, Magiae omnifariae, vel potius universae
naturae theatrum, in quo, a primis rerum principiis
arcessita disputatione, universa spirituum et
incantationum natura ... explicatur ... Ex italico
latinitaiti donatum opera et studio Caspari Ens,
Cologne, 1606   8°

551. Gulielmi Varignanae secreta medicinae   £0 03 0

**Gulielmus VARIGNANA, <u>Secreta Medicine ... secreta</u>
<u>sublimia ad varios curandos morbos verissimis</u>
<u>autoritatibus illustrata</u>, Lyons, 1533 ; 1539 ;
Basle, 1597**   8°

552. Davisoni Cursus Chymiatricus   £0 05 0

**Willielmus DAVISSONUS, <u>Philosophia pyriotechnia</u> ...
<u>seu Cursus chymiatricus</u>, Paris, 1641**   8°

553. Augusti Etzleri Isagoge Phisico magica medica £0 02 0

**Augustus ETZLERUS, <u>Isàgoge Physico-magico-medica, in qua</u>
<u>signaturae non paucorum vegetabilium et animalium tam</u>
<u>internae quam externae accurate depinguntur, ex quibus</u>
<u>mundi superioris astralis, cum inferiori elementali</u>
<u>mundo concordantia et influentia, mirabilisque ...</u>
<u>sympathia et antipathia rerum elucescunt</u>, Strassburg,
1631**   8°

554. Traite de la Peste (8°)   £0 02 0

555. Tho: Erasti de lamijs lib   £0 01 8

**Thomas ERASTUS, <u>Repetitio disputationis de Lamiis seu</u>
<u>strigibus</u>, Basle, 1578**   8°

556. Cornellij Drebelij de natura Elementorum   £0 01 4

**Cornelis Jacobszoon DREBBEL, <u>Tractatus de Natura</u>
<u>Elementorum ... in linguam latinam translatus et in lucem</u>
<u>emissus a J.E. Burggravio</u>, Frankfurt, 1628**   8°

557. Nich: Papinij de pulvere Sympathico   £0 01 0

**Nicholas PAPIN, <u>De Pulvere sympathico dissertatio</u>,
Paris, 1647 ; 1650**   8°

558. Scola Saliterna   £0 00 6

**SALERNO, Schola Salernitana, <u>Regimen sanitatis</u>
<u>Salernitanum</u>, Paris, 1513 ... Paris, 1672**   8°

559. 2 tractats of Glaubers   £0 01 8

Two volumes by **Johann Rudolph GLAUBER.**

560.   Hieronomi Rorarij qd: Bruta ratione utantur melius
       homine   £0 02 0

       **Hieronymus RORARIUS, Quod animalia bruta ratione
       utantur melius homine. Libri duo** (ed. Gabriel Naudé),
       Paris, 1648   8°

561.   Jo: Ernesti Burgravi Achilles redivivus   £0 02 0

       Johann Ernst BURGGRAV, Achilles Πανοπλος **redivivus,
       seu Panoplia physico-vulcania qua in proelio** φιλοπλος
       **in hostem educitur sacer etinviolabilis. Cui praemissa
       est Marcelli Vranckheim** ... ἐπικρισις στοχαστικη
       ad Achillem Πανυπεροπλομαχον, Amsterdam, 1612 8°

562.   Johuberti opuscula   £0 02 0

       **Laurent JOUBERT, Opuscula, olim discipulis suis
       publice dictata, quae nunc Johan. Posthius typis
       excudenda curavit**, Lyons, 1571   8°

563.   Hermanni Hugonis de prima scribendi origine £0 02 6

       **Hermannus HUGO, De prima scribendi origine et universa
       rei literariae antiquitate**, Antwerp, 1617   8°

---

f9r

564.   Taliacotij Chirurgia   £0 03 6

       Gaspar TALIACOTIUS, Cheirurgia nova ... **de narium,
       aurium, labiorumque defectu, per insitionem cutis ex
       humero** ... **sarciendo**, Frankfurt, 1598   8°

565.   Secreti Medicinali di; M: Pietro Bairo   £0 02 0

       Pietro BAIRO, Secreti medicinali di M. Pietro Bairo,
       Venice, 1561 ; 1592   8°

566.   Opera omnia Cl: Galeni lat in 5 vols   £0 15 0

       GALEN, Opera Omnia (ed. Agostino Ricci), 8 vols. (bound
       in 5?), Venice, 1541-45   8°

       (DS, pp.157-158,181 ; M, pp.28,70)

567.   Aurelij Cornelij Celsi de re medica lib 8 cum alijs
£0 05 0

**Aulus Cornelius CELSUS, De Re Medica, libri octo
eruditissimi. Q. Sereni Samonici praecepta medica,
versibus hexametris. Q. Rhemnij Fannij Palaemonis,
de ponderibus & mensuris, liber ... Hos libros D. Ioan.
Caesaris ... castigavit**, Hagenau, 1528 ... Lyons, 1566
8°

568.   Leonarti ffuchsij de ratione medendi lib   £0 03 6

**Leonhard FUCHS, De Curandi ratione libri octo,
causarum signorumque catalogum breviter continentes,
partim olim conscripti, et nunc postremum recogniti,
multisque locis aucti : partim recens adjecti**, Lyons,
1548 ; 1552 ; 1553 ; 1554 ; Basle, 1568   8°

569.   Caroli Clusij rariorum aliquot stirpium historia
£0 03 6

**Charles de L'ECLUSE, C. Clusii rariorum aliquot stirpium
per Hispanias observatarum historia, libris duobus
expressa**, Antwerp, 1576   8°

570.   Caspari Bauhini Anatomica historia   £C 01 8

**Caspar BAUHINUS, Anatomica corporis virilis et muliebris
historia Caspari Bauhini Hippocrat. Aristotel. Galeni
auctoritat. illustrata & novis inventis plurimis aucta**,
Lyons, 1597   8°

571.   Hieronomi Cardani methodus medendi cum alijs   £0 02 6

**Girolamo CARDANO, Ars curandi parva, quae est absolutiss.
medendi methodus, & alia, nunc primum aedita, opera, in
duos tomos divisa**, Basle, 1566   8°

572.   Phocillidis Phisica   £0 03 6

**Joannes Phocylides HOLWARDA, Philosophia Naturalis, seu
Physica Vetus-Nova. Ex optimis quibusque autoribus
antiquis pariter et neotericis deducta, propriisque
speculationibus et inventis aucta et illustrata**,
Franeker, 1651   8°

(AE, pp.78,106)

573.   Roberti Valensis de veritate Chimiae cum alijs   £0 02 6

**Robertus VALLENSIS, De veritate et antiquitate Artis
Chemicae et Pulveris sive Medicinae Philosophorum vel
Auri Potabilis ... Ex variis auctoribus sacris,
Theologis, Iurisperitis, Medicis, Philosophis, &
Poetis, ... selecta**, Leyden, 1593 ; Montbéliard, 1602 8°
First edition : Paris, 1561 (16°).

574. Bartholomei Carichteri de herbis lib: Germ: £0 01 6

**Bartholomaeus CARRICHTER, <u>Kreutterbuch ... Darin</u>
<u>begriffen under welchem zeichen Zodiaci, auch in welchem</u>
<u>gradu ein jedes Kraut stehe, wie sie in leib zu allen</u>
<u>schäden zu bereiten und zu welcher zeit sie colliegeren</u>
<u>sein</u>** (ed Michael Toxites), Strassburg, 1575   8°

(DS, p.158)

575. Raymundi Lullij de Quintessentia   £0 01 6

**Ramón LULL, <u>De secretis naturae ; sive, quinta essentia</u>
<u>libri duo</u>**, Venice, 1540 ; Strassburg, 1541 ; Venice,
1542 ; Cologne, 1567   8°
First edition : Augsburg, 1518 (4°).

576. Raymundi Lullij testamentum   £0 03 6

**Ramón LULL, <u>Testamentum ... universam artem Chymicam</u>
<u>complectens antehac nunquam excessum. Item ejusdem</u>
<u>Compendium Animae Transmutationis artis metallorum</u>**,
Cologne, 1566 ... Rouen, 1663   8°

(M, pp.181,386)

577. Paracelsi Chirurgia Germ: £0 01 4

**Philipp Aureol Theophrast BOMBAST VON HOHENHEIM,
<u>Wundtuund Leibartzenei, Die gantze Chirurgei belangend</u>,**
Frankfurt, 1555 ; 1561   8°
Later translations of Paracelsus' **Chirurgia** were
printed at Basle, 1573 ; 1579 ; Meissen, 1574 ; Schleswig,
1595? ; Strassburg, 1608 ; 1622 ; 1633 (all 8°).

578. Jo: ffieni de flatibus lib   £0 01 6

**Joannes FIENUS, <u>De Flatibus humanum corpus molestantibus</u>
<u>commentarius novus ac singularis</u>**, Antwerp, 1582 ;
Heidelberg, 1589 ; 1592   8°

579. Admonitio de fratribq Roseaecracis   £0 00 6

Henricus NEUHUSIUS, <u>Admonitio de fratibus</u>(sic) **<u>Roseae</u>
<u>crucis nempe an sint quales sint</u>**, Frankfurt, 1611 ;
1618 ; 1622 ; Danzig, 1628   8°

580. Jo: Ernesti Burgravi Biolichnium   £0 02 0

**Johann Ernst BURGGRAV, <u>Biolychnium seu Lucerna, cum vita</u>
<u>ejus, cui accensa est Mystice, vivens jugiter ; cum</u>
<u>morte ejusdem expirans ; omnesque affectus graviores</u>
<u>prodens. Huic accessit Cura Morborum Magnetica ex</u>
<u>Theophr. Parac Mumia : itemq; omnium venenorum</u>
<u>Alexipharmacum</u>**, Franeker, 1611 ; Frankfurt, 1629   8°

(DS, pp.268-269)

SECTION G

"Libri medici in 8vo:"

(Works on medicine in 8°)

581. Hen: Corn: Agrippae de vanitate scientiarum lib
£0 01 2

**Henricus Cornelius AGRIPPA, De incertitudine &
vanitate scientiarum & artium ; atque excellentia verbi
Dei, declamatio**, ?, 1530 ; Cologne & Paris, 1531 ;
?, 1537 ; ?, 1544 ; Strassburg?, 1622   8°
First edition : Antwerp, 1530 (4°).

(AE, p.35)

582. Jo: Munsteri contra capvicum lib   £0 01 4

**Joannes MUENSTERUS, Discussio eorum quae ab Abrahamo
Schopffio ... de Purgatione ... scripta sunt. Quibus
duae acceserunt .. appendices, una, contra Capovaceum,
altera contra Mercurialem**, Frankfurt, 1603   8°

583. Iatrionices libr   £0 0 10

**Otto BRUNFELS, Iatrion medicamentorum simplicium
continens remedia omnium morborum, quae tam hominibus
quam pecudibus accidere possunt .. digestum in libros
quatuor**, Strassburg, 1533   8°

584. Jo: Baptist: portae magiae naturalis lib 20   £0 03 6

**Giovanni Battista della PORTA, Magiae Naturalis libri
XX**, Frankfurt, 1607 ; Hanover, 1618 ; Rouen, 1650 8°
First edition : Naples, 1589, in folio.

(AE, p.69)

585. Nathan Carpenterij Philosophia libera   £0 01 8

**N(athanael) C(ARPENTER), Philosophia libera, duplici
exercitationum decade proposita ... Cui praeit paradoxon,
ignorantem docto praeferendum esse**, Frankfurt, 1621 ;
2nd ed., enlarged, Oxford, 1622 ; 3rd ed., Oxford,
1636 ; another ed., Oxford, 1675   8°

(STC : 4678-4680 ; C616)

586. Jo: Trithemij Poligraphiae lib 6   £0 03 6

Johann TRITHEIM, Polygraphiae libri sex, Cologne, 1564 ;
Strassburg, 1600   8°
First edition : Oppenheim, 1518, in folio.

(AE, p.24)

587. Jo: Baptist: portae de occultis literarum notis
£0 02 6

Giovanni Battista della PORTA, De occultis literarum
notis, seu artis animi sensa occulte alijs significandi
... libri III, Montbeliard, 1593   8°
Later editions, enlarged (**... Libri IV**), Strassburg,
1603 ; 1606 (8°).

588. Mercury or ye secret messenger   £0 01 8

J(ohn) W(ILKINS), Mercury, or the secret and swift
Messenger : shewing how a man may with privacy and
speed communicate his thoughts to a friend at any
distance, London, 1641   8°

(STC : W2202)

589. Tho: Erasti de auro potabili   £0 0 10

Thomas ERASTUS, Disputatio de auro potabili, in qua
accurate admodum disquiritur, num ex metallis, opera
Chemiae, concinnata pharmaca tutè utiliterque bibi
possint ... Adiectum est ... Iudicium eiusdem Authoris
de indicatione Cometarum, ex veris fundamentis & naturae
principijs erutum, Basle, 1578 ; 1584   8°

590. Thaumaturgus Phisicus   £0 01 6

Thaumaturgus Physici Prodromus, id est, problematum
physicorum liber singularis, Cologne, 1649   8°

591. Rodulphi Goclenij mirabilia cum alijs 3 vol   £0 05 0

Rudolphus GOCLENIUS the Younger, Mirabilium Naturae
Liber, concordias et repugnantias rerum in plantis,
animalibus, animaliumque morbis et partibus, manifestans,
nunc primo in lucem datus ... Adjecta est nova defensio
magneticae curationis vulnerum, Frankfurt, 1625 ;
1643*   8°
(*Nb. I have not been able to locate any 3 volume
edition of this work. It may have been split and
rebound in 3 volumes, or, the "cum alijs" in the
catalogue title may refer to other works by Goclenius).

592. Michael: Toxitae onomastica   £0 03 0

Michael TOXITES, Onomastica II. 1. Philosophicum
Medicum, synonymum en variis vulgaribusque linguis.
2. T. Paracelsi : hoc est, earum vocum quarum in scriptis
ejus solet usus esse, explicatio nunc primum ... publicata,
Strassburg, 1574   8°

(M, p.111)

593.　Dr Brownes Hidrotaphia etc　　　　　　£0 02 0

Sir Thomas BROWNE, Hydriotaphia, Urne–buriall, or, a
Discourse of the sepulchrall urnes lately found in
Norfolk. Together with the Garden of Cyrus,
London, 1658　　　　　　　　　　　　　　　8°

(STC : B5154)

594.　Hieronomi Capivaccei methodus　　　　　£0 02 0

Hieronymus CAPIVACCIUS, Methodus, seu ars curandi ...
cum prefatione de vita autoris, atque editionis
occasione, Frankfurt, 1594 ; 1596　　　　　8°
First published under the title, **Nova methodus
medendi**, Frankfurt, 1593 (8°).

595.　Johes Rhenani opera Chimiatrica　　　　£0 03 6

Joannes RHENANUS, Opera chymiatrica ... omnia, a ...
mendis vindicata et ... medicamentis aucta,
Frankfurt, 1635　　　　　　　　　　　　　　8°

596.　Leonard: Vairi de ffascino lib　　　　£0 03 0

Leonardus VAIRUS, De Fascino libri tres ... In quibus
omnes fascini species ... describuntur ... nec non
contra praestigias, imposturas, allusionesque daemonum,
cautiones et amuleta praescribuntur, Venice, 1589 8°
First edition : Paris, 1583 (4°).

(DS, p.324)

597.　Sam: Hafenreferi officina Iatrica　　　£0 02 6

Samuel HAFENREFFER, Officina iatrica, continens
pharmaca selecta hippocratico–galenica et hermetico–
paracelsica juxta morborum seriem ... disposita,
Ulm, 1653　　　　　　　　　　　　　　　　8°

---

f9v

598.　Mich: Majeri viatorium　　　　　　　　£0 03 0

Michael MAIERUS, Viatorium, hoc est, de montibus
Planetarum septem seu metallorum, Rouen, 1651　　8°
First edition : Oppenheim, 1618 (4°).

599. Brindelij Chymia   £0 02 0

Zacharias BRENDEL, **Chimia in artis formam redacta, ubi**
praeter methodum addiscendi ἐγχειρήσεις **chimicas**
facilimam, disquisitio curata de famosissima
praeparatione auri potabilis instituitur. Editio
secunda correctior et auctior post obitum autoris,
consilio Werneri Rolfinck, Jena, 1641   8°
First edition : Jena, 1630 (12°).

600. Hen: Wareni Nosologia Hermetica   £0 03 6

Henricus **WARENIUS**, Νοσολογια **, seu adfectuum humanorum**
curatio Hermetica et Galenica thesibus comprehensa ...
post obitum autoris collecta et publicata studio et opera
J. Tanchii, Leipzig, 1605   8°

601. Gassend: contra Aristotelē lib   £0 01 8

Pierre **GASSENDI**, **Exercitationum paradoxicarum adversus**
aristoteleos libri septem, in quibus praecipua totius
peripateticae doctrinae fundamenta excutiuntur,
opiniones vero aut novae, aut ex vetustioribus obsoletae
stabiliuntur, Grenoble, 1624 ; Amsterdam, 1649   8°

(AE, pp.35,66,86,88)

602. Septalij Animadvertiones   £0 04 6

Ludovico **SETTALA**, **Animadversionum et cautionum**
medicarum libri septem, Naples, 1627 ; Padua, 1628 ;
1630 ; and enlarged (**... libri novem**), Milan, 1626 ;
Padua, 1628, 1630 ; Dordrecht, 1640 ; 1650 ; Padua, 1652 ;
1659   8°
First edition : Strassburg, 1625 (12°).

603. Bapt Codronck de Cam Rabie etc   £0 03 6

Giovanni Battista **CODRONCHI**, **De rabie, hydrophobia**
communiter dicta, libri duo. De sale absynthij libellus.
De iis, qui aqua immerguntur, opuscula : et De elleboro
commentarius, Frankfurt, 1610   8°

(DS, p.94)

604. Jo: Steph: Strobelgeri de dentium Podagra   £0 02 6

Johann Stephan **STROBELBERGER**, **De Dentium Podagra seu**
potius de ὁδονταγρα **, dolorevè dentium, tractatus,**
Leipzig, 1630   8°

605.   Eiusdem Authoris Epistolaris concertatio   £0 02 0

Johann Stephan STROBELBERGER, **Epistolaris Concertatio**
super variis ... quaestionibus, febrim malignam seu
petichialem concernentibus, agitata inter D.I.S.S. ...
et D.J. Burserum ... Annexa est et disceptatio de
venenorum natura .. habita inter eundem D. Burserum
et M.V. Hertelium, Leipzig, 1625   8°

606.   Jo: Macolonis Iatria Chimica   £0 01 8

Joannes MACOLLO, **Iatria chymica, exemplo therapiae**
luis venereae illustrata, London, 1622   8°

(STC : 17175)

607.   Leon: Suavij sup: paracel: Comment: £0 03 6

Philipp Aureol Theophrast BOMBAST VON HOHENHEIM,
Theophrast Paracelsi philosophiae et medicinae utriusque
universae compendium, ex optimis quibus que ejus libris :
Cum scholiis in libros IIII, ejusdem de vita longa ...
auctore Leone Suaivo J.G. (i.e Jacques Gohorry, alias
Leo Suavius), Paris, 1567? ; Frankfurt & Basle, 1568 8°

608.   Petr Severini Idea medicinae etc   £0 03 6

Petrus SEVERINUS, **Idea medicinae philosophicae,**
fundamenta continens totius doctrinae Paracelsicae,
Hippocraticae, et Galenicae, Erfurt, 1616   8°
First edition : Basle, 1571 (4°).

(DS, p.9)

609.   Levini Lemnij Herb: Bibl: Explicatio   £0 02 0

Levinus LEMNIUS, **Herbarum atque arborum quae in Bibliis**
passim obviae sunt, et ex quibus sacri vates
similitudines desumunt, ac collationes rebus accommodant,
dilucida explicatio, Antwerp, 1566 ; 1569 ; Erfurt,
1581 ; Lyons, 1588 ; 1594 ; Frankfurt, 1596 ; 1626 8°

610.   Mich: Potier veredarium   £0 01 4

Michael POTIER, **Veredarius Hermetico–Philosophicus**
laetum et inauditum nuncium adferens ; id est, secreti
naturae secretissimi, de conficiendo nimirum lapide
philosophico, personalem et viviam revelationem veris
verae sapientiae filiis ... offerens, novis ad quorundam
literas et ... these responsionibus informatus,
Frankfurt, 1622   8°

611.   Hen: ab Heer Spadacrene   £0 00 8

**Henri de HEER, Spadacrene. Hoc est Fons Spadanus ;
ejus singularia, bibendi modus, medicamina bibentibus
necessaria**, Liège, 1614 ; 1622 ; 1635   8°

612.   Gerardi Dornei Philosophia magna   £0 02 0

**Philipp Aureol Theophrast BOMBAST VON HOHENHEIM,
Philosophiae magnae Aureoli Philippi Theophrasti
Paracelsi ... collectanea quaedam ... per Gerardum
Dorn è Germanico sermone ... Latinè reddita,**
Basle, 1569   8°

(DS, p.9)

613.   Isac: Phisica Hebraea   £0 02 0

**Joannes ISAAC Levita (i.e. Judah ben Saul aben Thibbon),
Physica Hebraea Rabbi Aben Tybbon ... nunc primum edita
& Latina facta, Joanne Isaac Levita auctore,**
Cologne, 1555   8°
Hebrew and Latin.

614.   Hen: Scheunemanni Paracelsia   £0 01 6

**Henningus SCHEUNEMANN, Paracelsia ... de Morbo Sulphureo
Cagastrico, quem febrem vulgus nominat, ex quintuplici
ente, Dei nimirum, astrorum, pagoyi, veneni et naturae
prognato, in qua omnes ejus species et vera curandi
ratio recensentur**, Frankfurt, 1610   8°

615.   Gerard: Dornei in vitam longam Paracel: £0 01 6

**Philipp Aureol Theophrast BOMBAST VON HOHENHEIM,
Theophrasti Paracelsi libri V. de vita longa, brevi,
& sana. Deq. triplici corpore. Iamdudum ab ipso
authore obscurè editi, nunc verò opera & studio
Gerardi Dornei commentarijs illustrati**, Frankfurt,
1583   8°

616.   Magni G: Phaedronis Iatro Chemica   £0 02 6

**Georgius PHAEDRO Rodocherus, Opuscula iatro-chemica
quatuor. I. Praxis medico-chemica. II. Halopyrgice,
sive pestis medica-chemica curatio. III. Chirurgia
Minor. IV. Furnus chymicus ... nunc latinitate donata
... curante J.A. Schenckio**, Frankfurt, 1611   8°

(DS, p.340)

617.   Tho: Bartholini insidiae structae   £0 01 6

**Olof RUDBECK the Elder, <u>Insidiae structae O. Rudbeckii</u>
<u>Seieci eluctibus hepaticis aquosis, et vasis</u>
<u>glandularum serosis ... a T</u>**(homas) **<u>Bartholino</u>**,
Leyden, 1654   8°

618.   Jo: Scharandaei de conservanda sanitate   £0 01 8

**Joannes Jacobus SCHARANDEUS, <u>De ratione conservandae</u>
<u>sanitatis liber</u>**, Amsterdam, 1649   8°

619.   Hen: Kunrach(sic) de Igne magorum   £0 02 0

**Henricus KHUNRATH, <u>De Igne Magorum Philosophorumque</u>
<u>secreto externo et visibli : das ist, Philosophische</u>
<u>Erklährung von und uber dem geheymen eusserlichen,</u>
<u>sichtbaren, Gludt und Flammen fewer der uhralten magorum</u>
<u>oder Weysen, und andern wahren Philosophen</u>**, Strassburg,
1608   8°

620.   Tulpij observacones   £0 05 6

Nicolaus TULPIUS, <u>Observationum Medicarum libri tres</u>,
Amsterdam, 1641 ; later editions enlarged (**<u>libro</u>**
<u>quarto</u>), Amsterdam, 1652 ; 1672   8°

(DS, pp.33,282)

621.   (a) Bartholini observacones Centur: 3:4   £0 04 6
       (b) Id: 2 3   £0 02 6

Two works from a larger edition by **Thomas BARTHOLINUS,
Prof. of Anatomy at Copenhagen**:

      (a) **<u>Historiarum Anatomicarum Rariorum Centuria</u>**
<u>III & IV. Ejusdem cura accessere Observationes</u>
<u>Anatomicae ... Petri Pawi</u>, Hague, 1657   8°
Volume 2 in a 2 volume edition issued by Adrian Vlacq
at the Hague, 1654-57, as well as volume 2 in a 3
volume composite edition issued by P. Hauboldt at
Copenhagen, 1654-61.

      (b) **<u>Historiarum Anatomicarum Rariorum Centuria</u>**
<u>II & III</u>, a composite edition formed from two separate
volumes : **<u>Centuria II</u>**, Hague, Amsterdam & Copenhagen,
1654 ; **<u>Centuria III</u>**, Hague, 1657   8°

(DS, pp.88,285-286,341 ; references are to (b)
<u>Centuria II</u>, Amsterdam, 1654).

622.   Medicina Magnetica   £0 02 0

**Christopher IRVINE, <u>Medicina Magnetica : or, the rare</u>
<u>and wonderful Art of Curing by Sympathy ; laid open by</u>
<u>Aphorismes ; proved in conclusions ; and digested into</u>
<u>an easy method</u>**, Edinburgh, 1656   8°

(DS, p.322 ; STC : I1053)

623.   Jo: Hartmanni praxis Chimiatrica   £0 04 0

Johann HARTMANN, Prof. of Chemistry at Marburg,
Praxis chymiatrica, Frankfurt, 1634 ; Geneva, 1635 ;
1639 ; 1659   8°
First edition : Leipzig, 1633 (4°).

624.   Pegasus ffirmamenti   £0 01 0

Joseph STELLATUS (i.e. Christoph HIRSCH), Pegasus
Firmamenti, sive introductio ... in veterum sapientiam ;
quae olim ab AEgyptiis ... magia ; hodie vero a ...
Fraternitate Roseae Crucis Pansophia recte vocatur,
?, 1619   8°

625.   The history of Genracon by Dr: Highmoore   £0 02 0

Nathaniel HIGHMORE, The History of Generation ;
examining the several opinions of divers authors, ... To
which is joyned, A discourse of the Cure of Wounds by
sympathy, ... especially by that powder, known chiefly
by the name of Sir Gilbert Talbots powder, London,
1651   8°

(M, p.357 ; STC : H1969)

626.   Glaubers bookes 4 vol (8°)   £0 05 6

Four volumes by **Johann Rudolph GLAUBER.**

627.   Gulielmi Johnsoni Lexicon Chimicum   £0 02 6

William JOHNSON, Lexicon Chymicum, cum obscuriorum
verborum et rerum Hermeticarum, tum phrasium
Paracelsicarum in scriptis ejus, et aliorum chymicorum
passim occurrentium ... explicationem continens,
London, 1652, 1653 ; 1657 ; 1660   8°

(STC : J855–J857)

628.   Jo: Issacii Hollandi Chimia   £0 03 0

JOANNES ISAACUS, called Hollandus, Opera Mineralia,
sive de Lapide Philosophico, omnia, duobos libris
comprehensa (trans. P.M.G.), Middleburg, 1600 ;
Arnhem, 1616   8°

(AE, p.70)

629.   Petr Pomponatij de Incantationibq lib   £0 02 6

Petrus POMPONATIUS, De naturalium effectuum causis,
sive, de Incantationibus, opus ... adjectis ... scholiis
a G. Gratarolo (ed.), Basle, 1556 ; enlarged, Basle,
1567   8°

(DS, p.336)

630. Davidis Crusi Theatrum morborum etc   £0 02 0

**David CRUSIUS, Theatri morborum hermetico–hippocratici.
Seu Methodicae morborum et curationis eorundem dispositionis
pars prior**, Erfurt, 1615, 1616   8°

---

f10r

631. Nicol: Hemmingij de superstitionibq Magisis lib
      £0 01 6

**Niels HEMMINGSEN, Admonitio de superstitionibus
magicis vitandis**, Copenhagen, 1575   8°

(DS, p.36)

632. Jo: Antonidae vander Linden medulla medicinae £0 03 6

**Joannes Antonides van der LINDEN, Medulla Medicinae,
partibus quatuor comprehensa ... tom 1**, Franeker,
1642   8°

633. Geor: Riplaei opera lat   £0 03 6

**George RIPLEY, Opera omnia chemica, ... quorum aliqua
jam primum in lucem prodeunt, aliqua ms. exemplarium
collatione ... repurgata atque integritati restituta
sunt**, (ed. L.H. Combachius), Cassel, 1649   8°

634. Hermanni ffollini Luis pestifera fuga   £0 03 0

**Hermannus FOLLINUS, Amuletum Antonianum, seu luis
pestiferae fuga ... cui accessit utilis libellus de
cauteris**, Antwerp, 1618   8°

635. Matthaei Martini de morbis mesenterij lib   £0 04 0

**Matthaeus MARTINI, De Morbis Mesenterii abstrusioribus,
in scholiis medicorum hactenus praetermissis, nec
scriptis veterum illustratis.   Item affectionum
Hypochondriacarum, ... historia & curatio**, Leipzig,
1630   8°

636. Phill: Gruelingij Centuria medica   £0 02 0

Philippus GRUELINGIUS, Curationum dogmatico-hermeticarum ... centuria prima, Leipzig, 1638   8°

637. Ludovici Combachij de salo vere secreto   £0 02 0

Clovis HESTEAU, Sieur de Nuysement, Tractatus de vero Sale Secreto Philosophorum & de Universali Mundi Spiritu Gothice primo scriptus, in supplementum diu desiderati tertii principii Cosmopolitae, sive ut vulgo creditur, M. Sendivogii ... quod des Sale promisit ... Liber ... tractans de cognitione verae medicinae chemicae ... nunc Latine versus a L(udovico) **Combachio**, Cassel, 1651 8°

(M, pp.164,284,297,299)

638. 5 bookes of Eugenius Philalethes   £0 06 6

Five of six volumes by **Eugenius PHILALETHES (i.e. Thomas VAUGHAN)**, published by Humphrey Blunden at London, 1650-51:

　　(a) **Anima magica abscondita**, 1650   8°
　　(b) **Anthroposophia Theomagica**, 1650   8°
　　(c) **Lumen de Lumine**, 1651   8°
　　(d) **Magia Adamica**, 1650   8°
　　(e) **The Man-Mouse taken in a trap**, 1650   8°
　　(f) **The Second Wash ; or the Moore scour'd once more**, 1651   8°

(DS, p.59 ; reference to (a) ; STC : (a) V142 ; (b) V143 ; (c) V150 ; (d) V151 ; (e) V153 ; (f) V154

639. Dr: ffrench booke of ye Spaw   £0 01 6

John FRENCH, The York-shire Spaw ; or, a treatise of four famous medicinal wells, ... near Knaresborou in York-shire, London, 1652 ; 1654   8°

(M, p.358 ; STC : F2175-F2176A)

640. Sr: Chr: Heydon of ye Influence of ye Starrs   £0 01 8

Sir Christopher HEYDON, An Astrological discourse with mathematical demonstrations proving the powerful and harmoniocal influence of the planets and fixed stars upon elementary bodies, in justification of the Validity of Astrology ... Published by N. Fiske, London, 1650 8°

(STC : H1663-H1663A)

641. Des Chartes of ye passions of ye soule   £0 02 0

René DESCARTES, The Passions of the Soule. In three books .. Translated out of French into English, London, 1650   12°*

(*Nb. There does not appear to be an edition in 8° ; First published in French at Paris, 1649 in octavo).

(STC : D1134)

642.   The marrow of Chyrurgeri   £0 03 6

**James COOKE, Mellificium chirurgiae. Or, the marrow of
many good authours, wherein is ... handled the art of
chyrurgery ... As also an appendix, wherein is ... set
down, the cure of those affects usually happening at
sea and in campe**, London, 1676   8°*
*Nb. Webster may possibly have owned an earlier edition
(London, 1648, 1662) published in duodecimo.

(STC : C6012-C6014)

643.   Whites Philosophy   £0 03 6

**Thomas WHITE (called Thomas BLACKLOW), Peripateticall
Institutions. In the way of that eminent Person and
excellent Philosopher Sr. Kenelm Digby. The Theoricall
Part. Also a Theologicall Appendix of the Beginning
of the World**, London, 1656   12°*
(*Nb. There does not appear to be an edition in 8°.
First published in latin at Lyons, 1646, in duodecimo).

(STC : W1839)

644.   A new methode of Phisicke by Nich: Culpeper   £0 02 6

**Simeon PARTLIZ von Spitzberg, A new Method of Physick :
or, a short view of Paracelsus and Galens practise : in
3 treatises ... Written in Latin by S. Partlicius ...
Translated into English by N**(icholas) **Culpeper**,
London, 1654   8°

(STC : P612)

645.   Chimicall Collections   £0 02 6

**Arthurus DEE, Fasciculus chemicus ; or, Chymicall
collections. Expressing the ingress, progress, and
egress of the secret Hermetick science, out of the
choisest and most famous authors ... Whereunto is added,
... the Arcanum or Grand Secret of Hermetick philosophy**
(by Jean d'Espagnet) **Both made English by James
Hasolle, Esquire** (i.e. Elias Ashmole), London, 1650 8°

(M, pp.165,172,223,375 ; STC : D810)

646.   A Treatise of ye Ricketts   £0 03 6

**Francis GLISSON, A Treatise of the Rickets ... Published
in Latin by F**(rancis) **G**(lisson)**, G. Bate, and A.
Regemorter. Translated by P. Armin. Enlarged** (and)
corrected by N(icholas) **Culpeper**, London, 1651 ; 1668 8°

(STC : G860-G861)

647.   2 bookes of ppareinge of medicines by Geo: Sarky(sic)
       £0 03 6

       Almost certainly the following two works by the
       English alchemist, **George STARKEY**:

           (a) **Natures Explication and Helmonts Vindication :
       or, a Short and sure way to a long and sound life : being
       a ... full apology for chymical medicaments**, London,
       1657   8°

       (M, p.340 ; STC : S5280)

           (b) **Pyrotechny asserted and illustrated, to be the
       surest and safest means for arts triumph over natures
       infirmities, being a ... discovery of the medicinal
       mysteries studiously concealed by all artists and onely
       discoverable by fire. With an Appendix concerning the
       nature, preparation and virtue of several specifick
       medicaments**, London, 1658   8°

       (M, p. 340 ; STC : S5284)

648.   The glass of Humors   £0 00 8

       **Thomas WALKINGTON, The Optick Glasse of Humors ; or,
       the touchstone of a golden temperature, or the
       Philosophers stone to make a golden temper**, London,
       1607 ; Oxford, 1631? ; London, 1639 ; 1664   8°

       (STC : 24967-24969 ; W459-W459A)

649.   Ars memoriae   £0 0 10

       **Henry HERDSON, Ars Mnemonica, sive Herdsonus Bruxiatus ;
       vel Bruxus Herdsoniatus (Ars memoriae : The art of Memory
       made plaine**, London, 1651 ; 1654   8°
       Latin-English. Nb. Webster may only have possessed the
       English half of this work.

       (STC : H1546-H1546A)

650.   The womans dockter   £0 01 8

       **Nicolaus FONTANUS, The Womans Doctour : or, an exact
       and distinct explanation of all such diseases as are
       peculiar to that sex**, London, 1652   8°

       (STC : F1418A)

651.   The Lawes of ye Rosie Cursioris   £0 01 6

       **Michael MAIERUS, Themis Aurea. The laws of the
       Fraternitie of the Rosie Crosse. Written in latin ...
       now in English**, London, 1656   8°

       (STC : M287)

652.   Lux veritatis   £0 01 4

William RAMESEY, Lux Veritatis : or, Christian judicial astrology vindicated and demonology confuted ; in answer to Nath: Homes ... Whereunto is annexed, a short discourse of that great eclipse of the sun, March 29. 1652,
London, 1651   8°

(STC : R209)

653.   Medicina diastatica   £0 01 8

Philipp Aureol Theophrast BOMBAST VON HOHENHEIM (supposititious), Medicina diastatica, or sympatheticall mumie : containing many mysterious and hidden secrets in philosophy and physick .. Abstracted from the works of Dr. Theophr. Paracelsus: by the labour of Andrea Tentzelius ... Translated out of the Latine by Ferdinando Parkhurst, London, 1653   small 8°

(STC : B3542)

654.   Speedy hope(sic) for rich and poore by Hermannus
        Vandr: Heyden -   £0 02 0

Hermannus van der HEYDEN, Speedy help for Rich and poor. Or, certain physicall discourses touching the Vertue of Whey, ... cold water, ... wine-vinegar, London, 1652 ;
1653   8°

(STC : V62-V63)

655.   Naturall Philosophy by J: A: Comenius   £0 02 0

Jan Amos KOMENSKÝ, Naturall Philosophie reformed by Divine Light or a Synopsis of Physics ... With a briefe appendix touching the diseases of the body, mind, and soul ; with their generall remedies, London, 1651   8°

(STC : C5522)

656.   Medicas medicatus   £0 01 2

Alexander ROSS, Medicus Medicatus : or, the physicians religion cured ... With some animadversions upon Sir. K. Digbies Observations on Religio Medici, London,
1645   8°

(STC : R1961)

657.   Paradoxes Phisiologiques   £0 03 6

Pierre BAILLY, Les Songes de Phestion, paradoxes phisiologiques. Ensemble un dialogue de l'immortalité de l'ame et puissance de nature, Paris, 1634   8°

658.   A Treatise of health   £0 01 6

Henry WINGFIELD, A compendious or shorte Treatise,
gathered out of the chyefe and principall Authors of
Phisycke, conteynynge certeyne preceptes necessary to
preservation of healthe, and longe continnuance of
the same, London, 1551?   8°

(STC : 25852)

659.   Jean Liebaut des Infirmitez des femmes   £0 03 8

Jean LIÉBAULT, Trois livres appartenant aux infirmitez
et maladies des femmes, Paris, 1582 ; Rouen, 1649 8°

660.   Petr: fforresti de incerto Urinarum Juditio   £0 04 0

Petrus FORESTUS, De incerto, fallaci urinarum judicio,
quo uromantes, ad perniciem multorum aegrotantium,
utuntur : & qualia illi sint observanda, tum praestanda,
qui recte de urinis sit judicaturus, libri tres,
Leyden, 1589   8°

661.   Hill of Phisiognomy by Dr: Bright of melancholly £0 03 6

Two works bound together in 1 volume:

        (a) **Thomas HILL, Londoner, A Pleasant History :**
declaring the whole Art of Phisiognomy, orderly uttering
all the speciall parts of man, from the head to the foot,
London, 1613   8°

(STC : 13483)

        (b) **Timothy BRIGHT, A Treatise of Melancholie ...**
Newly corrected and amended, London, 1613   8°

(STC : 3749)

662.   ffelicij Plateri Questiones medicae paradoxae   £0 02 0

Felix PLATERUS the Elder, Quaestionum medicarum
paradoxarum & endoxarum, iuxta partes medicinae
dispositarium, centuria posthuma. Opera Thomae Plateri
nunc primum edita, Basle, 1625   8°

663.   Helmont disguised   £0 01 0

James THOMPSON, Helmont disguised : or, the vulgar
errours of impericall ... practisers of physick confuted
... in a dialogue between Philiatrus, and Pyrosophilus,
London, 1657   8°

(STC : T999)

664. Tho: Bartholini de venis lacteis   £0 01 4

Probably the following edition of **Thomas BARTHOLINUS,
De Lacteis Thoracicis Vasa Lymphatica**:

**Joannes Alcidius MUNIERUS (ed.), De venis tam lacteis
thoracicis quam lymphaticis novissime repertis**, Genoa,
1654   8°
(Also includes Jean Pecquet, **Experimenta nova**).

665. The Waterstone of ye wise men & others   £0 02 0

**Philipp Aureol Theophrast BOMBAST VON HOHENHEIM,
Paracelsus his Aurora, & Treasure of the Philosophers.
As also the Water-stone of the Wise Men ; describing
the matter of, and manner how to attain the universal
tincture. Faithfully Englished. And published by
J**(ohn) **H**(arding) **Oxon.**, London, 1659   12°*
(*Nb. No edition in 8°).

(STC : B3540)

666. The English Phisitian   £0 02 0

**Nicholas CULPEPER, The English Physitian, or an
Astrologo-physical discourse of the vulgar herbs of
this nation ... enlarged**, London, 1653 ... London,
1681   8°
First edition : London, 1652 (12°).

(STC : C7502-C7511)

667. Man in Paradise   £0 01 6

**Richard BUNWORTH, Man in Paradise, or the Prerogative
of the Soul**, London, 1656   small 8°
Part 2 of Bunworth's Ομοτροπια **naturae ; a physical
discourse, exhibiting the cure of disease by signature**,
London, 1656.

(STC : B5475)

---

f10v

668. Apologia pro vasis lymphaticis   £0 03 0

**Martinus BOGDANUS, Apologia pro vasis lymphaticis
D. Thomae Bartholini ... contra insidias secundo
structas ab Olao Rudbek**, Copenhagen, 1654   12°*
(*Nb. No edition in 8°).

669. Jo: ffollini Synopsis tuende Sanitatis   £0 02 0

Joannes **FOLLINUS**, **Synopsis tuendae et conservandae**
bonae valetudinis, Cologne, 1646 ; 1648   12°*
(* Nb. No edition in 8°).

670. Petr: Borelli Bibliotheca Chimica   £0 02 0

Pierre **BOREL**, **Bibliotheca chimica : seu Catalogus**
librorum philosophicorum hermeticorum ... usque ad
annum 1653 ... cum eiusdem bibliothecae appendice &
corollario, Paris, 1654 ; Heidelberg, 1656   12°*
(*Nb. No edition in 8°).

671. Guil: Harvaei de Generatione Exercitatio   £0 03 6

William **HARVEY**, **Exercitationes de Generatione Animalium.**
Quibus accedunt quaedam de Partu : de Membranis ac
humoribus Uteri : & de Conceptione, London and
Amsterdam, 1651   12°*
(*Nb. No edition in 8°).

(M, p.357 ; STC : H1091A)

672. Levini Lemnij de occultis naturae miraculis lib £0 03 6

Levinus **LEMNIUS**, **Occulta naturae miracula, ac varia**
rerum documenta, probabili ratione atque artifici
coniectura duobus libris explicata, Antwerp, 1559 ...
Frankfurt, 1640   8°
Also 2 editions in 12° : Amsterdam, 1650 ; Leyden, 1666.

(DS, p.264)

673. Severini Pinaei de virgininitatis(sic) notis cum alijs
      £0 04 0

Severin **PINEAU**, **De integritatis et corruptionis virginum**
notis : de graviditate et partu naturali mulierum.
Ludov. Bonacioli Enneas muliebris ... Fel. Plateri ...
De origine partium, earumque in utero conformatione.
Pet. Gassendi De septo cordis pervio, observationes,
Leyden, 1639 ; 1640 ; enlarged (including Melchior
Sebizius, **De notis Virginitatis**), Leyden, 1641 ; 1644 ;
1650 ; Amsterdam, 1663   12°*
(*Nb. No edition in 8°).

674. Anatomia Sambusi   £0 02 0

Martinus BLOCHWITZ, **Anatomia sambuci, quae non solum**
sambucum & hujusdem medicamenta singulatim delineat,
verum quoque plurimorum affectuum, ex una fere sola
sambuco curationes breves, rationibus, exemplis ...
exhibet (ed. Johannes Blochwitz), Leipzig, 1631 ;
London, 1650   12°*
(*Nb. No edition in 8° ; translated into English by
Christopher Irvine, London, 1655, 1670, 1677, 12°).

(STC : B3198(latin) ; B3199-B3201(English))

675.   Jac: Primerosij de erroribus vulgi in medicina lib
       £0 02 0

       Jacobus PRIMEROSIUS, **De vulgi in medicina erroribus**
       libri quatuor, London, 1638 ; Amsterdam, 1639   12°*
       (*Nb. No edition in 8°).

       (STC : 20384)

676.   Jo: Pharamundi Rhumelij medicina Spagyrica   £0 05 6

       Johann Pharamund RHUMEL, **Medicina Spagyrica oder**
       Spagyrisch Artzneykunst in welcher I. Compendium
       hermeticum, darinnen die kranckheiten in Gemein in
       ihrem Ursprung zu erkenen und wie sie zu curiren.
       II. Antidotarium chymicum ... III. Iatrium chymicum,
       Frankfurt, 1648   8°
       Another ed., Frankfurt, 1662 (12°). The next entry
       would seem to suggest that what is indicated here is
       a Latin edition of Rhumel's **Medicina Spagyrica**. No
       such work is indicated in any of the bibliographical
       literature on alchemy. Moreover, Webster himself, in
       referring to Rhumel's writings in **Metallographia**,
       stated that they were "not translated that ever I could
       hear of," pp.118-119.

       (DS, p.158 ; M, pp.39,118-119,129,192,222)

677.   Id: Rhumelij Germanicae   £0 03 0

       ? Another copy of Item no. 676, above.

678.   Examen Phlebotomicum Germanicae (8°)   £0 03 0

       I have been unable to trace this work.

679.   Deusingij de motu cordis lib   £0 04 0

       Antonius DEUSINGIUS, **De motu cordis et sanguinis,**
       itemque de lacte ac nutrimento foetus in utero,
       dissertationes. Publicae ventilationi submissae in
       illustri Groningae & Omlandiae Academia. Accessere
       Disquisitiones & dissertationes variae, Groningen,
       1655   12°*
       (*Nb. No edition in 8°).

680.   Digby of ye Sympatheticke powder   £0 01 6

       Sir Kenelm DIGBY, **A late Discourse made in a solemne**
       assembly of nobles and learned men at Montpellier in
       France ... Touching the cure of wounds by the powder
       of sympathy ... Rendered faithfully ... into English
       by R. White, Gent, London, 1658 ... 4th ed., London,
       1664   12°*
       (*Nb. No edition in 8°).

       (STC : D1435-D1438)

SECTION H

"Libri Medici et alij in 12°"

**(Works on medicine and other
subjects in 12°)**

681.   Jouberti de erroribus vulgi etc   £0 01 6

**Laurent JOUBERT, Prime partis de Vulgi erroribus
medicine medicorumque dignitatem deformantibus librum
primum latinitate donabat et scholiis illustrabat
Joannes Bourgesius**, Antwerp, 1600   8°*
(* Nb. I can find no edition of this work in 12°).

682.   Nich: ffontani opera in 4 vol   £0 08 6

Probably a composite volume:

Nicolaus FONTANUS, Opera, 7 vols. in 4, Amsterdam,
1633-44   12°

   (a) Two works published by Charpentier, bound in
one volume :
(i) **Aphorismi Hippocratis Methodice dispositi**, 1633
(ii) **Institutiones pharmaceuticae, ex Bauderonio et
      Du Boys concinnatae**, 1633
   (b) Three works published by J. Janssonius,
bound in one volume:
(i) **Commentarius in Sebastianum Austrium**, 1642
(ii) **Responsionum et curationum medicinalium liber unus**,
1639
(iii) **Syntagma medicum de morbis mulierum**, 1644
   (c) Published by Bernardi:
Florilegium medicum, 1637
   (d) Published by Blaeu:
De Fons, sive Origo Febrium, 1644

683.   Multiplicity of worlds by Peter Borrell   £0 01 6

**Pierre BOREL, A New Treatise proving a Multiplicity of
Worlds, that the planets are regions inhabited, and the
earth a star, and that it is out of the center of the
world in the third heaven, and turns round before the
sun which is fixed** (trans. D. Sashott), London, 1658 12°

(STC : B3753)

684.   Petr: Molinaei vates   £0 04 0

**Pierre DU MOULIN the Elder, Vates ; seu, de praecognitione
futurorum bonis malisque prophetis libri V. In quibus
etiam explicantur difficiliores nonnullae veteris et
novi Testamenti prophetae**, Leyden, 1640 ; Gorinchem,
1672   small 8°

685.   Ja Du Bois veritas sacra   £0 02 0

**Jacob DU BOIS, Veritas et authoritas sacra in naturalibus
et astronomicis asserta et vindicata contra Wittichi
dissertationes duas de S. Scripturae in philosophicis
abusu. Adjuncta refutatione argumenti ab eodem authore
ex Cartesii principiis pro motu terrae desumpti,**
Utrecht, 1655   12°

686.   Jo: A: Comei(sic) Pansophiae prodromus   £0 01 8

**Jan Amos KOMENSKÝ, Pansophiae Prodromus, in quo
admirandi illius ... operis, necessitas, possibilitas,
utilitas, solide, perspicue, eleganter demonstrantur**
(ed. Samuel Hartlib), London, 1639 ; Leyden, 1644 12°

(STC : 15082)

687.   Artificia hominum miranda   £0 05 6

**Adam PREYEL, Artificiosa hominum, miranda naturae, in
Sina et Europa**, Frankfurt, 1655   12°

688.   Dillherri Eclogae Sacra Syriace, Grece et lat £0 07 0

**Johann Michael DILHERR, Eclogae sacrae Novi Testamenti,
syriacae, graecae, latinae cum observationibus
philologicis**, Jena, 1637 ; 1638 ; Halle, 1646 ; Jena,
1658 ; 1662   12°

689.   Galeotij martij de doctrina promiscua   £0 03 0

**Galeottus MARTIUS, De doctrina promiscua liber, varia
multiplicique eruditione refertus ac nunc primum in
lucem editus**, Lyons, 1552 ; Frankfurt, 1602   12°
First edition : Florence, 1548 (8°).

(DS, pp.161,331 ; reference is to the Frankfurt,
1602 edition).

690.   Gotofredi Zamelij studiosus Apodemicus   £0 01 2

**Godofredus ZAMELIUS, Studiosus apodemicus, sive de
peregrinationibus studiosorum discursus politicus,**
Bremen, 1651   12°

691.   Voces Greco Barbariae   £0 01 6

**Martinus Petrus CHEITOMAEUS, Graeco–barbara Novi
Testamenti quae Orienti originem debent. Selegit,
congesit, notis illustravit M.P. Cheitomaeus,**
Amsterdam, 1649   12°
Described in William Marsden, A Catalogue of Dictionaries,
London, 1796, as "Novi Testamenti Voces Graeco-Barbarae".

692.   Democritus Redivivus   £0 03 6

Joannes Chrysostomus MAGNENUS, Democritus reviviscens, sive, de Atomis.   Addita est Democriti vita, Leyden, 1648 ; Hague & London, 1658   12°
First edition : 1646 (4°).

(AE, p.78 ; STC : M255A)

693.   August: Alsteni de nobilis iuventutis institutione
        £0 02 0

Augustinus ALSTENUS, Singularis liber de nobilis et studiosae juventutis ·institutione, Amsterdam, 1653 12°

(AE, pp.86,89,93)

694.   ffranc: Baconi de Verulamio opera omnia in 8 vol
        £0 18 0

Francis BACON, Viscount St. Albans, Opera, 8 vols., Amsterdam, 1660-63   12°

An edition of Bacon's Works published at Amsterdam by the Elzevier (E) and Ravestein (R) presses :

        (a) **De Augmentis Scientiarum**, 1662 (R)
        (b) **Historia regni Henrici Septimi**, 1662 (E)
        (c) **Historia Ventorum**, 1662 (E)
        (d) **Historiae Vitae et Mortis**, 1663 (R)
        (e) **Novum Organon**, 1660 (R)
        (f) **Opuscula varia posthuma**, 1663 (R)
        (g) **Sermones fideles, ethici, politici, oeconomici** (i.e. the Essays), 1662 (E)
        (h) **Sylva Sylvarum** (including New Atlantis), 1661 ; 1663 (E)

(DS, pp.244,246,262,266,321,322 : all references are to (h)).

695.   Hen: Grotij et Aliorum disertationes de studijs
        instituendis   £0 04 0

Hugo de GROOT, H. Grotii et aliorum de omni genere studiorum recte instituendo dissertationes, Leyden, 1637 ; Amsterdam, 1645   12°

696.   Rabdologiae lib   £0 01 0

John NAPIER, Rabdologiae, seu numerationis per virgulas libri duo : Cum Appendice de expeditissimo Multiplicationis promptuario.   Quibus accesit et Arithmeticae Locatis Liber unus ... Authore ... Ioanne Nepero, Barone Merchistoni, Edinburgh, 1617   12°

(AE, p.41 ; STC : 18357)

697.   Jo: Vinc: ffranckij(sic) enkiridion   £0 01 4

**Joannes Vincentius FINCKIUS, Encheiridion dogmatico-
hermeticum morborum partium corporis humani praecipuorum
curationes breves continens**, Leipzig, 1618   12°

698.   Alberti magni de mineralibus lib   £0 01 8

**Saint ALBERT, Bishop of Ratisbon (i.e. Albertus
MAGNUS), De mineralibus et rebus metallicis libri
quinque**, Cologne, 1569   12°
First edition : Venice, 1495, in folio.

(M, p.250)

699.   Adolphi occonis Pharmacopoeia   £0 02 6

**Adolphus OCCO, Pharmacopoeia, seu medicamentorum pro.
Rep. Augustana. Cui accessere simplicia omnia officinis
nostris usitata & annotationes in eadem, et composita
... diligenter**, Augsburg, 1580   12°

700.   Jo: Velcarionis Phisica   £0 01 8

**Joannes VELCURIO, Commentarii in universam Physicam
Aristotelis libri quatuor, diligenter recogniti**,
Tubingen, 1539 ; 1540 ; 1547 ; Lyons, 1573   8°*
(*Nb. No edition in 12°. Possibly the London edition
of 1588, published in 16°).

---

f11r

701.   Medicina Saliterna cum Comm: Arnoldi Villanovum
£0 02 0

**ARNALDUS de Villa Nova, De conservanda bona valetudine,
opusculum Scholae Salernitanae ... cum Arnoldi
Novicomensis .. enarrationibus ... recognitis et auctis
per Joannem Curionem**, Antwerp, 1557 ; Venice, 1567 ;
1607 ; Rotterdam, 1649 ; 1657 ; 1667   12°
First edition : Cologne, 1480? (4°).

702. Iamblichus cum Trismegisti lib etc   £0 02 0

IAMBLICHUS of Chaleis, Iamblichus de Mysteriis ...
AEgyptiorum, Chaldaeorum, Assyriorum. Proclus in
Platonicum Alcibiadem de anima, atque demone. Idem de
sacrificio et magia. Porphyrius de Divinis atque
Daemonib. Psellus de Daemonibus. Mercurii
Trismegisti Pimander. Ejusdem Asclepius, Lyons, 1570 ;
1577 ; 1607   12°
First edition : Venice, 1497, in folio.

(DS, p.314)

703. Jo: Baptist montani Consultationes medicinales   £0 03 0

Joannes Baptista MONTANUS, Consultationes medicinales in
duos distinctae tomos, nunc primum post Valentini Lublini
... Hieronymi Donzellini Philippique Bechii editiones ac
castigationes summa diligentia D. Reineri Solenandri
medici recognitae. Accesit ejusdem Reineri Sol.
Consiliorum medicinalium sectio prima, Lyons, 1560   12°

704. Robert Hues de Globis   £0 01 8

Robertus HUES, Tractatus de Globis ... denuo auctior ...
editus, Heidelberg, 1613? ; Frankfurt, 1627   12°
First edition : London, 1594 (8°).

705. Jo: Hen: Alstedij Phisica Harmonica   £0 01 8

Johann Heinrich ALSTED, Physica harmonica, quatuor libellis
methodice proponens I. Physicam Mosaicam. II. Physicam
Hebraeorum. III. Physicam Peripateticam. IV. Physicam
Chemicam, Herborn, 1616 ; 1642   12°
Originally published under a different title, Herborn,
1612 (12°).

706. Id: Methodus mathematicorum   £0 02 0

Johann Heinrich ALSTED, Methodus admirandorum mathematicorum;
complectens novem libros mathesews universae, Herborn,
1613 ... 4th ed., Herborn, 1657   12°

707. L: Apuleij opera omnia   £0 03 0

Lucius APULEIUS Madaurensis, Opera omnia quae exstant,
Paris, 1601 ; ?, 1606 ; Leyden, 1623   12°
First edition : Rome, 1469, in folio.

708. Alberti magni de secretis mulierum cum alijs   £0 01 8

Saint ALBERT, Bishop of Ratisbon (i.e. Albertus MAGNUS)
(suppositious), Alberti magni, de secretis mulierum
Libellus, scholiis ... Ejusdem de virtitibus herbarum,
lapidum et animalium quorundam Libellus. Item de
mirabilibus mundi ... Adjecimus et ob materiae
similitudinem Michaelis Scoti philosophi de secretis
opusculum, Lyons, 1580 ; Amsterdam, 1648 ; 1655 ; 1669   12°

111

709. Phill Ulstadij Coelum Philosophorum   £0 01 4

Philipp ULSTADT, Coelum Philosophorum, seu de secretis naturae liber ... Nunc autem recens apposuimus Rosarium Philosophorum, M. Arnaldi de Villanova, Trier, 1630   12°
First edition : Strassburg, 1526, in folio

(M, pp.32,127)

710. Medicina Saliterna   £0 01 6

Another copy of Item no. 701, above.

711. Amati Lusitani Curationum medicinalium Centuriae
£0 02 6

Lusitanus AMATUS (i.e. João RODRIGUES de Castelo Branco), Amati Lusitani ... Curationum medicinalium centuriae II. priores, Lyons, 1560 ; enlarged, Lyons, 1580 ; Venice, 1653   12°

(DS, p.329 ; reference is to one of the later, expanded editions).

712. Andr: Mathioli opusculum   £0 01 6

Pietro Andrae MATTIOLI, Opusculum de simplicium medicamentorum facultatibus secundum locos & genera. Accesserunt quoque praefationes quaedam huic opusculo ... necessariae, Venice, 1569   12°

713. Macrobij opera   £0 03 0

Ambrosius Theodosius MACROBIUS, Opera, Florence, 1515 ... Leyden, 1670   small 8°*
(*Nb. No edition in 12°).

(M, pp.9,10)

714. Jo: Bachanelli de consensu medicorum lib   £0 03 6

Joannes BACCHANELLUS, De consensu medicorum in curandis morbis, libri quatuor, Paris, 1550 ; Venice, 1553 ; 1556   8°*
(*Nb. No edition in 12°. Possibly one of various editions published in 16° : Paris, 1554 ; Lyons, 1558 ; 1572).

715. Alberti magni de Secretis mulierum   £0 02 0

Another copy of Item no. 708, above.

716. The pisse prophet   £0 01 0

Thomas BRIAN, The Pisse-Prophet or, Certaine pisse-pot lectures. Wherein are newly discovered the old fallacies ... of the pisse-pot science, used by all those ... who pretend knowledge of diseases, by the urine, London, 1655 ; 1679   12°
First edition : London, 1637 (8°).

(STC : B4437-B4438)

717. Paradoxes   £0 01 0

718. Alphonsi ferri de ligno sancto   £0 01 0

Alphonsus FERRUS, De ligni sancti multiplici medicina et vini exhibitione, Paris, 1539 ... Paris, 1566 16°*
(*Nb. No edition in 12°).
First edition : Rome, 1537 (4°).

719. De purgatione lib   £0 00 6

Adam LONICER, De purgationibus libri III, ex Hippocrate, Galeno Aetio et Mesue depromti ... foras dati per Teuc. Annaéum Privatum, C. Adami Loniceri ... filium,
Frankfurt, 1596   12°

720. Aristot problemata cum alijs   £0 01 8

ARISTOTLE (supposititious), Aristotelis aliorumque Problemata : cui de novo accessere Iul. Caesaris Scaligeri Problemata Gelliana, Amsterdam, 1643 ;
1650   12°

721. Mr: Hochlams booke   £0 00 6

I have not been able to trace this author or work.
It could, however, be a reference to a work by either
Cornelius ab Hogelande or Ewaldus de Hoghelande.

722. Quinti Cursij lib   £0 01 6

Quintus CURTIUS RUFUS, De rebus gestis Alexandri Magni libri qui exstant, Leyden, 1595   12°
Numerous subsequent editions in 12°, including Oxford,
1672.

(STC : C7692-C7693)

723 C: Salustij opera   £0 00 8

Caius SALLUSTIUS CRISPUS, Opera, Lyons, 1536   12°
Numerous subsequent editions in 12°, including Oxford,
1678.

(STC : S401)

724. Epicteti Enchiridion   £0 00 8

EPICTETUS, 'Επικτητου 'Εγχειριδιον . **Idem Lat.,**
A. Politiano interprete, Basle, 1531 ; Paris, 1653   12°
Greek—Latin*
(*Nb. No latin edition of this work seems to have been
published in 12°).   (AE, pp.88,108)

725. L: Jul: fflori historia   £0 00 8

Publius Annius FLORUS, Epitome Rerum Romanorum, Oxford,
1631 ... Rotterdam, 1680   12°

(STC : 11101—11102)

726. Hypocrates Aphorismes Graece & lat   £0 01 6

HIPPOCRATES, Hippocratis ... Aphorismi Graece et Latine
(ed. J. Heurnius), Leyden, 1601   12°
Numerous subsequent editions in 12°.

727. Sanctorij Sanctorij de statica medicina   £0 01 8

Sanctorius SANCTORIUS, Ars Sanctorii Sanctorii, ...
de Statica medicina aphorismorum sectionibus septem
comprehensa. Accessit staticomastix, sive ejusdem
artis demolitio Hippolyti Obicii, Leipzig, 1624 ; Venice,
1634 ; Hague, 1657 ; 1664 ; Leipzig, 1670   12°

728. The Aphorismes of Hipp: in English   £0 01 0

HIPPOCRATES, The Whole Aphorismes of great Hippocrates
... faithfully translated into English (by S.H.),
London, 1610 ; 1655   12°

(STC : 13521 ; H2071)

729. Postelli Clavis   £0 01 0

Guillaume POSTEL, Absconditorum a constitutione mundi
clavis, qua mens humana tum in divinis quam in humanis
pertinget ad interiora velaminis aeternae veritatis,
Paris?, 1555? ; Amsterdam, 1646   12°

730. Jo: pecquetti Experimenta nova   £0 01 0

Jean PECQUET, Experimenta nova anatomica, quibus
incognitum hactenus chyli receptaculum, et ab eo per
thoracem in ramos usque subclavios vasa lactea deteguntur.
Ejusdem dissertatio anatomica de circulatione sanguinis
et chyli motu, Harderwijk, 1651 ; Amsterdam, 1661   12°

731.   Guliel: Harvaei Exercitatio Anatomica   £0 02 6

**William HARVEY, Exercitatio anatomica de motu cordis et
sanguinis in animalibus**, Padua, 1643 ; Rotterdam, 1648 ;
1649 ; London, 1649 ; Rotterdam, 1660 ; 1671   12°
First edition : Frankfurt, 1628 (4°).

(STC : H1087–H1089)

732.   Dr: Reads manuall of Anatomie   £0 03 6

Alexander READ, A Manuall of the Anatomy of Man,
London, 1633 ... 6th ed., London, 1658   12°

(STC : 20783.5–20784 ; R430–R433)

733.   Ant: possevini Cultura ingeniorum   £0 01 6

**Antonio POSSEVINO the Elder, Cultura Ingeniorum e
Bibliotheca Selecta A. Possevini**, Trevis, 1606   12°
All earlier and later editions of this work were
published in 8°.

734.   Jo: Reucklini de verbo mirifico   £0 01 6

Johann REUCHLIN, De Verbo Mirifico, Lyons, 1552   16°*
(*Nb. No edition in 12°. First edition : Basle, 1494?,
in folio. First edition published in 8° : Cologne, 1532).

735.   Tho: fieni de veribq imaginationis lib   £0 01 8

Thomas FIENUS, De viribus Imaginationis tractatus,
Leyden, 1635 ; London, 1657 ; Amsterdam, 1658   12°
First edition : Louvain, 1608 (8°).

(DS, p.336 ; STC : F843)

736.   Pharmacopoeia Londinensis   £0 02 6

**ROYAL COLLEGE OF PHYSICIANS OF LONDON, Pharmacopoaeia
Londinensis**, London, 1651 ... London, 1675   12°
Another copy of Item no. 354, above, in duodecimo.

(STC : R2112–R2117)

737.   Messis Aurea   £0 03 0

**Siboldus HEMSTERHUIS, Messis aurea triennalis, exhibens,
anatomica : novissima et utilissima experimenta**, Leyden,
1654   12°
An enlarged later edition appeared at Heidelberg,
1659 (8°).

738.   Reusneri Urinarum probacones   £0 02 0

**Jodocus WILLICH, Urinarum Probationes, ... illustratae
scholis medicis, H. Reusneri ... in quibus principia
solidae Uroscopiae ad solidae Philosophiae fontes
revocantur** (ed. Hieronymus Reusner), Basle, 1582   8°*
(*Nb. No edition in 12°).

739.   Leon: fuchsij Institutionum medicinae   £0 05 6

**Leonhard FUCHS, Institutionum Medicinae, sive methodi
ad Hippocratis, Galeni aliorumque veterum scripta recte
intelligenda ... libri quinque**, Lyons, 1555 ... Basle,
1618   8°*
(*Nb. No edition in 12°).

740.   Amicus medicorum   £0 03 0

Joannes GANIVETUS, Amicus medicorum, Leyden, 1550 ;
Frankfurt, 1614   12°
First edition : Lyons, 1494 (4°). First edition in
8° : Lyons, 1508.

741.   The Surgions Vade mecum   £0 01 8

**Thomas BRUGIS, Vade Mecum : or, a Companion for a
chyrurgion : fitted for times of peace or war ... To
which is added the maner of making reports before a
judge of assize, of any one that hath come to an
untimely end**, 3rd ed., London, 1657 ... 6th ed.,
London, 1679   12°
First and second editions : London, 1652, 1653 (8°).

(STC : B5227-B5228)

742.   Jo: Argenteri de Urinis   £0 01 6

Joannes ARGENTARIUS, De Urinis liber, Heidelberg?,
1591   8°*
(*Nb. No edition in 12°).

SECTION I

"Libri Historici: Philos:
Metaph: Logici etc in 4to"

**(Works on history, philosophy,
metaphysics, logic, etc in 8°*)**

743.   Geor: Buchannani historia Scotica   £0 06 0

George BUCHANAN, <u>Rerum scoticarum historia</u>, Frankfurt,
1584 ... Utrecht, 1668   8°
First edition : Edinburgh, 1582, in folio.

744.   Melch: Adami vitae germ: Theolog: £0 05 0

**Melchior ADAMUS, <u>Vitae Germanorum theologorum, qui
superiori seculo, ecclesiam Christi voce scriptisque
propagarunt et propugnarunt</u>**, Heidelberg, 1620 ;
Frankfurt, 1653   8°

745.   ffamiani Steradae de bello belgicae   £0 06 0

Famianus STRADA, <u>De Bello Belgico decas prima</u>, Rome,
1637 ... Rome, 1658   8°
First edition : Rome, 1632, in folio. First edition in
4° : Frankfurt and Mainz, 1651.

746.   C: J: Caesaris Comment: cum alijs   £0 03 6

Caius Julius CAESAR, <u>Opera cum Commentarii</u> (of Hirtius
and others), Florence & Lyons, 1508   8°
Numerous subsequent editions in 8°.   First edition in
4° : Paris, 1522.

747.   C: J: Caesaris Coment: cum alijs multis   £0 04 0

A later edition of the preceding entry.

748.   Laur: Surij historia   £0 04 0

**Laurentius SURIUS, <u>Commentarius brevis rerum in orbe
gestarum</u>**, Louvain & Cologne, 1566 ... Cologne, 1602 8°

*   The reference in the title of this section to works
in 4° is almost certainly an error in transcription.
The great majority of the works were published
exclusively in 8°.   However, where editions in 4° can
be established, these are referred to following the
main entry.

749. fflavi vegetij de re militari   £0 02 0

Flavius VEGETIUS RENATUS, De re militari, Lyons,
1523   8°
Numerous subsequent editions in 8°.
First edition : Utrecht, 1475? (4°).
Another copy of Item no. 222, above, in octavo.

750. M: Anton: mureti orationes   £0 03 0

Marc Antoine MURET, Orationes, Venice, 1571 ... Ursel,
1621   8°
First edition : Venice, 1555 (4°).

751. Rerum a Carolo 5to Gestarum authores varij   £0 03 4

**Cornelius Duplicius SCEPPER (ed.), Rerum a Carolo V.
Caesare Augusto in Africa bello gestarum commentarii,
elegantissimis iconibus ad historiam accommodis illustrati**
(by J.C. Calvete de Estrella, J. Etrobius, P. Giovio, etc),
Antwerp, 1554 ; 1555   8°

752. Natalis Comitis muthologiae lib 10   £0 05 6

**Natale CONTI, Mythologiae ; sive Explicationum
fabularum libri decem**, Frankfurt, 1581 ... Lyons,
1653   8°
First edition : Venice, 1567 (4°).

(DS, p.121)

753. Les images des Dieux des anciens etc   £0 12 0

**Vincenzo CARTARI, Les images des dieux anciens, contenans
les idoles, costumes, ceremonies & autres choses
appartenans à la religion des payens. Recuilles ...
en italien par ... Vincent Cartari ... & ... traduites
en françois & augmentées par Antoine Du Verdier,**
Tournon, 1606, 1607 ; Lyons, 1610 ; 1623, 1624   8°
First edition : Lyons, 1581 (4°).

754. Montirosarum historia   £0 03 0

**Agricola SOPHOCARDIO (i.e. George WISHART, Bishop of
Edinburgh), J(acobi) G(raemi) De rebus auspiciis ...
Caroli ... Magnae Britanniae ... Regis, &c sub imperio
... Jacobi Montisrosarum Marchionis, ... supremi Scotiae
gubernatoris annon 1644, & duobus sequentibus praeclare
gestis, commentarius**, Amsterdam?, 1647 ; Paris,
1648   8°

755.   Dionis Cassij Histor: Rom: cum Comment: £0 05 0

**DION CASSIUS, <u>Romanae historiae libri ... XXV, nimirum</u>
<u>XXXVI a ad LXI, quibus exponuntur res gestae a bello</u>
<u>cretico usque ad LXI ... Gulielmo Xylandro Augustano</u>
<u>interprete ... Additum est Joannis Xiphilini e Dione</u>
<u>compendium, Guli Blanco Albiensi interprete ab eodem</u>
<u>Xylandro diligenter castigatum</u>,** Lyons, 1559   8°
First edition : Lyons, 1558, in folio.

756.   C: Jul: Higini fabularum lib cum multis alijs
        ejusdm naturis   £0 05 0

**Caius Julius HYGINUS, <u>Fabularum liber ... nunc denuo</u>
<u>excusus. Ejusdem Poeticon astronomicon libri quatuor.</u>
<u>Quibus accesserunt similis argumenti : Palaephati de</u>
<u>Fabulosis narrationibus liber I ; P. Fulgentii Placiadis,</u>
<u>... Mythologiarum libri III ; Ejusdem de Vocum antiquarum</u>
<u>interpretatione liber I</u>...**(etc) (ed. J. Micyllus),
Paris, 1578 ; Geneva & Lyons, 1608   8°
First edition : Basle, 1535, in folio.

757.   Dionysij Gothofredi antiqua historia   £0 04 6

**Denis GODEFROY, Prof. at Heidelberg, <u>Antiquae historiae</u>
<u>ex XXVII authoribus contextae libri VI</u>,** Strassburg,
1604   8°
First edition : Basle, 1590 (32°).

758.   Assertiones Theol: Basilicon doron cum alijs   £0 02 6

Two tracts bound together in 1 volume:

        (a) **John GORDON, Dean of Salisbury, <u>Assertiones</u>
<u>Theologicae pro vera verae ecclesiae nota quae est</u>
<u>solius Dei adoratio, contra falsae Ecclesiae creaturarum</u>
<u>adorationem</u>,** La Rochelle, 1603   8°

        (b) **JAMES I, King of GB and Ireland, Βϰοιλικον
Δωροψ ; or His Maiesties instructions to <u>his dearest</u>
<u>sonne Henry the Prince</u>,** Edinburgh & London, 1603 ;
London, 1604 (latin ed.)   8°

        (STC : 1603 eds., 14349–14354 ; 1604 ed., 14355)

759.   Jo: Leonis Africani de descriptione Africae   £0 03 6

**Joannes LEO Africanus, <u>De totius Africae descriptione,</u>
<u>libri IX recens in latinam linguam conversi, Joan.</u>
<u>Floriano interprete</u>,** Antwerp, 1556 ; Zurich, 1559 8°

760.   Ammiani Marcellini   £0 03 6

**Ammianus MARCELLINUS, <u>Ammiani Marcellini rerum gestarum
libri XVIII, a decimo-quarto ad trigesimum primum</u>,**
Paris, 1554 ; Lyons, 1591 ; 1600   8°
First edition : Rome, 1474, in folio. First edition in
4° : Hamburg, 1609.

761.   Legationum Insigne   £0 03 0

**Fridericus de MARSELAER, Κηρυκειον <u>sive Legationum
insigne ; in duos libros distributum</u>,** Antwerp, 1618 8°
Another edition : Antwerp, 1626 (4°).

762.   Herodoti historia   £0 04 0

**HERODOTUS, <u>Historiae Libri VIII ... per L. Vallam
interpreti</u>** (trans. Conrad Heresbach), Lyons, 1542 ;
Basle, 1559 ; 1566 ; 1573 ; 1583 ; Frankfurt, 1584 ;
1595   8°
First edition : Venice, 1474, in folio. I have located
only 1 4° edition : Paris, 1510.

(M, p.9)

763.   Gulielmi Nabrigensis historia   £0 02 0

**Gulielmus PETIT Neubrigensis, <u>Historia Anglicana, sive
de regno et administratione regum Angliae</u>,** Paris,
1632   8°
Two earlier editions appeared under different titles
at Antwerp, 1567 and Paris, 1610 (8°).

764.   Pauli Jovij historia in 4 vol   £0 07 0

**Paolo GIOVIO the Elder, Bishop of Nocera, <u>Historiarum
sui temporis</u>,** 2 vols. split and rebound in 4, Paris,
1558-60 ; Lyons, 1561   8°
Also numerous 1 and 3 volume editions in 8° : ?, 1555
(1 vol) ; Basle, 1560 ; 1567 (3 vols) ; Strassburg,
1556 (1 vol).
Another copy of Item no. 119, in octavo.

765.   Thusididis historia   £0 03 6

**THUCYDIDES, <u>Thucydidis, ... Historiae de bello
Peloponnesiaco libri octo</u>,** Wittenberg, 1580 ; Frankfurt,
1589 ; Tubingen, 1596 ; Strassburg, 1614   8°
First edition : Treviso, 1483?, in folio.

766.   Pausaniae veteris Graeciae historiae   £0 05 0

**PAUSANIAS, <u>Pausaniae ... veteris Graeciae regionibus
commentarii a Romulo Amasaeo, ... conversi cum indice
et rerum et verborum</u>,** Basle, 1557 ; Lyons, 1558 ; 1559 ;
1577 ; Frankfurt, 1624   8°
First edition : Florence, 1551, in folio.

767.　Justi Lipsi de Crucae　　　　　　　　　　£0 01 6

Justus LIPSIUS, De Cruce libri tres, 2nd ed., Antwerp,
1595 ; 3rd ed., Antwerp, 1597 ; and later eds., Paris,
1598 ; 1606　　　　　　　　　　　　　　　　8°
First edition : Antwerp, 1593 (4°).

768.　Phill: Loniceri historia Turcita　　　　£0 03 6

**Philippus LONICERUS, Chronicorum turcicorum in quibus
Turcorum origo, principes, ... &c huc pertinentia
exponuntur et mahometice religionis instituta ;
judiciorumque processus, & aulae constitutio ... tomus
primus**, Frankfurt, 1584　　　　　　　　　　8°
First edition (3 vols) : Frankfurt, 1578, in folio.

---

f12r

769.　Herodoti Historia　　　　　　　　　　　£0 03 6

Another copy of Item no. 762, above.

770.　Historia Albigentium　　　　　　　　　£0 02 0

**PETRUS Sarnensis, A Monk of the Abbey of Vaux-de-Cernay,
Historia Albigensium, et sacri belli in eos anno MCCIX.
suscepti duce & principe Simone a Monte-Forti, dein
Tolosano comite, rebus strenve gestis clarissimo.　Ex
mss codicibus, in lucem nunc primum edita**, Trecis,
1615 ; 1617　　　　　　　　　　　　　　　　8°

771.　Barthol: ffacij et Joviani Pontani historia　£0 02 6

**Bartholomaeus FACIUS and Joannes Jovianus PONTANUS,
Rerum suo tempore gestarum libri sexdecim**, Basle, 1566,
1567　　　　　　　　　　　　　　　　　　　8°

772.　Diogenis Laertij de vita et moribus Philosophorum
£0 02 0

**DIOGENES Laertius, De vita et moribus philosophorum
libri X** (trans. St. Ambrose of Camaldoli), Lyons, 1541 ;
Cologne, 1542 ; Lyons, 1546 ; Antwerp, 1566　　8°
First edition : Brescia, 1485.　First edition in 4° :
Venice, 1490.

773.   Plutarchi opuscula in 2 vol   £0 04 6

PLUTARCH, Plutarchi Chaeronei ... Opuscula moralia, 2 vols.,
Lyons, 1542   8°
Numerous 1 and 3 vol. editions of this work were published
in octavo.

774.   Nichol: Videlij Rationale Theologicum   £0 03 6

**Nicolaus VEDELIUS, Rationale theologicum, seu de
Necessitate et vero usu principiorum rationis ac
philosophiae in controversiis theologicis libri tres,
pro veritate totius religionis christianae et speciatim
confessionum evangelicarum oppositi sophisticae
ultimorum temporum a Nicolao Vedelio**, Geneva, 1628 8°

775.   Jo: Sturmij Dialectices lib   £0 01 8

**Joannes STURMIUS Sleidanus, Partitionum dialecticarum
libri duo**, Paris, 1539 ... enlarged, Strassburg, 1549
(libri IIII) ... Strassburg, 1582   8°

776.   Jo: Bodini methodus historiarum   £0 03 0

**Jean BODIN, Methodus historica, duodecim eiusdem
argumenti scriptorum, tam veteram quam recentiorum,
commentariis adaucta**, Basle, 1576 ; Heidelberg, 1583 ;
Geneva, 1595 ; 1610   8°
First edition : Paris, 1566 (4°).

777.   Stekij Logica   £0 03 0

**Joannes STEKIUS, Methodus eruditionis, seu Cursus novus
systematicus et agonisticus logicae Aristoteleae, Organi
librorum omnium commentarium brevem facilem et methodicam
complectens**, Plancy, 1614   8°

778.   Jo: Magyri Phisica   £0 02 0

**Joannes MAGIRUS, Physica peripatetica ex Aristotele,
eiusque interpretibus collecta, et in sex libros
distincta, in usum Academiae Marpurgensis, studio &
opera Iohannis Magiri**, Frankfurt, 1597   8°

779.   Barthol: Keckermanni Systema Theolog   £0 01 8

**Bartholomaeus KECKERMANNUS, Systema S.S. Theologiae,
tribus libris adornatum**, Hanover, 1602 ; 1603 ; Geneva,
1611 ; Hanover, 1615   8°

780.   Andr: Alciati Emblemata   £0 03 0

Andreas ALCIATUS, <u>Emblematum liber</u>, Augsburg, 1531 ...
Padua & Paris, 1618   8°

781.   Casmanni Psychologia   £0 03 6

**Otho CASMANNUS, <u>Psychologia anthropologica ; sive animae
humanae doctrina</u>**, Hanover, 1594, 1596 (in 2 Parts) 8°

(DS, p.83)

782.   Thom de Aquino Sumae pars prima   £0 02 0

Saint THOMAS Aquinas, <u>Summa Theologica ... Pars Prima</u>,
Paris, 1520 ; Bergamo, 1590 ; Paris, 1639   8°

783.   Lamberti Danaei Ethicaes Christianae lib   £0 03 8

Lambert DANEAU, <u>Ethices christianae libri tres</u>, Geneva,
1577 ; 1579 ; 1582 ; 1583 ; 1588 ; 1601   8°

(AE, p.87)

784.   Severini Bortij(sic) de Consolatione   £0 02 0

**Anicius Manlius Torquatus Severinus BOETHIUS,
<u>De Consolatione Philosophiae</u>**, Florence, 1507 ...
Leyden, 1671   8°
First edition : Basle, 1474?, in folio.

785.   Jul: Caesaris Scaligeri Exercitat in Cardanum £0 04 0

**Julius Caesar SCALIGER, <u>Exotericarum Exercitationum
liber quintus decimus de Subtilitate, ad H. Cardanum</u>**,
Frankfurt, 1576 ; 1582 ; 1592 ; 1612 ; Lyons, 1615 ;
Hanover, 1620 ; 1634 ; Frankfurt, 1665   8°
First edition : Paris, 1557 (4°).

(DS, p.59,156 ; M, p.249)

786.   Tho: Hobbes Philosophia   £0 02 6

**Thomas HOBBES, <u>Elementorum philosophiae sectio prima :
de Corpore</u>, authore Thoma Hobbes**, London, 1655   8°
(STC : H2230)

787.   Barthol: Keckermanni Systema Logicae   £0 02 0

Bartholomaeus KECKERMANNUS, <u>Systema Logicae</u>, Hanover,
1600 ... Frankfurt, 1628   8°

788. Benedicti pererij Physica   £0 04 0

Benedictus Valentinus PERERIUS, Physicorum, sive de
principiis rerum naturalium libri XV, Lyons, 1585 ;
Paris, 1586 ; Lyons, 1588 ; Cologne, 1595 ; 1603 ;
1618   8°
First edition : Rome, 1562, in folio. First edition
in 4° : Paris, 1579.

(DS, pp.75,106,112)

789. M: Catonis T: Varronis Columella et aliorum de re
      rustica lib   £0 06 6

Marcius Porcius CATO, Libri de re rustica. M. Catonis
lib I. M. Terentii Varronis lib III. L. Junii
Moderati Columellae lib XII. Palladii lib XIIII,
Zurich, 1528 ... Heidelberg, 1595   8°
First edition : Venice, 1472, in folio.

790. Sommaire de la Philosophie   £0 03 0

Jean de CHAMPAIGNAC, Sommaire des quatre parties de la
philosophie, logique, ethique, phisique, et
metaphisique, Paris, 1606   8°

791. Hier: Cardani de subtillitate lib 21   £0 03 6

Girolamo CARDANO, De subtilitate libri XXI, Paris,
1550 ; 1551 ; Lyons, 1554 ; 1559 ; Basle, 1560 ; Lyons,
1580 ; Basle, 1582 ; 1611   8°

(DS, p.41 ; M, p.95)

792. Jo: Hen: Alstedij Logicae systema Harmonicum £0 04 0

Johann Heinrich ALSTED, Logicae systema harmonicum,
Herborn, 1614   8°

(DS, p.344)

793. ffr: Eustachij Summa philosophiae Quadripartita £0 04 0

EUSTACHIUS a Sancto Paulo, Summa philosophiae
quadripartita : de rebus dialecticis, moralibus, physicis
et metaphysicis, authore Fr. Eustachio a Sancto Paulo,
2 vols. in 1, Paris, 1609 ... Cambridge, 1649   8°

(STC : 10578 ; E3432-E3433)

794. Aristot: politicorum lib   £0 01 6

ARISTOTLE, Politica, Venice, 1543 ... Frankfurt, 1608 8°
First edition : Rome, 1492, in folio.

795.   Ja: Cheynei Physiologia   £0 01 8

**Jacobus CHEYNEIUS, Succincta in physiologiam
Aristotelicam analysis**, Paris, 1580   8°

796.   Barthol: Keckermanni Systema Logicae   £0 01 8

Another copy of Item no. 787, above.

797.   Alius ejusdem Authoris   £0 01 6

Another copy of Item no. 787, above.

798.   Aristot: Ethicorum lib graecae et lat   £0 01 8

ARISTOTLE, Ethica Nicomachea, Basle, 1556 ; Frankfurt,
1591 ; 1596 ; 1601 ; Hanover, 1610   8°
First edition : Paris, 1555, in folio.
Greek–Latin.

799.   Philosophia naturalis (8°)   £0 01 8

800.   Melch: Junij methodus Eloquentiae   £0 00 8

**Melchior JUNIUS (i.e. Johann SOMMER), Methodus
eloquentiae comparandae, scholiis rhetoricis tradita
a Melchiore Junio**, Strassburg, 1585 ; 1589 ; 1609 ;
Basle, 1589   8°

801.   Petr: Rami dialectico lib   £0 00 8

Pierre de LA RAMÉE, Dialecticae libri duo, Paris, 1560
... Frankfurt, 1600   8°

802.   Alius ejusdem authoris   £0 00 8

Another copy of Item no. 801, above.

803.   ffr: Titellmanni Logica   £0 01 0

**Franciscus TITELMAN, Compendium Dialecticae Francis
Titelmanni, ad libros Logicorum Arist. admodum utile
ac necessarium**, Paris, 1539 ... Paris, 1602   8°

804.   Theoph: Golij Ethica   £0 1 10

**Theophilus GOLIUS, Epitome doctrinae moralis, ex decem
libris Ethicorum Aristotelis**, Strassburg, 1592?   8°
Numerous subsequent editions in 8°, including a Greek-
latin edition published at Strassburg, 1617.

805.   Jo: Tho: ffreigij Questiones Log: et Ethic   £0 01 8

Joannes Thomas FREIGIUS, Quaestiones ἐωτιναι και
δειλιναι : **seu logicae & ethicae.   In Archigymnasio
friburgensi ad captum adolescentum praelectae**, Basle,
1574? ; 1576 ; 1584?   8°

---

f12v

806.   August Hunnaei Dialectica   £0 02 0

**Augustinus HUNNAEUS, Dialectica, seu generalia logices
praecepta**, Antwerp, 1570 ; 1581 ; 1585   8°

807.   Aristot Categoria   £0 00 8

ARISTOTLE, Categoriae, Cologne, 1551   8°
Numerous later editions in 8°.
First edition : Cologne, 1490, in folio.

808.   Barth: Keckermanni metaphisica   £0 0 10

**Bartholomaeus KECKERMANNUS, Scientiae Metaphysicae
compendiosum systema ; publicis in Gymnasio Dantiscano
praelectionibus adornatum, & in duas partes tributum**,
Hanover, 1609 ; 1611 ; 1615 ; 1619   8°

809.   Jac: Martinij Questiones metaphisicae   £0 03 6

**Jacob MARTINI, Partitiones et quaestiones metaphysicae,
in quibus omnium fere terminorum metaphysicorum
distinctiones accurate ... explicantur : ut et
praecipuae quaestiones ex Fr. Suaretz et Cl. Timplero
partim resolvuntur, partim examinantur et refutantur**,
Wittenberg, 1615   8°

810.   Comentar: de Anima   £0 00 8

An unidentified commentary on **ARISTOTLE, De Anima**,
in 8°.

811.   Geo: Downhami Coment: in Ram: dialectic: £0 01 6

**George DOWNAME, Bishop of Derry, Commentarii in P. Rami
... Dialecticam, quibus ex classicis quibusque auctoribus
praeceptorum Rameorum perfectio demonstrantur, sensus
explicatur, usus exponitur**, Frankfurt, 1601 ; 1606 ; 1610 ;
1616 ; 1631 ; London, 1669 ; Cambridge, 1672   8°

(STC : L434-L435)

126

812.   Summa Ethices   £0 00 8

Francesco PAVONE, <u>Summa ethicae, sive Introductio in</u>
<u>Aristotelis et Theologorum doctrinam moralem</u>, Lyons,
1620   8°

813.   Titellmanni Phisica   £0 0 10

Franciscus TITELMAN, <u>Compendium Physicae ..., ad libros</u>
<u>Aristo. de Naturali philosophia utilissimum. Cui libellus</u>
<u>accessit de Mineralibus, plantis et animalibus, ad</u>
<u>absolutiorem rerum naturalium scientiam ; et tabula</u>
<u>universam philosophiae partitionem continens</u>, Paris,
1545 ; 1588 ; 1607   8°

814.   Bath: Keckermanni Systema Logices   £0 02 0

Another copy of Item no. 787, above.

815.   Benedicti pererij phisica   £0 04 0

Another copy of Item no. 788, above.

816.   Hieronom: Cardani de Subtilitate et de varietate
       lib in 2 vol   £0 08 0

A 2 volume edition of **Girolamo CARDANO**, published by
Bartholomaeus Honoratus at Lyons, 1580:

       (a) **<u>De Subtilitate libri XXI</u>**, Lyons, 1580   8°
           Another edition of Item no. 791, above.
       (b) **<u>De rerum varietate</u>**, Lyons, 1580   8°

817.   M: Terentij Varonis opera cum alijs   £0 03 6

Marcus Terentius VARRO, <u>Opera quae supersunt. In lib.</u>
<u>de ling. Lat. conjectanea J. Scaligeri recognita & appendice</u>
<u>aucta. In libros de re rust. notae ejusdem Ios. Scal. non</u>
<u>antea editae. His adjuncti fuerunt A. Turn</u>(ebus)**<u>. Comment.</u>**
<u>in lib de lingua Latina cum emendationibus A. Augustini.</u>
<u>Item P. Victorii castigationes in lib. De re rustica</u>,
Geneva, 1573 ; 1581 ; Paris, 1585 ; Leyden, 1601 ;
Dordrecht, 1619 ; Amsterdam, 1623   8°

818.   fflagellum Daemonis cum alijs   £0 05 6

<u>Thesaurus exorcismorum atque conjurationem terribilium</u>
<u>... Authores et tractatus qui hoc volumine continentur :</u>
<u>F. Valerii Polydori, ... Practica exorcistarum ad daemones</u>
<u>et maleficia de Christi fidelibus pellendum, pars 1a.</u>
<u>Ejusdem dispersio daemonum ... pars 2a.   F. Hieronymi</u>
<u>Mengi ... Flagellum daemonum. Ejusdem Fustis daemonum.</u>
<u>F. Zachariae Vicecomitis, ... Complementum artis</u>
<u>exorcistiquae.   Petri Antoniii Stampae, ... Fuga</u>
<u>Satanae</u>, Cologne, 1608   8°

819. Hen: Conaelius(sic) Agripae opera omnia in 2 vol
      £0 13 4

      **Henricus Cornelius AGRIPPA, Opera omnia, in duos tomos
      digesta**, 2 vols., Lyons?, 1533? ; Lyons, 1590? ; 1600? ;
      Strassburg, 1630?   8°

      (AE, p.31 ; DS, p.335)

820. Antonij Ruvio opera in 3 vol: £0 08 0

      Either part of or the complete set of commentaries on
      Aristotle, written by **Antonius RUVIO,** and published at
      Lyons in 5 volumes by Joannis Pillehotte.

              (a) **Commentarii in libros Aristotelis ... de Anima,**
      1613 ; 1620
              (b) **Commentarii in libros Aristotelis ... de Coelo,
      et Mundo,** 1616 ; 1620
              (c) **Logica Mexicana ... Commentarii ... in Universam
      Aristotelis Dialecticam,** 1611
              (d) **Commentarii in libros Aristotelis, de ortu, et
      interitu rerum naturalium,** 1614 ; 1620
              (e) **Commentarii in Octo Libros Aristotelis de
      Physico Auditu,** 1618 ; 1620

821. Jo: Magyri Phisyologia   £0 02 6

      **Joannes MAGIRUS, Physiologiae peripateticae libri sex,
      cum commentariis, in quibus praecepta illius perspicue
      eruditesque explicantur, & ex optimis quibusque
      peripateticae philosophiae interpretibus, Platone,
      Aristotele, Zabarella ... & aliis disceptantur,**
      Frankfurt, 1603 ... Frankfurt & Geneva, 1638   8°

      (M, pp.87,357)

822. Jo: Magyri in Eth: Aristot: £0 03 6

      **ARISTOTLE, Ioannis Magiri ... Corona virtutum moralium,
      universam Aristotelis ... ethicen exacte enucleans :
      variasq; enodationes, quaestiones, obiectiones et
      dilutiones ... proponens : adiecto ubiq; Aristotelis
      contextu graeco-latino,** Frankfurt, 1601 ; 1614 ; 1628 ;
      Paris, 1663   8°
      Greek-Latin.

823. Sphinx Theologico Philosophica   £0 07 0

      **Joannes HEIDFELDIUS, Quartum renata, renovata Sphinx
      theologico-philosophica ; promens et proponens, pia ac
      arguta aenigmata, sive scrupos ex variis tum sacris tum
      profanis authoribus ... comportatos,** Herborn, 1604 ...
      9th ed., Herborn, 1631   8°
      First published as **Sphinx philosophica,** Herborn, 1600
      (8°).

824.   Jo: Lodov: Vivis et Phil: Malanchthonis de anima lib
£0 05 6

**Joannes Ludovicus VIVES, De anima et vita libri tres.
Eiusdem argumenti V. Amerbachii de anima libri IIII.
Ex ultima autorum eorundem recognitione (P. Melanthonis
de anima liber unus)**, Lyons, 1555 ; 1596   8°

825.   Barthol: Keckermanni Systema phisicum   £0 03 6

**Bartholomaeus KECKERMANNUS, Systema physicum, septem
libris adornatum et anno Christi 1607 publice propositum
in gymnasio dantiscano a Bartholomaeo Keckermanno**,
Hanover & Danzig, 1610 ; Hanover, 1612 ; 1617 ; 1623 8°

826.   Jo: Hen: Alstedij Lexicon Philosophicum   £0 04 0

Johann Heinrich ALSTED, Compendium Lexici philosophici,
Herborn, 1626   8°

827.   Jac: Martini metaphisicae lib in 2 vol   £0 05 6

Jacob MARTINI, Exercitationum metaphysicarum libri duo,
1 volume, split and rebound in 2, Wittenberg, 1608 ...
Wittenberg, 1624 (all 1 volume editions)   8°

828.   Jo: Garcaei Meteorologia   £0 03 6

**Johann GARCAEUS, Meteorologia ... Additae sunt tabellae,
quae totam meteorum doctrinam complectuntur, et exempla
historica**, Wittenberg, 1568 ; 1583   8°

829.   Jul: pacij in Phys: Aristot: Coment   £0 04 0

ARISTOTLE, ᾽Αριστοτελους φυσικης ἀκροασεως .
βιβλια θ᾽. ... **Aristotelis ... Naturalis auscultationis
libri VIII.   Iul. Pacius ... cum graecis ... codicibus
... contulit, latina interpretatione auxit, &
commentariis illustravit**, Frankfurt, 1596 ; Hanover,
1608   8°
Greek–Latin.

830.   Jo: Tho: ffreigij Questiones phisicae   £0 05 0

**Joannes Thomas FREIGIUS, Quaestiones physicae ; in
quibus methodus doctrinem physicam legitimi docendi
describendique rudi Minerva descripta est, libris XXXVI**,
Basle, 1579 ; 1585   8°

831.   Petr: Lombardi Sententiarum lib   £0 03 0

PETRUS Lombardus, Bishop of Paris, <u>Sententiarum</u>
<u>Libri IV</u>, Paris, 1510   8°
Numerous later editions in 8°. First edition :
Strassburg, 1470?, in folio. First edition in 4° :
Venice, 1507.

832.   Les Comentaires de Caesar des guerres de la gaule
£0 03 0

Caius Julius CAESAR, <u>Les Commentaires de Cesar des</u>
<u>guerres de la Gaule. Mis en françois par Blaise de</u>
<u>Vigenere</u>, ?, 1600   8°
First edition : Paris, 1576 (4°). There was an earlier
French translation of this work by Robert Gaguin.

SECTION J

"Lexicons, Grammers, bibles
and such like bookes in 4°: et 8°:"

833.   Dictionarium Italicum et lat   £0 02 6

Catharinus DULCIS, <u>Dictionariolum Italico Latinum ...</u>
<u>Scholae Italicae Annexum</u>, Cologne, 1631   8°

834.   Grammatica Gallica   £0 01 4

A French grammar, probably that produced by:

Robert ESTIENNE the Elder, <u>Grammatica Gallica</u>, Geneva?,
1558 ; Paris, 1569 ; Geneva, 1667   8°

835.   Dictionarum lat: Gre: gallicum   £0 03 6

<u>Dictionariolum latinograecogallicum</u> (ed. Orazio
Toscanella), Paris, 1551   4°
Later editions (8°) : Paris, 1573 ; Lyons, 1578 ; Paris,
1607, 1606. The same work, edited by Federicus Morellus:
Geneva, 1631 ; Rouen, 1636 ; Lyons, 1654 ; 1665 ; Rouen,
1669 (all 8°) ; Rouen, 1658 ; 1665 (both 4°).

836.   Alius ejusdem generis   £0 05 6

Another copy of Item no. 835, above.

837.   Dictionarium Hispanicum Gallicum   £0 03 6

A Spanish-French dictionary in either 4° or 8°. I have
not been able to trace a work with this exact title.
It may refer, however, to one of the following:

   (a) **ANTONIO de Lebrixa the Elder, Vocabularius
Nebrissensis**, Paris, 1516 ; Lyons, 1517 ; Paris, 1523   4°

   (b) **César OUDIN, Tesoro de las dos languas francesa
y española. Thresor des deux langues françoise et
espagnolle**, Paris, 1607 ... Paris, 1660   4°

838.   Junius et Tremellius lat: bible   £0 05 6

**Joannes Immanuel TREMELLIUS and François DU JON the Elder
(eds.), Testamenti Veteris Biblia Sacra sive libri
canonici, priscae Iudaeorum Ecclesiae a Deo traditi,
Latini recens ex Hebraeo facti, brevibusque scholiis
illustrati ab Immanuele Tremellio & Francisco Junio,**
London, 1580, 1579 ... Hanover, 1618   4°
Also published in 8° : Hanover, 1618.

(DS, pp.22,30, chapter VI, <u>passim</u> ; M, pp.2,146,147,148,
150 ; STC : 2056-2060)

839.   M. Ludovisi Lusij Dictionarium novi testament   £0 04 0

**Ludwig LUCIUS, Dictionarium Novi Testamenti, vocum
singularum significationes, origines ... exhibens ...
a M. Ludovico Lucio**, Basle, 1640   8°

---

f13r

840.   Geo: Pasoris Lexicon Grece lat   £0 04 0

**Georgius PASOR, Lexicon Graeco-Latinum in Novum ...
Testamentum**, Herborn, 1619 ... Herborn, 1663*   8°
(* including London, 1620 ; 1621 ; 1644 ; 1650)

(STC : 19443-19444 ; P649-P650)

841.   Jo: Buxtorfi Lexicon Hebraicum et caldiacum   £0 06 8

**Johannes BUXTORFIUS the Elder, Lexicon hebraicum et
chaldaicum ... Accessit lexicon breve rabbinico-
philosophicum**, Basle, 1615 ... Basle, 1676*   8°
(* including London, 1646)

(STC : B6348)

842.   Gregori Lexicon sanctum   £0 05 6

Gregorius FRANCUS, Lexicon Sanctum, Hanover, 1634   8°

(M, p.150)

843.   A large greeke testamt wth notes (4° or 8°)   £0 04 6

844.   Gramatica Hebrea Martinio Buxtorfiana   £0 03 0

**Petrus MARTINIUS, Grammatica Ebraea Martinio–Buxtorfiana.
Seu Grammatica P. Martinii Navarri, quam ex accuratissimis
aliorum Grammaticis, precipue vero Cl. Buxtorfii ... S.
Amama ... mutavit, correxit et auxit**, Amsterdam, 1625 ;
1634   8°

845.   ffra: Junij Gramat haebraea   £0 01 8

**François DU JON, Grammatica hebraeae linguae nunc primum
justae artis methodo ... conformata et in lucem edita
per Franc. Junium**, Frankfurt, 1580   4°
Second edition : Geneva, 1590 (8°).

846.   Petr: Rami grammat graeca   £0 01 8

**Pierre de LA RAMÉE, Grammatica Graeca, quatenus a Latina
differt**, Paris, 1562 ; 1567 ; Frankfurt, 1577 ; 1581 ;
1586   8°

847.   Willielmi Schicards Horologium Hebraeum   £0 02 0

**Wilhelmus SCHICKARD the Elder, Horologium hebraeum,
sive Consilium quomodo sancta lingua, spacio XXIV
horarum, ab aliquot collegis sufficienter apprehendi
queat, jam saepius comprobatum, et hac quinta vice
paulo acutius recusum**, Leipzig, 1633 ... London, 1675 8°

(STC : 21816 ; S866)

848.   The new testamt in low dutch   £0 05 6

Dat niewe Testament, Antwerp, 1523   8°
Numerous later editions in 4° and 8°.

849.   Tho: James Catalogus Bibliothecae Bodleiana   £0 03 6

Thomas JAMES, Catalogus ... Bibliotheca Bodleiana,
Oxford, 1620   4°
First edition (different title), Oxford, 1605 (4°).

(STC : 14449–14450)

850.   Bibliotheca hispanica   £0 02 6

Richard PERCYVALL, Bibliotheca hispanica. Containing a
Grammar with a dictionarie in Spanish, English, and
Latine ... Enlarged with the Latin by the advise and
conference of ... Thomas Doyley Doctor in Physicke,
London, 1591   4°

(STC : 19619)

851.   Dictionarium Teutonico Lat   £0 05 6

One of at least 3 possible works:

    (a) **Martinus BINNART, Dictionarium teutonico-**
latinum, reformatum ... et usui juventutis accomodatum,
Antwerp, 1635 ; 1660 ; 1661 ; Amsterdam, 1676   8°

    (b) **Cornelis van KIEL, Etymologicum Teutonicae**
Linguae : sive Dictionarium Teutonico-Latinum, Amsterdam,
? (2nd ed.) ; Antwerp, 1599 ; Utrecht, 1632   8°

    (c) **Matthias Martinus WAUCQUIER, Dictionarium**
Latino-Teutonicum novum, Amsterdam, 1663   8°

852.   Dictionarium Historicum, Geographicum, Poeticum   £0 08 6

Charles ESTIENNE, Dictionarium historicum, geographicum,
poeticum, gentium, hominum, deorum gentilium, regionum,
locorum, civitatum, equorum, fluviorum, sinuum, portuum,
promonorium, ac montium, Leyden, 1595 ... Geneva, 1660 4°

853.   Tho: Erpenij Gramatica Arabica   £0 03 6

Thomas ERPENIUS, Grammatica Arabica quinque libris ...
explicata, Leyden, 1613 ; Amsterdam, 1636 ; Leyden, 1636 ;
1656   4°

854.   Lexicon Syriacum   £0 06 6

One of at least 3 possible works:

    (a) **Christophorus CRINESIUS, Lexicon syriacum,**
Wittenberg, 1612   4°

    (b) **Aegidius GUTBIRIUS, Lexicon Syriacum,** Hamburg,
1667   8°

    (c) **Martinus TROSTIUS, Lexicon Syriacum,** Kothen,
1623   4°

855.   Theod: Bexis(sic) Graeke testamt: wth 2 lat versions
        & notes   £0 06 8

Théodore de BÈZE, Iesu Christi, D.N. Novum Testamentum,
gr. & lat. Theodoro Beza interprete ... Huic editioni,
praeter quorundam locorum recognitionem accesserunt breves
difficiliorum phrasewn expositiones, & aliae quaedam
annotatiunculae, cum ex maioribus ipsius Bezae
annotationibus, tum aliende excerptae, Geneva, 1580 ; 1590 ;
1604 ; 1611   8°
A polyglot edition of the New Testament : Greek & Latin.

856.   Dasypodij Dictionarium lat, Germ: £0 06 6

       Petrus **DASYPODIUS**, **Dictionarium Latinogermanicum, et vice versa Germanicolatinum, ex optimis Latinae linguae scriptoribus concinnatum**, Strassburg, 1537 ; 1538   4°
       Later editions in 8° : Strassburg, 1540 ; 1569 ; 1596.

857.   A ffrench bible (4° or 8°)   £0 05 6

858.   An English bible (4° or 8°)   £0 07 0

859.   A large lat: bible wth: notes*   £0 08 0
       (* presumably in 4°)

860.   2 Concordances (4° or 8°)   £0 03 0

861.   Clavis graecae linguae   £0 01 8

       Eilhard **LUBIN**, **Clavis Graecae Linguae cum sententiis Graecis, Latine explicatis, quibus inclusae sunt omnes predictae linguae radices primogeniae**, Rostock?, 1609?
       ... London, 1669   8°

       (STC : 16879–16881 ; L3386–L3386B)

862.   Janua linguarum latinae, grecae et galicae   £0 03 6

       Jan Amos **KOMENSKÝ**, **Janua linguarum reserata, cum Graeca versione Theodori Simonii ... emendata a Stephano Curcellaeo : qui etiam Gallicam novam adjunxit**, Amsterdam, 1649 ; 1665   8°
       Latin, Greek and French.

863.   Homeri Ilias   £0 02 8

       HOMER, **Iliad**, Cologne, 1522   8°
       Numerous subsequent editions.

864.   Poetae minores graecae   £0 03 0

       (Ralph **WINTERTON**), **Poetae Minores Graeci ... Quibus subjungitur ... index utilis.   Accedunt etiam nunc primum observationes Radulph Wintertoni in Hesiodum**, Cambridge, 1635 ; 1652 ; 1661 ; 1667 ; 1671 ; 1677 8°

       (STC : 12211 ; P2729–P2733)

865.   M: Terrentij varronis de lingua lat   £0 01 8

       Marcus Terrentius VARRO, **De Lingua Latina**, Rome, 1471? 4°
       Numerous subsequent editions in 4° and 8° (first in 8° : Paris, 1529).

866.   fformulae oratoriae   £0 02 0

**John CLARKE, Formulae Oratoriae in usum scholarum
concinnatae privatis olim Lincolniensis Scholae
exercitui accommodatae a J. Clarke,** London, 1630 ...
London, 1673 (12th ed.)   12°*
(*Nb. All extant editions appear to have been published
in 12°).

(STC : C4468B-C4470)

867.   Petr: Martinij Gramatica Hebraea   £0 01 8

Petrus MARTINIUS, Grammaticae Hebraeae libri duo,
Paris, 1567 ... Amsterdam, 1621   8°

868.   Jo: Buxtorfi Epitomae Grammaticae hebraea   £0 01 6

**Johannes BUXTORFIUS the Elder, Epitome grammaticae
Hebraeae ... Adjecta succincta de mutatione punctorum
vocalium instructio et Psalmorum aliquot Hebraicorum
Latina interpretatio,** Basle, 1613 ... Basle, 1669* 8°
(*including London, 1646 ; 1653 ; 1666 ; 1669)

(STC : B6343-B6346)

869.   Institution de la langue fflorentine et Toscaine £0 0 10

**François GUEDAN, Institution de la langue florentine et
toscane, pour apprendre .. la langue italienne,**
Paris, 1602   8°

870.   Janua linguarum lat: gallico teutonicum   £0 01 8

Almost certainly the following:

**Jan Amos KOMENSKÝ, Janua linguarum reserata aurea, sive
Seminarium linguarum et scientiarum omnium,** Amsterdam,
1638 ; 1642 ; 1662   8°
Latin, French and German.

871.   Caspar Cunradi Prosopographia   £0 01 4

**Caspar CUNRADUS, Prosopographiae melicae millenarius
I-II In quo virorum doctrina & virtute clarissimorum
vita ac fama singulis distichis utcunque delineatur,**
Frankfurt, 1615 ; Hanover, 1621   8°

872.   Grammatica, Caldeo Syrica   £0 01 6

A Chaldean-Syriac grammar. At least five works were
published under this title (by Georgius Amira ; Johannes
Buxtorfius the Elder; Johann Heinrich Hottinger the
Elder; Joannes Caspar Myricaeus and Joannes Immanuel
Tremellius).

135

873.   An Italian Grammer   £0 01 0

Scipio LENTULUS, An Italian Grammar ... Turned into
English by H. G(ranthan), London, 1575 ; 1587   8°

(STC : 15469-15470a)

874.   Osservationi della lingua Castiliana   £0 01 0

Juan de MIRANDA, Osservationi della lingua Castigliana
... divise in quatro libri : ne quali s'insegna ... la
... lingua Spagnuola. Con due tavole, Venice, 1566 ...
Venice, 1622   8°
Also an edition in 4° : Florence, 1601.

875.   Collequia familiaria Graecae et lat   £0 00 6

Joannes POSSELIUS the Younger, Οἰκείων Διαλόγων
βιβλίον ἐλληνιστὶ καὶ ῥωμαιστί . **Familiarum**
colloquiorum libellus graece et latine, Wittenberg,
1601 ; 1606 ; 1654 ; Leipzig, 1654 ; and London, 1622
... London, 1681 (10th ed.?)   8°

(STC : 20128.3-20128.7 ; P3017-P3020)

---

f13v

876.   Petr Martini gramatico hebraea   £0 01 6

Another copy of Item no. 867, above.

877.   Gallicae linguae institutio   £0 01 4

Joannes PILOTUS, Gallicae Linguae Institutio, latino
sermone conscripta ... per Joannem Pilotum, Paris,
1550 ; 1555 ; 1561 ; 1563   8°

878.   The Key of ye holy tongue by Jo Udall   £0 03 0

Petrus MARTINIUS, The Key of the Holy Tongue : wherein
is conteined, first the Hebrue Grammar ... woord for
woord .. out of P. M. Martinius. Secondly, a practize
upon the first, the twentie fift and the syxtie eyght
Psames ... Thirdly, a short dictionary conteining the
Hebrue woords that are found in the Bible ... All
Englished by I(ohn) **Udall**, Leyden, 1593 ; Amsterdam,
1645 ; 1648 ; 1650   8°

(STC : 17523 ; M858A-M858C)

879.   Jo: Buxtorfi Epitome, Gram: hebraea   £0 01 0

Another copy of Item no. 868, above.

880.   Gramaticae, Gall Compendium   £0 00 8

Gabriel DUGRÈS, Breve et accuratum Grammaticae Gallicae Compendium, Cambridge, 1636   8°

(STC : 7294)

881.   Erasmi Roteradami Coloquia   £0 01 6

Desiderius ERASMUS, Colloquia, Basle & Cologne, 1526 8°
Numerous subsequent editions in 8°.

882.   Nicol: Clenardi Gramat: hebraeae   £0 00 8

Nicolaus CLENARDUS, Tabula in grammaticen hebraeam,
Paris, 1533 ; 1534 ; 1540 ; 1544 ; 1552 ; 1564 ;
Cologne, 1567 ; Leyden, 1589   8°
Also an edition in 4° : Paris, 1559.

883.   The ffrench Alphabet   £0 01 2

G. DELAMOTHE, The French Alphabeth, teaching in a very short time ... to pronounce French naturally, to reade it perfectly, to write it truely, and to speake it accordingly. Together with The Treasure of the French tung, London, 1595, 1596 ; 1603 ; 1615 ; 1633 ; 1639 ;
1647   8°

(STC : 6546-6550 ; D886)

884.   A spanish and french gramer   £0 01 4

Antonio de CORRO, The Spanish Grammer : With certeine Rules teaching both the Spanish and French tongues. With a Dictionarie adioyned unto it, of all the Spanish wordes cited in this Booke ... by John Thorius,
London, 1590   4°

(STC : 5790)

SECTION K

"Historicall Poeticall and other
miscelanious bookes in 4°: & 8°:"*

885.   Du Bartas his Divine weekes & workes   £0 06 8

Guillaume de **SALUSTE DU BARTAS**, **Bartas his Devine
Weekes and Workes translated ... by I**(oshua)
Silvester, London, 1605, 1606 ; 1608 ; 1611 ; 1613   4°

(M, p.3 ; STC : 21649-21652)

886.   The history and proceedings about ye powdr: treason
£0 02 6

**Anon., A True and Perfect Relation of the whole
proceedings against the late ... Traitors, Garnet, a
Jesuit, and his confederats**, London, 1606 ; republished
in 1662 by J.H., Gent. at London   4°

(STC : 11618-11619a ; H82C-H83)

887.   Bales Pageant of popes   £0 02 0

John **BALE**, Bishop of Ossory, **The Pageant of Popes,
contayninge the lyves of all the Bishops of Rome, from
the beginninge of them to the yeare of Grace 1555 ...
now Englished with sondrye additions by I**(ohn)
S(tudley), London, 1574   4°

888.   A discourse of horsmanship and huntinge   £0 01 4

Gervase **MARKHAM, A Discource of Horsmanshippe. Wherein
the breeding and ryding of Horses for service ... is ...
... sette downe. Also the manner to chuse, trayne, ryde
and dyet, both Hunting-horses, and Running-horses,**
London, 1593 ; 1599 (different title)   4°

(STC : 17346)

889.   of Policy and Religion by Tho: ffitzherbert   £0 04 0

Thomas **FITZ-HERBERT, The first (-second) part of a
treatise concerning policy and religion**, 2nd ed.,
corrected and enlarged, Douai?, 1615, 1610   4°
First edition (Part 1 only) : Douai, 1606, in 8°.
Another edition of Part 1 was printed at London, 1652 (4°).

(STC : 11017-11019 ; F1102)

* On the whole, this section subdivides quite neatly into two
   smaller sections : a large number of works published in 4°,
   followed by a smaller category of works in 8° (and some 12°).

890.   A Compend of ye history of ye Church   £0 05 6

Patrick SYMSON, <u>A Short Compend of the historie of the</u>
<u>first ten persecutions moved against Christians, divided</u>
<u>into III. centuries. Whereunto are added ... treatises</u>
<u>... clearly declaring the novelties of Popish Religion</u>,
Edinburgh, 1613, 1616   4°
Later published, in slightly amended form, as <u>The</u>
<u>historie of the Church</u>, London, 1624, 1625.

(STC : 23601)

891.   The History of 7 Champions of Christendome   £0 03 0

Richard JOHNSON, <u>The most famous history of the Seven</u>
<u>Champions of Christendome : Saint George ... Saint</u>
<u>Denis ... Saint Iames ... Saint Anthony ... Saint Andrew</u>
<u>... Saint Patricke ... and Saint David ... Shewing</u>
<u>their Honorable battailes by Sea and Land</u>, London,
1596, 1597 ... London, 1680   4°

(STC : 14677-14683 ; J795A-J798A)

892.   Geographie by Peter Heylin   £0 05 6

Peter HEYLYN, <u>Microcosmus, or a Little Description of the</u>
<u>Great World. A treatise historicall, Geographicall,</u>
<u>politicall, theologicall</u>, Oxford, 1621 ... 9th ed.,
Oxford, 1639   4°

(STC : 13276-13284)

893.   Camdens Britania in lat   £0 06 0

William CAMDEN, <u>Britannia. Sive florentissimorum</u>
<u>regnorum, Angliae, Scotiae, Hiberniae, et Insularum</u>
<u>adiacentium ex ultima antiquitate Chorographica</u>
<u>descriptio</u>, London, 1594 ; 1600   4°
Also 3 editions in 8° : London, 1586 ; 1587 ; 1590.

(DS, p.287 ; STC : 4506-4507)

894.   Politick, morrall & martiall discourses   £0 02 6

Jean HURAULT, <u>Politicke, moral, and martial Discourses</u>
<u>... Translated into English by A. Golding</u>, London,
1595   4°

(STC : 14000)

895.   The ffrench Academy   £0 05 6

Pierre de LA PRIMAUDAYE, <u>The French Academie, wherein</u>
<u>is discoursed the institution of maners ... Newly</u>
<u>translated into English by T.B.</u>, London, 1586 ... 5th
ed., London, 1614   4°

(STC : 15233-15240)

896.   Cebetis Thebani tabula   £0 00 6

CEBES, Tabula, Frankfurt, 1507   4°
Numerous later editions in 4°, the majority of which
were Greek-latin versions.

897.   Jo: Prisei historia Britaniae defensio   £0 02 0

Sir John PRICE, Historiae Brytannicae defensio,
London, 1573   4°

(STC : 20309)

898.   Ricas Stanihursti de rebus Hibernicis lib   £0 02 0

**Richard STANIHURST, De Rebus in Hibernia gestis, Libri
quattuor. Accessit ... Hibernicarum rerum appendix,
ex S. Giraldo Cambrensi ... collecta**, Antwerp and
Leyden, 1584   4°

899.   Breviarium Rom: Pontificum   £0 01 0

Almost certainly an edition of the Tridentine Breviary:

**CHURCH OF ROME, Breviarum Romanum, ex decreto Sacrosancti
Concilij Tridentini restitutum, Pii V. Pont. Max. iussu
editum**, Venice, 1570   4°
Numerous subsequent editions in 4°.

900.   Hieroglyphica sacra   £0 02 0

I have not been able to trace a work with this exact
title. In all probability, however, it is an edition of:

**HORAPOLLO, Hieroglyphica hoc est de sacris Aegyptiorum
literis**, Bologna, 1517 ; Basle, 1518 ; Paris, 1548 4°
This work was included in a later collection of similar
writings by Giovanni Pierio Valeriano entitled
Hieroglyphica, sive de sacris AEgyptiorum aliarumque
gentium literis commentariorum libri LVIII, Frankfurt,
1614, 1613 (4°) ; republished in 2 volumes, Cologne,
1631 (4°).

901.   Ricas Stanihursti de rebq Hibernicis lib   £0 01 6

Another copy of Item no. 898, above.

902.   The history of Theogines & Cariclia in french wth
        brass catch   £0 07 6

**HELIODORUS, Bishop of Tricca, Les Adventures amoureuse
de Theagenes et Cariclee** (trans. Pierre Vallet), Paris,
1613 ; later editions, trans. J. de Montlyard, Paris,
1623 ; 1626 ; 1633   8°*
(* Nb. This, and the following six works in French,
were published exclusively in octavo).

903. Poliarchus and Argenis in french in ye same manner
      £0 07 6

      **John BARCLAY, L'Argenis, de Ian Barclay. Traduction
      nouvelle** (by Pierre de Marcassus) **Enrichie de figures**,
      Paris, 1623 ; 1624 ; 1625 ; 1633 ; 1638   8°

904. The history of Cassandra in french in 5 vol   £0 15 0

      Gautier de COSTES DE LA CALPRENÈDE, Cassandre, 10 vols.
      in 5, Paris, 1644-67 ; 1644-60 ; 1654-60   8°

905. Histoire le Interditt de Venise   £0 01 8

      **Paolo SARPI, Histoire des différens entre le pape
      Paul V et la république de Venise ès années 1605. 1606.
      et 1607. Traduite** (by Jean de Cordes) **d'Italien en
      françois**, Paris, 1625   8°

906. Rowland Amoreux   £0 03 0

      **Matteo Maria BOIARDO, Count di Scandiano, Histoire de
      Roland l'amoreux ... par M. Jacques-Vincent Du Crest-
      Arnaud**, Lyons, 1614 ; another ed., trans. F. de Rosset,
      Paris, 1619   8°

907. Jo: de Serres Cronockle of all ye Kgs: of ffrance till
      Hen: ye 4th   £1 02 0

      **Jean de SERRES, Inventaire général de l'histoire de
      France, depuis Pharamond jusques à Henri IIII aujourd'
      hui regnant ... par Jean de Serres**, 4 vols., Paris,
      1600-1608   8°*
      (* Nb. Although a 4 vol. edition is not stipulated in
      the catalogue, the value accorded to this item certainly
      suggests more than a single volume).

908. Le Astree de mesire Honore D'Urfe   £0 05 0

      **Honore D'URFÉ, L'Astrée de messire Honoré d'Urfé ... où,
      par plusieurs histoires et sous personnes de bergers et
      d'autres, sont déduits les divers effets de l'honeste
      amitié**, Paris, 1607 ; 1612 ; Lyons, 1617 ; Paris, 1624 ;
      1627 (2 vols) ; 1633, 1632 (5 vols)   8°

909.   Auli Gellij noctium Atticarum lib   £0 01 0

Aulus GELLIUS, Noctes Atticae, Paris, 1508   4°
Numerous subsequent editions in both 4° and 8°.
First edition : Rome, 1469, in folio.

910.   ffaciculus temporum   £0 01 0

Wernerus ROLEWINCKIUS, Fasciculus temporum omnes antiquorum cronicas succincte complectens, Paris,
1512   4°
Another ed., Paris, 1525 (8°).
First edition : Cologne, 1474, in folio.

911.   Illustrium virorum Epistolae p(er) Angelum Politianum
£0 01 0

Angelo AMBROGINI Poliziano, Illustrium virorum Epistolae,
Antwerp, 1510   4°
Numerous subsequent editions in 4° and 8°.

912.   The history of Palmeri of England*   £0 04 6

The (First) – Seconde Part, of the Historie, of the Princes Palmerin of England, and Florian du Desart his brother ... Translated out of French by A. M(unday),
London, 1596 ; 1616 ; 1639 ; 1664   4°
Part 3 was published separately at London, 1602 (4°).
* Variously ascribed to either Francisco de MORAES or Luis HURTADO.

(STC : 19161-19165 ; M2613A-M2613B)

913.   The history of Arthur of ye round table   £0 05 6

Sir Thomas MALORY, The most Ancient and Famous History of the renowned Prince Arthur ... Wherein is declared his life and death ... As also the noble acts and heroicke deeds of his valiant knights of the Round Table, London, 1634   4°

(STC : 806)

914.   The Anatomy of Witt by Jo: Lilly   £0 02 6

John LYLY, Euphues. The Anatomy of Wyt ... wher in are contained the delights that Wyt followeth in his youth by the pleasuntnesse of Love, and the happynesse he reapeth in age, by the perfectnesse of wisedome, London,
1578? ... London, 1636   4°

(STC : 17051-17067)

142

915.   Of ye Advancemte of Learninge   £0 01 6

**Francis BACON, Viscount St. Albans, The Twoo Bookes of
Francis Bacon. Of the proficience and advancement of
Learning, divine and humane**, London, 1605 ; 1629 ;
Oxford, 1633   4°

(DS, p.15 ; STC : 1164–1166)

916.   A booke of playes (4°)   £0 06 0

917.   A Mirror for Magistrates   £0 05 6

**William BALDWIN, A Myrroure for Magistrates. Wherein
may be seen by example of other, with howe grevous
plages vices are punished**, London, 1559 ... London,
1578   4°
In 1574, this work was incorporated into a larger
work by **John HIGGINS** entitled **The first parte of the
Mirrour for Magistrates**, London, 1574 ; 1575 ; 1587 (4°).
Finally, in 1578 appeared **The second part** by **Thomas
BLENERHASSET,** London, 1578 (4°). A complete edition
by all three authors appeared at London, 1610, 1609 (4°).

(STC : 1247–1252 ; 13443–13446 ; 3131)

918.   The Destruction of Troy   £0 02 0

**Raoul LEFÈVRE, The Auncient Historie of the destruction
of Troy. Translated out of French into English, by
W. Caxton. Newly corrected, and the English much
amended, by William Fiston**, London, 1596 ... 10th ed.,
London, 1680   4°

(STC : 15379–15382 ; L929–L941)

919.   The naturall and morrall history of ye East & west
        Indies   £0 06 0

**Joseph de ACOSTA, The naturall and morall historie of
the East and West Indies, tr**(anslated) **by E.G.,**
London, 1604   4°

(M, pp. 1,132,143,149 and passim ; STC : 94)

920.   A forme of prayer for ye 30th of January   £0 00 6

**CHURCH OF ENGLAND, A Form of Common Prayer, to be used
upon the thirtieth of January, being the Anniversary-
Day appointed by Act of Parliament for fasting and
humiliation**, London, 1661   4°

(STC : C4113–C4114)

921. The booke of Cannons   £0 01 0

**CHURCH OF ENGLAND, A Booke of Certaine Canons
concerning some parte of the discipline of the Church
of England**, London, 1571 ; revised, London, 1604, with
numerous subsequent editions, and revised again in
1640   4°

922. Camdens remaynes   £0 03 0

**William CAMDEN, Remaines of a Greater Worke, concerning
Britaine, the inhabitants thereof, their languages,
names, surnames, empreses, wise speeches, poesies, and
epitaphes**, London, 1605 ... London, 1657   4°

(STC : 4521–4526 ; C374–C375)

923. The Travailes of Wm: Lithgow   £0 03 6

**William LITHGOW, A most delectable, and true discourse,
of an admired and painefull peregrination from Scotland
to the most famous Kingdomes in Europe, Asia and
Affricke**, London, 1614 ; 1616 ; 1623 ; 1632 ; 1640 4°

(STC : 15710–15714)

924. Valentine & Orson   £0 01 8

**Anon., The Hystory of the two valyaunte Brethren
Valentyne and Orson, sonnes unto the Emperour of
Greece** (trans. H. Watson), London, 1510? ...London,
1671   4°

(STC : 24571.3–24573 ; V28–V28A)

925   Lamberts perambulacon of Kent   £0 04 6

**William LAMBARD, A Perambulation of Kent, containing the
description, Hystorie, and Customes of the Shyre,**
London, 1576 ; 1596   4°
Another ed., London, 1656 (8°).

(DS, p.271 ; STC : 15175–15176)

926. Gondibert by Sr: Wm: Davenant   £0 03 6

Sir William DAVENANT, Gondibert : an heroick poem,
London, 1651   4°

(STC : D325)

927.   The new found pollitick   £0 02 0

Traiano BOCCALINI, **The New-Found Politicke ... wherein
the governments, greatnesse and power of the most notable
Kingdomes and common-wealths of the world are discovered
and censured** (translated by John Florio, Thomas Scott
and William Vaughan), London, 1626   4°

(STC : 3185)

928.   The history of ye boy of Bilson   £0 01 0

Richard BADDELEY, **The Boy of Bilson ; or a true
discovery of the late notorious impostures of certaine
Romish Priests in their pretended Exorcisme or expulsion
of the Divell out of a young boy, named W. Perry ... of
Bilson**, London, 1622   4°

(DS, pp.252,265,274,275 ; STC : 1185)

929.   Romaines Antiquityes   £0 02 6

Thomas GODWIN, **Romanae Historiae Anthologia. An English
Exposition of the Romane Antiquities, wherein many Romane
and English Offices are paralleld and divers obscure
phrases explained**, Oxford, 1614 ... Oxford, 1680   4°

(STC : 11956–11964 ; G985–G995)

930.   Moses and Aron by Tho: Goodwin   £0 02 6

Thomas GODWIN, **Moses and Aaron. Civil and ecclesiastical
rites used by the ancient Hebrewes ; observed, and at
large opened, for the clearing of many obscure texts
thorowout the whole Scripture**, London & Oxford, 1625
... 11th ed., London, 1678   4°

(DS, p.114 ; STC : 11951–11955 ; G976–G983)

931.   Sr: Edw: Deeringe Speeches in Parliamte: £0 01 2

Sir Edward DERING, **The Speeches of Sr. Edward Deering
in the Commons House of Parliament. 1641**, London,
1641   4°

(STC : D1116–D1117)

932.   The end and begininge of Popery   £0 00 8

Walter LYNNE, **The beginning and endynge of all popery,
or popish kyngedome (being taken oute of certaine olde
prophecies more then CCC yeres agone, here faythfully
set forth to the amendement of this present worlde,
out of hye Almayne by Gwalter Lynne)**, London, 1548? ;
1588   4°

(STC : 17115–17116)

933.   A Survey of London   £0 04 0

John STOW, A survay of London, contayning the originall antiquity, increase, moderne estate, and description of that citie ... also an apologie ... against the opinion of some men, concerning the citie, the greatnesse there of, London, 1598 ; 1603 ; 1618   4°

(STC : 23341-23344)

934.   The History of Trebizond   £0 01 8

Thomas GAINSFORD, The Historie of Trebizond. In foure bookes, London, 1616   4°

(STC : 11521)

935.   A Dicourse(sic) concirninge Prophesies   £0 01 4

John HARVEY, A Discoursive Probleme concerning Prophesies, how far they are to be valued, or credited ... Devised especially in abatement of the terrible threatenings ... denounced against the kingdoms and states of the world, this present ... yeere, 1588, London, 1588   4°

(STC : 12908)

936.   A Compend of Church history   £0 01 0

Another copy of Item no. 890, above.

937.   The English Schoolemaster   £0 00 8

Edmund COOTE, The English Scholemaister, teaching all his schollars, of what age soever, the most easie short and perfect order of distinct readinge & true writinge our Englishe tonge, London, 1596 ... 40th ed., London, 1680   4°

(STC : 5711-5716 ; C6067-C6075)

938.   The Catholique Moderator   £0 00 4

H.C. (i.e. Jacques DAVY DU PERRON), The Catholike Moderator : or a Moderate Examination of the Doctrine of the Protestants, London, 1623 ; 1624   4°

(STC : 6377-6380)

939.   Of ye advancemt of learnige(sic)   £0 01 6

Another copy of Item no. 915, above.

940.   A discription of ye whole World   £0 01 0

(George ABBOT, Archbishop of Canterbury), <u>A Briefe</u>
<u>Description of the whole worlde.   Wherein is</u>
<u>particularly described, all the Monarchies, Empires,</u>
<u>and Kingdomes of the same</u>, London, 1599 ... 6th ed.,
London, 1624   4°

(STC : 24-30)

941.   The Accedence of Armory   £0 02 6

Gerard LEGH, <u>The Accedens of Armory</u>, London, 1568 ;
1576 ; 1591 ; 1597 ; 1612   4°
First edition : London, 1562 (8°).

(STC : 15389-15393)

942.   The Armory of Honour   £0 01 8

John BOSSEWELL, <u>Works of Armorie, devyded into three</u>
<u>bookes, entituled, the Concordes of Armorie, the</u>
<u>Armorie of honor, and of Coates and creastes</u>, London,
1572 ; 1597   4°
Book 2, "The Armorie of honor", comprises virtually
the whole work (i.e. pp.18-136).

(STC : 3393-3394)

943.   Starr Chamber Cases   £0 00 6

Richard CROMPTON, <u>Star-Chamber Cases. Shewing what</u>
<u>causes properly belong to the cognizance of that Court.</u>
<u>Collected for the most part out of Mr. Crompton, his</u>
<u>booke, entituled the Iurisdiction of divers Courts</u>,
London, 1630 ; 1641   4°

(STC : 6056 ; C7030)

944.   Lysimmatha Nicanor   £0 00 6

Lysimachus NICANOR (i.e. John CORBET), <u>The Epistle</u>
<u>congratulatorie of Lysimachus Nicanor of the Societie of</u>
<u>Jesu, to the Covenanters in Scotland : wherin is</u>
<u>paralleled our sweet Harmony and correspondency in</u>
<u>... Doctrine and Practice</u>, Oxford, 1640   4°

(STC : 5751-5752)

945.   Tobacco tortured   £0 01 0

John DEACON, <u>Tobacco tortured, or, the Filthie fume of</u>
<u>tobacco refined : shewing ... that the inward taking of</u>
<u>tobacco fumes, is very pernicious</u>, London, 1616   4°

(STC : 6436)

946. An Abridgmt of all Sea lawes   £0 01 0

William WELWOOD, <u>An abridgement of all Sea-Lawes gathered</u>
<u>forth of all writings and monuments, which are to be</u>
<u>found among any people or nation, upon the coasts of the</u>
<u>great Ocean and Mediterranean Sea</u>, London, 1613   4°
Another ed., London, 1636 (8°).

(STC : 25237)

947. A peice of Aristot: £0 00 4

An extract from a work by **ARISTOTLE** in 4°.

948. Heliodorus History in Greeke   £0 01 6

HELIODORUS, Bishop of Tricca, ʽΗλιοδωρου Αἰθιοπικης
ʽΙστοριας βιβλια δεκα.   **Heliodori Historiae**
AEthiopicae libri decem, nunquam antea in lucem editi
(ed. V. Obsopaeus), Basle, 1534   4°

949. Herodotus history in lat   £0 01 0

Another copy of Item no. 762, above.

950. The Ethiopian history   £0 02 0

HELIODORUS, Bishop of Tricca, <u>An AEthiopian Historie</u>
<u>written in Greeke by Heliodorus : very wittie and pleasaunt,</u>
<u>Englished by Thomas Underdoune. With the Argumente of</u>
<u>every Booke, sette before the whole Woorke</u>, London, 1569? ;
1577 ; 1587 ; 1605 ; 1606 ; 1622   4°

(STC : 13041-13046)

951. Gods revenge agst: murther   £0 05 0

John REYNOLDS, Merchant of Exeter, <u>The Triumph of Gods</u>
<u>Revenege, against the crying, and execrable Sinne of</u>
<u>Murther ... in thirty severall Tragicall Histories,</u>
<u>digested in sixe bookes, acted in divers Countries beyond</u>
<u>the Seas</u> (Books 1-3), London, 1621, 1622, 1624 ; another
ed., London, 1629, 1622, 1623   4°
Later eds. in 8° : London, 1640 ; 1662.

(STC : 20942-20943.7)

952. The Tragedy of Guy of Warwick   £0 00 8

Probably an edition of the following:

Samuel ROWLANDS, The famous historie of Guy Earle of Warwick, London, 1609 ... London, 1667   4°

(STC : 21378-21380 ; R2084-R2085)

However, another possibility is:

B.J., The tragical history ... of Guy Earl of Warwick, a tragedy, London, 1661   4°

(STC : J5)

953. Palmerin d'oliva   £0 04 0

Anon., Palmerin d'Oliva. The Mirrour of nobilitie, Mappe of honor, Anotamie of rare fortunes, Heroycall president of Love, Wonder for Chivalrie, and most accomplished Knight in all perfections ... turned into English by A(nthony) **M**(unday), London, 1588 ; 1597 ; 1616 ; 1637   4°

(STC : 19157-19160)

954. The Gentle craft wth others   £0 02 0

T(homas) **D**(ELONEY), **The Gentle Craft. A discourse containing many matters of delight ... Shewing what famous men have beene shoomakers in time past in this land** (Parts 1 and 2), London, 1637, 1639   4°
Numerous subsequent editions of Part 1 only in 4°.
The "with others" in the catalogue title probably refers to other works by Deloney.

(STC : 6555-6556 ; D953-D955)

955. Englands Helicon   £0 01 4

(John BODENHAM), Englands Helicon, London, 1600   4°
A miscellany, probably edited by Nicholas Ling and planned by John Bodenham.
Another edition : London, 1614 (8°).

(STC : 3191)

956. The history of Dr: ffaustus   £0 00 8

One of two treatments of the Faust legend:

(a) **P.F., The historie of ... Doctor John Faustus**, London, 1592 ... London, 1674   4°
(b) **Ch**(ristopher) **MAR**(LOW), **The Tragicall Historie of the Life and Death of Doctor Faustus**, London, 1604 ... London, 1663   4°

(STC : (a) 10711-10714 ; H2151-H2152 ; (b) 17429-17436 ; M700)

957.   The history of palmendos   £0 01 8

**Anon., The Honorable, pleasant and rare conceited
Historie of Palmendos. Sonne to the famous and
fortunate Prince Palmerin d'Oliva ... Translated out
of French by A**(nthony) **M**(unday), London, 1589 ; 1653 ;
1663 ; 1664   4°

(STC : 18064 ; F377-F378 ; M2613A-M2613B)

958.   The wandringe Knight   £0 0 10

**Jean de CARTHENAY, The Voyage of the Wandring Knight.
Shewing al the course of mans life, how apt he is to
follow vanitie, and how hard it is for him to attaine
to Vertue. Devised by J. Carthenie ... and translated
out of French ... by W**(illiam) **G**(oodyeare) **of
Southampton, Merchant**, London, 1581 ; 1607 ; 1609? ;
1626? ; 1650 ; 1661 ; 1670   4°

(STC : 4700-4703 ; C681-C682)

959.   Mathematicall recreations   £0 03 0

**Hendrik van ETTEN, Mathematicall recreations. Or A
Collection of sundrie problemes, extracted out of the
ancient and moderne philosophers, as secrets in nature,
and experiments in arithmeticke, geometrie,
cosmographie, ... lately compiled in French, by
Henry van Etten, gent** (trans. William Oughtred),
London, 1633 ; 1653 ; 1674   8°

(STC : 10558.5 ; L1790-L1791)

960.   The history of Magicke   £0 03 0

**Gabriel NAUDÉ, The History of Magick, by way of
apology for all the wise men who have unjustly been
reputed magicians, from the creation to the present age
... Englished by J. Davies**, London, 1657   8°

(DS, pp.6,7,8-9 ; STC : N246)

961.   Knowledge of beasts   £0 03 0

**Marin CUREAU DE LA CHAMBRE, A Discourse of the
Knowledg of Beasts, wherein all that hath been said for,
and against their ratiocination, is examined ...
Translated into English by a person of quality**,
London, 1657   8°

(STC : L131)

962. 2 of Mr: Boyles bookes   £0 06 6

Two works by **Robert BOYLE.** Given that Webster cited
Boyle on numerous occasions in his published works (see
below), but made reference to only two works, it might
seem logical to assume that these were the works owned
by Webster. They were:

> (a) **The sceptical chymist**, London, 1661   8°
> (b) **Some Considerations touching the Usefulnesse
> of Experimental Natural Philosophy**, 2 vols. (in 1?),
> Oxford, 1663–71 ; 1664–71   4°

((a) M, pp.47,50,54,57–59,79,122 ; (b) DS, pp.158,
248 ; M, p.339)
(STC : (a) B4021 ; (b) B4029–B4031)

963. Arcana Microcosmi   £0 02 0

**Alexander ROSS, Arcana Microcosmi or, the hid secrets
of mans body disclosed ... With a refutation of Doctor
Browns Vulgar Errors, the Lord Bacons Natural History,
and Doctor Harveys Book de Generatione**, London, 1652 8°

(DS, p.3 ; STC : R1947)

964. The Univsall Caracter   £0 02 0

**Cave BECK, The Universal Character, by which all the
nations in the world may understand one anothers
conceptions, reading out of one common writing their
own mother tongues**, London, 1657   8°

(STC : B1647)

965. The Art of Gunery   £0 01 6

**Nathaniel NYE, The Art of Gunnery. Wherein is described
the true way to make all sorts of gunpowder, gun–match,
the art of shooting in great and small ordnance ... To
make divers sorts of artificiall fire–works**, London,
1647 ; 1648 ; 1670   8°

(STC : N1481–N1483)

966. Tabulae Britanicae   £0 01 8

**Jeremy SHAKERLEY, Tabulae Britannicae : the British
Tables : wherein is contained logistical arithmetick,
the doctrine of the Sphere, astronomicall chronologie
... Together with the calculation of the motions of the
fixed and wandering stars, and the eclipses of the
luminaries. Calculated ... from ... Bullialdus, and
... Mr. Horrot**, London, 1653   8°

(STC : S2912)

967.   Poems by Mich: Drayton   £0 03 0

Michael DRAYTON, Poems. By M. Draiton Esquire, London,
1605 ; 1606 ; 1609? ; 1610 ; 1613 ; 1630   8°

(STC : 7216-7221 ; 7224)

968.   The history of ffenise   £0 01 8

**Francisco de QUINTANA, The history of Don Fenise.
A new romance, written in Spanish by Francisco de las-
Coveras** (pseud.) **And now englished by a person of honour**,
London, 1651   8°

(STC : Q220)

969.   The Unfortunate Spaniard   £0 02 6

**Gonzalo de CÉSPEDES Y MENESES, Gerardo the Unfortunate
Spaniard.   Or a Patterne for lascivious lovers ...
Made English by L**(eonard) **D**(igges), London, 1653   8°
First edition : London, 1622 (4°).

(STC : C1783)

970.   The Lancashire lovers   £0 01 8

**Musaeus PALATINUS (i.e. Richard BRATHWAIT), The Two
Lancashire Lovers : or The Excellent History of
Philocles and Doriclea**, London, 1640   8°

(STC : 3590-3590a)

971.   Cottoni posthuma   £0 03 6

**Sir Robert Bruce COTTON, Cottoni Posthuma : divers
choice pieces of that renowned antiquary Sir Robert
Cotton ... preserved from the injury of time, and
expos'd to public light, for the benefit of posterity,
by J**(ames) **H**(owell) **Esq.**, London, 1651 ; 1672 ; 1679 8°
(STC : C6485-C6487)

972.   Rabelais his Romance   £0 02 6

**François RABELAIS, The first (-second) book of the
works of Mr. Francis Rabelais, doctor in physick : containing
five books of the lives, heroick deeds, and sayings of
Gargantua, and his sonne Pantagruel** (trans. Sir Thomas
Urquhart), London, 1653 ; reissued, London, 1664   8°

(STC : R103 ; R105 ; R108)

973. Restitution of decayed intelligence   £0 02 6

**Richard VERSTEGAN the Elder, A Restitution of Decayed
Intelligence : In Antiquities. Concerning the most noble
and renowned English nation**, London, 1652 ; 1653 ;
1655 ; 1673   8°
First edition : Antwerp, 1605 (4°), with subsequent
editions published in 4° at London, 1628 ; 1634.

(STC : V268–V271)

974. Mores Cabbala   £0 02 6

**Henry MORE, Conjectura Cabbalistica : or, a conjectural
essay of interpreting the minde of Moses according to a
threefold Cabbala, viz. literal, philosophical, mystical,
or, divinely moral**, London, 1653   8°

(STC : M2647)

975. A Banquet of Jests   £0 02 0

(Archibald ARMSTRONG), A Banquet of Jests, 4th ed.,
London, 1634 ; 1660 ; 1665   8°
First edition : London, 1630 (12°)

(STC : 1369 ; A3706–A3707)

976. The Church & Church porch   £0 01 0

**George HERBERT, The Temple. Sacred poems and private
ejaculations**, Cambridge, 1633 ... London, 1679   12°*
(* Nb. All editions in 12°).

(STC : 13183–13188 ; H1516–H1523)

977. Witts recreations   £0 02 0

**(George HERBERT), Witts Recreations. Selected from the
finest Fancies of Moderne Muses. With a Thousand out
Landish Proverbs (selected by Mr. G**(eorge) **H**(erbert)**)**,
London, 1640   8°

(STC : 25870)

978. Lucans Pharsalia   £0 01 6

**Marcus Annaeus LUCANUS, Lucan's Pharsalia : or the
Civil Warres of Rome, betweene Pompey the Great and
Julius Caesar. The three first Bookes. Translated
into English by T**(homas) **M**(ay), London, 1626   8°
Later editions, enlarged (**... the whole ten Books**),
London, 1627 ; 1631 ; 1635 ; 1659 ; 1679 (8°).

(STC : 16886–16889 ; L3388–L3389)

153

979.   Poems by Tho: Carew   £0 01 6

Thomas CAREW, <u>Poems</u>, London, 1640 ; 1642 ; 1651 ;
1670 ; 1671   8°

(STC : 4620 ; C564–C567)

980.   Abuses stript and whipt   £0 01 4

**George WITHER, <u>Abuses Stript, and Whipt ; or, Satirical
Essayes</u>**, London, 1613 ; 1614 ; 1615 ; 1617   8°

(STC : 25891–25897)

981.   Nosce teipsum   £0 0 10

**Sir John DAVIES, <u>Nosce teipsum. This oracle expounded
in two elegies. 1. Of humane Knowledge. 2. Of the
soule of man, and the immortalitie thereof. ...
Whereunto is added, Hymns of Astraea in acrosticke
verse</u>**, London, 1619 ; enlarged, London, 1622   8°

(STC : 6358–6359)

982.   Herodians Imperiall history   £0 02 0

**HERODIAN the Historian, <u>Herodian of Alexandria his
imperiall history of twenty Roman Caesars and Emperours
of his time ; first writ in Greek, and now converted
into an heroick Poem, by C.B. Stapylton</u>**, London,
1652   4°*
(* Nb. There were numerous earlier translations of
this work, but none with the catalogue title).

(STC : H1582–H1583)

983.   Planometria   £0 01 0

**William LEYBOURN, <u>Planometria ; or, The Whole art of
surveying of land</u>**, London, 1650   8°
Published under the pseudonym **Oliver WALLINBY**.

(STC : L1928A)

---

f15r

984.   The Ideot   £0 01 4

**Nicolaus KHRYPFFS de Cusa, <u>The Idiot in four books ;
the first and second of wisdome, the third of the minde,
the fourth of statick experiments</u>**, London, 1650   12°*
(* Nb. No edition in 8°).

(STC : K394)

985.   Esop ffables in English   £0 01 6

AESOP, The Fables of Esope, London, 1550 ... London,
1674   8°
First edition : London, 1484, in folio. The STC lists
only one edition in 4° (London, 1651), and three editions
in 12° (London, 1650 ; 1651 ; 1655).

(STC : 178–184 ; A686–A687)

986.   A description of the new world   £0 01 6

**George GARDYNER, A description of the New World ; or,
America islands and continent ; and by what people those
regions are now inhabited**, London, 1651   8°

(STC : G252aA)

987.   The Common wealth of England   £0 01 8

**Sir Thomas SMITH, The Common–Welth of England, and
maner of government thereof**, London, 1633 ; 1635 ;
1640   ·12°*
(* Nb. The STC lists no edition in 8°. First edition
under this title : London, 1589, 4°. Originally
published as De Republica Anglorum, London, 1583).

(STC : 22865–22867)

988.   Εἰκὼν βασιλικη   £0 01 0

Anon.*, Εἰκὼν βασιλική . **The pourtraicture of his
Sacred Maiestie in his solitudes and sufferings,**
London, 1648 ; 1649 (numerous eds.)   8° & 12°
*** Sometimes attributed to John GAUDEN, Bishop of
Exeter and Worcester.**

(STC : E268–E311)

989.   Rudiments of governmt by Tho: Hobbes   £0 03 0

**Thomas HOBBES, Philosophicall Rudiments concerning
Government and Society ... containing the Elements of
Civill Politic in the agreement which it hath both with
Naturall and Divine Lawes**, London, 1651   12°*
(* Nb. No edition in 8°).

(AE, p.88 ; STC : H2253)

990.   A discription of ye low Countryes   £0 01 8

**Lodovico GUICCIARDINI, The description of the Low
Countreys and of the provinces thereof, gathered into
an epitome out of the Historie of L. Guicchardini** (by
Thomas Danett), London, 1593   8°

(STC : 12463)

991.   The workes of Salust   £0 02 0

**Caius SALLUSTIUS CRISPUS, The Workes of Caius Crispus
Salustius** (trans. W. Crosse), London, 1629   12°*
(* Nb. No edition in 8°. First edition : London,
1608, 1609, in folio).

(STC : 21624)

992.   The golden booke of Marcus Aurelius   £0 01 8

**Antonio de GUEVARA, Bishop of Guadix and Mondonedo,
The golden booke of Marcus Aurelius, emperour and
eloquent oratour** (trans. from French by John Bourchier),
London, 1546 ... London, 1586   8°
First edition : London, 1535 (4°).

(STC : 12440-12447)

993.   The history of Sr: Wm: Wallace   £0 01 8

**(HENRY the Minstrel), The Life and Acts of the most
famous and valiant Campion, Sir William Wallace,
knight of Ellerslie, Maintainer of the Libertie of
Scotland**, Edinburgh, 1618 ... Glasgow, 1665   8°
First edition : Edinburgh, 1570 (4°). Also two
editions in 12° : Edinburgh, 1666 ; 1673.

(STC : 13152-13153 ; 13155 ; L1981-L1984)

SECTION L

"Schoole bookes history and other
miscelanious bookes in 8°: & 12mo:"

994.   Jo: Baptist: Mantuani poemata   £0 01 8

Baptista SPAGNUOLI Mantuanus, Bucolica, Paris, 1507 8°
Numerous subsequent editions in 8°, including many
published at London, 1569 ... 1679.

(STC : 22980-22989 ; S4786-S4790)

995.   Q: Aureli Symmachi Epistol: lib 10   £0 03 0

**Quintus Aurelius SYMMACHUS, Epistolarum ad diversos
libri decem. Jacobus Lectius restituit, auxit notis.
Additae item notae Fr. Jureti iam ante vulgatae**,
Geneva, 1587 ; 1598 ; Naples, 1617 ; Frankfurt, 1642 8°
First edition : Paris, 1580 (4°). Also an edition
in 12° : Leyden, 1653.

996. Dictionario vulgare et lat   £0 03 6

**Filippo VENUTI, Dittionario volgare et latino nel
quale si contiene, come ; voacoboli italiani si possano
dire et esprimere latinamente, per M. Filippo Venuti,**
Venice, 1562 ; Bologna, 1578 ; Venice, 1583 ; 1587 ;
1589 ; 1592 ; Rome, 1597   8°

997. Nicol: Clenardo gramatica graeca   £0 02 0

Nicolaus CLENARDUS, Grammatica graeca, Paris, 1619 ...
Paris, 1669   8°
Another (later?) copy of Item no. 476, above. First
published under the title, **Institutiones in linguam
graecam**, Paris, 1540 (8°), etc.

998. Isocratis orationes et Epistolae   £0 03 6

**ISOCRATES, Isocratis ... orationes et epistolae ...
in Latinum pridem conversae, nunc recognitae per H.
Wolfium**, Paris, 1553   8°
There were also numerous editions of this work in
Greek and latin : Basle, 1571 ; ?, 1604 ; Paris &
Geneva?, 1615 ; Paris, 1621 ; 1631 ; Geneva, 1651 (8°).

(STC : 14272)

999. The psalmes of David in Latin verse wth: a Comment: (8°)
£0 01 6

1000. M: Anto: Majoragij orationes   £0 03 6

**Antonio Maria de' CONTI (later known as Marco Antonio
MAJORAGIO), Orationes et praefationes**, Münster, 1599 ;
Leipzig, 1600 ; 1606 ; Cologne, 1608 ; 1614 ; Leipzig,
1628   8°
First edition : Venice, 1582 (4°).

1001. P: Virgilij poemata   £0 01 8

Publius VIRGILIUS MARO, Poemata   8°
There were at least three separate editions of
Virgil's Poemata (Collected works) in 8° : 1st ed.,
Philipp Melanchthon, Zurich, 1561 ; 2nd ed., Henri
Estienne, Geneva, 1576?, etc. including editions at
London, Cambridge, Edinburgh and Aberdeen ; 3rd ed.,
Joannes Ludovicus de la Cerda, Frankfurt, 1610.

(STC : 24790.7-24795)

1002. Pet: Bembi Card: Epist: familiar: lib   £0 03 0

**Cardinal Pietro BEMBO, Epistolarum familiarum libri VI.
ejusdem Leonis X, Pont. Max., nomine scriptarum lib.
XVI** (ed. C. Gualteruzzi), Venice, 1552 ; Cologne, 1582   8°

1003.   Dan: Heinsij orationes   £0 02 6

Daniel HEINSIUS, <u>Orationes</u>, Leyden, 1612 ; 1615 ;
1620 ; 1627   8°
First edition : Leyden, 1609 (4°). Also published in
12° : Leyden, 1612 ; 1642 ; 1657.

1004.   Q: Horatii fflacci poemata   £0 01 8

Quintus HORATIUS FLACCUS, <u>Poemata</u>, Venice, 1509   8°
Numerous subsequent editions in 8°.

1005.   P: Virgilij poemata cum comentarijs   £0 04 6

Another copy (with Commentaries) of Item no.1001, above.

1006.   Jo: Phill. Parei Thesaurus lingua lat   £0 03 6

**Johann Philipp PAREUS, <u>Lexicon Criticum, sive Thesaurus
Linguae Latinae</u>**, Nuremburg, 1645, 1646   8°

1007.   Demosthenis orationes   £0 00 8

An unspecified edition of **DEMOSTHENES**, presumably in
latin (8°).

1008.   Synonimorum silva   £0 02 0

Simon PELEGROMIUS, <u>Synonymorum Sylva</u>, London, 1580 ...
London, 1663   8°
English—Latin—Greek.

(STC : 19556–19564 ; P1067–P1067A)

1009.   Jo: Tho: ffreigij Colloquia   £0 01 6

**Joannes Ludovicus VIVES, <u>Colloquia, sive Exercitatio
latinae linguae Joannis Lodovici Vivis ... Joan. Thomae
Freigii notis, ex praestantissimus quibusque autoribus
desumtis illustrata</u>**, Nuremburg, 1582   8°

1010.   Jos: Scaligeri appendix virgilij   £0 01 4

**Publius VIRGILIUS MARO, <u>Appendix ... cum supplemento
multorum antehac nunquam excusorum Poematum veterum,
J. Scaligeri in eandem appendicem commentarij &
castigationes</u>**, Lyons, 1572 ; 1573 ; Leyden, 1595   8°

1011. Tho Linacri de Emendata structura latini sermonis
£0 01 4

**Thomas LINACRE, De emendata structura Latini sermonis
libri sex**, 2nd ed., Paris, 1532 ... Lyons, 1559   8°
First edition : London, 1524 (4°).

1012. The Nomenclater of Adrianus Junius   £0 01 6

**Adrianus JUNIUS, The Nomenclator, or Remembrancer ...
in Latine, Greeke, French ... and now in English by
J. Higins. With a dictional index**, London, 1585 8°

(STC : 14860)

1013. M: ffab: Quint: Institutes orator   £0 02 6

Marcus Fabius QUINTILIANUS, Institutiones Oratoriae,
Lyons, 1510   8°
Numerous subsequent editions in 8° (and 12°).
Another copy of Item no. 63, in 8° (or 12°).

1014. M: T: Ciceronis Epist: famil   £0 01 4

Marcus Tullius CICERO, Epistolae familiares, Venice,
1502   8°
Numerous subsequent editions in 8°. First edition :
Rome, 1467 (4°).

1015. M: Acci Plauti Comoediae 20   £0 02 0

**Titus Maccius PLAUTUS, M. Plauti Sarsinatis Comediae
XX. Varronianae ex antiquis recentioribusque exemplaribus
invicem collatis diligentissime emendate** (ed.
S. Charpentarius), Lyons, 1513   8°
Numerous subsequent editions in 8°. First edition :
Venice, 1472, in folio.

1016. Jul: Caesar Scaligeri Poetices lib 7   £0 05 0

Julius Caesar SCALIGER, Poetices libri septem, 2nd ed.,
Heidelberg, 1581 ... 5th ed., Heidelberg, 1617   8°

1017. M: Andr: Wilki orationes   £0 01 8

**Andreas WILKE, Orationum M. Andreae Wilkii, ... pleias
II. philologicas versa pagina indiculo praeferens, in
publicis examinum et aliis conventibus, diversis
temporibus, dictas**, Hanover, 1614   8°

1018.   Geo: Buchanani poemata   £0 01 8

George BUCHANAN, Poemata, Edinburgh, 1615 ; Saumur &
Leyden, 1621 ; Leyden, 1628 ; Amsterdam, 1641 ; 1665 ;
1676 ; Edinburgh, 1677   12°*
(* Nb. No edition, with catalogue title, in 8°. First
published as **Operum poeticorum**, 2 vols., Heidelberg,
1594-97 (8°).

(STC : 3990 ; B5290-B5291)

---

f15v

1019.   Virtutum vitiorumque Exempla   £0 00 8

**Nicolas de HANNAPES, Patriarch of Jerusalem, Virtutum
vitiorumque exempla ... per Nicolaum Hanapum**, Antwerp,
1524 ; 1535 ; Cologne, 1544 ; Paris, 1576 ; Antwerp,
1634   8°
Also published in 12° : Paris, 1608 ; Leyden, 1608 ;
1677 ; 1680.

1020.   St: Johns Gospell in Greek verse   £0 01 0

Νοννου Ποιητου Πανοπολιτου μεταβολη του κατα
Ἰωαννην ἁγιου Εὐαγγελιου.   **Nonni ...
tralatio Sancti Evangelij, secundam Ioannem**, Hagenau,
1527 ; ?, 1541 ; Paris, 1556 ; Cologne, 1566   8°
First edition : Venice, 1501 (4°).
A Greek translation of the Gospel of St. John by
Nonnus of Panopolis.

1021.   Rog: Aschami Epist: lib   £0 02 0

Roger ASCHAM, Familiarum epistolarum libri tres,
London, 1576 ; 1578 ; 1581 ; 1590   8°
Also published in 12° : Hanover, 1602 ; 1610 and
Geneva, 1611.

(STC : 826-829)

1022.   The Apocrapha in Greeke & latine   £0 01 6

The Apocryphal books of either the Old or New Testament
in Greek and latin:

        (a) **Bibliorum Graecorum Latinorumque. Pars quarta,
continens Tobit, Iudeth, Baruch ... Seirach sapientiam**,
Basle, 1550 ; Antwerp, 1584 ; Leyden, 1612   8°
        (b) **Apocrypha : hoc est, narrationes de Christo, Maria,
Joseph ... exposita & edita graecolatine a Michaele Neandro**,
Basle, 1564 ; 1567   8°

1023.   M: T: Ciceronis Sententiar: lib   £0 01 0

Marcus Tullius CICERO, <u>Sententiae illustriores,</u>
<u>**apophthegmata item et parabolae sive similia, aliquot**</u>
<u>**praeterea ejusdem piae sententiae, authore Petro**</u>
<u>**Lagnerio**</u>, Paris, 1546 ; 1548   8°
Another edition in 12° : Venice, 1565. There were
numerous later editions of this work in 8° under
different titles.

1024.   Terentius Christianus   £0 03 0

Cornelius SCHONAEUS, <u>Terentius Christianus. Utpote</u>
<u>**comoediis sacris transformatus**</u> (ed. C. Loosaeus),
Cologne, 1592   8°
Later editions appeared under two titles:
        (a) **<u>Terentius Christianus, sive comoediae duae</u>**
<u>**Terentiano stylo conscriptae ad usum scholarum seorsim**</u>
<u>**excusae ... Tobaeus, Juditha**</u>, London, 1595 ... London,
1674   8°
        (b) **<u>Terentius Christianus. Seu comoediae sacrae</u>**
<u>**sex, Terentiano stylo conscriptae**</u>, Cologne, 1596 ...
Amsterdam, 1646   8°

(STC : 21821-21824 ; S879 ; S881)

1025.   Pueriles fabulae Clausd after the method of Dr: Webbe
         £0 01 8

Joseph WEBBE, <u>Pueriles confabulatiunculae, or childrens</u>
<u>**talke : claused and drawne into lessons, after the**</u>
<u>**method of Dr. Webbe**</u>, London, 1627   4°*
(* Nb. No edition in 8° or 12°).
Latin and English.

(AE, p.23 ; STC : 25170.5)

1026.   M Annaei Lucani de bello Civili cum scholijs lib £0 02 0

The first edition to fit the catalogue description
would seem to be:

Marcus Annaeus LUCANUS, <u>De Bello civili apud Pharsaliam</u>
<u>**libri X, doctissimis argumentis et scholiis ornati**</u>,
Cologne, 1560   8°
Numerous subsequent editions in 8° and 12°.

1027.   Erasmi Roterodami de copia verborum lib   £0 01 6

Desiderius ERASMUS, <u>De Duplici Copia Verborum ac rerum</u>,
?, 1516   8°
Numerous later editions in 8°.   First edition :
Strassburg, 1513 (4°).

1028.   Erasmi Roterodami adagiorum Epitome   £0 02 0

Desiderius ERASMUS, Adagiorum epitome, Paris, 1523 ;
Antwerp, 1544 ; ?, 1593   8°
Also published in 12° : Cologne, 1530 ; Amsterdam,
1649 ; 1650 ; 1663 ; Oxford, 1666.

(STC : E3187-E3187B)

1029.   Erasmi Roterodami Apophthegmata   £0 01 6

Desiderius ERASMUS, Apophthegmata, Lyons, 1531 ...
Antwerp, 1564   8°
First published in 12° : Antwerp, 1543 (with numerous
subsequent editions in 12°).

1030.   Laur: Vallae Ellegentiarum lib   £0 01 6

Laurentius VALLA, Elegentiarum libri sex, Mainz,
1522 ... Basle, 1562   8°

1031.   The new testamt: in Italian   £0 01 8

Il Nuovo Testamento (trans. Antonio Brucioli), Venice,
1530   8°
Numerous subsequent editions in 8°, all of which were
either re-publications of the above translation by
Brucioli, or were closely modelled on the original.

1032.   Theod: Gazae Grammatica Graeca   £0 01 8

Theodorus GAZA, Grammaticae institutionis libri duo,
Basle, 1518 ; later eds. enlarged (**... libri quatuor**),
Paris, 1521 ... Venice, 1545   8°

1033.   Beati Rhenani anotat: in T: Livis   £0 01 0

**Beatus BILDIUS Rhenanus, Annotationes Beati Rhenani et
Sigismundi Gelenii, ... in exstantes T. Livii libros**,
Lyons, 1537 ; 1542 ; 1555   8°

1034.   Commentarium in Hesiodum   £0 02 0

Probably the following edition of:

HESIOD, Commentarius in Hesiodi Ascraei ᾽Εργα καὶ
῾Ημερας   **magno studio ... collectus est ... nunc
primum editus a S. Riccio ... Accesserunt Ulpii
Franekerensis Frisii et N. Vallae translationes**,
Wittenberg, 1590   8°
A **Greek-latin** edition of Hesiod's Works, first published
in 8° at Basle, 1542.

1035.   Erasmi Roterdami Colloquia   £0 02 6

Another copy of Item no. 881, above.
Nb. First edition in 12° : Leyden, 1636 (with numerous
subsequent editions in 12°).

1036.   Erasmi Roterdami Elegentiarum lib   £0 01 6

**Desiderius ERASMUS (ed.), Elegantiarum e Plauto et
Terentio libri II. P. Syri mimorum et sententiarum ex
poetis similium lib. I.,** Basle, 1555   12°*
(* Nb. I have not been able to locate any other edition
of this work).

1037.   M: T: Ciceronis Epist: famil: £0 00 6

Another copy of Item no. 1014, above.

1038.   Luciani Dialogi Coelestes   £0 00 8

**LUCIAN of Samosata, Luciani ... dialogi coelestes,
marini & inferni, ... editi in usum puerorum,** Basle,
1550   8°
(Nb. A Greek-latin edition was also published at
Strassburg, 1550, ed. J. Sambucus).

1039.   Q: Horatij poemata   £0 0 10

Another copy of Item no. 1004, above.

1040.   Ovidij Epistolae   £0 00 8

**Publius OVIDIUS NASO, P. Ovidii Nasonis Heroides
epistolae,** Paris, 1533 ; 1541   8°

1041.   Ovidij de tristibus lib   £0 00 8

**Publius OVIDIUS NASO, De Tristibus libri V, cum
annotationibus minime rejiciendis,** Antwerp, 1573   8°
Later editions in 8° : London?, 1574 ; 1581 ;
Edinburgh, 1612 ; Cambridge, 1638.

(STC : 18976.4-18977)

1042.   Virgilius Evangelicus   £0 01 0

**Publius VIRGILIUS MARO, Virgilius Evangelisans. Sive
historia domini & salvatoris nostri Jesu Christi,
Virgilianis verbis & versibus descripta. Operâ A.
Rossaei** (i.e. Alexander Ross) **(A. Rossaei peroratio
seu Hymnus ad Deum Patrem),** London, 1633 ; 1634 ;
1638 ; 1659   8°
Also published in 12° : Zurich, 1664.

(STC : 24826-24827 ; V628)

1043.   Ovidij Metamorphosion lib   £0 01 0

Publius OVIDIUS NASO, Ovidii Metamorphoseon libri XV,
Lyons, 1505?   8°
Numerous later editions in 8° and 12°.

(DS, p.121)

1044.   Geo: Macropedij Epistolica   £0 00 8

**Georgius MACROPEDIUS, Epistolica G. Macropedii
studiosus Trajectinae scholae tyrunculis nuncupata,
quae nihilominus quicquid ad prima rhetorices elementa
attinet, brevibus praeceptis plane complectitur**,
Antwerp, 1543 ; 1546 ; 1559   8°

1045.   Poetae Graecae minores   £0 07 6

Another copy of Item no. 864, above.

1046.   Homeri Ilias et Odissea   £0 05 0

HOMER, Ilias et Odyssea   8°
First latin edition in 8° : ?, 1528 (trans. Laurentius
Valla and Raphael Volaterranus). In all probability,
this is the Greek-latin edition published by Henri
Estienne at Geneva, 1617, in 8°.

1047.   Justiniani Institutiones   £0 01 6

Emperor JUSTINIAN I, Institutiones, Venice, 1503 8°
Numerous subsequent editions in 8°. First edition :
Mainz, 1468, in folio.

1048.   Textoris Dialogij   £0 01 6

Joannes RAVISIUS Textor, J. Ravisii Textoris Dialogi,
Paris, 1530 ; 1534 ; 1536 ; 1542   8°
Later editions in 12° : Paris, 1558 ; Rotterdam, 1651.

1049.   Euripedis Tragoediae   £0 00 6

EURIPIDES, Tragoediae, Basle, 1541 ; 1558   8°
First Greek-Latin edition in 8° : Heidelberg, 1597 ;
First Greek edition in 8° : Basle, 1537.

1050.   A latine testamt: (8° or 12°)   £0 01 0

1051.   Dan: Heinsij poemata   £0 01 8

Daniel HEINSIUS, Poemata, Leyden, 1606   12°
Numerous later editions in 8° and 12°.

1052.   Illustrium poetarum flores   £0 01 8

**Octavianus MIRANDULA (ed.), <u>Illustrium Poetarum Flores</u>
<u>per O. Mirandulam collecti, et a studioso quodam in</u>
<u>locos communes nuper digesti, ac castigati ...</u>
<u>P. Beroaldi de hisce floribus iudicium</u>**, Strassburg,
1538 ... Lyons, 1586   8°
Also published in 12° : Venice, 1565 ; 1574.

1053.   C: Suetonij Caesares   £0 01 4

Caius SUETONIUS TRANQUILLUS, <u>Duodecim Caesarum Vitae</u>,
Lyons, 1508   8°
Numerous later editions in 8°.

1054.   M: T: Ciceronis Epist Lat: et Gallicae   £0 02 6

**Marcus Tullius CICERO, <u>M.T.C. aliquot epistolae, cum</u>
<u>latina simul et gallica interpretatione Maturino</u>
<u>Corderio authore</u>**, Paris, 1542 ; 1549   8°
Latin-French.

1055.   M: T: Ciceronis Orationis   £0 01 8

Marcus Tullius CICERO, <u>Orationes</u>, Lyons, 1508   8°
Numerous subsequent editions in 8°.

---

f16r

1056.   fflores Doctorum   £0 02 6

**THOMAS Hibernicus, <u>Flores omnium pene doctorum, qui</u>
<u>cum in theologia, tum in philosophia, hactenus</u>
<u>claruerunt, alphabetico ordine digesti</u>**, Lyons, 1555 ;
Paris, 1556   8°
Later editions in 12°: Cologne, 1606 ; Paris, 1664.

1057.   Petronij Abitri Satyricon   £0 00 8

Titus PETRONIUS ARBITER, <u>Satyricon</u>, Lyons, 1575   8°
Numerous later editions in 8° and 12°.

1058.   Terentius Christiani   £0 01 0

Another copy of Item no. 1024, above.

1059.   Jonstoni Parerga   £0 00 8

   Arthur JOHNSTON, Parerga, Aberdeen, 1632   8°

   (STC : 14714)

1060.   Idaea togatae Constantiae   £0 01 8

   **Joannes MOLANUS of Cork, Idea togatae constantiae,
   sive Francisci Tailleri, dubliniensis praetoris, in
   persecutione congressus et religionis catholicae
   defensione interitus ... Epitome tripartita martyrum
   fere omnium qui in britannicis insulis nostra
   patrumque memoria de haeresi gloriose triumpharunt,**
   Paris, 1629   12°

1061.   Busbequi Epist   £0 01 0

   **Angerius GISLENIUS, Seigneur de Bousbecq, Legationis
   Turcicae Epistolae quatuor. Quarum priores duae ...
   in lucem prodierunt sub nomine Itinerum Constantinopolitani
   et Amasiani. Adjectae sunt duae alterae. Ejusdem de re
   militari contra Turcam instituenda consilium,** Paris,
   1589 ; 1595 ; Frankfurt, 1595 ; Hanover, 1605 ; 1629   8°
   Also 1 edition in 12° : Munich, 1620.

1062.   M: T: Ciceronis de officijs lib   £0 01 0

   Marcus Tullius CICERO, De Officiis libri tres,
   Strassburg, 1545   8°
   Numerous later editions in 8°.

1063.   Carmina proverbialia   £0 00 6

   **S.A.I., Carminum Proverbialium, totius humanae vitae
   statum breviter delineatium, ... loci communes, in
   gratiam juventatis selecti** (by S.A.I.), London, 1577
   ... London, 1670   8°

   (STC : 14059-14065 ; I11-I13)

1064.   Jo: Posselij Syntaxis graeca   £0 01 6

   Joannes POSSELIUS the Elder, Σύνταξις **linguae Graecae,**
   Wittenberg, 1565 ... Cambridge, 1640   8°

   (STC : 20130)

1065.   Junij Juvenalis Satyrae   £0 01 0

   Decimus Junius JUVENALIS, Satirae, Venice, 1501   8°
   Dozens of later editions in 8°.

1066.   Dialouges in latine & french (8° or 12°)   £0 0 10

1067.   Valerij maximi memorabilium lib   £0 01 4

VALERIUS MAXIMUS, Valerii Maximi dictorum et factorum memorabilium libri novem, Venice, 1502   8°
Numerous later editions in 8°.

1068.   The ffrench Schoolemaster   £0 01 6

Claude de SAINLIENS (i.e. Claude HOLLYBAND), The French Schoolemaister, wherein is ... shewed, the true ... way of pronouncinge of the Frenche tongue ... Unto the which is annexed a Vocabularie ... by C. Hollybande, London, 1573 ... London, 1660   8°
Also 1 edition in 12° : London, 1641.

(STC : 6748-6757 ; S293A-S293C)

1069.   Colloquia 7 linguarum   £0 01 4

Noel van BARLEMENT, Colloquia et dictionariolum septem linguarum, Liège , 1589 ... Antwerp, 1616 obl.8°

1070.   An Hebrew psalter (8° or 12°)   £0 01 6

1071.   The Spanish Schoolmaster   £0 01 2

William STEPNEY, The Spanish Schoole-maister ... Now newly corrected by a new author (i.e. J. Grange), London, 1619   12°
First edition : London, 1591 (16°).

(STC : 23257-23258)

1072.   Talaei Rhetorica*   £0 00 6

Audomarus TALAEUS, Rhetorica ad Carolum Lotharingum cardinalem Guisianum, Paris, 1548 ... Berne, 1670 8°
* According to W. J. Ong, Ramus and Talon Inventory, pp. 82-86, this work should be attributed at least in part to Pierre de La Ramée.

1073.   L: Annaei Senecae tragoediae   £0 01 0

Lucius Annaeus SENECA, Tragoediae, Florence, 1506 8°
Numerous later editions in 8°.

1074. Esops fables in Greeke, latine & french 3 bookes
£0 04 0

AESOP, Aesopi fabulae gallicae, latinae, graecae, cum facillimis in contextum graecum scholiis. Versio utraque nova et elaborata per I(ean) **Meslier. Liber pueris linguam graecam capessentibus utilis, facilis, atque iucundus**, Paris, 1629 ; 1679   8°
A 1 volume edition, presumably split and rebound in 3 volumes.

1075. Jo: Row Grammatica hebraea   £0 01 6

John ROW, Hebraeae Linguae Institutiones compendiosissimae et facillimae, Glasgow, 1644   12°

(STC : R2060)

1076. The french Litleton   £0 01 2

Claude de SAINLIENS (i.e. Claude HOLLYBAND), The French Littelton. A most easie, perfect and absolute way to learne the french tongue, London, 1581 ... London, 1630   12°
Also published in 8° : London, 1593. First edition : London, 1576 (16°).

(STC : 6740-6747)

1077. D: Magni Ausonij opera   £0 0 10

Decimus Magnus AUSONIUS, Opera, Venice, 1501 ... Amsterdam, 1671   8°
Also published in 12° : Geneva, 1608.

1078. The Psalmes in greeke (8° or 12°)   £0 01 0

1079. A Greeke testamt: (8° or 12°)   £0 01 6

1080. Historia tragicomica   £0 02 0

Francisco LOUBAYSSIN DE LA MARCA, Historia tragicomica de Don henrique de Castro, en cuyos estraños succesos de veen los varios ... efectos del amor y de la guerra, Paris, 1617   8°

1081. Le Bouquet de l'Eloquence   £0 02 6

Jean PUGET DE LA SERRE, Le Bouquet des plus belles fleurs de l'éloquence, cueilly dans les jardins des sieurs Du Perron, Coiffeteau, Du Vair, Bertaud, d'Urphé, Malerbe, Daudiguier, La Brosse, Du Rousset, La Serre, Paris, 1624   8°

1082.   Traite de le escritture saintte   £0 02 0

Jean MESTREZAT, Traitté de l'Escriture saincte, où est monstrée la certitude et plénitude de la foy et son indépendance de l'authorité de l'Eglise, contre les prétendues démonstrations catholiques du jésuite Regourd, en quoy est comprise la réfutation du troisiesme livre de la Réplique du cardinal Du Perron touchant les traditions, Geneva, 1633   8°

1083.   Le bon pasteur   £0 02 0

Pierre de BESSE, Le bon pasteur ; c'est a dire les qualitez et conditions necessaires pour la perfection d'un bon pasteur, Paris, 1639   8°

1084.   La Cour saincte p(er) Nic: Caussin in 2 vol   £0 03 0

Nicolas CAUSSIN, La Cour sainte, ou l'Institution chrestienne des grands, avec les exemples de ceux qui dans les cours ont fleury dans la saincteté, par le R.P. Nicolas Caussin, Paris, 1624 ; Rouen, 1624 ; Paris, 1640 ; 1641*   8°
(* Nb. All editions in 8° appear to be in one volume. A 1 volume edition, split and rebound in 2 volumes?)

1085.   pie de la Rosa fragrante   £0 01 6

Jeronimo de SAN PEDRO, Libro de Cavalleria Celestial del pie de la Rosa Fragrante, Antwerp, 1554 ; Venice, 1584   8°

1086.   Conseiles militaires   £0 01 6

Cosimo BARTOLI, Conseils militaires ... fort utiles et nécessaires à tous generaulx, colonnels, capitaines et soldats (trans. Gabriel Chappuys), Paris, 1586   8°

1087.   Les Oeuvres de Cornelius Tacitus   £0 04 0

Publius Cornelius TACITUS, Les Oeuvres de C. Cornelius Tacitus, Paris, 1584 ; Geneva, 1594 ; Douai, 1609 ; Paris, 1619 ; Rouen, 1650   8°
Also published in 12° : Amsterdam, 1663 ; Paris, 1664.

1088.   Du Vrai usage des peres   £0 02 0

Jean DAILLÉ the Elder, Traicté de l'employ des Saincts Peres pour le iugement des differands, qui sont auiourd' hui en la religion (running title : "Du vrai usage des peres"), Geneva, 1632   8°

1089.   Le prince des princes   £0 02 6

**Claude BOITET DE FRAUVILLE, Le Prince des Princes, ou
l'art de régner, contenant son instruction aux sciences
et à la politique contre les orateurs de ce temps,**
Paris, 1632   8°

1090.   Le Secretaire de la Cour   £0 02 0

**Jean PUGET DE LA SERRE, Le secretaire de la cour ; ou,
La maniere d'escrire selon le temps**, Paris, 1624 ;
1632   8°
Also published in 12° : Paris, 1634 ; 1641 ; Rouen,
1645 ; 1650 ; 1675 ; Amsterdam, 1645, 1646 ; 1650 ;
1655 ; 1662.

1091.   Dialogues in Italian (8° or 12°)   £0 02 0

1092.   L'historia di Palmerino in 2 vol   £0 03 0

**Anon., La Historia, dove si ragiona de i valorosi ...
gesti ... dell' invitto Cavalliero Palmerino d'Oliva,**
2 vols., Venice, 1620   8°

1093.   Historia Settentrionale   £0 02 0

**Olaus MAGNUS, Archbishop of Upsala, Storia d'Olao Magno
arcivescovo d'Upsali, de' costumi de' popoli
settentrionali. Tradotta par M. Remigio Fiorentino.
Dove s'ha piena notitia delle genti della Gottia, della
Norvegia, della Suevia, e di quelle che vivono sotto
la Tramontana**, Venice, 1559 ; 1561   8°

(DS, p.32 ; M, p.370)

f16v

1094.   Della Republica di venetia   £0 01 8

**Gasparo CONTARINI, Cardinal and Bishop of Belluno,
Della republica et magistrati di Venetia libri V,**
Venice, 1591   8°
First edition : Venice, 1589 (4°).

1095.   Amadis de Gaule in french in 7 vol   £0 05 0

AMADÍS de Gaula, Le premier (–septiesme) livre d'Amadis de Gaule, mis en francoys par ... Nicolas de Herberay, 7 vols., Groulleau edition, Paris, 1555 8°

1096.   Diana de Geor: de monte major in 2 vol   £0 02 6

Jorge de MONTEMAYOR, La Diana de Iorge de Monte Maior ... Parte primera (–segunda), 2 vols., Venice, 1574 12°
Later 2 volume eds., Antwerp, 1580 (8°) ; Milan, 1616 (12°), etc.

1097.   Del grand Reyno de la China   £0 01 6

Juan GONZALEZ DE MENDOZA, Historia de las cosas mas notables, rites y costumbres, del gran Reyno de la China .. con un Itinerario del nuevo mundo (del Padre Custodio Fray Martin Ignacio ... que paso ala China), Rome, 1585 ; Valencia, 1585 ; Madrid, 1586 ; Medina del Campo, 1595 ; Antwerp, 1596   8°

1098.   Don Quxote(sic)   £0 01 0

Miguel de CERVANTES SAAVEDRA, Don Quixote   8°
Part 1 first published in 8° at Lisbon and Valencia, 1605 ; Parts 1 and 2, first published in 8° at Brussels, 1607, 1616.   Numerous later editions in 8°.

1099.   La some de Theologie   £0 01 4

Philipp MELANCHTHON, La Somme de Théologie ; ou lieux communs, reveuz et augmentés de nouveau ... ce qui estoit en la précédente édition improprement traduict ... a esté ... conferé à l'original (with a preface by Jean Calvin), Geneva, 1551   8°

1100.   6 small french bookes (8° or 12°)   £0 02 8

1101.   3 bookes in Italian (8° or 12°)   £0 01 4

1102.   6 other bookes in Italian (8° or 12°)   £0 02 0

1103.   8 other bookes in french (8° or 12°)   £0 02 0

1104.   2 in high dutch (i.e. German) (8° or 12°) £0 01 6

1105. Jo: Webb mare ovidianum   £0 03 6

**Joseph WEBBE, Usus et Authoritas, Id est Liber Loquens,
feliciter incipit, sub titulo Entheati Materialis
primi Hexametra & Pentametra** (half-title reads :
"Entheatus Materialis Primus, Mare Ovidianum Totum"),
London, 1626   12°

(STC : 25171)

1106. Euphormioni Lusinij Satyricon   £0 02 6

**Lusininus EUPHORMIO (i.e. John BARCLAY), Euphormionis
Lusinini Satyricon** (Parts 1 and 2), Paris, 1605, 1609 ;
1613 ; Leyden, 1637 ; 1655 ; Amsterdam, 1658   12°

1107. Rhetorum Collegij Porsensis orationis   £0 01 8

**Nicolaus VERNULAEUS, Rhetorum Lovaniensium Collegii
Porcensis orationum Tomi duo, sub Nicalao Vernulaeo
habitae**, Cologne, 1618 ; 1645 ; 1671 ; Liège, 1671 12°

1108. C: Plinij Epist: lib: 9   £0 01 0

**Caius PLINIUS CAECILIUS SECUNDUS, C. Plinii ... Epist.
lib IX** (ed. H. Estienne), Paris, 1581 ; Geneva, 1591 ;
Paris, 1598 ... Geneva, 1638   small 12° or 16°

1109. Phrases poeticae   £0 01 8

**Anon., Phrases Poeticae, seu sylvae poeticarum lectionum
uberrimae. – Multo quam antea meliores ... locupletioresque
redditae**, Frankfurt, 1620?   12°

1110. M Val Martialis epigramata cum anotat   £0 02 0

The first edition of this work, with annotations;in either 8° or 12°:

Marcus Valerius MARTIALIS, Epigrammata, Lyons, 1518 8°
Numerous subsequent editions in 8°.

1111. P: Virgilij opera   £0 01 6

Publius VIRGILIUS MARO, Opera, Venice, 1501   8°
First published in 12° : Paris, 1537.   Numerous
subsequent editions in both 8° and 12°.

1112. Dialogi sacri   £0 00 8

Sébastien CHÂTEILLON, Dialogorum sacrorum libri quatuor,
Basle, 1551 ... Edinburgh, 1676   8°

(STC : 4770-4774 ; 4775-4776 ; C3732-C3732D)

1113.   Owens Epigrams   £0 01 0

**Joannes OWEN, the Epigrammist, Epigrams of that most
wittie and worthie epigrammatist Mr. J. Owen** (trans.
from latin by J. Vicars), London, 1619   8°
Later editions in 12° : London, 1677 ; 1678.

(STC : 18993 ; 0825E-0825F)

1114.   Nicol: Taurelli metaphisica   £0 0 10

**Nicolaus TAURELLUS, Philosophiae triumphus, hoc est,
Metaphysica philosophandi methodus, qua divinitus
inditis menti notitijs, humanae rationes eo deducuntur,
ut firmissimis inde constructis demonstrationibus
aperte rei veritas elucescat, & quae diu philosophorum
sepulta fuit authoritate philosophia victrix erumpat,**
Basle, 1573 ; Arnhem, 1617   8°

1115.   Adolphi Scribonij Ethica   £0 00 6

**Gulielmus Adolphus SCRIBONIUS, Philosophia ethica ex
Aristotele et aliis methodice repetita,** Lemgo, 1584 ;
Basle, 1586 ; 1588? ; Frankfurt, 1589 ; 1606 ;
Hanover, 1593   8°

1116.   Lamberti Danaei Phisica Christiana   £0 01 4

**Lambert DANEAU, Physica christiana, sive de Rerum
creatarum cognitione et usu, disputatio e Sacrae
Scripturae fontibus hausta ... per Lambertum Danaeum,**
Geneva, 1576 ; 1580, 1582 ; 1580 ; 1602, 1606   8°

1117.   Jo: Setoni dialectica   £0 01 6

Joannes SETONUS, Dialectica, London, 1545 ...
London, 1639   8°

(STC : 22250-22257.5)

1118.   Rob: Baronij opuscula   £0 01 8

**Robert BARON, Prof. of Divinity at Marischal College,
Aberdeen, Metaphysica generalis ; accedunt nunc primum
quae supererant ex parte speciali. Omnia ad usum theologiae
accomodata. Opus posthumum. Ex museo Antonii Clementii
Zirizaei,** Leyden, 1657 ; London, 1657? ; Oxford, 1658 ;
Oxford, 1669?   12°

(STC : B882-B884)

173

1119.   Guidonis Pancerolli rerum memorabilium lib   £0 02 6

**Guido PANCIROLI,Rerum memorabilium jam olim
deperditarum : & contra recens atque ingeniose inventarum
: libri duo** (trans. into latin by H. Salmuth), 2 vols.in 1,
Hamburg, 1599, 1602 ; 1607 ; 1612 ; 1622   8°
Another copy of Item no. 263, in octavo.

1120.   Gilberti Jacchaei Phisicae et metaphisicae Institucon
£0 03 0

Two works by **Gilbertus JACCHAEUS** bound together in
one volume:

        (a) **Institutiones physicae**, Leyden, 1614 ; Erfurt,
1619 ; Leyden, 1624   8°
Later editions in 12° : Amsterdam, 1644 ; Jena, 1646.

        (b) **Primae philosophiae institutiones (...
Institutionum metaphysicarum libri sex)**, Leyden, 1616 ;
1628   8°
Later editions in 12° : Leyden, 1640 ; Cambridge, 1649.

(STC : J57)

1121.   Jo: Rigeri Ethica   £0 01 4

**Johannes RIGER, Ethicorum libri duo, quibus vera bene
vivendi ratio continetur**, Frankfurt, 1589 ;
Hanover, 1605   8°

1122.   Adolphi Scribonij Phisica   £0 01 2

**Gulielmus Adolphus SCRIBONIUS, Rerum physicarum,
Iuxta Leges Logices Methodica Explicatio**, Frankfurt,
1577 ; 1579 ; London, 1581 ; Basle, 1583 ; Cambridge,
1584 (with Timothy Bright's Animadversiones) ;
Frankfurt, 1593 ; 1600   8°

(STC : 22109.5-22110.5 ; 3745)

1123.   Bar: Keckerm: systema logicae cum alijs   £0 02 6

Another copy of Item no. 787 (with other works by
Keckermannus), above.

1124.   ffr: Burgersdicij logica   £0 01 6

**Franco BURGERSDIJCK, Institutionum Logicarum Libri
duo**, Leyden, 1626 ... Cambridge, 1680   8°

(STC : 4108 ; B5630-B5636)

1125.   Philosophia Epicurea per Nic: Hill   £0 02 0

**Nicolaus HILL, Philosophia Epicurea, Democratica,
Theophrastica, proposita simpliciter, non edocta**,
Paris, 1601   8°
Another edition : Geneva, 1619 (12°).

(AE, p.38)

1126.   Symths(sic) Logick   £0 01 0

       **Samuel SMITH, <u>Aditus ad logicam in usum eorum qui
primo academiam salutant</u>**, London, 1613   8°
All subsequent editions, Oxford, 1615 ... 7th ed.,
Oxford, 1656, published in 12°.

       (STC : 22825-22833 ; S4194-S4195)

1127.   Philosophia libera   £0 02 0

       Another copy of Item no. 585, above.

1128.   Platonis Alcibiades   £0 00 8

       **PLATO (suppositious), <u>Platonis Alcibiades Primus,
vel de Natura Hominis</u>, M. Ficino interprete**, Paris,
1560   4°*
(* Nb. I have not been able to trace an edition of
this work in either 8° or 12°).

1129.   ffr: Hottmanni Logica   £0 01 6

       François HOTMAN, <u>Dialecticae Institutionis libri IIII</u>,
Geneva, 1573 ; ?, 1593 ; Frankfurt, 1586 ; 1665   8°

---

f17r

1130.   Val: Maximi memorabilium lib   £0 01 6

       Another copy of Item no. 1067, above.

1131.   Polidori Virgilij de rerum Inventoribq   £0 02 0

       **Polydorus VERGILIUS, <u>De rerum inventoribus libri octo,
... Eiusdem in dominicam precem commentariolum</u>**,
Basle, 1532 ... Cologne, 1626   8°
Later editions in 12° : Antwerp, 1562 ; Basle, 1570 ;
Amsterdam, 1671.
First edition : Venice, 1499 (4°).

1132.   ffr: Patritij de reipublicae institutionae   £0 01 6

       **Francesco PATRIZI, Bishop of Gaeta, <u>De Institutione
reipublicae libri novem historiarum sententiarumque
varietate refertissimi</u>**, Paris, 1569 ; 1575 ; 1578 ;
1585 ; Strassburg, 1594 ; 1608   8°
First edition : Paris, 1518, in folio.

1133.   Venerabilis Bedae historia Ecclesiastica   £0 01 6

Venerable BEDE, Historia Ecclesiastica, Louvain,
1566 ; Cologne, 1601   12°
First edition : Essling, c.1475, in folio.

1134.   Pauli Manutij epistolae   £0 01 4

**Paolo MANUZIO, Epistolae, et Praefationes quae
dicuntur**, Venice, 1558   8°
Numerous subsequent editions in both 8° and 12°.
This work was repeatedly enlarged, from four to
fourteen books.

1135.   Chronicon Carionis   £0 01 4

**Johann CARION, Chronica ... conversa ex Germanico in
Latinum a doctissimo viro Hermano Bono, & ab authore
diligenter recognita**, Schweinfurt (in Halle), 1537 ;
1539 ; Paris, 1543   8°
Later published in 12° as **Carionis chronicon liber**,
Venice, 1556.

1136.   ffr: Petrarchi de remidio utriusque fortunae   £0 01 8

Francesco PETRARCA, De Remediis utriusque Fortunae,
Heidelberg?, 1485? ; Venice, 1515   8°
First edition in 12° : Rotterdam, 1649.

1137.   Chronicon Phil: melanthonis   £0 01 6

**Johann CARION, Chronicon absolutissimum ab orbe condito
usque ad Christum deductum, in quo non Carionis solum
opus continentur ... Philippo Melanthone autore**,
Basle, 1559   8°
Another edition, expanded, Lyons?, 1560 (16°). An
updated edition of Item no. 1135 above. All editions
after 1560 included contributions from Caspar Peucer
as well as Philipp Melanchthon.

1138.   Suetonij Tranquilli de 12 Caesaribus   £0 01 6

Another copy of Item no. 1053, above.

1139.   Alciati Emblemata   £0 01 0

Another copy of Item no. 780, above.

1140.   Theatrum mundi minoris   £0 01 2

**Pierre BOAISTUAU, called LAUNAY, Theatrum mundi minoris,
sive humanae calamitatis oceanus. Ex Gallico in Latinum
translatus sermonem, interprete F. Lauren. Cupaero**,
Antwerp, 1576 ; 1589   12°

1141. Computus Ecclesiasticus £0 00 8

Two possible works published in 12°:

(a) **Johann SPANGENBERG, Computus ecclesiasticus in pueriles questiones redactus**, Wittenberg, 1539

(b) **Christophorus CLAVIUS, Computus ecclesiasticus per digitorum articulos mira facilitate traditus**, Rome, 1597 ; Mainz, 1599 ; Rome, 1603

1142. Nichodemi ffrischlini facetiae £0 01 6

Nicodemus FRISCHLIN, Facetiae selectiores : quibus ob argumenti similitudinem accesserunt H. Bebelii, P.L. Facetiarum Libri Tres : Sales item, seu facetiae ex Poggii Florentini Oratoris libro selectae. Nec non Alphonsi Regis Arragonum et Adelphi Facetiae, ut et Prognostica J. Heinrichmanni, Strassburg & Leipzig, 1600 8°
All subsequent editions in 12° : Strassburg, 1603 ; 1609 ; 1615 ; 1625 ; Amsterdam, 1651 ; 1660.

1143. Hadriani Junij Emblemata £0 00 8

Adrianus JUNIUS, Emblemata ... Ejusdem aenigmatum libellus, Antwerp, 1565 ; 1566 ; 1569 8°
All subsequent editions in 12° : Antwerp 1569 ; 1575 ; 1585 ; Leyden, 1596.

1144. Herodiani Historia £0 00 6

HERODIAN the Historian, Historia Libri VIII, Florence, 1517 ; Colmar, 1523 ; Paris, 1529 ; 1539 ; 1544 8°
Subsequent editions in 12° : Lyons, 1559 ; Antwerp, 1585.

1145. Justini historia £0 0 10

TROGUS POMPEIUS, Justini Historia ex Trogo Pompeio quatuor & triginta epithomatis collecta, Lyons, 1510 ... Amsterdam, 1669 8°
Also published in 12° : Lyons, 1551 ... Hamburg and Amsterdam, 1678.
An edition of the Epitome historiarum Trogi Pompeii by Justinus the historian.

1146. L: fflori historia £0 0 10

Publius Annius FLORUS, Epitome Rerum Romanorum, Strassburg, 1528 ... Utrecht, 1680 8°
Also published in 12° : Oxford, 1631 ... Rotterdam, 1680.
Another copy of Item no. 725 above, in either 8° or 12°.

1147. Scutum Regium   £0 00 8

George HAKEWILL, Scutum regium, id est, adversus omnes
regicidas et regicidarum patronos, ab initio mundi usque
ad interitum Phocae Imp. ... Ecclesiae Catholicae
consensus orthodoxus, London, 1612   8°
Another ed., London, 1613 (12°).

(STC : 12618-12619)

1148. Mercurius Gallobellicus   £0 01 4

Michael Caspar LUNDORP, Breviarii historici continuatio,
hoc est succincta descriptio historica, omnium rerum
memorabilium toto terrarum orbe gestarum, alias sub
titulo Mercurii gallo-bellici typis publicis divolgata,
in qua penes dilucidam historicam commemorationem res
inter imperatorem ... Ferdinandum II et serenissimum
principem electorem palatinum ... explicantur ... per
Michaelem Gasp. Lindorpium (ed. Theobaldus Schoenwetterus),
Frankfurt, 1620   8°

1149. Car: Sigonij de Rep: Hebriorum   £0 02 0

Carlo SIGONIO, De Republica Hebraeorum libri VII,
Bologna, 1582 ; Frankfurt & Cologne, 1583 ; Speyer,
1584 ; Frankfurt, 1585 ; Hanover, 1608   8°

1150. Pauli manutij Antiquitatum Rom: lib 2   £0 02 6

Paolo MANUZIO, Antiquitatum romanorum Pauli Manutii
libri duo, unus de legibus, alter de senatu,
Cologne, 1582   8°

1151. Mundus alter et idem   £0 01 0

MERCURIUS BRITANNICUS (i.e. Joseph HALL, Bishop of
Exeter and Norwich), Mundus alter et idem sive Terra
Australis antehac semper incognita longis itineribus
peregrini Academici nuperrime lustrata. Auth.
Mercurio Britannico (ed. William Knight), London,
1605? ; Hanover, 1607 ; Frankfurt, ?   8°

(STC : 12685)

1152. Jo: Sleidani de 4 imperijs   £0 01 8

Joannes PHILIPPSON Sleidanus, De quatuor summis imperiis,
Babylonico, Persico, Graeco, et Romano, libri tres,
Strassburg, 1556 ... Cambridge, 1646   8°
Also published in 12° : Geneva, 1559 ... Frankfurt, 1672.

(STC : 19847 ; S3988)

1153.   Eliae Reusneri flores   £0 02 6

Elias REUSNERUS, <u>Florum hortuli historico-politici</u>
<u>coronae VI. ... Opus incremento posthumum recensente</u>
<u>Cyriaco Lentulo</u>, Herborn, 1651   8°
Earlier edition, different title-page, Herborn, 1618 12°
(ed. Abraham de la Faye).

1154.   Dioginis Laertij cum alijs de vitis Philosophorum
        £0 02 6

DIOGENES Laertius, <u>Diogenis Laertii de vitis, dogmatis</u>
<u>et apophthegmatis eorum qui in philosophia claruerunt,</u>
<u>libri decem. Hesichii, ... de iisdem philosophis, et</u>
<u>de aliis scriptoribus liber. Pythagoreorum</u>
<u>philosophorum fragmenta</u>, Geneva, 1595   12°
Various Greek-Latin editions of this work were
published by Henri Estienne at Geneva, 1593 ; 1594 ;
1616 ; 1617, all in 8°.
Another copy of Item no. 772, above, in 12°.

1155.   Auli Gellij noctes Atticae cum notis   £0 02 0

        Possibly the following edition:

Aulus GELLIUS, <u>Noctes atticae, seu vigilliae atticae</u>
<u>... Henrici Stephani ... cum notis Lud. Carrionis</u>,
Paris, 1585   8°
However, there were numerous other editions of this
work, many with commentaries.
Another copy of Item no. 909, above, in 8° (or 12°).

1156.   fflores politici   £0 02 0

Pietro Andrea CANONIERO, <u>Flores illustrium axiomatum,</u>
<u>sententiarum ac similitudinum politicarum, ex optimis</u>
<u>scriptis collecti</u>, Antwerp, 1615   8°
("Running title reads "Flores politici")

1157   Bellum Tartaricum   £0 01 8

Martinus MARTINI, <u>Bellum Tartaricum, or the conquest of</u>
<u>the great and most renowned Empire of China, by the</u>
<u>invasion of the Tartars ... Together with a map of the</u>
<u>Provinces and Chief Cities of the countries</u>, London,
1654   8°
First published in latin as <u>De bello tartarico historia</u>,
Antwerp, Rome and Cologne, 1654.

(STC : M858)

1158.   Dictijs Cretensis et daretis Phrygij de bello
        troicano   £0 01 6

**DICTYS Cretensis, Dictys Cretensis et Daretis Phyrgii,
De bello Troiano historia** (ed. Franciscus Faragonius),
Lyons, 1552 ; Paris, 1560 ; 1564 ; Lyons, 1569   12°
Later edition (ed. Josias Mercerus) : Paris, 1618 ;
Amsterdam, 1630 ; 1631 (12°).
First edition : Messina, 1498 (4°).

1159.   Alex: Sardi de moribq et ritibq gentium   £0 02 0

**Alessandro SARDI of Ferrara, De moribus ac ritibus
gentium libri III. nunc primum in lucem editi,**
Venice, 1557 : Mainz, 1577   8°
Also published in 12° : Mainz, 1577 ; Hamburg, 1599.

1160.   Erasmi Roterodami vita et Epist   £0 01 6

**Desiderius ERASMUS, Magni D. Erasmi ... vita, partim
ab ipsomet Erasmo, partim ab amicis ... descripta.
Accedunt Epistolae ... plus quam septuaginta, quas
aetate provectiore scripsit, nec inter vulgatas in
magno volumine comparent,** Leyden, 1615   8° & 12°
Another edition : Leyden, 1642 (12°).
First edition : Leyden, 1607 (4°).

1161.   Apiani Alexandrini historia   £0 02 6

APPIAN of Alexandria, Historia romana, Venice, 1526 ;
Geneva, 1560   8°
Another copy of Item no. 104, above, in 8°.

1162.   Dionisij Hallicarnasses Antiquit: Rom: historia
        £0 03 0

**DIONYSIUS of Halicarnassus, Antiquitates Rom. libri XI
ab Aemilio Porto ... redditi,** Cologne, 1614   12°
An edition of the **Archaeologia Romana,** first published
at Trevis, 1480, in folio.

1163.   C: Julij Caesaris quae extant omnia   £0 02 0

**Caius Julius CAESAR, Omnia quae exstant. Accessere
Imperij Romani, Galliarumque & Hispaniarum tabulae
A. Orteli** (ed. J.J. Scaliger), Leyden, 1593 ; 1606 ;
1651 ; Amsterdam, 1661 ; 1670   8°
Also published in 12° : ?, 1595 ; Leyden, 1635 ;
Amsterdam, 1635 ; 1644 ; 1657 ; 1661 ; 1675.
An edition of Caesar's **Works** with the commentaries of
Hirtius and others.

1164.   Lasari soranzi de rebus   lib   £0 01 4

**Lazzaro SORANZO, Ottomannus L. Soranzi ... sive de rebus
Turcicis liber unus, in tres partes divisus ... Nunc
primum Latio donatus** (ed. J. Geuderus ab Heroltzberga),
Hanover?, 1600   12°
Another edition (different title-page) : Frankfurt,
1601 (8°).

1165.   Polianaei Stratagematum lib 8 graecae et lat   £0 03 0

POLYAENUS, Πολυαινου Στρατηγηματων Βιβλοι ὀκτω.
**Polyaeni Stratagematum libri octo. I. Casaubonis
Graece nunc primum edidit, emedavit et notis illustravit.
Adjecta est etiam J. Vulteii Latina versio,** Lyons,
1589   16°*
No edition in 8° or 12°.
Greek-Latin.

1166.   Barth: Caranze summa Consiliorum   £0 03 6

**Bartholomé CARRANZA, Archbishop of Toledo, Summa
Conciliorum et Pontificum a Petro usque ad Paulum
Tertium,** Venice, 1546 ... Louvain, 1681   8°
One edition in 12° : Paris, 1555.

---

f17v

1167.   Mores leges et ritus omnium gentium   £0 02 0

**Joannes BOEMUS Aubanus, Omnium gentium mores, leges,
& ritus,** Lyons, 1535 ... Lyons, 1621   8°
Also published in 12° : Lyons, 1570 ; Antwerp, 1571 ;
Lyons, 1576 ; Geneva, 1604 ; 1610.

1168.   Noches de invierno   £0 00 6

**Antonio de ESLAVA, Parte primera del libro intitulado
Noches de Invierno,** Pamplona & Barcelona, 1609 ;
Brussels, 1610   12°
Only the first part of this work seems to have been
published.

1169.   Antiquae historiae ex 27 historibq Contexte   £0 05 0

Another copy of Item no. 757, above (nb. edition
published in 12° : Lyons, 1591).

1170.   Epitaphie Jocoseria   £0 01 8

**Franciscus SWEERTIUS, Epitaphia joco-seria Latina,
Gallica, Italica, Hispanica, Lusitanica, Belgica.
F.S. posteritati et urbanitati collegit**, Cologne,
1623 ; 1645   8°

1171.   Camdeni Britania   £0 05 6

Another copy of Item no. 893, above.

1172.   Tho: mori Utopia cum alijs   £0 02 0

Sir Thomas MORE, Utopia, Paris, 1517?   8°
First edition in 12° : Frankfurt, 1601. Numerous
further editions in 8° and 12°. The reference to "cum
alijs" in the catalogue description may refer to other
works by More, or commentaries on Utopia (e.g. the
1517? edition included the annotations of Erasmus).
First edition : London, 1516 (4°).

(AE, sig.Bv)

1173.   Comparatio Rom: pontificum et regum Ethnicorum
£0 01 4

**(Jean DU TILLET, Bishop of Saint Brieuc and Meaux),
Pontificum aliquot Roman. Christi Vicariorum exempla.
cum Ethnicorum principum gestis comparata**, London?,
1576   8°

(Not listed in STC)

1174.   Justi Lipsi de rebus Rom   £0 00 8

**Justus LIPSIUS, Tractatus ad historiam Romanam
cognoscendam apprime utiles**, Cambridge & Leyden,
1592 ; Cambridge, 1607 ; Frankfurt, 1609 ; and reissued
as **Roma Illustrata**, Leyden, 1645 ; 1650 ; Amsterdam,
1657   12°

1175.   Quinti Curtij historiarum lib   £0 02 0

**Quintus CURTIUS RUFUS, Historiarum magni Alexandri
Macedonis libri octo**, Cologne, 1579   8°
First edition with catalogue title. First published
in 8° (**Historia Alexandri Magni**), Florence, 1507.
Another copy of Item no. 722, above, in 8° or 12°.

Catalogue

"Bookes lent & omitted in
ye formr Catalogue"

(Book sizes unknown)

1176.   2 my owne Sermon bookes   £0 05 0

Presumably 2 copies of Item no. 451, above.

1177.   Alexand: ab Alexand Genialium dierum   £0 03 6

**Alexander ab ALEXANDRO, Genialium dierum libri sex ...
accuratius quam antehac excusi, cum duplici indice,**
Paris, 1532   folio
Numerous subsequent editions in various book sizes.

(DS, p.286)

1178.   The history of ye yron age   £0 06 6

**Jean Nicolas de PARIVAL, The History of this Iron Age :
wherein is set down the true state of Europe, as it was
in the year 1500 ... rendred into English, by B. Harris,**
London, 1656 ; 1659   folio

(STC : P361)

1179.   The history of Sweethland   £0 07 0

**John FOWLER, The History of the troubles of Suethland
and Poland, which occasioned the expulsion of
Sigismundus the Third ... with his heires ... from
the Suethish crown,** London, 1656   folio

(STC : F1731-F1732)

1180.   Plato in latine   £0 07 6

Probably an edition of:

PLATO, Opera (ed. M. Ficino), Florence, 1484, 1485 ...
Lyons, 1588   folio

1181.   Peuceri de divinatione   £0 03 6

**Caspar PEUCER, Commentarius de praecipuis divinationum
generibus,** Wittenberg, 1553 ... Hanover & Frankfurt,
1607   8°

1182.   Holy oake upon Rider   £0 10 0

**John RIDER, Bishop of Killaloe, <u>Riders dictionarie
corrected and augmented</u>** (English-latin)<u>. Wherein
Riders index is transformed into a dictionarie
etymologicall. **Many words added**</u> (Latin-English) **By
F̲**(rancis) **<u>Holyoke</u>**, London, 1606 ... London, 1659   4°

(STC : 21032-21036b.7 ; R1442-R1443)

1183.   A Greeke Lexicon   £0 08 6

1184.   3 of Glaubers bookes   £0 03 6

3 volumes by **Johann Rudolph GLAUBER.**

1185.   A peice of paracelsus   £0 04 6

An unspecified work by **Philipp Aureol Theophrast
BOMBAST VON HOHENHEIM.**

1186.   Terrence in English   £0 02 6

**Publius TERENTIUS Afer, <u>Terence in English. Fabulae
... Anglicae factae primumque hac nova forma nunc
editae : opera ac industria R. B</u>**(ernard), Cambridge,
1598 ; 1607 ; London, 1614 ; 1629 ; 1641 (6th ed)   8°
Latin-English.

(STC : 23890-23893 ; T751)

1187.   Walesij infinitorum Arithmetica   £0 04 6

John WALLIS, <u>Arithmetica Infinitorum</u>, Oxford, 1655   4°
Part 3 of Wallis' **<u>Operum mathematicorum</u>**, published in
4 Parts at Oxford, 1655-56 (each part with a separate
title-page and pagination).

(STC : W598-W598A)

1188.   Piquet in English   £0 02 6

**Jean PECQUET, <u>New Anatomical Experiments of J. Pecquet,
by which the hitherto unknown receptacle of the chyle,
and the transmission from thence to the subclavical
veins by the now discovered lacteal chanels of the
thorax, is plainly made appear in brutes</u>**, 2 vols. (in
1?), London, 1653   12°

(STC : P1045)

1189.   Brevis disquisitio & Racovian Cathechisme   £0 02 0

Two separate works bound together in 1 volume:

(a) **(John BIDDLE)**, <u>**Brevis Disquisitio : or a**</u>
<u>**brief enquiry touching a better way then is commonly**</u>
<u>**made use of, to refute Papists, and reduce Protestants**</u>
<u>**to certainty and unity in religion**</u>, London, 1653   8°

(STC : B2870)

(b) **(William DUGARD)**, <u>**The Racovian Catechisme : or**</u>
<u>**the substance of the confession of those Churches, which**</u>
<u>**in the Kingdom of Poland ... and other provinces**</u>
<u>**appertaining to that kingdom, do affirm that no other**</u>
<u>**save the Father of our Lord Jesus Christ is that one**</u>
<u>**God of Israel**</u>, Amsterdam & London, 1652   8°

(STC : R121)

1190.   The history of parismus   £0 02 6

Emanuel **FORDE**, <u>**Parismus, the Renowned Prince of Bohemia.**</u>
<u>**His most famous, delectable, and pleasant Historie.**</u>
<u>**Conteining his Noble Battailes fought against the Persians.**</u>
<u>**His love to Laurana ... and his strange adventures in**</u>
<u>**the Desolate Iland**</u>, London, 1598, 1599 ... 11th ed.,
London, 1681   4°

(STC : 11171-11175 ; F1531A-F1536)

1191.   Ovidij metamorphos: lib   £0 02 0

Publius **OVIDIUS NASO**, <u>**Metamorphoses**</u>
Dozens of editions in various book sizes. First published
in folio : ?, 1472? ; in 4° : Lyons, 1510 ; in 8° :
Lyons, 1505.
Another copy of Item no. 1043, above.

1192.   Marchams booke wth: ye Art of venery   £0 12 6

Two separate works bound together in 1 volume:

(a) A work by Gervase **MARKHAM**. Given the subject
of 1192(b), and the wording in the catalogue, this is
probably an edition of the following:
<u>**Markhams maister-peece. Or what doth a horse man**</u>
<u>**lacke**</u>, London, 1610 ... London, 1636   4°

(STC : 17376-17379.5)

(b) **(George TURBERVILLE)**, <u>**The Noble Arte of**</u>
<u>**Venerie or Hunting. Wherein is handled and set out the**</u>
<u>**Vertues, Nature, and Properties of fivetene sundrie**</u>
<u>**Chaces together, with the order and maner how to Hunte**</u>
<u>**and Kill every one of them. Translated and collected**</u>
<u>**... out of the best approved Authors**</u>, London, 1575 ;
1611   4°

(STC : 24328-24329)

1193. ffieni methodus medendi lib   £0 06 0

I can find no work of this title under either Joannes
or Thomas Fienus. In all probability, this is an
error in transcription for:

GALEN, Methodus medendi, 1st ed., Paris, 1519   folio
Numerous later editions in various book sizes.
(Another copy of Item no. 37, above?)

1194. ffelix Wurtzius in English   £0 03 6

**Felix WUERTZ, An experimental treatise of surgerie
in four parts ... Faithfully translated ... out of
the ... German tongue ... by Abraham Lenertzon Fox**,
London, 1656   4°
Another edition of this work appeared under the
title **The surgeons guid**, London, 1658 (4°).

(STC : W3733 ; W3734)

1195. 2 bookes of Cleopatra   £0 03 0

Probably two works by the medical writer **CLEOPATRA**.
This might also, however, be a reference to:

**Thomas MAY, Two Tragedies, viz. Cleopatra Queene of
AEgypt : and Agrippina, Empress of Rome**, London,
1654   12°

(STC : M1416)

1196. Bellerminus enerbatus   £0 03 6

William AMES, Bellarminus enervatus, Amsterdam, 1628 ;
Oxford, 1629 ; 4 vols., London, 1633, 1632   12°

(DS, p.46 ; STC : 550-551)

1197. H: N: Workes   £0 07 6

The works of the founder of the sect known as the
Family of Love, **H(endrik) N(ICLAS)**, first published
in English at Cologne, 1574-75 in 15 small volumes in
8° (trans. Christopher Vitell). Many of these works
were subsequently republished at London between 1648
and 1656.

1198. Tenzelij exagesis etc   £0 03 0

**Angelo SALA, Ternarius Bezoardicorum et Hemetologia
seu Triumphus vomitoriorum, e gallico sermone latinitate
κατα ποδας donati, cum exegesi Chymiatrica A**(ndreas)
Tentzelii, Erfurt, 1618 ; 1630   8°

1199.   Blundeviles Excercise   £0 06 6

**Thomas BLUNDEVILLE, <u>M. Blundevile His Exercises,
containing sixe Treatises ... verie necessarie to be
read and learned of all young Gentlemen that ... are
desirous to have knowledge ... in Cosmographie,
Astronomie and Geographie, as also in the Arte of
Navigation</u>**, London, 1594 ... 7th ed., London, 1636   4°

(STC : 3146-3151a)

1200.   Historia Waldensis   £0 03 0

One of two possible works:

    (a) **Scipio LENTULUS, <u>Memorabilis historia
persecutionum, bellorumque in populam vulgo Valdensem
appellatum ... nunc vero a Christophoro Richardo ...
Latinitate donata</u>**, Geneva, 1581   8°

    (b) **Balthasar LYDIUS, <u>Facula accensa Historiae
Waldensium</u>**, Dordrecht, 1618   book size unknown*

* Work referred to in Georg Draud, <u>Bibliotheca Classica,
Sive Catalogus Officinalis</u>, 2 vols., Frankfurt, 1625,
I, p.650.   I have not been able to trace an extant
edition of this work.

1201.   A poeticall Dictionary & Hebrew grammer   £0 07 0

In all probability, two separate works published by
Robert Estienne the Elder at Paris in the 1530s, and
now bound together in 1 volume:

    (a) **Hermannus TORRENTINUS, <u>Dictionarium poeticum
quod vulgo inscribitur Elucidanus Carminum</u>**, Paris,
1530 ; 1535 ; 1550   8°

    (b) **(Robert ESTIENNE the Elder), <u>Alphabetum
Hebraicum. De pronuntiatione literarum Heb., ...
decem ... Domini praecepta, Hebraice et Latine</u>**,
Paris, 1539   8°

1202.   Moores Arithmeticke   £0 03 6

**Sir Jonas MOORE, <u>Moores Arithmetick : discovering the
secrets of that art, in Numbers and Species</u>**, London,
1650 ; 1660   8°

(STC : M2563-M2564)

1203.　　Bakers Arithmetick　　　　　　　　　£0 01 8

**Humphrey BAKER, The Well springe of Sciences, which
teacheth the perfect worke and practise of Arithmeticke,**
London, 1568 ... London, 1670*　　　　　　　8°
(* Nb. The 1670 edition was entitled **Bakers
Arithmetick**).

(STC : 1210–1218 ; B492)

1204.　　Regij Arithmetica　　　　　　　　　£0 01 4

**Ulricus REGIUS, Utriusque arithmetices epitome ex variis
authoribus concinnata, per Hudalrichum Regium,** Strassburg,
1536 ; Freiburg im Breisgau, 1543 ; 1550　　　　8°

SECTION N
"Libri Theologici in 4to: et 12mo:"*

(Works on theology in all book sizes*)

1205.　　Bishop King upon Jonas　　　　　　　£0 07 0

**John KING, Bishop of London, Lectures upon Jonas,
delivered at Yorke,** Oxford, 1597 ; 1599 ; 1600 ;
London, 1611 ; 1618　　　　　　　　　　　4°

(STC : 14976–14981)

1206.　　Lewes of Granada, The Sinners guide　　£0 03 6

**LUIS de Granada, Dominican (i.e. Luis SARRIA),
The Sinners Guyde. A worke contayning the whole
regiment of a Christian life ... Compiled in the
Spanish tongue ... And nowe ... digested into English,
by Francis Meres,** London, 1598 ; 1614　　　　4°

(STC : 16918–16919)

*　This is clearly an error in transcription for "4to: 8vo:
et 12mo:".　Once again, this section would appear to fall
into two fairly well defined sub-divisions, the first half
mainly consisting of works in 4°, the second half of works
in 8° and some 12°.

1207.   The way of ye Church by ffr: White   £0 03 0

Francis WHITE, Bishop of Carlisle, Norwich and Ely,
The Orthodox Faith and Way to the Church explained and
justified : in answer to a Popish treatise entituled,
White died Blacke, London, 1617   4°

(STC : 25380)

1208.   Downehams defence   £0 0 10

George DOWNAME, Bishop of Derry, A Defence of the
Sermon preached at the consecration of the L. Bishop of
Bath and Welles against a Confutation thereof by a
namelesse Author. Divided into 4 bookes, London,
1611   4°

(STC : 7115)

1209.   A Retractive from ye Romish Religion by Tho: Beard
£0 04 0

Thomas BEARD, A Retractive from the Romish Religion :
Contayning Thirteene forcible motives disswading
from communion with the Church of Rome, London, 1616 4°

(STC : 1658)

1210.   Jo: Randall upon ye Lord supper   £0 04 0

John RANDALL, Three and twentie Sermons, or, catechisticall
lectures upon the Sacrament of the Lords Supper, London,
1630   4°

(STC : 20682-20682a)

1211.   Incouragemts agst afflictions by Tho: Peirson £0 03 0

Thomas PIERSON, Excellent Encouragements against
Afflictions : or Expositions of four select Psalmes,
the 17, 84, 85 and 87 (ed. C. Harvey), London, 1647 4°

(STC : P2216)

1212.   Bishop Babingtons workes   £0 05 0

The **Works** of Gervase BABINGTON, Bishop of Llandaff,
Exeter and Worcester.   Presumably 4 volumes published
by Thomas Charde at London, 1596 (4°) and bound in 1 vol.:

        (a) **A brief conference betwixt mans Frailtie and Faith**
        (b) **Certaine Plaine, briefe and comfortable notes**
upon every chapter of Genesis
        (c) **A profitable Exposition of the Lords Prayer**
        (d) **A very fruitfull Exposition of the Commaundements**
Another copy of Item no. 159, above, in 4°.

(STC : (a) 1084 ; (b) 1087 ; (c) 1091 ; (d) 1098

1213.   Smithes Sermons   £0 03 6

Henry **SMITH**, Minister of St. Clement Danes, **The Sermons of Maister Henrie Smith, gathered into one volume**, London, 1594 ... London, 1675   4°
First edition : London, 1592 (8°).

(STC : 22720-22734 ; S4044-S4046)

1214.   Mr: Wm: Bartons workes   £0 05 0

I have been unable to trace any edition of the <u>Works</u> of **William BARTON** in 4°. This may well be a composite edition of Barton's two main works:

    (a) **The Book of Psalms in metre**, London, 1644 ; 1646 ; 1651 ; 1654   12°
    (b) **A Century of Select Hymns**, London, 1659 ; enlarged, London, 1668 ; 1670 ; 1672   12°

(See under Wing, STC : Barton, William)

1215.   of Divorce by Edm: Bunny   £0 00 8

Edmund **BUNNY**, **Of Divorce for Adulterie, and Marrying againe : that there is no sufficient warrant so to do. With a note ... that R(obert) P(arsons) many yeeres since was answered**, Oxford, 1610 ; 1613   4°

(STC : 4091-4092)

1216.   The 2 wittnesses   £0 00 6

Francis **WOODCOCK**, **The two witnesses discovered in severall sermons upon the eleventh Chapter of the Revelation**, London, 1643   4°
(Nb. Also the title of a work published by Thomas Tillam, but in octavo).

(STC : W3343)

1217.   The way to true peace & rest by Rob: Bruce   £0 02 0

Robert **BRUCE**, **The Way to True Peace and Rest. Delivered at Edinborough in XVI. Sermons : on the Lords Supper : Hezechiahs Sicknesse : and other select Scriptures**, London, 1617   4°

(STC : 3925)

1218.   Meditacons on ye Lords Supper by Edw: Reynolds £0 01 6

Edward **REYNOLDS**, Bishop of Norwich, **Meditations on the Holy Sacrament of the Lords Last Supper**, London, 1638 ; 2nd ed., London, 1639 ; 3rd ed., London, 1647   4°

(STC : 20929-20930a ; R1267)

1219.   Lectures upon ye prophet Hosea by Jo: Downhame
£0 03 6

John **DOWNAME**, **Lectures upon the foure first chapters of the prophecie of Hosea**, London, 1608   4°

(STC : 7145)

1220.   The peace of Roome(sic) by Jos: Hall   £0 01 6

Joseph **HALL**, Bishop of Exeter & Norwich, **The Peace of Rome, proclaimed to all the world by her famous Cardinall Bellarmine, and the Casuist Navarre** (i.e. M. de Azpilcueta), London, 1609   4°

(STC : 12696–12697a)

1221.   Essex dove by Mr: Jo: Smith   £0 00 6

John **SMITH**, Minister of Clavering, **Essex Dove, presenting the world with a few of her olive branches : or, a taste of the works of ... Mr. John Smith**, London, 1629 ; 1633 ; 1637   4°

(STC : 22798–22800.5)

1222.   A defence of ye Liturgy of ye Church of England   £0 02 0

Ambrose **FISHER**, **A defence of the Liturgie of the Church of England, or booke of Common Prayer, in a dialogue betweene Novatus and Iraeneus**, London, 1630   4°

(STC : 10885)

1223.   Antea Arminianisme   £0 0 10

William **PRYNNE**, **Anti-Arminianisme, or the Church of Englands old antithesis to new Arminianisme**, London, 1630   4°
First published under a different title (**The Church of Englands old Antithesis to new Arminianisme**), London, 1629 (4°).

(STC : 20458)

1224.   A Justification of separation by Jo: Robinson £0 02 6

John **ROBINSON**, Pastor of the English Congregational Church at Leyden, **A justification of separation from the Church of England : against Mr. R. Bernard his invective intituled The Separatists schisme**, Amsterdam, 1610 ; 1639   4°

(STC : 21109–21110)

1225.   The Diocesans triall   £0 00 8

Paul BAYNES, The Diocesans Tryall : Wherein all the sinnews of D. Downams Defence are brought unto three heads, and orderly dissolved, London, 1621 ; 1641 ; 1644   4°

(STC : 1640 ; B1547–B1548)

1226.   Jo: Drusij praeteritorum lib   £0 03 6

Joannes DRUSIUS the Elder, Annotationum in totum Jesu Christi Testamentum, sive praeteritorum libri decem, Franeker, 1612 ; 1616   4°

(DS, p.40)

1227.   Altare Christianum   £0 01 4

John POCKLINGTON, Altare Christianum : or, the dead Vicars Plea Wherein the Vicar of Gr(antham) **being dead, yet speaketh, and pleadeth out of Antiquity against him that hath broken doune his Altar**, London, 1637 ; 2nd ed., London, 1637   4°
A reply to J. Cotton's A Coale from the Altar.

(STC : 20075–20076)

1228.   Lectures on ye 15 psalme by Geo: Downhame   £0 02 0

George DOWNAME, Bishop of Derry, Lectures on the XV. psalme : read in the Cathedrall Church of S. Paule, in London, London, 1604   4°

(STC : 7118)

1229.   A Comentary upon ye Revelacon   £0 01 8

William COWPER, Pathmos : or, a Commentary on the Revelation of Saint Iohn, divided into three severall prophecies, London, 1619   4°

(STC : 5931)

1230.   Didaci a Stunica Coment: in Job   £0 06 6

Jacobus LOPIS STUNICA, Didaci a Stunica ... In Job commentaria, quibus triplex eius editio vulgata Latina, Hebraea, & Graeca septuaginta interpretum, necnon & Chaldaea explicantur, Toledo, 1584 ; Rome, 1591   4°

1231. Rich: ffeild of ye Church   £0 02 0

Richard **FIELD**, Dean of Gloucester, **Of the Church.
Five bookes**, London, 1606, 1610   4°

(STC : 10856-10857)

1232. of ye Covenants in Scotland   £0 03 0

Probably an edition of the following:

**CHURCH OF SCOTLAND, The Profession of the true
Protestant Religion : or the Protestation of the Kirk
of Scotland, with a Confession of the Faith, and
Solemne Covenant, or Oath of that kingdome**, Edinburgh,
1641 ; London, 1642   4°

(STC : P3645)

1233. The holy table name and thinge   £0 01 6

(John **WILLIAMS**, Bishop of Lincoln and Archbishop of
York), **The Holy Table, Name and Thing, more anciently,
properly and literally used under the New Testament,
then that of an Altar : written long ago by a minister
in Lincolnshire in answer to D. Coal**, London, 1637   4°

(STC : 25724-25726)

1234. Brotherly reconceilmt: by Egeon Ashero(sic) £0 01 8

Egeon **ASKEW, Brotherly Reconcilement : preached in
Oxford for the union of some, and now published with
larger meditations ... With an apologie of the use of
Fathers, and secular learning in sermons**, London,
1605   4°

(STC : 855)

1235. Reasons for reformacon   £0 00 8

Possibly the following small work in 4°:

Henry **JACOB**, Independent Minister, **Reasons taken out
of Gods Word and the best humane testimonies proving a
necessitie of reforming our Churches in England**,
Middelburg?, 1604   4°

(STC : 14338)

1236. The pastor & ye prelate   £0 00 8

David **CALDERWOOD, The Pastor and the Prelate**, Holland?,
1628   4°

(STC : 4359)

1237. A reexaminacon of ye Articles of Perth   £0 01 4

David CALDERWOOD, A Re-examination of the five Articles enacted at Perth anno 1618, ?, 1636   4°

(STC : 4363)

---

f18v

1238. The Passions of ye mind by Tho: Wright   £0 02 0

Thomas WRIGHT, The Passions of the minde in generall. Corrected, enlarged, and with sundry new discourses augmented. ... With a treatise ... of the Clymatericall yeare, occasioned by the death of Queene Elizabeth, London, 1604 ; 1620 ; 1621 ; 1630   4°
First edition : London, 1601 (8°).

(STC : 26040-26043)

1239. Christ ye great wondr by Mat: Barker   £0 01 6

Matthew BARKER, Jesus Christ The Great Wonder. Discovered for the Amazement of Saints, London, 1651   4°

(STC : B776)

1240. Articuli religionis   £0 00 8

CHURCH OF ENGLAND, Articles of Religion of the Church of England (Thirty-Nine Articles), London, 1553   4°
Dozens of subsequent editions, many revised, in 4°

(STC : 10034-10061)

1241. A replie to Dr: Mortons defence   £0 01 0

(William AMES), A Reply to Dr. Mortons Generall defence of three nocent Ceremonies. Viz. the Surplice, Crosse in Baptisme, and Kneeling at the receiving of the sacramentall elements of Bread and Wine, London, 1622 ; 1623   4°

(STC : 559-560)

1242.   A vindication of ye Presbiteriall governmt   £0 01 6

Anon., A Vindication of the presbyteriall-government, and ministry : together with an exhortation, to all the ministers, elders, and people within the bounds of the province of London, whether joyning with us, or separating from us, London, 1650   4°

(STC : V523)

1243.   A relacon of ye State of ye Kirk of Scotland   £0 01 8

Anon., A Short Relation of the state of the Kirk of Scotland since the reformation of religion to the present time, for information and advertisement to our brethren in the Kirk of England. By an hearty well-wisher to both kingdomes, Edinburgh?, 1638   4°

(STC : 22039)

1244.   Sti: Bernardi Sermones   £0 01 6

A collection of sermons in 4° by **Saint BERNARD, Abbot of Clairvaux,** possibly taken from an edition of his **Opera.**

1245.   The Sermons of Bishop Edwin   £0 01 8

Edwin SANDYS, Bishop of Worcester and London, and Archbishop of York, Sermons made by the most reverende Father in God, Edwin, Archbishop of Yorke, London, 1585 ; 1616   4°

(STC : 21713-21714)

1246.   Cartwright agst: Whitgift   £0 03 0

Thomas CARTWRIGHT was the author of three works directed against Archbishop Whitgift:

(a) **A Replye to an answere made of M. Doctor Whitgifte**, ?, 1573 ; ?, 1574   4°
(b) **The Second Replie of Thomas Cartwright : against Maister Doctor Whitgiftes second answer, touching the churche discipline**, Zurich, 1575   4°
(c) **The Rest of the Second Replie ... against M.D.W.**, ?, 1577   4°

These three works may have been bound together in one volume, or Webster may simply have owned any one of them.

(STC : (a) 4711-4712 ; (b) 4714 ; (c) 4715)

1247.   A bride bush by Wm: Wheatley   £0 01 6

William WHATELY, Vicar of Banbury, A Bride–Bush or a
wedding sermon for married persons, plainly describing
the duties common to both, and peculiar to each of them,
London, 1617 ; 1619 ; 1623   4°

(STC : 25296–25298)

1248.   A key for ye Revelation   £0 02 6

Richard BERNARD, A Key of Knowledge for the Opening of
the Secret Mysteries of St. Iohns Mysticall Revelation,
London, 1617   4°

(STC : 1955)

1249.   The Anatomy of a Christian by Mr: Cowper   £0 01 4

William COWPER, The anatomie of a Christian man.
Wherin is plainelie shewed out of the Word of God,
what manner of man a true Christian is in all his
conversation, both inward and outward, London, 1611 ;
2nd ed., London, 1613   4°

(STC : 5912–5913)

1250.   A disproofe agst Dr: Abott   £0 01 2

William BISHOP, Bishop of Chalcedon, A Disproofe of
D. Abbots Counterproofe against D. Bishops Reproofe
of the defence of M. Perkins reformed Catholicke.
The first part, Paris, 1614   4°*
(* Also published in 8° : Paris, 1614)

(STC : 3094)

1251.   The Confession of ye Church of Scotland   £0 02 0

CHURCH OF SCOTLAND, The Confession of Faith of the
Church of Scotland, Edinburgh, 1561 ... London,
1641 and ?, 1647   4°

(STC : 22016 ; 22023 ; 22024.5 ; 22026–22026.2 ;
22026.4 ; 22026.6–22026.8 ; 22027 ; C4202B–C4202CA)

1252.   Balme for England by Mr: Lockier   £0 01 8

Nicholas LOCKYER, Baulme for bleeding England and
Ireland ; or, seasonable instructions for persecuted
Christians : delivered in severall sermons, London,
1646 ; 1649   4°
First edition : London, 1643 (8°).

(STC : L2785–L2786)

1253.   Calvin upon ye Psalmes   £0 03 6

Jean CALVIN, The Psalmes of David and others. With
M. John Calvins Commentaries (trans. from latin by
Arthur Golding), London, 1571   4°

(STC : 4395)

1254.   An Answer to Campians Epistle   £0 01 8

William WHITAKER, An Answere to the Ten Reasons of
Edmund Campian (Running title, pp. 5-16 : "An Answere
to Campians Epistle"), London, 1606   4°

(STC : 25360)

1255.   Englands second Summons   £0 00 4

Thomas SUTTON, Englands second summons. A sermon,
London, 1615
(*Nb. No edition in 4°).   8°*

(STC : 23501)

1256.   The Serpent Anatomized by Ed: Sutton   £0 00 4

Edward SUTTON, The serpent anatomized. A morall discourse
wherein that foule serpentine vice of base creeping
flattery is manifestly discovered, and justly reproved,
London, 1626   4°

(STC : 23497)

1257.   A Discovery of Romish Doctrine   £0 00 4

T(homas) M(ORTON), An Exact Discoverie of Romish
Doctrine in the case of Conspiracie and Rebellion,
London, 1605   4°

(STC : 18184-18184.5)

1258.   The downefall of popery   £0 00 6

Thomas BELL, The Downefall of poperie : proposed by
way of a new challenge to all English Iesuits and
Iesuited or Italianized Papists : daring them ... to
make answere thereunto if they can, London, 1604 ;
1605   4°

(STC : 1825-1826)

1259.   4 Treatasies by Jo: Downeham   £0 01 6

John DOWNAME, Foure treatises tending to disswade all
Christians from ... the abuses of Swearing, Drunkennesse,
Whoredome, and Bribery ... Whereunto is annexed a
treatise of Anger, London, 1609 ; 1613   4°

(STC : 7141-7142)

1260. Cure for ye Comfortless   £0 00 8

Thomas **BARNES**, Minister of St. Margarets, New Fish
Street, London, Needfull helps : against Desperate
Perplexitie ; and Deepe Securitie. As they have been
delivered in sundry Sermons (Cure for the Comfortles,
etc - The Wise-Mans Forecast against the Evill time -
Sions Sweets : or the Spouses spikenard ; and mysticall
myrrhe), London, 1624   4°
"Cure for the Comfortless" forms Part 1 of this work,
with separate pagination.

(STC : 1477)

1261. The Popes funerall   £0 00 8

Thomas **BELL**, The Popes Funerall. Containing a plaine,
succinct, and pithy reply, to a pretensed answere of a
shamelesse and foolish Libell, intituled, the forerunner
of Bels downfall (by Philip Woodward), London, 1605 ;
another ed., enlarged, London, 1606   4°

(STC : 1825-1826)

1262. A forme of Prayer (4°)   £0 00 6

1263. Sacriledge sacredly handled   £0 0 10

Sir James **SEMPILL**, Sacrilege Sacredly Handled. That is
according to Scripture onely ... An Appendix also added,
answering some Objections mooved, namely, against this
Treatise, and some others, I finde in Jos. Scaligers
Diatribe and Joh. Seldens Historie of Tithes, London,
1619   4°

(STC : 22186)

1264. The baiteinge of ye Popes Bull   £0 0 10

Henry **BURTON**, Rector of St. Matthew's, Friday Street,
The Baiting of the Popes Bull. Or an unmasking of the
mystery of iniquity folded up in a ... Breeve or Bull,
sent from the Pope lately into England (with the text
of the brief dated 30th May 1626, in latin and English),
London, 1627   4°

(STC : 4137)

1265. Matth: Sladi exagesis   £0 01 0

Matthaeus **SLADUS**, M. Sladi ... cum C. Vorstio ... de
blasphemiis, haeresibus & atheismis, a ... rege Iacobo,
hujus nominis Primo, ... in ejusdem Vorstii de Deo
tractatu, & Exagesi apologetica nigro Theta notatis,
scholasticae disceptationis pars prima, Amsterdam,
1612 ; another ed. (Pars prima ... (altera)), Amsterdam,
1615, 1614   4°

1266.   Vocabularius (4°)   £0 02 0

1267.   Dominicalia Leonard Culman   £0 06 0

Leonhard CULMAN, <u>Contiones sacrae ac variae</u>
<u>predicandorum Evangeliorum, quae Dominicis Diebus et</u>
<u>in festis legi solent, fromulm</u>, Nuremburg, 1551 folio*
(* Nb. No edition in 4°).

1268.   Introductio in Ethicen Aristot p(er) Jac: Stapulens
        £0 04 0

Jacques LE FÈVRE d'Étaples, <u>Ars moralis philosophie.</u>
<u>In hoc opusculo continentur epitome moralis philosophie</u>
<u>in ethicem Aristotelis introductoria (ex morali</u>
<u>introductione Iacobi fabri Stapulensis ... deprompta</u>
<u>adjectis ... commentariis</u>, Deventer, 1500 ; Vienna,
1501 ; Paris, 1560   4°

1269.   Jo: Calvini in Isai Coment   £0 06 0

Jean CALVIN, <u>Ioannis Calvini Commentarii in Isaiam</u>
<u>Prophetam</u>, Geneva, 1551 ; 1559 ; 1563 ; 1570 ; 1583
folio*
(* Nb. No edition in 4°).

(DS, pp.75,130–131,225)

1270.   Jo: Piscatoris in Job lib: Coment   £0 04 6

Johann PISCATOR of Herborn, <u>In Librum Jobi commentarius.</u>
<u>In quo, praeter novam versionem, versioni Tremellio–</u>
<u>Junianae e regione adjectam, ordine & distincte</u>
<u>proponuntur. I. Analysis logica singulorum capitum.</u>
<u>II. Scholia in singula capita. III. Observationes locorum</u>
<u>doctrinae e singulis capitibus depromtae</u>, Herborn,
1612   8°*
(* Nb. No edition in any other size).

(M, p.148)

1271.   Matth: Sutlivij de purgatorio lib   £0 00 6

Matthew SUTCLIFFE, <u>M. Sutlivii Adversus R. Bellarmini</u>
<u>de Purgatorio Disputationem Liber</u>, London, 1599   4°

(STC : 23449)

1272.   Jo: Tarnovij in 10   Psalmos Comm: £0 01 0

Joannes TARNOVIUS, <u>Commentarius in decem primos</u>
<u>Psalmos Davidis</u>, Rostock, 1621 ; 1633   4°

1273.   Ro: Rolloci in Daniel lib: Coment   £0 02 0

Robert ROLLOCK, In librum Danielis Prophetae Roberti Rolloci ... commentarius, Edinburgh, 1591 ;
Heidelberg, 1594   4°

(DS, p.95 ; STC : 21280)

---

f19r

1274.   Jo: Melfickreri in Epist: ad Phillipenses Comm
£0 02 0

Joannes MEELFÜHRERUS, Monk of the Abbey of Heilbronn, S. Pauli epistola ad Philippenses commentationibus perspicuis enarrata, Nuremburg, 1628   4°

1275.   ffr: Junij Animadversiones   £0 01 6

One of a series of works, all entitled **Animadversiones**, and written by **Francois DU JON the Elder** as part of an on-going controversy with Bellarmine, Heidelberg, 1600-1608 (8°).

1276.   De la Gloria de los Cantos(sic)   £0 01 6

Diego de la VEGA, Parayso de la Gloria de los Santos, donde se trata de sus prerogativas y eccellencias, 2 vols. in 1, Toledo, 1602 ; Medina, 1604 ; Barcelona, 1604 ; Valladolid, 1607 ; Barcelona, 1611   4°

1277.   Ro: Rolloci in Epist ad Ephesios Comm   £0 02 0

Robert ROLLOCK, In Epistolam Pauli Apostoli ad Ephesios, Roberti Rolloci ... commentarius, Edinburgh, 1590 4°
Numerous later editions published at Geneva in octavo.

(STC : 21278)

1278.   A: N: Catachismus   £0 0 10

A(lexander) N(OWELL), Catechismus, sive prima Institutio, Disciplinaque pietatis Christianae, Latinè explicata,
London, 1570 ; 1571 ; 1572 ; 1574 ; 1576 ; 1580   4°

(STC : 18701-18706)

1279.   Guel: Sclateri in Epist ad Corinthos Com   £0 02 0

William SCLATER, Vicar of Pitminster, Utriusque
Epistolae ad Corinthios explicatio analytica, una cum
scholiis ; authore G. Sclatero ... Nunc tandem a filio
suo (William Sclater the Younger) **... in lucem edita**,
Oxford, 1633   4°

(STC : 21848)

1280.   Lectiones decem Jo: Prideaux   £0 02 6

John PRIDEAUX, Bishop of Worcester, Lectiones decem.
De totidem Religionis capitibus praecipue hoc tempore
controversis prout publice habebantur Oxoniae in
Vesperijs, Oxford, 1626   4°

(STC : 20357)

1281.   Guli: Perkinsi problema   £0 01 8

William PERKINS, Problema de Romanae Fidei ementito
Catholicismo. Estque antidotum contra Thesaurum
Catholicum J. Coccii ... Editum ... opera ... S. Wardi,
Cambridge, 1604   4°

(STC : 19734)

1282.   Andr: Riveti disputationes 13   £0 01 6

André RIVET, Disputationes tredecim de justa et gratiosa
Dei dispensatione circa salutem generis humani,
Leyden, 1631   8°*
(* Nb. No edition in 4°).

(DS, pp.192–193)

1283.   Dunel: ffenneri Theol: Sacra   £0 01 6

Dudley FENNER, Sacra Theologia ... ad unicae & verae
methodi leges descripta, London?, 1585 ; Geneva,
1586 ; 1589 ; Amsterdam, 1632   8°*
(* Nb. No edition in 4°. Also published in 12° :
Geneva, 1604)

1284.   De Sacramentis lib (4° or 8°)   £0 00 6

1285.   Manipulus florum ex criptis(sic) patrum   £0 03 6

THOMAS Hibernicus, Manipulus florum, seu sententiae
Patrum, Venice, 1495?   4°
First edition : Piacenza, 1483, in folio.
An earlier edition of Item no.1056, above.

1286.   Ad Policarpi Lyseri in Genes: lib Expositio   £0 04 0

**Polycarp LEYSER, Adamus ... hoc est, theologica
expositio primae partis Geneseos quae continet
historiam Adami**, Leipzig, 1604   4°

1287.   Collectio habitae Hagae de praedestinatione   £0 04 0

**Henricus BRANDIUS, Collatio scripto habita Hagae
comitis anno ... 1611, inter quosdam Ecclesiastas de
divina Praedestinatione ... Latina facta interprete
Henrico Brandio ... Huic est etiam subiecta Collatio
inter sex ecclesiastas Delphis habita anno 1613,**
Middelburg, 1615   4°

1288.   Apologia remonstrantium   £0 05 6

**Anon., Apologia pro confessione sive declaratione
sententiae eorum qui in foederato Belgio vocantur
remonstrantes, super praecipuis articulis religionis
Christianae contra censuram quatuor professorum
Leidensium**, Leyden?, 1629   4°

1289.   Barthol: Camerarij de gratia et libero arbitrio
        £0 02 0

**Bartholomaeus CAMERARIUS Beneventanus, De gratia et
libero arbitrio cum Joanne Calvino disputatio,**
Paris, 1556   4°

1290.   Jo: Piscatoris in Ezekiell: Com: £0 01 8

**Johann PISCATOR of Herborn, In Prophetam Ezechielem
commentarius. In quo praeter novam versionem, ordine
et distincti proponuntur. I. Analysis logica
singulorum capitum. II. Scholia in singula capita.
III. Observationes locorum doctrinae e singulis capitibus
depromtae**, Herborn, 1614   small 4°

1291.   Abr: Sculteti Idea Consionum   £0 06 0

**Abraham SCULTETUS, Idea concionum dominicalium ad
populum Haidelbergensem habitarum, confecta opera et
studio Balthasaris Tilesii**, Hanover, 1607 ; 1608 ;
Geneva, 1610 ; 1616 ; Hanover, 1651   8°*
(* Nb. No edition in 4°).

1292.   Dionysij Juberi dominica   £0 03 0

Dionisio JUBERO, Sermones de todas las Dominicas,
Barcelona, 1610 ; Salamanca, 1612   4°
I have not been able to trace a latin edition of
this work.

1293.   Tho: Brightmanni Apocalyp: Apocalipseos   £0 05 6

**Thomas BRIGHTMAN, Apocalypsis Apocalypseos. Id est,
Apocalypsis D. Ioannis analysi et scholiis illustrata ;
ubi ex scriptura sensus, rerumque predictarum ex
historijs eventus discutiuntur. Huic synopsis
praefigitur universalis : & refutatio Rob. Bellarmini
de Antichristo**, Frankfurt, 1609   4°
Another edition in 8° : Heidelberg, 1612.

1294.   Tho: Cartwriti historia Evangelica   £0 02 6

**Thomas CARTWRIGHT, Harmonia Evangelica per analysin
logicam, et metaphrasin historicam quatuor Evangelistas
explicans & concinnans**, Amsterdam, 1627 ; London?,
1630 ; Amsterdam, 1644 ; Leyden, 1647   4°

1295.   Theod: Bezae theses Theolog: £0 01 8

**Théodore de BÈZE, Theses theologicae in Schola Genevensi
ab aliquot sacrarum literarum studiosis ... sub D.D.
Theodoro Beza, & Antonio Fayo ... propositae &
disputatae**, Geneva, 1586 ; 1591   4°

1296.   Leon: Lessij quae fides etc sit capesenda   £0 03 6

**Leonardus LESSIUS, Quae fides et religio sit capessenda,
consultatio, auctore Leonardo Lessio**, Antwerp, 1609 ;
1610   8°

1297.   AEgidij Topiarij in Evangel: et Epist. Conciones 2 vol
£0 05 0

**Laurentius a VILLAVICENTIO, Conciones in Evangelia et
Epistolas, quae festis totius anni diebus populo in
Ecclesia proponi solent ... e tabulis D. Laurentii a
Villavicentio Xeresano elaboratae, nunc vero plurimis
in locis ... auctae et locupletatae per D. Aegidium
Topiarium**, 2 Parts in 1 volume, split and rebound in
2 vols., Antwerp, 1566 ; Paris, 1571 ; 1577   8°

1298.   Jo: Rainoldi de Rom: Eccles Idololatria   £0 02 6

**John RAINOLDS, De Romanae Ecclesiae Idololatria in
cultu sanctorum, reliquiarum, imaginum, aquae, salis
... aliarumque rerum consecratorum & sacramenti
Eucharistiae, operis inchoati libri duo, in quibus
cum alia multa variorum papismi patronorum errata
patefiunt**, Amsterdam?, 1598   8°
First edition : Oxford, 1596 (4°).

(STC : 1596 ed., 20606)

1299.   Isagoges Christianae Lamberti Danaei   £0 03 6

Lambert DANEAU, Christianae isagoges ad Christianorum theologorum locos communes, libri II.   Cum praefatione Theodori Besae, Geneva, 1583 ; 1584 ; 1586 ; 1588 ; 1591   8°

(DS, pp.193,227)

1300.   Lambert Danaei de duobq in Christ: naturis lib
        £0 04 0

Lambert DANEAU, Examen libri De duabus in Christo naturis, de earum hypostatica unione, & varia, quae ex illa unione sequitur, communicatione, a Martino Kemnitio conscripti, Geneva, 1581   8°

1301.   Jo: Calvini Institutiones   £0 04 0

Possibly an abridged version of:

Jean CALVIN, Christianae Religionis Institutio, 1st ed., Basle, 1536 (8°), with numerous subsequent editions in 8°.
The first abridged edition, entitled **Epitome Institutionis christianae religionis**, appeared at London, 1579 (8°), with numerous subsequent editions in 8°.

(STC : 4427-4428)

1302.   Postilla Melantholiana   £0 02 0

Philipp MELANCHTHON, Postilla Melanthoniana ; hoc est, Lectionum Evangelicarum, quae more recepto & usitato, in plaerisque ecclesiis christianis, diebus Dominicis & festis proponuntur explicationes ... collectae a Christophoro Pezelio, 4 vols*., Heidelberg, 1594-95 8°

* Webster presumably owned only 1 volume of this very large work.

1303.   Theod Bezae homiliae   £0 03 0

Théodore de BÈZE, Homiliae in historiam Domini resurrectionis ... Latinae factae, Geneva, 1586 ; 1593 ; Berne, 1601   8°

1304.   Car: Scribani amor divinus   £0 02 0

Carolus SCRIBANIUS, Amor divinus, Antwerp, 1615 8°

1305. Sam: Rhaetorfortis Exercitat pro divina gratia
       £0 02 0

**Samuel RUTHERFORD, Exercitationes apologeticae pro
divina gratia, in quibus vindicatur doctrina orthodoxa
de divinis decretis, & Dei tum aeterni decreti, tum
gratiae efficacis operationis, cum hominis libertate
consociatione & subordinatione amica. Adversus
I. Arminium ejusque asseclas, & Iesuitas, imprimis
vero F. Suarezium, G. Vasquezium, L. Molinam,
L. Lesium, P. Fonsecam & R. Bellarminum** (with a
preface by C. Schotanus), Amsterdam, 1636 ;
Franeker, 1651   8°

1306. Amandi Polani in Daniel Com   £0 03 0

Amandus POLANUS, In Danielam prophetam commentarius,
2nd ed., Basle, 1606   8°
First edition : Basle, 1600 (4°).

(DS, pp.93,95,136 ; M, p.148)

1307. Dan: Tileni Syntagma disput: Theol: £0 04 0

**Daniel TILENUS, Syntagmatis disputationum theologicarum
in Academia Sedanensi,** Heidelberg, 1606? ; Herborn,
1607 ; Sedan, 1611 ; 1613 ; Geneva, 1618 ; 1622 ;
Harderwijk, 1656   8°

1308. Theod: Bezae annotationes majores in N: T: £0 05 0

**Théodore de BÈZE, Theodori Bezae annotationes maiores
in novum dn. nostri Jesu Christi testamentum. In duas
distinctae partes, quarum prior explicationem in
quatuor Evangelistas & Acta Apostolorum : posterior
vero in Epistolas & Apocalypsin continet,** Geneva,
1594   8°

(DS, pp. 126,141-142,178,179,223,235,316,335)

1309. Sti: Hieronomi biblia sacra lat   £0 03 6

An edition of the Vulgate Bible, first published in
8° at Basle, 1491, with numerous subsequent editions.

1310. Hierem: Bastingij in Cataches Exegemata   £0 02 6

**Hieremias BASTINGIUS, In Catechesin religionis
christianae, quae in ecclesiis et scholiis tum Belgij
tum Palatinatus traditur, exegemata sive commentarii,
auctore Hieremia Bastingio,** Heidelberg, 1590   8°
First edition : Dordrecht, 1588 (4°).
An edition of the Heidelberg Catechism.

1311.   Jo: Winckelmanni in Epist: ad Rom: notationes £0 02 0

Joannes **WINCKELMANNUS**, Notationes in Epistolam B.
Pauli Apostoli ad Romanos, quibus loci praecipui a
Tho. Stapletoni, et aliorum corruptelis vindicantur,
Frankfurt, 1614   8°

1312.   Tho: Cartwright in Ecclesiast: homiliae   £0 02 0

Thomas **CARTWRIGHT**, Metaphrasis et homiliae in librum
Salomonis qui inscribitur Ecclesiastes, autore Thoma
Cartwright, Marburg, 1604   8°
Later editions in 4° : London, 1604 ; Amsterdam,
1647 ; 1663.

(STC : London, 1604 ed., 4710)

1313.   Amandi Polani de ratione legendi cum fructu   £0 02 0

Amandus **POLANUS**, De Ratione legendi cum fructu autores,
in primis sacros et dignoscendi in illis proposita,
themata et argumenta tractatus cui adjuncta est
Analysis logica et Exegesis theologica psalmorum
tredecim, Basle, 1603 ; 1611   8°

1314.   Theod: Bezae Epist   £0 01 8

Théodore de **BÈZE**, Epistolarum Theologicarum ... liber
unus, Geneva, 1573 ; 2nd ed., Geneva, 1575   8°

1315.   Apologia Belarmini pro Jure principum   £0 02 0

Roger **WIDDRINGTON** (i.e. Thomas Preston, Benedictine
Monk), Apologia Cardinalis Bellarmini pro Jure
Principum. Adversus suas ipsius rationes pro
auctoritate papali Principes saeculares in ordine ad
bonum spirituale deponendi, London, 1611 ; Paris, 1611 8°

(STC : 25596-25596.5)

1316.   Jo: Mestrezat opera gallice 3 vol   £0 06 0

3 volumes of works in French by **Jean MESTREZAT**. This
may in fact be a set of three works by Mestrezat
published at Sedan in 1625 by the printer J. Janon:

        (a) De la communion à Jesus Christ, 2nd ed.   8°
        (b) De fruict qui nous revient de la communion à
Jesus-Christ   8°
        (c) Meditation sur l'incarnation de J. Christ, et
sur le legitime honneur de la bienheureuse Vierge   8°

1317.   Examen le Sacrifice de la misse   £0 02 0

**Josue de LA PLACE, Examen des raisons pour et contre
le sacrifice de la messe, pour servir d'eschantillon
du vray moyen de nous réunir en mesme religion, par
J. de la Place**, Saumur, 1639   8°

1318.   Historia Waldensium   £0 03 6

Another copy of one of those works listed under
Item no. 1200 (a–b).

1319.   Rod: Gualtheri in Epist: ad Rom: Comm: £0 01 6

**Rudolph WALTHER, Archetypi homiliarum in Epistolam
S. Pauli ad Romanos Rodolphi Gualtheri, ... ex ejus
autographo primum opera et studio Heinrichi Wolphii,
... collecti, nunc vero ex eodem correcti, notis et
indice aucti**, Zurich, 1608   8°
First edition : Zurich, 1566, in folio.

1320.   Jo: Piscatoris in Genes: com   £0 02 0

**Johann PISCATOR of Herborn, Commentarius in Genesin,
id est librum primum Mosis, in quo distincte et ordine
proponuntur : I. Analysis logica singulorum capitum.
II. Scholia. III. Observationes locorum communium**,
Herborn, 1601 ; 1611   8°

(DS, p.149 ; M,pp. 2,146)

1321.   Episcop: Cicestriensis tortura torti   £0 02 6

**Lancelot ANDREWES, Bishop of Chichester, Ely and
Winchester, Tortura Torti : sive ad Matthaei Torti**
(i.e. Robert Bellarmine) **librum responsio, qui nuper
editus contra Apologiam ... Iacobi ... Regis, pro
iuramento fidelitatis**, London, 1609   4°*
(* Nb. No edition in 8°)

(STC : 626)

1322.   Jo: Piscatoris Exegesis   £0 03 6

**Johann PISCATOR of Herborn, Exegesis, sive Explicatio
aphorismorum doctrinae christianae**, Herborn?, 1622 ;
1650   8°

(DS, pp.193,228)

1323.   Les Six livres du Sacrament   £0 01 4

Jean d'ALBIN DE VALSERGUES (called de SERES),
<u>**Les Six Livres du sacrement de l'autel, pour la**
confirmation du peuple françoys ... composez par
Jean d'Albin de Valserge, dit de Seres</u>, Paris, 1566
... 5th ed., Paris, 1576   8°

1324.   Jo Geo: Grossij de Christiana Rebublica   £0 01 0

Johann Georg GROSS, <u>**De Christiana republica, seu de**
Felici gubernatione populi Dei, libri tres ...
Adjuncta est Expositio ... praecepti ... christiani :
Reddite quae sunt Caesaris, Caesari, et quae sunt
Dei, Deo</u>, Basle, 1612   8°

1325.   Theod: Beze de veris Eccles: notis   £0 00 8

Théodore de BÈZE, <u>**De veris et visibilibus Ecclesiae**
Catholicae notis tractatio</u>, Geneva, 1579   8°

1326.   Phill mornaei de Eccles: et de veritate religionis Chr:
£0 05 0

Two separate works by **Philippe de MORNAY,** bound
together in 1 volume:

        (a) <u>**Tractatus de Ecclesia ... quo praecipuae quae**
hoc nostro tempore de hoc capite agitatae fuerunt
quaestiones excutiuntur</u>, ?, 1579 ; ?, 1581 ; Geneva,
1585 ; Heidelberg, 1594 ; Geneva?, 1599   8°

        (b) <u>**De Veritate Religionis Christianae liber ...**
A. P. Morneo ... Gallice primum conscriptus, nunc
autem ab eodem Latine versus</u>, Antwerp, 1583 ...
Frankfurt, 1632   8°

1327.   Ro: Rolloci in Evangelium Jo: Com   £0 04 6

Robert ROLLOCK, <u>**In Evangelium Domini Nostri Jesu—Christi**
secundum sanctum Johannem commentarius Roberti Rolloci
... Accessit Harmonia ex quatuor evangelistis, in
historiam mortis, resurrectionis et Ascensionis Domini,
ab eodem Rolloco concinnata et luculenter exposita</u>,
Geneva, 1599 ; 1608   8°

(DS, pp.98,103,220,222)

1328.   Conciliorum liber   £0 03 4

François HOTMAN, <u>**Consiliorum liber. Cum indice**
locupletissimo</u>, Geneva, 1578   8°

1329.   Cathechesis Heidelbergensis   £0 01 6

Catechesis Heidelbergensis Orthodoxa contra censuram,
& ut ipse vocat Excalvinizationem Ioannis Andreae
Coppensteinij ... opera & studio Iacobi Laurentii,
Amsterdam, 1625 ; Leyden, 1626 ; Hanover, 1656   8°
First published under a different title, Heidelberg,
1563 in octavo.

1330.   Jo: Piscatoris Analisis in Evang: sec: Lucam   £0 02 0

Johann PISCATOR of Herborn, Analysis logica Evangelii
secundum Lucam.   Una cum scholiis et observationibus
locorum doctrinae, London & Siegen in Nassau, 1596 ;
Siegen, 1597 ; Herborn, 1603 ; 1608   8°

(STC : 19952)

1331.   Gabr: Povelli de Antichristo lib   £0 01 8

Gabriel POWEL, G. Poveli ... Disputationum theologicarum
et scholasticarum de Antichristo et ejus Ecclesia,
libri II, London, 1605   8°

(STC : 20147)

1332.   Rod: Gualtheri in Ep: ad Galathas   £0 01 6

Rudolph WALTHER, In D. Pauli Apostoli epistolam ad
Galatas homiliae LXI, Zurich, 1590   8°
First edition : Zurich, 1576, in folio.

1333.   ffr: Junij de peccato primo Adami lib   £0 02 0

François DU JON the Elder, F. Junii De Peccato primo
Adami, et genere causae qua ad peccandum adductus est,
Liber in Quaestiones quatuor distributus, Leyden,
1595   8°

(DS, p.190)

1334.   Petr: Rami de Religione Christiana Comm   £0 01 8

Pierre de LA RAMÉE, Commentariorum de religione
Christiana libri quatuor.   Ejusdem vita a T. Banosio
descripta, Frankfurt, 1576 ; 1577 ; 1583 ; 1594   8°

1335.   Jo: Scharpij tractatus de peccato   £0 0 10

Joannes SCHARPIUS, Tractatus de misero hominis statu sub
peccato, in duos libros distinctus, quorum priori de
peccato ejusque poena : posteriori vero de viribus in
homine per peccatum reliquis, seu de libero arbitrio
agitur, Geneva, 1610   8°

(DS, p.185)

1336.   Ro: Rolloci in Psalm: Aliq: Com   £0 01 2

Robert ROLLOCK, Commentarius in selectos aliquot psalmos, Geneva, 1599 ; 2nd ed., Geneva, 1610   8°

1337.   Guliel: Perkinsi armilla aurea   £0 01 8

William PERKINS, Armilla aurea, id est, Miranda series causarum et salutis & damnationis iuxta verbum Dei : eius synopsin continet annexa tabula, Cambridge, 1590 ; Cambridge, 1591? ; Cambridge, 1592 ; Basle, 1596 ; 1599   8°

(STC : 19655-19656)

1338.   Jo: Piscatoris de praedestinatione disputatio £0 01 6

Johann PISCATOR of Herborn, Disputatio theologica de praedestinatione, ac nominatim de tribus quaestionibus hodie controversis ... opposita disputationi Andreae Schaafmanni, cui titulum fecit de Divina pro singulorum hominum salute, voluntate ... per Johan. Piscatorem, Herborn, 1595   8°

1339.   Lamb: Danaei in Evang: marci questiones   £0 01 6

Lambert DANEAU, Quaestiones et scholia in evangelium secundum Marcum, Geneva, 1594   8°

1340.   Martini Beccani de Deo et Atributis divinis   £0 01 8

Martinus BECANUS, Tractatus de Deo et attributis divinis : in quo Catholicorum sententia breviter explicatur, et novi quorundam Calvinistarum atheismi refelluntur, Mainz, 1611   8°

1341.   Theod: Beze question: et Respons: £0 01 4

Théodore de BÈZE, Quaestiones et responsiones Christianae, Geneva & London, 1571 ; Geneva, 1576 ; 1577 ; 1580 ; 1587 ; 1600   8°

(STC : 2036)

1342.   Jo: de Spina de providentia Dei   £0 01 2

Jean de L'ESPINE, Tractatus de Providentia Dei, Geneva, 1591   8°

(DS, p.193)

1343.   Catachismus Romanus   £0 01 6

COUNCIL OF TRENT, Catechismus Romanus, Ex decreto
Concilij Tridentini, Ad Parochos, Pii Quinti Pont.
Max. Iussu Editus, Nunc vero primum ..., Dillingen,
1567   8°
Numerous later editions in 8°.
First edition : 1566 in folio.

1344.   Phil: Paraei Catachesis   £0 01 8

Johann Philipp PAREUS, Catechesis religionis
Christianae : in plerisque ecclesiis & scholiis reformatae
religionis usitata. Succincta analysi logica, &
exegesi theologica illustrata, studio J. P. Parei,
Hanover, 1624   8°
First edition : Neostadt, 1615 (4°).

1345.   Jo: Piscatoris thesium theologic: lib   £0 02 0

Johann PISCATOR of Herborn, Volumen Thesium
theologicarum ; in illustri schola nassovica, partim
Herbornae, partim Sigenae disputatarum : praeside J.
Piscatore (Volumen alterum, praeside B. Textore),
2 vols. in 1, Siegen in Nassau, 1596, 1597   8°

1346.   Guil: Barclaij de potestate papae   £0 01 8

William BARCLAY, Prof. of Civil Law at Angers,
De potestate Papae : an & quatenus in reges & principes
seculares ius & imperium habeat ... Liber posthumus
(ed. John Barclay), Pont-a-Mousson, 1609   8°

1347.   Da: Chitraei de morte et vita eterna   £0 01 8

David CHYTRAEUS the Elder, De morte, et vita aeterna,
2 vols. in 1, Wittenberg, 1581, 1582 ; 1583 ; 1590 8°

---

f20r

1348.   Amanda Polani de praedestinacone   £0 01 6

Amandus POLANUS, De Aeterna Dei praedestinatione
didascalia, Basle, 1598 ; 2nd ed., Basle, 1600   8°

1349. Ro: Rolloci in Epist ad Thesoloniensis Com   £0 01 8

**Robert ROLLOCK, In epistolam Pauli Apostoli ad
Thessalonicenses priorem (-posteriorem) commentarius,**
Edinburgh, 1598 ; Herborn, 1601   8°

(DS, pp.235,236,237 ; STC : 21279)

1350. Lambert Danaei de Antichristo lib   £0 01 0

**Lambert DANEAU, Tractatus de Antichristo recens editus,
in quo Antichristiani regni locus, tempus, forma,
munstri, fulcimenta, progressio, & tandem exitium,
& interitus ex Dei verbo demonstrantur, ubi etiam
aliquot difficiles antea & obscuri tum Danielis, tum
Apocalypseos loci perspicue iam explicantur,** Geneva,
1576 ; 2nd ed., Geneva, 1582   8°

1351. 4 litle bookes of pdestinacon & such like (8°) £0 01 6

1352. Martiralogium   £0 03 0

**Anon., Martyrologium. Complectens memorabilissima
praecipuorum martyrum, dicta et facta, ab ipsis
apostolorum temporibus ad haec usq; nostra hinc-inde
per Germaniam, Galliam, Angliam, Scotiam, Belgiam,
Italiam, Hispaniam, Lusitaniam, &c ob evangelicae
veritatis confessionem, post gravissimarum persecutionem
ac tormentorum variorum perpessionem, misere tandem ut-
plurimum interfectorum,** Hanover, 1600?   8°

1353. Jam: Gryneus upon ye prophet Haggai   £0 01 6

**Johann Jacob GRYNAEUS, Haggeus, the Prophet. Where-unto
is added a most plentifull commentary, gathered out of
the publique lectures of ... D. Iohn Iames Gryneus ...
and now first published ... translated ... into English
by Christopher Fetherstone,** London, 1586   8°

(STC : 2790)

1354. The Pathway to prayer by Rob: Hill   £0 01 8

**Robert HILL, Minister of St. Bartholomews, London,
The Pathway to Prayer and Pietie,** London, 1610 ; 1613 ;
1615, 1616 ; 1617   8°
First published as Christs prayer expounded, London,
1606 (8°).

(STC : 13473-13476)

1355. The Reward of Religion by Edw: Topsell   £0 01 4

**Edward TOPSELL, The Reward of Religion. Delivered in
sundrie lectures upon the Booke of Ruth,** London, 1596 ;
1597 ; 1601 ; 1613   8°

(STC : 24127-24130)

1356.   The Immage of booth Churches by Jo: Baile   £0 01 8

John BALE, Bishop of Ossory, The Image of bothe Churches after the moste wonderfull and heavenly Revelacion of Sainct Iohn the Evangelist, contayning a very frutefull exposicion or paraphrase upon the same, London, 1548? ; 1550? ; 1551? ; 1570   8°

(STC : 1297-1298 ; 1300-1301)

1357.   The Tryumph of a Christian by Wm: Cooper   £0 01 0

William COWPER, The Triumph of a Christian, contayning three excellent and heavenly Treatises. 1. Iacobs wrestling with God. 2. The Conduit of Comfort. 3. A Preparative for the Lords Supper, London, 1608 ... London, 1639   8°

(STC : 5937-5942)

1358.   An English Psalter (8°)   £0 00 8

1359.   An Expossition of Daniell ye Prophet   £0 00 6

George JOYE, The Exposicion of Daniel the Prophete gathered oute of Philip Melancthon, Johan Ecolampadius, Chonrade Pellicane, & out of Iohan Draconite, etc By George Joye, Antwerp, 1545 ; London, 1550   8°

(STC : 14823-14825)

1360.   Certayne treatasies by Mr: Dudley ffenner   £0 00 8

Dudley FENNER, Certain godly and learned treatises, written ... for the behoofe and edification of all those that desire to grow and increase in true godlines, Edinburgh, 1592   8°

(STC : 10769)

1361.   Remidyes against discontentmts: £0 00 4

ANONYMUS, Remedies against Discontment, drawen into severall discourses from the writinges of auncient philosophers, by Anonymus, London, 1596   8°

(STC : 20869)

1362.   Edicts of Pacification in french   £0 00 6

P.D.B., Recueil des edicts de pacification, ordonnances et declarations par les roys de France, ?, 1612   8°

1363. The Conviction of novelty   £0 00 2

**R.B., Roman Catholike (i.e. Richard LASCELLES, alias
BOLD), The Conviction of Noveltie and Defense of
Antiquitie. Or demonstrative arguments of the
falsitie of the newe Religion of England : and trueth
of the Catholike Roman faith ... Author R.B. Roman
Catholike**, Douai, 1632   8°

(STC : 1056)

1364. The Creation and fall of Adam   £0 00 8

Captain Robert EVERARD, The creation and fall of Adam,
London, 1649   8°

(STC : E3537)

1365. The Nature of truth by ye Lord Brookes   £0 01 6

**Robert GREVILLE, 2nd Baron Brooke, The Nature of Truth,
its union and unity with the soule, which is one in its
essence, faculties, acts ; one with truth** (ed. J.S.),
London, 1640   8°
Another edition : London, 1641 (12°).

(STC : 12363 ; B4913)

1366. of ye Originall of ye Soule   £0 01 6

**H(enry) W(OOLNOR), The true Originall of the Soule.
Proving ... that the production of mans soule is neither
by creation nor propagation, but by a certain meane way
between both** (ed. E. Palmer), London, 1641 ; 1642 12°*
(* Nb. No edition in 8°).

(STC : W3526-W3527)

1367. Salmons workes   £0 00 8

Probably works by the English radical, **Joseph SALMON**.
Salmon was the author of three extant volumes, in
various book sizes:

      (a) **Antichrist in Man**, London, 1647   8°
Later editions : London, 1648 (12°) and London, 1649
(24°).
      (b) **Heights in Depths and Depths in Heights**,
London, 1651   8°
      (c) **A Rout, a Rout**, London, 1649   4°

(STC : (a) unrecognised ; (b) S415 ; (c) S416-S416A

1368. A peece of Jacob Beamonds workes   £0 01 8

An unidentified work by **Jacob BOEHME** in English.

1369.   Hermes Trismegistus his Pimander   £0 01 4

HERMES TRISMEGISTUS, Hermes Mercurius Trismegistus, his Divine Pymander ... Together with his second book, called Asclepius ... with a commentary. Translated ... by ... Dr. (John) **Everard** (with a preface by John French), London, 1657   12°
First edition (different title-page) : London, 1650 (8°).

(STC : H1565 ; H1566–H1567)

1370.   of the Life of Christ   £0 01 0

Valentin WEIGEL, Of the Life of Christ : that is of true faith, which is the rule, square, levell, or measuring-line of the holy city of God, and of the inhabitants thereof here on earth ... Written in the German language by V.W., London, 1648   12°*
(* Nb. No edition in 8°).

(STC : W1256)

1371.   The way to Christ by Jac: Behemen   £0 01 4

Jacob BOEHME, The Way to Christ discovered ... (A letter from J. Behmen ... 20 April, 1624 – An Explication of some words in the writings of J. Behmen), London, 1648 ; 1654 ; 1656   12°*
(* Nb. No edition in 8°).

(STC : B3426–B3427)

1372.   An Abstract of dutyes commanded & forbiden by God   £0 0 10

George DOWNAME, Bishop of Derry, An Abstract of the duties commanded, and sinnes forbidden in the law of God (ed. Basil Nicoll), London, 1620 ; 1625 ; 1626 ; 1635   8°

(STC : 7104–7107)

1373.   Of Sysme(sic) by Mr: Owen   £0 01 4

John OWEN, Of Schisme : the true nature of it discovered and considered, with reference to the present differences in religion, Oxford, 1657   8°

(STC : O780)

1374.   Seaven sobbs of a sorrofull Soule   £0 00 8

William HUNNIS, Seven Sobs of a Sorrowfull Soule for Sinne.   Comprehending those seven Psalmes of David ... called Poenitentiall : ... reduced into meeter by W. H(unnis) **... Whereunto are also annexed his Handful of Honisuckles ; the Poore Widowes Mite ; a Dialog betweene Christ and a Sinner**, London, 1583 ... London, 1629   12°*
(*Nb. No edition in 8°).

(STC : 13975–13984)

1375.   Wm: Schickardi Astroscopium   £0 01 4

**Wilhelmus SCHICKARD the Elder, Astroscopium ... Cum
tabella synoptica ad faciliorem investigationem locorum
planetarum hoc proximo decennio, pro iis qui Ephemeridibus
sunt destituti, curante J. Ruffio,** Nördlingen, 1655 12°*
(* Nb. No edition in 8°)

1376.   15 litle treatasies in English (in 12°)   £0 01 6

1377.   The Scourge of Sacralidge   £0 0 10

Samuel GARDINER, The Scourge of Sacriledge, London,
1611   8°

(STC : 11580)

1378.   An Answer to Mr: Reynolds refutation by Wm: Whittacre
£0 01 6

**William WHITAKER, An answere to a certaine Booke,
written by ... W. Rainolds ... entituled, a Refutation
of sundrie reprehensions, cavils ...,** London, 1585 ;
Cambridge, 1590   8°

(STC : 25364-25365)

1379.   Christs testamt unfoulded by Mr: Symson   £0 0 10

**Archibald SIMSON, Christes Testament unfoulded : or
seaven godlie and learned sermons on our Lords seaven
last words, spoken on the Crosse,** Edinburgh, 1620 8°

(STC : 22565)

1380.   A short Catachisme (8° or 12°)   £0 00 6

1381.   The glory of man   £0 00 4

**Edward RABAN, The glorie of man consisting in the
excellencie and perfection of woman. Gathered out of
Holie Scriptures, and most renowned writers. Whereunto
is annexed the duetie of husbands,** Aberdeen, 1638 8°

(STC : 20596)

1382.   Mr: Perkins his sermons   £0 0 10

Probably the following edition:

**William PERKINS, M. Perkins, his exhortation to
repentance, out of Zephaniah : preached in 2 sermons.
Together with two treatises of the duties and dignitie
of the ministrie,** London, 1605   8°
Later editions in 12° : London, 1607 ; 1609.

(STC : 19706.5-19706.7 ; 19707.5-19708)

1383.   of ye Lords Supper   £0 00 6

      One of two works:

          (a) Pierre **VIRET**, **The principal points which are at this daye in controversie, concerning the Holy supper and of the masse** (Running title : "Of the Lords Supper and against ye masse" ; trans. J. Shute), London, 1579   8°

          (b) **(Henry SMITH), A Treatise of the Lords Supper, in two sermons**, London, 1591   8°

      (STC : (a) 24782 ; (b) 22704-22705)

---

f20v

1384.   The Apelation of Jo: Knoxe   £0 00 6

      John **KNOX**, **The Appellation of John Knox from the cruell ... sentence pronounced against him by the false bishoppes and clergey of Scotland ; with his supplication and exhortation to the nobilitie, estates and comunaltie of the same realme (An admonition to England and Scotland to call them to repentance, written by A. Gilby)**, Geneva, 1558   8°

      (STC : 15063)

1385.   8 ould bookes (8° or 12°)   £0 01 0

1386.   The true way to Salvation   £0 00 8

      I have been unable to trace any work in English with this exact title.

1387.   De officio Pastorum et animum(sic)   £0 0 10

      Franciscus **PONISSONUS**, **De officio pastorum et ovium, ad exemplar Jesu Christi, Boni Pastoris ; super Psalmum vigesimum secundum**, Toulouse, 1550   8°

1388.   Oratorium Religiosorum (8° or 12°)   £0 01 6

I have been unable to trace any work with this title.

1389.   Erasmi Roterodami Enchiridion militis Christ: £0 0 10

Desiderius ERASMUS, Enchiridion Militis Christiani,
Basle, 1519   8°
Numerous later editions in 8° and 12° (1st edition in
12° : Cologne, 1563).
First edition : Louvain, 1515 (4°).

1390.   opera Jo: Wigandi   £0 01 0

Unspecified works by the German theologian **Johann
WIGAND.**

1391.   A Rule to know true Religion   £0 00 6

**John HAMILTON, A facile traictise contenand ane
infallible ruel to discerne true from fals religion**
(Running title : "A RUEL TO KNAU TREU RELIGION"),
Louvain, 1600   12°

(STC : 12730)

1392.   The posie of Godly prayers   £0 00 6

Nicholas THEMYLTHORP, The posie of godlie prayers,
London, 1611 ... London, 1676   12°

(STC : 23934.2-23936 ; T847-T848)

1393.   Dayly prayers by Tho: Rogers   £0 00 6

**Saint AUGUSTINE, Bishop of Hippo (supposititious),
A right Christian Treatise, entituled S. Augustines
Praiers : Published in more ample sort than yet it hath
bin in the English tong ... by Thomas Rogers.
Whereunto is annexed Saint Augustines Psalter,** London,
1581 ; 1591 ; 1600 ; 1604 ; 1607   12°

(STC : 950-953)

1394.   Dominicalia p(er) Nic: Selneccerum et Tho:(sic) Pelugium
         £0 02 4

Two separate works bound together in one volume:

        (a) **Nicolaus SELNECCER, Evangeliorum et epistolarum
dominicalium, explicationis pars secunda,** Frankfurt,
1575   8°
        (b) **Christoph PFLUG, Sylva thematum epistolarum
dominicalium et festorum per totius anni curriculum
explicationi inservientium,** Wittenberg, 1611   8°

218

1395.   Sacrae Scripturae Phrases   £0 01 0

**Laurentius a VILLAVICENTIO, Phrases Scripturae sacrae
... collectae per fratrem Laurentium a Villavicentio,**
Antwerp, 1571   8°

1396.   Theophilacte in 4 Evangelia narrationes   £0 02 6

**THEOPHYLACT, Archbishop of Achrida, Theophylacti ...
in quatuor Evangelia enarrationes ... revisae atque
recognitae. Ioanne Oecolampadio interprete,** Zurich,
1527 ; Antwerp, 1531 ; Cologne, 1532 ; 1536 ;
Antwerp, 1564   8°
First edition : Cologne, 1525, in folio.
Another copy of Item no. 142, in octavo.

1397.   Valentini Hellopaei de tota re sacramentaria lib
        £0 02 6

**Bálint HELLOPOEUS, De Sacramentis in genere, sive,
de tota re sacramentaria, tractatio,** Geneva, 1585 8°

1398.   Daniel: Syntagma disputationum   £0 02 0

Another copy of Item no. 1307, above.

1399.   Nicho: Machiavelli de rebublica lib   £0 01 6

**Niccolò MACHIAVELLI, Disputationum, De Republica, quas
Discursus nuncupavit, Libri III ... Ex Italico Latini
facti** (trans. Joannes Nicolaus Stupanus), Mompelgard,
1591 ; 1599   8°

1400.   Will: Zepperi de Politia Ecclesiastica   £0 02 0

**Wilhelm ZEPPER, De Politia ecclesiastica, sive Forma ac
ratio administrandi et gubernandi regni Christi quod
est Ecclesia in his terris, demonstrata ex forma et
facie primitivae Ecclesiae per apostolos fundatae, et
illustrata ex decretis conciliorum, historiis
ecclesiasticis,** Herborn, 1595 ; 2nd ed., Herborn,
1607   8°

1401.   Enchiridion Theol: pasturalis   £0 01 8

**Petrus BINSFELD, Enchiridion theologiae pastoralis et
doctrinae necessariae sacerdotibus curam animarum
administrantibus, conscriptum a Petro Binsfeldio ...
nunc de novo recognitum,** Trier, 1594 ; 2nd ed.,
?, 1602   8°

1402.   Petr: Rami de Religione Christiana   £0 02 0

Another copy of Item no. 1334, above.

1403.   Petr Chrysologi dominicalia   £0 02 0

Saint PETER Chrysologus, Archbishop of Ravenna, Sermones, Paris, 1544 ; Mainz, 1607 ; Cologne, 1627 ; Lyons, 1627 ; Paris, 1632 ; Lyons, 1636 ; Rouen, 1640   8°
First edition : Bologna, 1534 (4°).

1404.   Rod: Gualtheri in Epist: ad Ephes: Comm   £0 01 6

Rudolph WALTHER, In epistolas D. Pauli Apostoli ad Ephesios, Philippenses, Colossenses et Thessalonicenses, D. Rudolphi Gualtheri ... homiliarum archetypi, Zurich, 1590   8°

1405.   Ejusdem authoris in Evangel: S: Jo: £0 02 6

Rudolph WALTHER, Archetypi homiliarum in evangelium Dn. N. Iesu Christi, secundum Ioannem. Rudolphi Gualtheri ... nunc primum ex eius autographo collecti, correcti, notis & indice aucti a Rodolpho Simlero, Zurich, 1605 8°
First edition : Zurich, 1565, in folio.

1406.   Jo: Cochlei de Authoritatae Ecclesiae   £0 0 10

Johann DOBNECK Cochlaeus, De autoritate Ecclesiae et Scripturae in Calvini errores & blasphemias, Mainz, 1549   8°
First edition : Rome & Strassburg?, 1524 (4°).

1407.   Exposition in Genesis   £0 01 6

Alexander ROSS, An Exposition of the fourteene first Chapters of Genesis by way of Question and Answere, London, 1626   8°

(STC : 21324)

1408.   Solem: Gesneri in Oseani Proph: Comm: £0 01 4

Solomon GESNER, Oseas propheta, duplici Latina versione, una Hieronymi, altera Montani, redditus, et commentario Hieronymi illustratus ; praemissa praefatione additisque notiunculis a S. Gesnero, Wittenberg, 1601   8°

1409.   Expositio Symboli Apostolorum   £0 01 0

Caspar OLEVIAN, Expositio symboli apostolici, sive articulorum fidei in qua summa gratuiti foederis aeterni inter Deum et fideles breviter ... tractatur, Frankfurt, 1576 ; 1580   8°

1410.   Barth: Keckerm: Rhetoric: Eccles: lib   £0 0 10

Bartholomaeus KECKERMANNUS, Rhetoricae Ecclesiasticae, sive Artis formandi et habendi conciones sacras libri duo, Hanover, 1600 ; 1604 ; 1606 ; 1616   8°

1411.   Rod: Gualtheri in Epist: ad Timotheum Com   £0 01 8

Rudolph WALTHER, In Epistolas D. Pauli apostoli ad Timotheum, Titum et Philemonem D. Rodulphi Gualtheri, ... homiliarum archetypi, cum indice rerum et verborum copiosissimo, Heidelberg, 1601   8°

1412.   Jo: Piscatoris in Evang: Jo: Analysis logica   £0 02 6

Johann PISCATOR of Herborn, Analysis logica evangelii secundum Johannem, London, 1591 ; 1595 ; Siegen, 1597 ; Herborn, 1603 ; 1608 ; 1609   8°

(STC : 19953-19954)

1413.   Da: Parei Epist: Jac: Explicatio   £0 01 0

David PAREUS, In Jacobi apost. Epistolam catholicam explicatio ... scripta et evulgata a Davide Pareo, Heidelberg, ?   8°

1414.   Rod: Gualtheri in Epist: ad Hebreos Com   £0 01 8

Rudolph WALTHER, In Epistolas D. Pauli apostoli ad Hebraeos D. Rodolphi Gualtheri, ... homiliarum archetypi, cum indice rerum et verborum copiosissimo, Heidelberg, 1601   8°

1415.   Jo: Garetij de vera presentia corporis Christi   £0 01 0

Joannes GARETIUS, De vera praesentia corporis Christi in sacramento Eucharistiae classes IX. contra Sacramentarium pestem ... collectae, Antwerp, 1561   8°

1416.   Dudlaei Sacra Theologiae   £0 01 0

Another copy of Item no. 1283, above.

1417.   Da: Chytraei in Genesin: Comm   £0 01 8

David CHYTRAEUS the Elder, In Genesin enarratio,
tradita Rostochii, ut ad lectionem textus Bibliorum
auditores invitarentur, Wittenberg, 1557 ; 1561 ;
1568 ; 1576   8°

1418.   Ro: Baronij Apodixis Catholica   £0 02 6

Robert BARON, Prof. of Divinity at Marischal College,
Aberdeen, Ad Georgii Turnebulli Tetragonismum
pseudographum apodixis catholica, sive apologia pro
disputatione de formali objecto fidei, Aberdeen,
1631   8°
Another edition published in 12° : London, 1657.

(STC : 1493 ; B880)

1419.   De disciplina Ecclesiastica   £0 00 8

(Daniel TILENUS), De Disciplina Ecclesiastica, brevis
& modesta dissertatio ad Ecclesiam Scoticam.   Autore
Gallo quodam Theologo, Aberdeen, 1622   8°

(STC : 24067)

---

f21r

1420.   Unio Dissentium(sic)   £0 00 6

Hermannus BODIUS, Unio dissidentium libellus, omnibus
unitatis & pacis amatoribus utilissima, ex praecipuis
Ecclesiae Christianae doctoribus ... selectus,
Cologne, 1527   8°
Numerous later editions in 8°.

1421.   Erasmi Sarcerij in Epist: ad Phill: Collo: et Thes:
         £0 01 8

Erasmus SARCERIUS, In Epistolas D. Pauli ad
Philippenses, Colossenses, & Thessalonicenses scholia,
Frankfurt, 1542   8°

1422.   Acta concilij Tridentini   £0 00 6

COUNCIL OF TRENT, Acta Concilii Tridentini, Antwerp
& Wittenberg?, 1546   8°

1423.   Ro: Rolloci in Ep: ad Hebraeos Analysis etc   £0 0 10

**Robert ROLLOCK, Analysis Logica in Epistolam ad
Hebraeos, autore D. Roberto Rolloco, ... Accessit
brevis et utilis tractatus de justificatione, eodem
authore**, Geneva & Edinburgh, 1605 ; Geneva, 1610 8°

(STC : 21270)

1424.   Am: Polani in Malachiam prophetam analysis   £0 01 0

Amandus POLANUS, Analysis libelli Prophetae Malachiae,
Basle, 1597   8°
With the text of Malachi in Hebrew and latin.

1425.   ffr: Junij Eirenicum   £0 01 0

**François DU JON the Elder, Eirenicum de pace Ecclesiae
catholicae inter christianos ... colenda atque continenda,
in Psalmos Davidis CXXII et CXXXI meditatio Francisci
Junii**, Leyden, 1593   8°

1426.   Medicina animae   £0 00 4

**Joshua MULLARD, Medicina Animae, or the Lamentation and
Consolation of a Sinner. Together with severall
collections out of the Holy Scriptures**, London, 1652 12°

(STC : M3056)

1427.   Ro: Rolloci in Ep: ad Galatas Analysis   £0 00 8

**Robert ROLLOCK, Analysis logica in Epistolam Pauli
Apostoli ad Galatas, authore D. Roberto Rolloco** (ed.
H. Charteris), London, 1602 ; Geneva, 1603 ; Herborn,
1603 ; Geneva, 1610   8°

(STC : 21269-21269.5)

1428.   Ad ffrancisci margarita Theologica   £0 01 4

**Adamus FRANCISCI, Margarita theologica, continens
methodicam explicationem praecipuorum capitum doctrinae
Christianae ... Accesserunt e Compendio Heerbrandio
disputationes ... J. Schröderi XIII**, Wittenberg,
1601   12°

1429. Jo: Piscatoris Aphorismi Doctr: Christ: £0 00 8

Johann PISCATOR of Herborn, Aphorismi doctrinae Christianae ex Institutione Calvini excerpti, Herborn, 1589   8°
Numerous later editions in 8° and 12°, including editions at London, 1595 and Oxford, 1630 (8° and 12° respectively).

(STC : 4372.5–4373)

1430. Gemmae regum   £0 00 6

Lodowick LLOYD, Regum gemma e sacris Biblijs desumpta, London, 1600? ; 1602   12°
(STC : 16628–16629)

1431. Labarinthus Amoris (8° or 12°)   £0 00 6

I have been unable to trace any work with this title in latin.

1432. Jo: Gersonis de imitatione Christi cum alijs £0 02 0

Jean CHARLIER DE GERSON (supposititious), De Imitatione Christi, Brescia, 1485   8°
Numerous subsequent editions in 8°, with various additions, etc.
First edition : Venice, 1483 (4°).

1433. Ant: de Sales praxis Spiritatis (8° or 12°)   £0 01 6

I have been unable to trace either the author or the work.

1434. Jo: Reynolds Theses   £0 02 6

John RAINOLDS, Sex theses de Sacra Scriptura et Ecclesia, publiciis in Academia Oxoniensi disputationibus propositae, explicatae, London, 1580 ; 1602 ; Herborn, 1603   8°
(STC : 20624–20625)

1435. Da: Parei de iure Regum   £0 01 4

David PAREUS, Quaestiones controversae theologicae, de jure regum et principum, contra papam romanum, magnum illum Anti-Christum ... Adversus Bellarminum, Becanum & id genus ... Procurante editionem Joachimo Ursino (pseud.), Hamburg, 1612   8°

1436.   Defentio regia   £0 02 6

Claude de SAUMAISE, Defensio Regia, pro Carolo I. ad Serenissimum Magnae Britanniae Regem Carolum II,
? and Leyden, 1649   12°
Numerous subsequent editions in 12°.

1437.   Jo: David lapis Lydius   £0 01 6

Jan DAVID, Lapis Lydius seu delitiarum Spiritualium hortulum animae ad perfectionem contendentis ... editum nunc latio sermone donatum a F. Theodoro Petreio ... cum figuris aere incisis, Cologne,
1610   12°

1438.   Gul: Amesij Coronis   £0 01 6

William AMES, Coronis ad Collationem Hagiensem, qua argumenta Pastorum Hollandiae adversus Remonstrantium quinque articulos de divina praedestinatione, & capitibus ei adnexis, producta, ab horum exceptionibus vindicantur,
Amsterdam, 1628   8°
Numerous subsequent editions in 8° and 12°, including London, 1630 and 1632 (12°).

(STC : 553-554)

1439.   Jo: Lanspergij Ench: militiae Chr: £0 01 6

Johann JUSTUS Landsberger, Enchiridion militiae christianae, ad novitatem vitae, quae in Christo est, perfecte instituens, authore Jo. Justo Lanspergio,
Paris, 1545 ; 1546 ; Antwerp, 1550   8°
Also published in 12° : Cologne, 1607.

1440.   Guli: Amesij Animadversiones in Synodalia etc £0 01 0

William AMES, Animadversiones in Synodalia Scripta Remonstrantium, quoad Articulum primum ... Disp. XXVIII. in Academia Franekerana propugnatae a studiosis theologiae,
Franeker, 1629   8°
Later editions in 12° : Amsterdam, 1633 ; 1646.

1441.   Consolatio e sacris literis   £0 00 6

François HOTMAN, Consolatio e Sacris Literis petita,
Geneva & Lyons, 1593 ; Geneva, 1594   8°

1442.   Ro: Rolloci in Ep: ad Rom: Analysis   £0 01 0

Robert ROLLOCK, Analysis dialectica Roberti Rolloci in Pauli apostoli epistolam ad Romanos, Edinburgh, 1593 ;
1594 ; Geneva, 1608   8°

(STC : 21267-21268)

1443.   ffr: Hottmanni de Jure civili   £0 01 0

François HOTMAN, Partitiones juris civilis elementariae,
Basle, 1560 ; 1561   8°
Later editions in 12° : Lyons, 1565 ; 1589 ; London,
1624 ; Bremen, 1626.

(London edition not listed in STC)

1444.   Gul: Amesij in Ep: Petr: Analysis   £0 01 0

**William AMES, Utriusque Epistolae Divi Petri Apostoli
explicatio analytica ... Nec non III.   conciones in
selectiora quaedam S. Scripturae loca.   Authore ...
Dn. Guilielmo Amesio**, Amsterdam, 1635   12°
Another edition in 8° : London, 1647 (8°).

(DS, pp.225-226 ; STC : A3004)

1445.   Petr Du Moulin de Cognitione Dei   £0 01 0

Pierre DU MOULIN the Elder, De cognitione Dei tractatus,
London, 1624 ; Bremen, 1626   12°

(STC : 7320)

1446.   Hispanus Reformatus   £0 00 4

**Juan NICHOLAS Y SACHARLES, Hispanus Reformatus ...
Omnibus Ecclesiis reformatis ... et praecipue ...
Archiepiscopis, Episcopis, Pastoribus et Doctoribus
... in ... Synodo Londinensi, anno 1621 jam
congregatis**, London, 1621   12°

(STC : 18529)

SECTION O

"Some Law Bookes wth: divers others"

(Book sizes unknown)

1447.   Swinburne of wills & Testaments   £0 03 6

**Henry SWINBURNE, A briefe Treatise of Testaments and
last willes**, London, 1590, 1591 ; 1611 ; 1633 ; 1635 ;
1640 ; 1677   4°

(STC : 23547-23551 ; S6261)

1448.   The termes of the Law   £0 03 6

John RASTELL, **The exposicions of the termes of the lawes
of England, with divers ... rules and principles of the
lawe, as well out of the bookes of ... Littleton, as of
other ... Whereunto are added the olde tenures**, London,
1563 ... 23rd ed., London, 1671   8°

(STC : 20703.5-20718 ; R286-R291)

1449.   Martinij Beccannus questiones   £0 01 8

Martinus **BECANUS, Quaestiones miscellaneae de fide
haereticis servanda. Contra quendam Calvinistam
Batavam, qui se faederatorum inferioris Germaniae
defensorem appellat**, Mainz, 1609   8°

1450.   fflores voluntatum ultimarum   £0 01 4

Rolandinus **RUDOLPHINUS DE PASSAGERIIS, Flores
ultimarum voluntatum, non sine sudore collecti per
dominum Rolandinum bononiensem ... cum additionibus
... magistri Gerardi Mulert**, Lyons, 1524   4°
Another edition in 8° : Speyer, Bavaria, 1598.
Other editions of this work appeared under slightly
different title (Flos ultimarum voluntatum).

1451.   An Abridgmt: of ye Statutes   £0 02 0

(John RASTELL), **An Abridgement of the Statutes,
translated from the French and Latin by J. Rastell**,
London, 1527 ... London, 1551   8°

(STC : 9518-9526)

1452.   Tractatus te(sic) literis gratiae   £0 01 0

Joannes **STAPHYLEUS, Bishop of Sebenico, Tractatus de
literis gratiae**, Paris, 1547 ; Lyons, 1573   8°

1453.   Jul: Pacij definit: juris civilis   £0 01 6

Julius **PACIUS, J. A. Corvini ... Posthumus Pacianus ;
seu, Definitiones ... Juris utriusque ... Julii Pacii
... posthumae, insigni auctu ; et divisionum, integrorum
titulorum, aliaque accessione planae novatae**,
Amsterdam, 1643 ; 1659   12°

1454.   Magna Charta cum alijs Statutis   £0 02 0

Magna Carta, cum aliis antiquis statutis, London, 1531 ;
1540 ; 1556 ; 1560? ; 1576 ; 1587 ; 1602 ; 1608 ; 1618   8°

(STC : 9271 ; 9274 ; 9277-9285)

1455.　　ffr: Hotmanni questiones　　　　　　£0 01 8

François HOTMAN, Quaestionum illustrium liber,
Paris, 1573 ; 1576 ; Lyons, 1579 ; Leimar, 1585　　8°

1456.　　Justi Lipsi politicorum lib　　　　　　£0 01 4

**Justus LIPSIUS, J. Lipsii Politicorum sive Civilis
Doctrinae libri sex,** Leyden, 1589　　　　　　　4°
Numerous later editions published in 4°, 8°, 12° and
16°.

1457.　　Le Court Leet & Baron p(er) Jo: Kitchin　£0 01 6

**John KITCHIN, Le Court Leete, et Court Baron, collect
per J. Kitchin ..., et les cases et matters necessarie
pur Seneschals de ceux courts a scier,** London, 1580
... London, 1623　　　　　　　　　　　　　　　8°

(STC : 15017-15025)

1458.　　The young Clerkes guide　　　　　　　£0 02 6

(Sir Richard HUTTON), The young clerks guide, London,
1649 ... 14th ed., London, 1673　　　　　　　8°

(STC : H3847B-H3854)

1459.　　Melchior: Adami de vitis Theol: exterorum　£0 01 8

**Melchior ADAMUS, Decades duae continentes vitas
theologorum exterorum principum, qui ecclesiam Christi
superiori seculo propagarunt et propugnarunt,**
Frankfurt, 1618 ; 2nd ed., Frankfurt, 1653　　　8°

1460.　　A manuall or Analecta　　　　　　　　£0 02 0

Anon., A manuall or analecta, London, 1641 ; 1642 ;
1646 ; 1648 ; 1660　　　　　　　　　　　　12°

(STC : M545B-M547A)

1461.　　Actions for Slander　　　　　　　　　£0 01 6

**John MARCH, Actions for Slaunder, or a methodicall
collection under certain grounds and heads, of what
words are actionable in the law, and what not? ...
To which is added, Awards or Arbitrements methodised
under severall grounds and heads,** London, 1647 ;
1648 ; 1655 ; 1674　　　　　　　　　　　　　8°

(STC : M571-M573)

228

1462.   natura brevium in English   £0 01 6

Natura brevium newly corrected in Englisshe, London,
1532 ... London, 1580?   8°

(STC : 18403–18411.5)

1463.   Les tenures de Litleton   £0 01 0

Sir Thomas LITTLETON, Les Tenures de Lyttelton,
London, 1545 ... London, 1639   8°
First edition : London, 1481, in folio.
Norman French.

(STC : 15733 ; 15739–15759)

1464.   A booke of sundry instruments   £0 00 8

Possibly the following:

**Anon., A new book of instruments fitted for the use of
attornies, ecclesiastical persons, scriveners, &c**,
London, 1680   8°

(STC : N584)

1465.   de Glanvilla de legibq Anglicae lib £0 01 0

**Ranulphus de GLANVILLA, Tractatus de legibus et
consuetudinibus regni Anglie, tempore Regis Henrici
Secundi compositus, Justicie gubernacula tenente ...
R. de G.**, London, 1554? ; 1604   8°

(STC : 11905–11906)

1466.   Litletons tenures in English   £0 00 6

**Sir Thomas LITTLETON, Lyttilton tenures truely
translated into Englysshe**, London, 1538 ... London,
1661   8°
First edition : London, 1525, in folio.

(STC : 15761–15783 ; L2586–L2587)

1467.   Haenigi Arnisaei Epitomie metaphys:(sic)   £0 01 0

**Henningus ARNISAEUS, Epitome doctrinae physicae,
continens brevem et dilucidam explicationem
fundamentorum Aristotelicorum, adjecto succincto examine
et decisione plerarumque quaestionum quae circa doctrinam
Aristotelis et veritatis fundamenta excitari solent**,
Frankfurt, 1607   8°

1468.   Tho: Brightmanni in Cantica canticorum Com   £0 01 4

**Thomas BRIGHTMAN, <u>Commentarius in Cantica canticorum
Salomonis, analysi & scholiis illustratus</u>**, Basle,
1614   8°

1469.   Nicol: Hemmingij Methodus Philos: et Theolog: £0 01 0

**Niels HEMMINGSEN, <u>De Methodis libri duo : quorum prior
... omnium methodorum ... quarum usus est in philosophia
... declarationem, posterior ... ecclesiasten sive
methodum theologicam interpretandi, concionandique
continet, authore Nicolao Hemmingio</u>**, Wittenberg, 1562 ;
Leipzig, 1565 ; 1570 ; 1578   8°

1470.   Elenchus motuum nuperorum in Anglia   £0 01 6

George BATE, <u>Elenchus motuum nuperorum in Anglia</u>,
Edinburgh, 1650   12°
Later editions in 8° : London, 1661 ; 1663 ; Amsterdam,
1663 ; London, 1676.

(STC : B1079-B1082)

1471.   Disquisitio de preadamitis   £0 01 6

**Johann HILPERT, <u>Disquisitio de Preadamitis anonymo
exercitationis et systematis Theologici auctori
opposita</u>**, Utrecht & Amsterdam, 1656   12°

1472.   A Justice of peace his vade mecum   £0 00 8

**Walter YOUNG, <u>A vade mecum, or tables containing the
substance of such statutes, wherein any one or more
justices of the peace are inabled to deale in, at the
session of the peace</u>**, London, 1643 ; 1650 ; 1660 8°
Another edition in 12° : London, 1663.

(STC : Y94-Y96)

1473.   A Closset for Ladies   £0 00 4

**Anon., <u>A Closset for Ladies and Gentlewomen, or, the
Art of preserving, conserving and candying. With the
manner howe to make divers kinds of syrups : and all
kind of banquetting stuffes. Also divers soveraigne
medecines and salves</u>**, London, 1608   12°
With numerous subsequent editions in 8° and 12°.

(STC : 5434-5440)

1474.   Auli Gellij noctes Atticae   £0 01 6

Another copy of Item no. 909, above.

1475.   Suetonij tranquilli 12 Caesares   £0 01 6

Another copy of Item no. 1053, above.

1476.   C: Julij Solini Polihistor: £0 01 0

**Caius Julius SOLINUS, Polyhistor sive de mirabilibus
mundi opus**, Bologna, 1505   4°
Numerous subsequent editions in 4° and 8°.

1477.   Philostrati de vita Apollonij Tianei lib   £0 01 6

**PHILOSTRATUS the Elder, Phylostratus de vita Apollonii
Tyanei Scriptor luculentus a P. Beroaldo castigatus**
(trans. from Greek into latin by A. Rinucinnus),
Lyons, 1504? ; Cologne, 1532   8°
Another edition in 16° : Paris, 1555.

(AE, p.2 ; DS, p.21)

1478.   Legum antiquarum Catalogus etc   £0 02 0

**Joannes Udalricus ZASIUS, Catalogus legum antiquarum,
una cum adjuncta summaria interpretatione, per J.U.
Zasium ... collectus, cum annotationibus L. Charondae
... Accesserunt alia ejusdem argumenti opuscula,**
Frankfurt, 1551   8°
Another edition : Paris, 1555 (16°).

1479.   Vellei paterculi historia Romm: £0 01 6

**Marcus VELLEIUS PATERCULIS, Historiae Romanae libri
duo**, Venice, 1571   8°
Numerous subsequent editions in 8°, 12° and 16°.
First edition : 2 vols., Basle, 1520, in folio.

1480.   Pauli manutij antiquitatum Rom: £0 01 4

Given the subject area of this section of the
catalogue, this is probably an edition of:

Paolo MANUZIO, Antiquitatum romanorum ... liber de legibus,
Paris, 1557 ; Venice, 1559 ; 1569 ; Cologne, 1570   8°

1481.   De Rom: et Venetor: magistrat: Comparatione   £0 01 4

**Guerinus PISO SOACIUS, <u>De Romanorum et Venetorum</u>
<u>Magistratuum inter se comparatione libellus</u>**, Padua,
1563   4°

1482.   Jurisprudentiae politicae   £0 01 6

Possibly:

**Franciscus RAGUELLUS, <u>Leges Politicae, ex sacrae</u>
<u>jurisprudentiae</u>**, Frankfurt, 1577 ; 1586   8°

1483.   Hieronomi Osorij de regis Institutione   £0 01 8

**Jeronimo OSORIO DA FONSECA, Bishop of Silves,
<u>De regis institutione et disciplina lib. VIII</u>,**
Lisbon, 1571 ; Cologne, 1572 ; 1574   8°
Another edition in 16° : Cologne, 1588.

1484.   Mercurius Gallobellicus   £0 00 6

Another copy of Item no. 1148, above.

1485.   Sibillina oracula Cum anotation   £0 0 10

**<u>Sibyllina Oracula, de Graeco in Latinum conversa, et</u>
<u>in eandem annotationes S. Castalione, interprete</u>,**
Basle, 1546 ; Paris, 1599 ; 1607   8°
Also a Greek-latin edition published at Basle,
1555 (8°).

1486.   Arcandum   £0 00 8

**ARCANDAM, pseud., <u>Arcandam doctor peritissimus ac</u>
<u>non vulgaris Astrologus, de veritatibus &</u>
<u>praedictionibus Astrologiae ... nuper per Richardum</u>
<u>Roussat ... aeditus, recognitus</u>**, Paris, 1541 ;
1542   8°
Another edition in 16° : Paris, 1553.

1487.   Syciliae descriptio   £0 00 6

I have been unable to trace any work of this title in
latin.

1488.   Sphera Jo: de Sacra bosco   £0 00 6

Another copy of Item no. 503, above.

1489.   Alfragani Astronomia   £0 00 6

AḤMAD IBN MUḤAMMAD IBN KATHĪR al-Farghāni, **Alfragani astronomorum peritissimi compendium**, Paris, 1546 8°

f22r

1490.   Cor: Valerij de Sphera   £0 00 6

Cornelius **VALERIUS**, **De Sphaera et primis astronomiae rudimentis libellus ... Cui adjecta sunt brevia quaedam de Geographia praecepta**, Antwerp, 1561 ; 1568 ; 1575 ; 1585   8°

1491.   Chiromantia   £0 01 4

1492.   Hudalrici Regij Arithmetica   £0 01 2
         Another copy of Item no. 1204, above.

1493.   A booke of palmestrie   £0 00 6

Johannes ab **INDAGINE** of Steinheim, **The Book of Palmestry and Physiognomy ... Being brief introductions ... unto the art of Chiromancy .. and Physiognomy**, London, 1651 ... London, 1676   8°
First translated into English as **Brief introductions ... unto the art of chiromancy** by F. Withers, London, 1558 (8°).

         (STC : I141-I143)

1494.   Jo: Piscatoris Arithmetica   £0 0 10

Joannes **PISCATOR** of Wittenberg, **Arithmeticae compendium ... denuo recognitum et locupletatum per J. Piscatorem**, Leipzig, 1582 ; 1592   8°

1495.   Bakers Arithmetiq   £0 00 8
         Another copy of Item no. 1203, above.

233

1496.   Cronologia sacra   £0 00 6

Philipp NICOLAI, Chronologia sacra, lib. 2. De regno Christi. Shortly collected and augmented by Niels Michelsone. Newly translated, out of the German ... into the English, by David Forbes, Edinburgh, 1630 ; 1631   16°

(STC : 18572-18573)

1497.   Jo: Claij Gramatica Germanica   £0 01 8

Joannes CLAIUS Hertzbergensis, Grammatica Germanicae linguae, Leipzig, 1578   8°
Numerous later editions in 8° and 12°.

1498.   The Psalter in high dutch   £0 01 6

Der psalter zu teütsch, Strassburg, 1475?   4°
Numerous subsequent editions in all book sizes.

1499.   Tho: Thomasij Dictionarium   £0 07 0

Thomas THOMASIUS, Dictionarium linguae Latinae et Anglicanae, Cambridge, 1587   8°
Numerous subsequent editions in 4° and 8°(... 13th ed., London, 1631, 4°).

(STC : 24008-24017.5)

1500.   Janua Linguarum   £0 01 6

Various works appeared under this title in England. Probably one of two works:

    (a) **William BATHE, Janua linguarum, sive modus maxime accommodatus. Cum translatione Anglicana** (by W. Welde), London, 1615 ... 1623   4°
Latin-English.

    (b) **John HARMAR the Younger, Rector of Ewhurst, Janua linguarum**, London, 1626   4°
Translated into English as **Janua linguarum, an easy method for the attaining all tongues, especially the Latine**, London, 1631 (4°).
Later editions : London, 1634 ; 1645 (8°), edited by Thomas Horne, with additions from Timothy Poole.

(STC : (a) 14466-14468.5 ; 15077.7 ; (b) 14469 ; 14471 ; 14472 ; H2812A)

1501.   Brinsleyes grammer schoole   £0 02 0

John BRINSLEY the Elder, Ludus Literarius : or the Grammar Schoole ; shewing how to proceede from the first entrance into learning, to the highest perfection required in the grammar schooles, London, 1612 ; 1627 4°

(AE, pp.24,99 ; STC : 3768-3770b.2)

APPENDIX 1

THE WILL AND INVENTORY OF DR JOHN WEBSTER

In the name of God Amen I John Webster of Cliderow in the County of Lancaster Physician knowing the certainty that it is appointed for all men ones [*sic*] to dye & that the houre of death is uncertain being something crazy of body but of right understanding perfect judgment & sound memory doe make this my last Will & Testament thereby revoking & disanulling all other Wills & Testaments by me made anytime heretofore in manner & forme following First I doe bequeath my soule & spirit unto the hands of Jesus Christ my onely Saviour & Redemer trusting by faith onely in His blood to have everlasting peace & salvation   Item I doe bequeath my body unto the earth hoping for its glorious resurrection according to the articles of the Christian Faith to be buried at the discretion of my most deare & loving Wife[1]   And for my temporall estate & worldly goods I dispose of them in this manner following   As for my lands & inheritance that I have purchased in the Borrow & Township of Cliderow to wit one Burgage or Messuage and one fourth part of a burgage paying yearly one shilling eight pence burgage rent called Keyes House with one garden and two crofts there unto belonging   Also one Burgage or Messuage of the yearly Borrow rent of one shilling fourepence now called my studdy[2] one stable & one building ioyned unto it called my furnace house one fold one garden & one croft or meadow with one barne on it commonly called the School house croft one meadow called Corbetts meadow one field of arable ground called the great Hey with one meadow adjoyning unto it also certaine closes called Muckland with one barne standing in one one of them & one field thereto adioyning called the little Hey all lying in the townshipe Cliderow aforesaid & being all freeland & of Burgage tenure as also one house or cottage in the little garden & backside comonly called Kenyon house in Cliderow aforesaid   All these Burgages cottage barnes with all the aforesaid premises with all the profits priviledges & apurtenances thereunto in any wise appertaining or belonging I doe give bequeath grant & confirm unto my most deare & loving Wife Elizabeth Webster for & dureing her life naturall without restriction condition or limitation to possesse & inioy the same for the aforesaid terme as fully as I myselfe have done and further my mind and will is that after the decease of my said wife then I doe give bequeath grant & confirme unto Edward Webster my nephew that Burgage or messuage with the garden & two crofts thereunto belonging called Keyes house with that house or cottage & the backside with all the rights priviledges & appurtenances in any wise belonging or appertaining & to

---

[1] Webster was married, probably for the first time, to Elizabeth Aspinall on 6 November 1667. She later remarried the minister of Clitheroe, William Bankes, in 1686. See William Self Weeks, 'John Webster, author of *The displaying of supposed witchcraft', TLCAS*, 1921, **39**: 102–103.

[2] Study House, along with Webster's "furnace house", originally stood beside the parish church in Clitheroe. The site is today occupied by the offices of J. L. Lumley, Solicitors. I should like to thank Mr. Lumley for kindly confirming many details relating to Webster's residence in Clitheroe.

[Webster's will and inventory are taken from Weeks, op. cit., note 1 above, pp. 98–101. A copy of the originals are to be found today in the Lancashire Record Office, Preston.]

his heyres males of his body lawfully begotten or to be begotten   And for want of such heyres (male) then to John Webster my nephew & to the heyres males of his body lawfully begotten for ever Itm my mind and Will is that after the decease of my said Wife then I doe give bequeath grant & confirme unto Richard Webster another of my nephewes & to the heyres male of his body lawfully begotten that Burgage or messuage comonly nowe called my studdy with the stable & furnace house thereunto adioyning with the fold garden & one croft or meadow with a barne in it comonly called the Schoolhouse croft & for want of such heyres male then to Nicholas Webster & his heyres male for ever with all the rights priviledges & apurtenances in any wise belonging or appertaining   Item it is my mind & will that after the decease of my said Wife then I doe give bequeath grant & confirme unto John Webster my nephew all my other lands in Cliderow aforesaid to witt the two fields called Muckland with a barne in one of them the little Hey thereunto adioyning the field of arable ground called the Great Hey with a meadow adioyning to it & also one meadow called corbet meadow to him & his heyres males for ever provided always that if the said Edward Webster Richard Webster or John Webster or any of them shall sue molest hinder or trouble my said deare & loveing wife Elizabeth dureing her life naturall for the said house or land or forming any part or parcell thereof or for or concerning anything in this my last Will & Testament to her my deare wife given and bequeathed then the first gift & grant to any of three fore named persons shall be null & void to all intents & purposes whatsoever & the part or parts of him or them so offending I doe give bequeath grant & confirme unto Nicholas Webster & his heyres for ever   And as for my goods cattels & chattels I conceive the one halfe of them by the custome of the province of Yorks doth belong to my deare & lovinge wife Elizabeth Webster of which I wish her much happy inioyment & for the other halfe comonly called the deads part or the Testators part I doe frely give & bequeath them to my said deare & loveing wife & I doe hereby nominate make constitute & appoint my said deare & loveing wife Elizabeth Webster sole & onely Executrix of this my last Will & Testament   Item I give fourty shillings to the poor of the township of Cliderow to be distributed within one month after my death at the discretion of my said Executrix   Item I give fourty shillings to the poore of the townshipp of Grindleton in Yorkshire to be distributed within one month after my death at the discretion of Henry Wallace & Thomas Hodgson of the said towne Item I give to Ann Slater my servant maid ten shillings January the third Anno Regni Caroli secundi dei gratia Angliae Scotiae Franciae &c. trycessimo secundo annoq: Domini 1680.

The will was signed "Jo: Webster" and was "published and declared . . . in the sight & presence of Jo. Townley, Nicholas Manroe . . . Richard Dugdale [and] Thomas Whittaker"

There follows "A True and p'fect Inventorie of all the goodes rights cattles and chatteles of Doctor Webster of Clitherow late deceased apprised the 19th day of July 1682 by these whose names are subscribed"

	£	s	d
Imp his apparell and money in his purse	10	00	00
Ite Brasse	05	00	00
Ite Pewter	05	00	00

	£	s	d
Ite Bedding	12	00	00
Ite Bedstockes	02	00	00
Ite Seeld Beds	03	00	00
Ite Linning	05	10	00
Ite Seeld Chists	02	05	00
Ite Strkes (Sic)	01	10	00
Ite Tables	02	06	00
Ite Seeld Chairs	02	00	00
Ite Buffet Stooles	00	12	00
Ite Cubbords	03	00	00
Ite Comon Chaires	00	13	00
Ite Woodden Vessell	01	05	00
Ite Earthen potts & bottles	00	05	00
Ite Fire Irons & tongues	01	00	00
Ite Spitts & Racks	00	05	00
Ite Dripping Pann	00	03	00
Ite One Warming Pan	00	05	00
Ite One Cow	03	00	00
Ite One Whye	02	00	00
Ite One Twinter & a Stirke	01	00	00
Ite one chist Bedd	00	10	00
Ite Meale & Malt	01	10	00
Ite Wheat	01	00	00
Ite Beef & Bacon	00	10	00
Ite Deskes	00	15	00
Ite Two Trunkes	00	10	00
Ite a Copper Vessel with its Toppe & worme	06	00	00
Ite Seu'all boxes	00	06	00
Ite one nest of Draw Boxes	00	10	00
Ite Chirurgicall Instruments	20	00	00
Ite [. . .] last . . . &c. alliis medicamentis	05	00	00
Ite Glasses	02	00	00
Ite Chimicall glasses	04	00	00
Ite The Library	400	00	00
[Total value]	[507	00	00]

APPENDIX 2

THE EPITAPH OF DR JOHN WEBSTER

Hic jacet ignotus mundo, mersusque tumultu
Invidiae, semper mens tamen aequa fuit
multa tulit, veterum ut sciret Secreta Sophorum
Ac tandem vires noverit ignis Aquae

Johannes Hyphantes alias Webster
natus in parochia Silvae cuculatae[1] in
Agro Eboracensi Anno Dom 1610
Ergastulum reliquit 1682

Sicque peroravit moriens, et mundo huic valedicens:
Aurea pax vivis, requies aeterna Sepultis

[1] The translation of Cuxwold as Silvae cuculatae in Latin was almost certainly an alchemical pun on Webster's part; cuculatum majus = aqua vitae.

A rough translation might read as follows:

Here he lies unknown to the world, and buried under a mound of odium,
But his mind was always patient and endured much,
So that it might know the secrets of the ancient sages,
And finally learn of the powers of the fire.

Johannes Hyphantes alias Webster
Born in the parish of the cuckoo wood [Coxwold]
In the county of York in the year of our Lord 1610
Left his prison in 1682.

And so, dying, he bade farewell to this world:
"Golden peace to the living, eternal rest to the buried".

[This epitaph is to be found appended to the Catalogue of Webster's Library, Chetham Library MS. A.6.47, f.22v. A fuller version is to be found on a monument in Clitheroe parish church erected in memory of Webster.]

<u>INDEX TO THE CATALOGUE</u>

<u>OF THE LIBRARY OF DR. JOHN WEBSTER</u>

All items cited by author or editor in the main body of the Catalogue are referred to in this Index by bold capitalised script, e.g. **FLUDD, Robert : 1(a–e)**. In the case of works and authors which are not mentioned in the main entry, but which nonetheless form part of the volume, these are referred to in bold, uncapitalised script, e.g. **Tagaultius, Joannes : see 18**. Translators, editors, publishers, etc are referred to in similar fashion in ordinary type, e.g. Ireton, John : see 164.

In the case of entries where more than one author has been suggested in the Catalogue, or where there is some uncertainty surrounding any given ascription, this is indicated in the index by a question mark, e.g. **SALTZMANN, Johann Rudolph? : 24?**

Unidentified works in the Catalogue are referred to in inverted commas, e.g. "Syciliae descriptio": **1487**.

<u>Note:</u>

(1)   Commentaries on single books of the Bible, except for Psalters, are referred to under the relevant author(s).

(2)   Throughout the Index, as with the Catalogue, I have tried wherever possible to adhere to the style adopted in the Catalogue of the Printed Books division of the British Library.

HEINSIUS, Daniel : 1003 ; 1051
HELBACH, Friedrich : 348
HELIODORUS, Bishop of Tricca : 902 ; 948 ; 950
HELLOPOEUS, Bálint : 1397
HELMONT, Jan Baptista van : 307 ; 330
HELVICUS, Christophorus : 165
HEMMINGSEN, Niels : 631 ; 1469
HEMSTERHUIS, Siboldus : 737
Henrichmannus, Jacobus : see 1142
(HENRY the Minstrel) : 993
Herberay, Nicolas de,
  Seigneur des Essars : see 105 ; 1095
HERBERT, George : 976 ; 977
HERBERT, Sir Thomas : 185(a)
HERDSON, Henry : 649
HERESBACH, Conrad : 363
.... : see also 762 ; 769 ; 949
HERIGONE, Pierre : 478
HERMES TRISMEGISTUS : 1369
.... : see also 36 ; 313 ; 383 ;
  702
HERO of Alexandria : 419
HERODIAN the Historian : 982 ; 1144
HERODOTUS : 762 ; 769 ; 949
Hertelius, Valentinus : see 605
HESIOD : 1034
HESTEAU, Clovis, Sieur de
  Nuysement : 637
HEURNIUS, Joannes : 7 ; 355
.... : see also 726
Hexham, Henry : see 77
HEYDEN, Hermannus van der : 654
HEYDON, Sir Christopher : 640
HEYLYN, Peter : 892
HEYWOOD, Thomas : 468
.... : see also 172
HIBNER, Israel : 342
HIGGINS, John? : 917?
.... : see also 1012
HIGHMORE, Nathaniel : 625
HILL, Nicolaus : 1125
HILL, Robert : 1354
HILL, Thomas : 361 ; 661(a)
HILPERT, Johann : 1471
HIPPOCRATES : 10 ; 515 ; 726 ; 728
HIRSCH, Christoph : see STELLATUS, Joseph,
  pseud.
Hirtius, Aulus : see 746 ; 747 ; 1163
HOBBES, Thomas : 786 ; 989
"Mr. Hochlams booke"? : 721
HOCUS POCUS JUNIOR : 388
Hogelande, Cornelius ab? : see 721?
Hoghelande, Ewaldus de? : see 721?